LIFE OF LORD KITCHENER

THE MACMILLAN COMPANY
NEW YORK · BOSTON · CHICAGO · DALLAS
ATLANTA · SAN FRANCISCO

MACMILLAN & CO., Limited
LONDON · BOMBAY · CALCUTTA
MELBOURNE

THE MACMILLAN CO. OF CANADA, Ltd.
TORONTO

London Stereoscopic Co., photographers.

Kitchener of Khartoum

LIFE OF
LORD KITCHENER

BY
Sir GEORGE ARTHUR

IN THREE VOLUMES
VOL. III

New York
THE MACMILLAN COMPANY
1920

All rights reserved

COPYRIGHT, 1920,
BY THE MACMILLAN COMPANY

Set up and electrotyped. Published May, 1920.

**LIBRARY
FLORIDA STATE UNIVERSITY
TALLAHASSEE, FLORIDA**

CONTENTS

CHAPTER XC
Secretary of State for War—A General Staff . . . . PAGE 1

CHAPTER XCI
The New Armies—Home Defence 7

CHAPTER XCII
Confidence in Kitchener—"Kitchener's Armies" 12

CHAPTER XCIII
Preliminary Work—French Plans—Kitchener's Views—Maubeuge or Amiens 16

CHAPTER XCIV
Sir John French—Kitchener's Advice to Soldiers—Sir John's Arrival 24

CHAPTER XCV
British Concentration—Retreat from Mons 31

CHAPTER XCVI
Smith-Dorrien—The Sixth Division 37

CHAPTER XCVII

Cambrai-Landrecies—De Lanrezac at Guise—Proposed British Retreat—Sir John's Explanation 42

CHAPTER XCVIII

The Danger of Cleavage—Kitchener's hurried Journey—The Meeting in Paris—Maunoury and Foch—The British Advance 50

CHAPTER XCIX

Battle of the Marne—Von Kluck's Retreat—Battle of the Aisne . 60

CHAPTER C

Antwerp—Lille—Indian Troops—With French President at Dunkirk 67

CHAPTER CI

Trench Warfare—Sir John and Joffre—Sir John's Plan . . . 77

CHAPTER CII

Ostend and Zeebrugge—The Allied Left Flank—Veto of the War Council—Co-operation with Joffre 85

CHAPTER CIII

Sir John Maxwell—The War Council—The Middle East . . . 95

CHAPTER CIV

Mr. Lloyd George's Project—The Dardanelles—The Suez Canal . 102

CONTENTS

CHAPTER CV

Balkans and Greece—The Twenty-ninth Division—Germany and the East—Dardanelles Plans 108

CHAPTER CVI

The Twenty-ninth Division released—Sir Ian Hamilton . . . 117

CHAPTER CVII

Military Co-operation—A Landing decided on 125

CHAPTER CVIII

Plans for Gallipoli—The Landing effected—The Anzacs—Krithia—Italy joins the Entente 130

CHAPTER CIX

General Gouraud—Hamilton's Reinforcements—Kilid Bahr . 141

CHAPTER CX

Effects of a Withdrawal—Suvla Bay 148

CHAPTER CXI

Arab Independence—Sheikh-Sayed—Checks and Delays . . . 153

CHAPTER CXII

Suvla Bay—Difficulties of Terrain—Sari Bair—Want of Water . 161

CHAPTER CXIII

Byng, Maude, and Fanshawe—Reinforcements promised—Unity of Command—Australian Engineers 170

CHAPTER CXIV

Evacuation mooted—Sir Charles Monro 179

CHAPTER CXV

Journey to Gallipoli—Reception by Anzacs—Evacuation considered—Ayas Bay—Salonika 185

CHAPTER CXVI

Athens—General Sarrail—Ayas Bay ruled out—King Constantine 196

CHAPTER CXVII

The King of Italy—Evacuation—Birdwood on Evacuation—Anzac Evacuation—Evacuation accomplished—Birdwood's Narrative 205

CHAPTER CXVIII

The Western Front—Haig and Smith-Dorrien—Neuve Chapelle . 220

CHAPTER CXIX

After Neuve Chapelle 227

CHAPTER CXX

Poison Gas—Second Battle of Ypres 231

CONTENTS

CHAPTER CXXI
PAGE
Festubert 237

CHAPTER CXXII
Preparing an Offensive—Rôle of the British Army—Vimy Ridge . 241

CHAPTER CXXIII
Mr. Churchill's Note—Reinforcing East and West—The Guards' Division 248

CHAPTER CXXIV
Loos—The Fifteenth Division—"Reparation" of the Front—Reinforcements for Salonika 254

CHAPTER CXXV
Pre-War Economies—The Cabinet Committee—Enormous Requirements 263

CHAPTER CXXVI
A Five Years' War—High Explosives—Amatol—Output of Gun Ammunition—Sir Stanley von Donop—M. Millerand . . . 270

CHAPTER CXXVII
Labour—The Trades Unions—Munitions Committee—Ministry of Munitions—Kitchener and Sir John 282

CHAPTER CXXVIII
Sir Douglas Haig Commander-in-Chief—Sir William Robertson—The Army Council 293

CHAPTER CXXIX

Mesopotamia—Verdun 301

CHAPTER CXXX

Seventy Divisions—Recruiting 307

CHAPTER CXXXI

Mr. Arthur Henderson—The Derby Scheme—The Kitchener Armies—Infantry Divisions 313

CHAPTER CXXXII

Conscientious Objectors—Mr. Lloyd George—The House of Commons—The New Force—Equipment—Ammunition—Compulsory Service—Transport—Health of the Army—Men on Leave—Mr. William Crooks 322

CHAPTER CXXXIII

France—Russia—The Emperor—A Visit to Russia 344

CHAPTER CXXXIV

Departure for Russia—The *Hampshire*—Tributes—St. Paul's Cathedral 352

CHAPTER CXXXV

Breadth of Mind—Sense of Duty—Abhorrence of Enemy Methods—Friend of Children—The Throne—Religion 361

INDEX 373

ILLUSTRATIONS

Field-Marshal Earl Kitchener. From a Photograph by the London Stereoscopic Company . . . . *Frontispiece*

FACE PAGE

Facsimile, Correspondence as to Grant of Honours on the Field . 65

Gallipoli and the Dardanelles 130

Lord Kitchener and the Members of his Staff bidding Farewell to Admiral Jellicoe. From a Photograph taken on June 5, 1916 354

CHAPTER XC

In August 1914 Kitchener was to envisage the great emprise of his career in the great hour when the country accepted a tremendous challenge.

Over the first days of the Great War brooded that atmosphere of fate which is seldom absent from great transactions. Events resulting from more than human cunning and wickedness unrolled themselves with apocalyptic majesty and inevitableness; and this savour of preordination attaches to the almost accidental presence of Kitchener in England in August 1914. He had arrived from Egypt in July, intending to stay till September; but he had hardly landed when he heard that Austria was presenting a pistol to Serbia's head, and he knew that Germany's finger would be on the trigger. He was not likely to belittle the significance of this. A German menace to European peace had long been present to his mind, and he felt that our military arrangements were dangerously inadequate to our responsibilities. He had refrained from an appeal to Caesar of the many heads; where Lord Roberts's persuasive eloquence had failed, he could hardly hope to succeed. But if he had said little, he had done much. India he had left prepared, as never before, for war; he had won for us the heart and hand of South Africa; Australia and New Zealand owed him their complete military organisation; up to the margin of his means, Egypt had been made secure. If the future filled him with disquiet, he could at least look back on his own personal past without a stab of conscience.

An insignificant entry in a pocket diary records Kitchener's engagement to luncheon at the German Embassy on July 21. From some rather sad words dropped by the Ambassador, Kitchener then and there was persuaded of the imminence of European war. During the tense days that followed, Kitchener's movements suggest a simple contentment with the duty lying nearest. Going on July 30 to bid him farewell, Maxwell and Rawlinson told their old chief that he would certainly not be allowed to return to Egypt should England become involved. He replied that he was going back to Egypt as arranged, and that the only thing that would prevent him would be "the wish of the country that he should stay." He advised that friends who were in Germany should return immediately: "You can use my name when you telegraph." This seasonable hint served to bring home many English travellers who would otherwise have been forcibly detained. On Friday, July 31, all heads of missions abroad were ordered to repair immediately to their posts, and Kitchener at once made ready to return to Cairo. After drafting a proclamation to be issued in Egypt should the declaration of war precede his arrival, he went down to Broome, intending to cross from Dover on the Monday. On Saturday he satisfied himself, through the village telephone, that nothing had happened to affect his own journey, and early on August 3, the day on which the Foreign Minister was to make his pronouncement, he went on board the Channel steamer, there to be told that the officers who were to accompany him had been detained in London, and that he himself should postpone his crossing. In default of direct official instructions Kitchener, aware that a special train awaited him on the other side, had decided to start without his Staff, when a message arrived from the Prime Minister requiring him to remain in England.

Mr. Asquith, having secured himself against Lord Kitchener's departure, felt safe in forgetting him for another twenty-four hours, and it was on the next afternoon that Kitchener, while engaged with his solicitors, received a summons to the Foreign Office. Thinking that he might not soon have another chance to deal with his private affairs, and that probably no special mandate awaited him, he deferred the call till later in the afternoon. The visit was quite inconclusive, and it was not until the next day that the Prime Minister—whose mind was largely made up for him by the persistence of Lord Northcliffe and the insistence of the public—asked him to take over his responsibilities of Secretary of State for War.[1] Kitchener agreed to accept the seals on the understanding that he served as a soldier for the duration of the war, and that the day peace was signed he would pass for ever from the War Office. Thus no political party could claim him, while senior officers could not regard him as delaying their passage to the high military posts.

The task imposed on him was one only to be accepted in the spirit of the soldier. It was no

[1] It is on record that Lord Haldane pressed this appointment on the Premier.

matter of meeting the grave difficulties which must always beset a Secretary of State in time of war. The main work—though Kitchener alone recognised it at that moment—was to found, build, and furnish a huge military fabric. After fighting had actually begun, he must set himself to mould Great Britain into a first-class military power. The Fleet—thanks to much preliminary care—could be placed on a war basis, and an Expeditionary Force could be smoothly mobilised and rapidly shipped to France, while each of the great departments of State had to some extent provided for the particular changes which might occur on the outbreak of war. But this was all; fighting had been regarded as the business of the Navy and Army, and the conception of a *national* war had not coloured the thoughts of those in authority. The War Office and the General Staff had concentrated on an honest literal fulfilment of our bargain with the French: to send them six divisions and a cavalry division, with possibly one or two more divisions later, so soon as the Territorial Force was steady on its own legs. To determine even this modest military contribution had been abundantly difficult. The immediate task completed, the senior officers of the General Staff hurried across the Channel, leaving large blanks in the War Office, regarded as the military General Headquarters of the Empire, and rendering it necessary to summon officers from retirement to fill important places.

There had been no serious consideration of the possible multiplication of theatres of war, of the defence of the Empire as a whole, or of the systematic enlargement of its military resources. Moreover, the Government, in placid nescience of the real nature of an emergency of which the vague shadow had long been projected, had formed no plans for its own war organisation. No attempt had been made to define or delimit the respective functions of the statesman, the soldier, and the sailor in the higher control and conduct of naval and military operations. There existed a vague body of doctrine that the Government, being responsible to Parliament and the people, must be supreme, and that its business was to get the best professional advice; the notion that any fundamental change in the mechanism of State, as existing in time of peace, was either requisite or desirable in time of war, had not yet occurred to any one in authority. To the Ministry, professional advice meant simply the individual opinions of certain eminent soldiers and sailors, checked by the opinions of such other soldiers and sailors as the Ministry as a whole, or some Ministers in particular, might desire to consult. Nor seemingly had the point suggested itself that, as the war might rapidly become world-wide, there should be domiciled at the War Office a great General Staff charged with the preparation of considered counsel to the Secretary of State and through him to the Government. With the outbreak of war the term "General Staff" became little more than a term. There was no security for quick military decisions; there was every inducement to leisurely political debate; the fact seemed to have been blinked that naval and military counsel, to be of value in war time, should be prepared by a scientifically contrived organisation, and presented by a single responsible authority ready to carry out the advice offered.

So long as France was the only theatre of active

war, the need for an expert and established General Staff was not so acute as it became later; but early difficulties arose which a scientifically organised constitution would have quickly detected and quietly dealt with.

Before the war was a few weeks old the War Office suffered badly in the death of Sir Charles Douglas, the very competent Chief of the Imperial General Staff whose place it was peculiarly difficult to fill. From that time until the arrival at the War Office of Sir William Robertson the Secretary of State practically doubled his part with that of Chief of the Staff, an undertaking which his wide knowledge and boundless energy went far to justify, but which tested unduly even his abnormal capacity for work. Comment on this matter seldom escaped his lips, but he felt that our preparedness for war was clearly proved by the lack of that machinery for carrying it on which he might have expected to find to his hand in the Office.[1]

[1] In his Memorandum submitted to the Government in 1904 Kitchener had laid great stress on the importance of a competent General Staff for and in war.

CHAPTER XCI

AT ten o'clock on the Thursday morning the new Minister entered the War Office for the first time as its Chief. During the two hours which were to elapse before his visit to Buckingham Palace to be sworn in of His Majesty's Privy Council and to receive the Seals of the War Office, he was formally introduced to the higher officials of his department. His first remark is burnt into many memories—"There is no Army!"[1]

The meaning of that trenchant observation is open to no sort of misunderstanding. The Regular Army, inclusive of Reserves and Special Reserves, numbered at this time 450,000 men. The Territorial Force, who were not liable—save as volunteers—for foreign service, contributed 250,000 more. But of these 700,000 men 110,000 were serving in India or at other stations abroad. There remained 600,000 men, all told, for the Defence of the Realm and for the Expeditionary Force; and of this total one-half were—not to overstate the case—imperfectly trained.

Kitchener's words were intended to convey that, for the titanic task the country had undertaken,

---

[1] In the course of the morning his private secretary handed him a pen with which to give his signature for the official stamp. The pen declined to function. "Dear me," murmured Kitchener, "what a War Office! Not a scrap of Army and not a pen that will write!"

our miniature Expeditionary Force was ludicrously inadequate. What that Force—known in future history as "the Contemptible Little Army"[1]—could do and dare was presently to receive convincing demonstration on the well-trodden battlefields of Flanders, where its predecessors for more than two centuries had reaped so many laurels. But, as regards the vast purpose in Kitchener's mind, it was the literal truth that we had "no Army." If it was to his undying fame that he created the armies to carry out that purpose, it was not less to his credit that he was the one statesman who perceived—or at least had the courage to declare—that England must strip herself to fight to the death.

Until the moment when Sir Edward Grey announced to an excited House of Commons that an ultimatum had been presented to Germany, the dominant notion among politicians had apparently been that we could wage war on some principle of limited liability. The accepted military plan was that in certain eventualities—and on urgent demand—we should despatch overseas an Expeditionary Force of six divisions of infantry, with a cavalry division and artillery,[2] that the Territorial Force should take over the military defence of these islands, and that the Special Reserve should feed the Expeditionary Force. On this basis the business of the War Office in the event of war was limited to

---

[1] The phrase—attributed to the German Emperor—was accepted and appropriated with the same derisive gaiety that killed the Hymn of Hate.

[2] It was currently said that in 1912, when General Foch was asked what troops he expected England would furnish in the event of war with Germany, he replied, "Send me one Englishman. I will take care he is killed, and I shall have the British nation in arms."

keeping the force in the field up to strength, and perfecting the arrangements for home defence.

Kitchener saw the truth at a glance; he knew that the views of the politicians were wholly untenable, and the provisions of the military authorities hopelessly insufficient. Whether our troops advanced, retired, or held their ground, it was not a question of reinforcing the miniature army appointed to take the field and of maintaining garrisons at home and in India, but of creating a real army which should pit itself in the near future fearlessly and effectively against the forces of the German Empire. He immediately laid his plans for an army of seventy divisions, coolly calculating that its maximum strength would be reached during the third year of the war, just when the enemy would be undergoing a sensible diminution of his resources in manpower.

His scheme, of course, ran clean contrary to all accepted ideas. It had always been held that in time of war, though armies could be expanded, they could not be created. To imagine otherwise seemed equally surprising to our friends and to our enemies. The French General Staff gracefully remarked that men had called new armies into being, and men had utilised and maintained existing armies; but that for Lord Kitchener it was reserved to perform the two feats simultaneously. The Germans scornfully derided the Kitchener plan as impracticable, and, despite the hard knocks they received at the hands of his New Armies, they repeated their mistake when they sneered at the military potentiality of America.[1]

[1] Kitchener did not live to see America's entry into the war; he told Colonel House, the emissary of the President, who sought an interview

Kitchener himself was under no illusions as to its difficulties. While his new millions were being raised, equipped, and made efficient, the Expeditionary Force had to be kept going, and the Territorial Home Garrison to be maintained to strength and afforded such training as would enable it to cope with its equivalent in Continental troops. These two requirements absorbed nearly the whole of the existing Staffs, and drained dry the sources of military supplies which had sufficed under the modest pre-war calculations.

The efficiency of the Home Garrison was a matter of vital importance in view of the possibility of an enemy invasion. Kitchener was plied with scornful arguments to prove the impracticability of an enemy descent on our coast. "I am only prepared," was his habitual reply, "to rule out the feasibility of an invasion if I can learn that the Germans regard it as an impossible operation." The Territorial divisions must be kept intact and standing to arms for an emergency, of which it was thought that the East Coast might be the possible scene.

In a word, England's honour had been at stake, and with something like fine recklessness England had flung herself into a fearful struggle with little thought of its possible duration and no calculation of its ultimate cost. With our dearly-bought experience one may well wonder how our responsibilities could have been so under-rated and our possible requirements so under-estimated; how these misconceptions originated; why they persisted for so long a

with him in the autumn of 1915, that only America herself could decide whether it was right or wrong for her to take up arms. "But," he added, "one thing is certain—if America bears no part in the waging of war, she will be allowed no voice in the making of peace."

period; and what our fate as a nation must have been had there been no Kitchener to seize and size the real situation.

It is within just surmise that steady thinkers and efficient strategists may have shared intellectually his estimate of our commitments. But the one man bold enough to publish it was also the one man to make that estimate effective, and to commend it to his countrymen with peculiarly persuasive force.

CHAPTER XCII

THE new Secretary of State entered upon his duties in possession of one priceless asset. He enjoyed the confidence of everybody who mattered—from his Sovereign down to the humblest barbarian native among the King-Emperor's subjects. The trust in Kitchener, which almost savoured of religious allegiance, was a factor in the resolve of the British people to spare nothing and shrink from nothing if only victory could be secured. And for those who saw the Finger of God in history, the belief that their country had joined issue to vindicate Divine Justice and Human Right found its complement in the conviction that a great leader had been providentially called to the work.

Although in this country not one person in a hundred thousand had ever set eyes on Kitchener, the people knew him for a great soldier and a great organiser. Yet in neither of these capacities could he have commanded their entire faith unless they had been assured of his singleness of aim and strength of motive. The masses are prone to suspect any leader, often quite unjustly, of working for his own ends and interests; Kitchener appealed to them as supremely trustworthy because supremely selfless. This was in the minds of Labour Members when, after his death, they declared in the House of

Commons that the workers trusted Kitchener "because they had found him to be straight." To know the British people at all is to know how difficult is this kind of confidence to win, but that once conceded it is never withdrawn. Instinct rather than reasoning selects the fit recipient of this rare gift, but the instinct is generally sound and the conclusion always sincere.

As an old friend, Lady Wantage, when placing her house in Carlton Gardens at his disposal, wrote:

> Nothing has done more to tranquillise public feeling than the knowledge that you are at the War Office. Your task is indeed a heavy one, but the heart of the nation is with you. (12.8.14.) [1]

The closeness of the bond subsisting between the big soldier and his countrymen was just now of peculiar importance. England must take her place in an armed world, and she stood as the one conspicuous adherent of the principle of voluntary military service, as contrasted with any form of compulsory recruiting. The only existing machinery for raising a large military force was voluntary enlistment. The deeply-rooted mutual trust between Kitchener and the masses possessed a value of the most tangible kind and figured largely in the shaping of a great army, enrolled as no army ever was before in the world's history. Posterity, remembering him, will remember that at a great emergency he called his fellow-countrymen to the Colours, and that three millions of them answered the call. They were moved by the instinct of self-preservation, by a gen-

---

[1] "I hope your Chief stands it well. We all depend on him, and it is the greatest mercy that he is at the head of things." (Lord Milner to Col. FitzGerald, 8.9.14.)

erous impulse to help a victim of aggression, by all that stirs English blood when liberty is threatened and right is insulted. But the signal to which they responded was a personal summons:

YOUR KING AND COUNTRY NEED YOU.
A Call to Arms!

An addition of 100,000 men to His Majesty's Regular Army is immediately necessary in the present grave National Emergency. Lord Kitchener is confident that this appeal will be at once responded to by all those who have the safety of our Empire at heart.

So ran the posters and the advertisements throughout the length and breadth of the land. And the men came because Kitchener asked them. At his word they leapt to arms from city and town and village and countryside, from moor and mine, from field and factory—rich men and poor men, squire and yokel, peer and peasant, cultured and unlearned, of every class and station and grade in life, of every profession and trade. The call was authoritative with all. Their formations were soon known as "Kitchener's Armies," and even official documents became cognisant of military units labelled "K" Divisions![1]

The marvel of the thing grows as it recedes into the past. We were even now at war, yet we had "no Army!" The Army had still to be created—the men enrolled, housed, fed, clothed, trained, armed, and equipped; the guns and rifles, with their ammunition, manufactured; the whole organisation and machinery of a mighty military force extemporised.

[1] Mr. Lloyd George in a Cabinet Memorandum of 1915 alludes to them as "Kitchener Armies," as did Joffre in General Orders of this year.

Kitchener shouldered his load with the calm which belongs to conscious strength. He knew and believed in his human material; he had decided exactly how he meant to use it, with the free hand which the country insisted on giving him. The declaration that "we had no Army" was one which the politicians could scarcely have heard unmoved. It implied the calling of vast armaments into being, the unlearning of a stereotyped national tradition, the acceptance of a radically novel conception of the whole position and mission of England in the world. It was not only that, as regards troops, Kitchener was thinking in millions where those who thought at all had been thinking in thousands; it was also that Great Britain, already supreme on the seas, must now, without hesitation, undertake the new character of a military power of the first rank. The unquestioning readiness to accept so fateful a decision was the measure of the people's confidence in the man who had just been admitted to power.

CHAPTER XCIII

WHEN Kitchener came into the War Office he found that the arrangements for the mobilisation and despatch to France of our Expeditionary Force had been completed, that the Commander-in-Chief had been nominated, and that the scheme for the co-operation of our troops with the Army entrusted by the French Government to General Joffre had been outlined. Lord Haldane should have his due; during his tenure of office he had made it possible to send across the Channel, at a few days' notice, a compact and self-contained force of superfine quality and really "equipped to the last button." Further, he had prevailed on the then Prime Minister and the Foreign Secretary to allow the British and French Staffs to discuss co-operation between their respective Armies in the event of an enemy throwing down the glove. The arrangements so arrived at were to be precautionary and preparatory only, and were non-committal as regards either Government. But even if the conversations were naïvely accounted informal and the hostilities hypothetical, the occasion was none the less valuable, as securing a step, if a short one, towards preparedness.

A Continental Army which at the sound of the Rally can concentrate on its own ground may hardly appreciate the difficulties which beset an Insular

Power when engaged in mobilising and shipping overseas even a small body of troops. It behoved us to prepare bases at the ports both of embarkation and of disembarkation, to fit in our time-tables—which depended mostly on movements by sea—with the French time-tables, to arrange the lines of communication in a foreign country, to provide for the orderly and timely despatch over them of all the multifarious requirements of our Army, and tactfully to adjust our military methods, particularly as regards the billeting of troops, to those of our Allies.

To the careful preliminary work—of which a large proportion fell to the Quartermaster-General's department—the smooth arrival of the British troops at the indicated rendezvous in France bore the best testimony. Kitchener, who never favoured pulling up a plant to examine its roots, had little to add to the prepared programme, except to impose strict secrecy as to movements of troops.[1] His injunction in this respect provoked both pungent and pathetic comments as to denying "good-byes" and "send-offs"; but when it was suddenly announced that the entire Expeditionary Force had been landed in France without a single mishap, it was, then and thereafter, admitted that sentiment must be subordinated to safety.

As the British force formed but a small proportion of the Allies' strength in the West, our early plans were naturally and necessarily subject to those of General Joffre, the French Commander-in-Chief.

[1] An important personage said to Kitchener just then, "Is there any harm in my asking when the —— Brigade is likely to go to France?" "Oh no, there is not the least harm in your *asking*," was the courteous, if unsatisfying, answer.

Both General Staffs had made up their minds that in a European war Germany would set out to overrun and crush France quickly, while with the aid of Austria she held off the slow-moving masses of Russia. It was also fairly certain that she would not confine operations at the opening of the war to the comparatively narrow strip of the Franco-German frontier, but that, to give full play to her military might, she would defiantly violate the neutrality of both Luxemburg and Belgium. The moot point was whether she would cross the Meuse and march through Brussels to South-East Belgium, or, keeping south of the Meuse as far at least as Namur, would bring the right of her line through the Ardennes. Here opinions differed, the unknown factor being the force which Germany could bring to the West. It was known that the active army which she maintained in peace time consisted of 25 corps or 50 divisions, and of a large force of cavalry; and it was also known that she would at once supplement them with a number of reserve formations. But it was not known how many divisions would be ready to jump off, or what proportion of her army could be detailed to watch the Russians on the Eastern frontier.

The French General Staff had at their disposal $22\frac{1}{2}$ corps or 45 active divisions and a number of reserve formations. Once assured of five or six British divisions, and allowing for the contingent which Germany must set apart for her Eastern frontier, the French believed themselves strong enough to carry the war into the enemy's country.

As the French Government had no right, nor mind, to send troops across the frontiers of Belgium or Luxemburg until invited to do so, a French offensive could only be directed into Alsace and Lorraine. The original plans for the deployment of the French armies placed one-half of their total available strength on the Franco-German frontier, while other troops watched the *débouchés* from Luxemburg and the Ardennes. One whole army was kept in reserve, ready to back up the advance or to deal with any sudden occurrences in the north.

The French were unable to put their full weight into one great combined offensive, chiefly because Alsace-Lorraine did not afford room to manœuvre their entire force. Thus their military policy was in great degree bound to be opportunist. But the distribution shows that the General Staff did not at first contemplate the Germans traversing Belgium north of the Meuse in great masses.

After some preliminary skirmishes, the main French offensive began on August 14; Mulhouse was occupied, the outskirts of Colmar were reached, patrols were pushed forward to the Rhine, and a considerable portion of the main chain of the Vosges secured. In Lorraine the French armies fought their way slowly forward, and by August 19 had occupied Saarburg on the main line of railway connecting Strasbourg and Metz; but, as the Germans had calculated, this frontal advance was through difficult country, and the delaying power of modern quick-firing arms of precision made progress slow. Before any substantial success could be scored, happenings in the north necessitated a change in Joffre's programme. The enemy had in fact deployed his armies along the whole stretch of the Franco-Belgian frontier from Alsace to Aix-la-Chapelle. The Germans, estimating more accurately than we did the pace at which the Russian armies could be mobilised and brought forward, were content to leave only four of their twenty-five active corps with some reserve formations on their Eastern frontier; all the others they brought to the West, and supported them with many more reserve corps than they had been expected to produce in so short a time. Of this total force a large proportion was brought up on the frontier of Belgium, ready to cross the Meuse, pour down into Flanders, and roll up the Allied left wing.

Until Belgium should declare war and definitely appeal to the Allies for help, the French Commander could not, of course, so much as allow his aircraft to fly over Belgium territory. Thus he never discovered either the true strength of the German armies opposed to him or their general plan of campaign until the eve of their assault. The Germans had then perfectly veiled their arrangements, and had established an effective screen against the enterprises of the French cavalry, who could pick up but scanty information. By August 5 the German guns were trained on Liége: its forts were reported to be holding out bravely, but the appearance of large bodies of enemy cavalry in northern Belgium indicated pretty surely an advance in strength.

Joffre thereupon promptly extended his left northwards to the neighbourhood of the Belgian frontier near Maubeuge, and stiffened it by transferring troops from Alsace and Lorraine, simultaneously moving his reserve army forward to fill the gap. His general impression at this time was that the Germans could not bring to the West a force sufficient for three concurrent purposes—to oppose an offensive in Lorraine, to hold the Ardennes in strength, and to carry out the great attack through Belgium north of the Meuse. He believed that, if the Germans were strong on the Ardennes front, they would be weak north of the Meuse, and that his left, with the help of our little Army, could advance towards Brussels, combine with the Belgian Army under King Albert, and drive them back. The resistance of Liége warranted the hope that the Belgian fortresses of the Meuse, backed by the Belgian Army, would sufficiently detain the Germans for the execution of his manœuvre. On the other hand, should there be a great German advent north of the Meuse, the French Commander conceived that his enemy would be weak on the Ardennes front, and in that case he would order his left, with British support, to stay the German advance into Flanders while he would strike through the Ardennes against their flank. In either event he desired that the British Army should be concentrated as quickly as possible behind the fortress of Maubeuge, in readiness to act in unison with the French left.

These were the propositions unfolded to Lord Kitchener. He had enjoyed little opportunity of studying the problem in its complexities, and he had made no very exact calculations as to the strength of the enemy's forces and their probable distribution. But he was well informed as to the ideas prevalent in the German Army; he knew of their belief in the efficacy of attack by envelopment, and he did not think it probable that they would have attacked Liége, and thus taken the risk of bringing us into the war, unless they intended to hurl themselves through Belgium upon the Allied left flank.

It had been arranged that the British Army should concentrate about Amiens, but happenings on the Belgian frontier in the early days of August impelled Joffre to ask that its rendezvous should be fixed farther forward at Maubeuge. A party of French officers were sent over to London to press on Kitchener this plan—which Sir John French favoured—and a conference took place in the Secretary of State's room at the War Office on August 12. He listened carefully to the views expounded by the French and British Staffs, and then replied that he had understood and accepted that the concentration of troops was to be at Amiens, that he had already advised the Cabinet in that sense, and had drafted the instructions of His Majesty's Government to Sir John accordingly. He protested strongly against a concentration so far forward as Maubeuge; nothing, he urged, could be worse for the moral of our troops than that the result of their first meeting for over fifty years with a European enemy should be a compulsory retirement, which he regarded as the too likely sequel to detraining so far forward.

Kitchener then gave reasons for his belief that the German armies would penetrate Belgium north of the Meuse. His arguments were met with the polite but positive assurance that the plan propounded to him was the outcome of long and close study of local and strategical conditions, and was supported unanimously by French and British military opinion. With his finger on the mammoth map which hung in his room Kitchener dwelt and enlarged on the dangers of a great German enveloping movement against the Allied left flank, the brunt of which he shrewdly suspected would fall upon the British Army. His theory was met by counter-theory, and by an assurance that our troops would be in no danger. He was unconvinced, but felt that he could not oppose such a combination of experts, nor force his opinion on men who had devoted themselves to a study of the West, while his own attention had been so largely absorbed in the East. He yielded the point with the reservation that he must secure the consent of the Prime Minister. Mr. Asquith very naturally declined to overrule the experts, and so began and ended Kitchener's responsibility for a rendezvous which resulted in the heroic retreat from Mons. He believed his military instinct and logic to be correct, but he felt that, without much closer and more detailed study than he had been able to give to the problem, he could not speak authoritatively on the initial plan of campaign.

CHAPTER XCIV

KITCHENER could feel nothing but pleasure in the choice of Sir John French to command the British Army in France. He had watched and weighed his work in South Africa, and had understood that alike at Aldershot and in Whitehall Sir John had been the arch-apostle of modernism for the training and equipment of troops. From Pretoria the Commander-in-Chief had written to the War Secretary: "I am very glad you have selected French [for the Aldershot Command]; you could not have picked a better man. French is the most thoroughly loyal, energetic soldier I have, and all under him are devoted to him—not because he is lenient, but because they admire his soldier-like qualities."

To Roberts he had insistently commended him: "French is quite first-rate, and has the absolute confidence of all serving under him, as well as mine."

That the confidence was mutual is happily shown in a letter which, even in the stress of the Aisne battle, the Commander-in-Chief in France wrote:

G.H.Q., September 18, 1914.

MY DEAR LORD KITCHENER—Amongst my most treasured possessions at home is an old letter I have from you, written hurriedly on a telegraph form, telling me what you thought of our Kimberley and Paardeberg work with the Cavalry. It reached me when we were fighting. I think I've told you about this before. As a soldier I value your opinion and good word before anything. You can then well understand what I feel about your generous words in the House of Lords. I thank you with all my heart. You have given me incalculable encouragement and help.—Yours always,

J. D. P. FRENCH.

The original instructions, issued by the Secretary of State for War in the name of His Majesty's Government, were:

INSTRUCTIONS FOR THE GENERAL OFFICER COMMANDING THE EXPEDITIONARY FORCE PROCEEDING TO FRANCE

Owing to the infringement of the neutrality of Belgium by Germany, and in furtherance of the Entente which exists between this country and France, His Majesty's Government has decided, at the request of the French Government, to send an Expeditionary Force to France and to entrust the command of the troops to yourself.

The special motive of the Force under your command is to support, and co-operate with, the French Army against our common enemies. The peculiar task laid upon you is to assist (1) in preventing, or repelling, the invasion by Germany of French territory, and (2) in restoring the neutrality of Belgium.

These are the reasons which have induced His Majesty's Government to declare war, and these reasons constitute the primary objective you have before you.

The place of your assembly, according to present arrangements, is Amiens, and during the assembly of your troops you will have every opportunity for discussing with the Commander-in-Chief of the French Army the military position in general and the special part which your Force is able, and adapted, to play. It must be recognised from the outset that the numerical strength of the British Force—and its contingent reinforcements—is strictly limited, and with this consideration kept steadily in view it will be obvious that the greatest care must be exercised towards a minimum of losses and wastage.

Therefore, while every effort must be made to coincide most sympathetically with the plans and wishes of our Ally, the gravest consideration will devolve upon you as to participation in forward movements where large bodies of French troops are not engaged and where your Force may be unduly exposed to attack. Should a contingency of this sort be contemplated, I look to you to inform me fully and give me time to communicate to you any decision to which His Majesty's Government may come in the matter. In minor operations you should be careful that your subordinates understand that risk of serious losses should only be taken where such risk is authoritatively considered to be commensurate with the object in view.

The high courage and discipline of your troops should, and certainly will, have fair and full opportunity of display during the campaign, but officers may well be reminded that in this—their first—experience of European warfare a greater measure of caution must be employed than under former conditions of hostilities against an untrained adversary.

You will kindly keep up constant communication with the War Office, and you will be good enough to inform me as to all movements of the enemy reported to you as well as to those of the French Army.

I am sure you fully realise that you can rely with the utmost confidence on the whole-hearted and unswerving support of the Government, of myself, and of your compatriots, in carrying out the high duty which the King has entrusted to you, and in maintaining the great traditions of His Majesty's Army.

Kitchener thought that a homely word of advice from him might prove useful to soldiers suddenly thrust into strange circumstances and exposed to new forms of temptation, and that it would be taken in good part. The whirl of work did not prevent his drafting with his own hand a short message which he asked every soldier going on active service to keep in his Pay Book:

ADVICE TO SOLDIERS

[*This paper is to be considered by each soldier as confidential, and to be kept in his Active Service Pay Book.*]

You are ordered abroad as a soldier of the King to help our French comrades against the invasion of a common Enemy. You have to perform a task which will need your courage, your energy, your patience. Remember that the honour of the British Army depends on your individual conduct. It will be your duty not only to set an example of discipline and perfect steadiness under fire but also to maintain the most friendly relations with those whom you are helping in this struggle. The operations in which you are engaged will, for the most part, take place in a friendly country, and you can do your own country no better service than in showing yourself in France and Belgium in the true character of a British soldier.

Be invariably courteous, considerate, and kind. Never do anything likely to injure or destroy property, and always look upon looting as a disgraceful act. You are sure to meet with a welcome and to be trusted; your conduct must justify that welcome and that trust. Your duty cannot be done unless your health is sound.[1] So keep constantly on your guard against any excesses. In this new experience you may find temptations both in wine and women. You must entirely resist both temptations, and, while treating all women with perfect courtesy, you should avoid any intimacy.

        Do your duty bravely.
        Fear God.
        Honour the King.

                          KITCHENER,
                          Field-Marshal.

---

[1] Kitchener, in India, had warned the men under his command: "Although a soldier is no good unless he can use his rifle effectively in the fighting line, he has to get there, and must therefore be able to stand the strain and fatigue of a campaign. It is the duty of every soldier to keep himself fit and healthy. Wanton negligence of this important duty is quite as culpable as neglect to learn how to shoot." (At Meerut, November 1906.)

Meanwhile the mobilisation of our Army was proceeding smoothly, the advanced parties starting for France on August 11. Sir John with the Headquarters Staff followed a few days later, and after a rapturous reception in Paris and a cordial meeting with General Joffre, reached his Headquarters at Le Cateau on August 17.

Kitchener's earnest reminder to the Commander-in-Chief as to forward movements where he might be exposed to attack was prompted by his anxiety lest a German onslaught through Belgium should fall upon our slender Army in what he regarded as a perilous position. On August 17, anxious to know what French forces were covering our concentration near Maubeuge, he wired to Sir John: "Please let me know the number of French troops now lying west of the line Givet—Namur—Brussels, and where they are in touch with the Belgians." Sir John telegraphed: "Our concentration area amply covered by numerous French troops west of the line mentioned by you." He wrote the same day, giving full details of the French dispositions, and concluded:

I left Paris on Sunday morning (16th) by motor and reached the Headquarters of General Joffre at 12. They are at Vitry-le-François.

He quite realises the value and importance of adopting a waiting attitude. In the event of a forward movement by the German corps in the Ardennes and Luxemburg, he is anxious that I should act in échelon on the left of the Fifth French Army, whose dispositions I have given you. The French Cavalry Corps now north of the Sambre will operate on my left front and keep touch with the Belgians.

I spent the night at Rheims and motored this morning to Rethel, the Headquarters of General de Lanrezac, commanding the French Fifth Army. I had a long talk with him, and arranged for co-operation in all alternative circumstances. I then came to my headquarters at this place (Le Cateau) and found everything proceeding satisfactorily and up to time. . . .

P.S.—I am much impressed by what I have seen of the French General Staff. They are very deliberate, calm, and confident. There was a total absence of fuss and confusion, and a determination to give only a just and proper value to any reported successes. So far there has been no conflict of first-rate importance, but there has been enough fighting to justify a *hope* that the French Artillery are superior to the German. . . .

The French Fifth Army referred to in this letter was that which Joffre had sent northwards on the news of a German advance into Belgium, and was at this time marching to its new place of concentration in the angle between the Sambre and the Meuse, bounded roughly by the triangle Dinant—Namur—Charleroi. This movement, when completed, would place de Lanrezac immediately on the right of the British Army.

None the less, Kitchener was still anxious as to the German movement towards Brussels, news of which began to come in. On August 19 he wired to French: "The movement of the German right flank, north of the Meuse—which, if you will remember, I mentioned as likely to happen—seems to be definitely developing. Their Second and Tenth Corps, with three cavalry divisions, are now north of the Meuse, and are possibly being followed by reserve formations." He wrote next day:

War Office, *August* 20, 1914.

I see the German right flanking movement is being pressed in force. I do not know what is behind the Second and Tenth Corps—probably reserve formations. You may be in action about Sunday—on the Sambre, I presume. I have accelerated the despatch of a fifth division; as a matter of fact, they follow on as quickly as possible the last of your troops.

I hope you will let me have on Saturday an idea of how your own and the neighbouring French forces are disposed. I think the French ought to reinforce all they can, so as not to allow penetration between Maubeuge and Lille without considerable resistance. If held there, and you are on their flank, they ought to be in an awkward position. All depends on the French holding on to the south of Namur: that is vital. Best wishes.

But the German flanking movement was even more formidable than Kitchener presumed. The Sunday referred to was August 23, the day of the battle of Mons. The concentration of the British Army to the south of Maubeuge was completed on August 20, and on the 21st it marched for Mons. On that day Sir John replied to Kitchener's letter of the 20th:

Friday, August 21, 1914.

Thank you for yours of 20th. I fear I may be a little remiss in writing to you, but the situation changes with such rapidity, and false reports are so constant, that I defer sending you my real appreciation till I am fairly sure.

I don't think really serious fighting will commence before Monday (perhaps Sunday, but I don't think so now). I promise you to write my views at full length to-morrow (Saturday).

Our Cavalry have been nearly in touch with the enemy's Cavalry in the neighbourhood of Mons to-day. I was with Allenby up till 6 P.M. I say "nearly" because they were not actually in contact. I think I know the situation thoroughly, and I regard it as quite favourable to us.

Please be content with this till to-morrow.

We are all fit and well but working at high pressure day and night.

Thank you for the Fourth Division.

CHAPTER XCV

THE first four divisions of the Expeditionary Force to leave England were the First and Second, which formed the First Corps under Sir Douglas Haig; and the Third and Fifth, which made up the Second Corps entrusted to a distinguished and popular soldier, Sir James Grierson, who died in the train near Amiens, and was succeeded by Sir Horace Smith-Dorrien. The Government had decided that the two remaining divisions of our Regular Army, the Fourth and Sixth, should be kept in England for Home Defence until the Territorials should have had some training; but Kitchener persuaded the Cabinet to agree to the despatch of the Fourth Division—which is the "fifth division" he mentions in his letter—as quickly as transport would allow. It arrived at a most opportune moment.

On August 22, the eve of the battle of Mons, Sir John, after consultation with Joffre, sent Kitchener a formal review of the situation. The strength of the German turning movement through Belgium—inclusive of troops masking Namur, and others which must turn towards Antwerp—was estimated at 6 army corps, 3 cavalry divisions, and 2 or 3 reserve divisions. Opposed to these were the Fifth French Army composed of 5 army corps, 3 cavalry divisions, and 2 reserve divisions; and the British force of 2 army corps, 1 cavalry division—stronger by one cavalry brigade than any German cavalry division—and, in addition, 1 cavalry and 1 infantry brigade. On this estimate, after allowing for the German forces which would be detained before Antwerp and Namur, the Allies might reckon to range about 7 army corps and 4 cavalry divisions against about 5½ German corps and 3 cavalry divisions—quite a comfortable superiority, the more so as behind them stood the strongly garrisoned fortress of Maubeuge, and the French garrison of Reserve and Territorial troops holding Valenciennes.

General Joffre's general plan [Sir John went on to say] has been in course of operation since yesterday, during which time the Third and Fourth French Armies east of the Meuse have made considerable advances. His intention is to attack in force in a northerly direction east of the Meuse with 9½ corps (Third and Fourth French Armies), 3 or 4 Cavalry divisions and Reserve divisions.

The Fifth French Army west of the Meuse and the British forces are to hold back in their present positions until the Third and Fourth Armies come into line, and then a general advance north is to be made.

In other words, Joffre had decided definitely on a great offensive through the Ardennes against the flank of the German forces marching through Belgium. The rôle of his left—composed of his Fifth Army and the British divisions—was to await the result of this offensive, to hold up the German advance—if it were pressed—and at the psychological moment, when the attack of the Third and Fourth Armies had begun to take effect, to sweep forward and thrust the enemy right back through Belgium.

Sir John completed a very lucid story late in the evening:

Since I dictated this at 3 or 3.30 P.M. I have more news to report. I find the French Third Army in rear of our right, east of the Meuse, is not quite so far forward as I thought. They are in échelon on the right of the Fourth Army, and were this morning engaged with three German Corps on their front. The Germans do not appear to be pressing their attacks between Charleroi and Namur. The latter place was heavily attacked at 12 to-day, but seems all right. German cavalry with their usual Jäger supports have been hammering away at Gough and Chetwode [1] most of the day. We have captured several prisoners, and our losses are very slight.

All quiet to-night. The spirit and dash of our Cavalry is splendid. Horses are very good and in good condition. I have laid the strictest injunction on Allenby to save them and nurse them to the utmost, and not to commit them to any appreciable extent. We get all the information that is possible from the aircraft. The concentration is complete, except two ambulances which come up to-morrow. All are in the best of condition and in the highest spirits. The billets are excellent. I have given you the best information at my disposal, but the fog of war has not yet lifted.

Kitchener received the letter at 8 P.M. on Sunday, August 23, and after reading it felt much relieved. The concentration of the British Army had been accomplished, and with it was dissipated one danger which he had apprehended. He had always been anxious lest the Germans might descend upon us in force before we had made ready to accept battle. But now Joffre's plan was in full swing, and on that left flank, which concerned us so vitally, the Allies seemed in superior force to the enemy. As he had said in his letter of the 20th, all depended on the

[1] Sir Hubert Gough and Sir Philip Chetwode, both then commanding cavalry brigades.

French holding on to the south of Namur; but the French Fifth Army was in place, and our Commander-in-Chief had reported that the Germans did not appear to be pressing their attacks on the Sambre between Namur and Charleroi. The Minister congratulated himself all that evening that perhaps, after all, his fears had been groundless. He was late in retiring to rest, and as he mounted the stairs turned round to a friend and said, "Nothing is certain, but I think we may have really good news in the morning."

But that very afternoon "the fog of war" had lifted in Belgium and the storm had burst. The force brought by the Germans through Belgium, north of the Meuse and against Namur, was not 6 army corps, 3 cavalry divisions, and 2 or 3 reserve divisions, as had been supposed; but 7 active and 5 reserve corps, and 5 cavalry divisions—nearly double the strength the Allies had calculated to be threatening their left. The enemy, leaving sufficient troops to watch the Belgian Army in Antwerp, were launching two great armies—the first under von Kluck against the British, the second under von Bülow against de Lanrezac; a third army was moving through the Northern Ardennes against de Lanrezac's right flank, between Namur and Dinant.

Kitchener had rightly surmised that the Germans would not violate the neutrality of Belgium for nothing, and now they had sprung their great surprise on us. As Sir John explained in his first despatch, he had accepted battle at Mons on the strength of an assurance received from the French Headquarters that he was opposed by only one, or at most two, of the enemy army corps, with perhaps one cavalry division. At 5 P.M. on the afternoon of August

23 he learned from Joffre the unpleasant truth that Namur had fallen, its forts smashed by the fire of the heavy Austrian howitzers; that the French Fifth Army had been driven back from the Sambre and the Meuse by the German Second and Third Armies, and was in retreat; and that the force confronting the British Army consisted of at least three German corps, while a fourth was endeavouring to get round our left flank.

Joffre's offensive through the Ardennes had been delayed by the difficulties of the country, in which the famous French 75's could find little scope, and the favourite German device of envelopment had—as Kitchener expected that it might—so far justified itself that it had taken effect more quickly than the French frontal advances. By skill and secrecy, by a bold acceptance of risk on their Eastern frontier, and by an unscrupulous violation of Belgian neutrality, the Germans had succeeded in turning the whole Allied line from the north, and our little Army on the extreme left was in the post of greatest danger. There was nothing for it but retreat—the retreat which Kitchener had all too correctly feared.

In the early hours of the 24th Sir John telegraphed that he must retreat from Mons:

> My troops have been engaged all day on a line roughly E. and W. through Mons; the attack was renewed after dark, but we hold our ground tenaciously. I have just received message from G.O.C. Fifth Army that his troops have been driven back; that Namur has fallen; and that he is taking up a line from Maubeuge to Rocroy. I have therefore ordered a retirement to the line Valenciennes—Longueville—Maubeuge, which is being carried out now. It will prove a difficult operation if the enemy remain in contact. I re-

member your precise instructions as to method and direction of retirement if necessity arises. I think that immediate attention should be directed to defence of Havre; will keep you fully informed.

The instructions as to the direction of retirement had laid down that, if it became a question of falling back upon the Channel ports so as to cover them, or of preserving touch with the French Armies, the ports must be abandoned, and everything staked upon keeping line with our Allies. Kitchener saw that, if once the Germans succeeded in driving a wedge between us and the French, they would be in a position either to hold off Sir John with a small force, while throwing their weight against Joffre, or else to annihilate us and then bear down upon the French—alternatives equally disastrous in their effect upon the public temper in France. He had no difficulty in persuading the Government that, having put our hand to the plough, we must at all hazard support our Allies; and after Mons the Channel ports were, as a matter of fact, let go, and lay at the enemy's mercy.

But the German High Command was then trying for bigger game, and—aiming at nothing less than the complete destruction of the Allied Forces in France and the occupation of Paris—postponed any diversion to the sea. Whether the Germans were strong enough to hold the ports if they had occupied them, and what would have been the effect upon the course of the war if they had held them, will remain an attractive theme of military debate; but no doubt can be cast on the wisdom of Kitchener's decision. Had we fallen back upon the coast instead of upon Paris, there would have been no battle of the Marne.

CHAPTER XCVI

THE news of the retreat from Mons caused great perturbation at home; but Kitchener, who saw his worst fears realised, retained his usual calm. Nothing could be more foreign to him than to hint an "I told you so," and his first act on hearing of the battle was to pencil a telegram to Sir John—"Congratulate troops on splendid work. We are all proud of them." To this the Commander-in-Chief replied on the 25th:

Thanks for your wire of to-day congratulating the troops. They really have behaved quite magnificently. . . . You will remember all I told you in my letter of the 22nd. Had the advance been commenced on Sunday, as I was led to suppose it would, we should have got well into Belgian territory before we came to close quarters with the Germans. We should probably have hampered their deployment and secured many advantages which this unfortunate delay has now made impossible. . . . From 6 P.M. on Sunday 23rd to daybreak on Monday we were engaged in making dispositions for retiring to a position which had been previously reconnoitred, between Maubeuge and Jenlain, south-east of Valenciennes.

I have not time to go into details here, but the enemy tried hard to hold us to the position and was vigorous in following up. In spite of this the retirement was effected and the new position occupied at nightfall, when the enemy drew off and firing ceased.

I am sure the Germans in the afternoon made a vigorous attempt to drive us under the forts at Maubeuge and shut us up there. Their attack on our left was pushed so hard with that object only. I understand from prisoners and from other more reliable sources that the German losses were tremendous. I cannot speak too highly in praise of all ranks; but particularly I must mention the two Army Corps Commanders and Allenby. They directed their commands with the utmost skill. . . .

This letter was supplemented by a telegram:

Retirement continued to-day without serious hindrance from the enemy. Am halting for the night on the line Landrecies—Le Cateau—Cambrai. To-morrow will continue retiring in the direction of Peronne. Our casualties roughly 2500. Condition of the troops is excellent. They are convinced of their superiority and most unwilling to retire further. I shall explain to them that the operations of our Allies are the cause of this.

On the 26th Kitchener wired to Sir John: "It is vital that at the earliest possible moment we should have reliable information as to Joffre's intentions."

Have had long interview [Sir John promptly answered] with Joffre, who admits failure of his first plan, but now intends to retire with the English Army and the Third, Fourth, and Fifth French Armies to the line Amiens—Rheims. He hopes thus to secure a valuable delay and to draw the Germans from the wooded country of the Ardennes frontier, and then to attack and drive them back. At Amiens another French Army Corps is being detrained coming from the south, which will make attacking line 17 army corps and 9 cavalry divisions.

Joffre attributes failure of his first plan to precipitous and wooded nature of the country in the Ardennes and near the Meuse. He expects under present plan to get better advantages from his unquestionably superior artillery.

The spirit of the French regular troops is high. They are very good, and are well and efficiently led by their officers.

After some details as to the day's operations, he added:

I do not recommend troops landing in Belgium. I feel absolutely certain all reinforcements should be devoted to the Army in France. To divert the Sixth Division would be most disappointing and injurious. I hope to have them at once, having been terribly hampered by my losses, increased by the weakness of my force.

The interview with General Joffre recorded in this telegram took place at St. Quentin at about noon on the 26th. While Sir John was at St. Quentin he heard from Smith-Dorrien that he had been unable to continue his retreat towards Peronne, as the Commander-in-Chief had intended, but had been obliged to stand and fight in a position to the west of Le Cateau with the two divisions, Third and Fifth, of his own Corps, Allenby's Cavalry, the 19th Infantry Brigade, and the Fourth Division, just arrived from England. With this force Smith-Dorrien met the attacks of the major portion of von Kluck's Army, held them off through the burden and heat of the day, and in the late afternoon effected his retreat.

Kitchener's reply of the 27th shows how sorely he was put to it to reinforce the heroic troops who were battling for every inch of ground—and this quite apart from the raising and equipping of his New Armies:

When the Defence Committee and the General Staff decided on sending a force abroad, it was laid down that the Sixth Division, though kept quite in readiness, should not leave England until the Territorial Force had had time to do some training. If this Sixth Division had gone, you know what Regular forces would have been left here; besides which there would only be immobile Reserve Battalions in Coast defences, and the unfit and untrained Territorials.

Every effort has been made to increase the Regular forces at home in order to release the Sixth Division. I could not relieve the Malta garrison at once, as the situation in Egypt looked bad, owing to the attitude of Turkey. The General there, after finding the necessary guards, had only 1000 men to deal with internal disorder, and could only be supported from Malta. A division was sent from India as soon as the escort and transport could be provided. On their arrival, native troops will relieve Malta, and the troops in Gibraltar, Malta, and Egypt will come home.

The whole of the forces in South Africa have been sent home as quickly as possible. The garrisons of Hong-Kong, with China, Singapore, Mauritius, and Bermuda, will be relieved by native troops from India; and troops from Canada and corresponding British battalions will be withdrawn from India without waiting for relief.

By these means I hope to get a Seventh Regular Division together here between September 12 and 15, and some time later an Eighth Division as well as a Cavalry Division. As soon as the first troops of the Seventh Division arrive I have little doubt but that the Sixth Division will join you. In the meantime your wastage shall be fully filled up.

When the despatch of the Expeditionary Force was decided upon by the Government, its strength was to be four divisions, two remaining in England for eventualities. But as soon as it was seen that the Germans were moving their main forces north of the Meuse, and that you would therefore bear the brunt of the attack, a fifth division was sent to strengthen you, and practically joined up with the last troops of the original four.

I will communicate your telegram to the Cabinet to-day, and the matter of the Sixth Division will be again discussed here.

We all feel what a splendid effort you and your troops are making against superior odds. We are all determined to support you to the utmost, and to see that, as soon as possible, you shall be provided with an adequate force, which will increase as we go on. Our first thought is for your needs. I only wanted your opinion on the Belgian project, and you can rely upon me not only upon this occasion, but on all others, to follow your opinion wherever I can possibly do so. But pray do not increase my troubles by the thought that if the Division had been with you, some of your men's lives might have been saved. Do remember that we shall have to go through much more fighting before we are out of the war, and that by prematurely putting all our eggs in one basket we might incur far greater losses. Believe me, had I been consulted on military matters during the last three years, I would have done everything in my power to prevent the present state of affairs in which this country finds itself.

To this Sir John answered on the 28th:

I understand entirely and fully appreciate your reasons for postponing for a while the despatch of the Sixth Division.

Against our force of five divisions and one cavalry division, von Kluck had at this time ten divisions and three cavalry divisions; even if the despatch of our Sixth Division immediately after the Fourth had been possible, they would only have become involved in the retreat without materially affecting the issue, and the Commander-in-Chief would not have enjoyed the potent contribution which they brought to the battle of the Marne.

CHAPTER XCVII

THE Commander-in-Chief's first reports of the battle of Le Cateau and of the subsequent retirement were far more cheerful than Kitchener had dared to expect:

August 27.—The troops under my command were again heavily engaged yesterday. We were forced during our retirement to stand and fight on the line roughly Cambrai—Landrecies. My troops were opposed to the attack on this line of no less than 5 German Army Corps and 2 Cavalry Divisions. . . . Throughout the day and night hardly any support was forthcoming from the French Army. All along the line the retirement has been going on since 2 P.M. yesterday, with short rests. Considering the overpowering force in front of them the troops have been wonderfully steady. I have at last been able to induce the Fifth French Army on my right and 3 Divisions French Cavalry on my left to move up and take the pressure off me. There is now no sign of further German advance in my direction, and we have retired far enough to shake off further molestation. I therefore presume that the action of the French forces on my flank has accomplished this most necessary object. To-morrow I hope to be in a position of comparative safety south of the Somme River near to Ham. From there I intend to retire behind the river Oise near Noyon. Joffre has assigned this point in the new line to the British Army as the starting point in the new dispositions which I communicated to you to-day, and as telegraphed to me in terms of deep gratitude.

A letter of the same date gave further detail:

CAMBRAI—LANDRECIES

Noyon, *August* 27, 1914.

My dear Lord K.—You must bear with me if I do not write privately as often as I could wish, but you know well what all this work means. I earnestly hope that the enemy are now shaken off our front for a few days, and that I shall have a little time and thought to spare.

Of course I have had a terribly anxious time. You know the circumstances under which we were left in a more or less isolated position, and I feel sure that a determined and vigorous attempt has been made by the Germans (1) to drive us under the forts at Maubeuge and surround us, and (2) having failed in (1) to concentrate an overwhelming force in our front and practically destroy us. I believe the Emperor in his rancour and hate has really risked weakness in other parts of the field in order to finish off the British forces.

In the course of a few days you will have my full official despatches covering the fighting which has gone on continuously from noon on Sunday, 23rd August, up to 6 p.m. yesterday, 26th August. It really constituted a three days' battle.

You know in outline of the events of Sunday, the 23rd, on the "Mons" position; of Monday, the 24th, in the retirement of the "Maubeuge" position; and of Tuesday, the 25th, in the retirement to the "Cambrai" position.

I have sent you a telegraphic despatch to-day recounting the events of yesterday, the 26th. The position "Cambrai —Landrecies" was occupied very hurriedly.

The men were exhausted and wanted food. I wanted to keep all their power for marching and not to fatigue them with digging, but we had previously got some local labour and done a certain amount of entrenching. . . . Both Army Commanders have proved themselves most efficient and intrepid leaders of troops in war. I am deeply indebted to them. . . .

The next day Sir John could say, "My concentration near Noyon is nearly complete. No fighting to-day, and am nearly sure of securing two or three days' rest. The spirit of the troops is quite wonderful. I know your anxiety about casualties and will do my very best to ascertain them."

The Army Corps described by Sir John on the 26th as having come from the south and detrained at Amiens was the Seventh French Corps, which formed the nucleus of Maunoury's Sixth Army, soon to figure in forbidding the first great German offensive. From this time onwards Joffre was continually transferring troops from his right to his left. He had been hoping to take the offensive on the line Amiens—Rheims from which his Armies had been forced back by the attempted engirdling of their left, but our abandonment of Le Havre and the transfer of our base to St. Nazaire on the Atlantic had seriously increased the congestion of the French railways in and around Paris. Besides the transport of French troops through the capital to the Allied left flank, they had to supply all our requirements, and by lines which crossed the French movements. Delay was inevitable, and before Maunoury could muster sufficient force to hold the line of the Somme to the east of Amiens, von Kluck had driven him back and compelled him to retire on Paris.

On August 29 de Lanrezac on our right had made a successful counter-attack on von Bülow near Guise, and next day Sir John telegraphed to Kitchener:

August 30.—It is reported this morning that the right of the Fifth French Army attacked and threw back in the neighbourhood of Guise the three German Army Corps which were advancing on their flank from the north. The French are also reported to be holding their own well from

Guise to their left, which is near Beney and north-west of La Fère.

The German Army Corps which was moving south yesterday on Guiscard, through Ham, appears to have turned its attention to a considerable extent to the left of the Fifth French Army and is not pressing on. The Seventh French Army Corps holds the same position on our left as last night, but it appears that its right has been thrown more forward. About 2 P.M. yesterday the two or three German Army Corps opposite to it appear to have discontinued their attack and to have retreated some miles towards the Somme and Péronne. The German Army Corps which were reported to be defeated near Guise consist of the Tenth Corps, the Guard, and a Reserve Corps. I am now proceeding to refit and reorganise with all speed in a position south of the Oise. The anxiety caused by ignorance as to casualties is felt by none more than myself.

This information from the Commander-in-Chief tended to convey the impression that our little Army was in process of extricating itself from what had seemed to be a terrible plight. Our losses, as given by Sir John, were smaller than Kitchener had feared, and he had despatched to France more than sufficient to make them good.[1] De Lanrezac's success at Guise on our right and the arrival of French reinforcements on our left showed that close contact between the two Armies was assured; cordial co-operation had not only survived the early difficulties to which Allies are prone when strange to one another's ways, but had been proof against the strain and jars inherent in an enforced retirement. It was therefore a rude shock to him to receive from Gen-

[1] On August 25 the I.G.C. telegraphed to G.H.Q. asking if he could send forward from the advanced base the men forming the reinforcements, and the guns, up into the line; but was told to keep them in hand for the moment.

eral Robb, the Inspector-General of Communications in France, a message that he had heard from G.H.Q. of the Commander-in-Chief's decision to make a definite and prolonged retreat due south, passing by Paris to the east or west. Kitchener at once repeated this message to Sir John, anxiously inquiring its meaning, and early the next morning his fears were confirmed. Sir John telegraphed:

The French Army advanced yesterday from the line of the Oise River with the result that the left of the advance fully held its own with the Germans and the right won a great success. It appears that the three German Corps, the Tenth, the Guard, and the Reserve Corps, moved from the direction of Le Cateau south in order to attack in the neighbourhood of Guise the right of the Fifth French Army. The French drove them back in disorder and with great losses, and I have every reason to believe that the Commander of the Tenth German Corps was killed. From the situation to-day on my front I should gather that the pressure on our centre and left has been relieved by the success, although there are still some German troops remaining in front of the Seventh French Corps to the south-west of Peronne. The Fifth and Fourth French Armies have been ordered to retire on the river Serre, the right of the Fourth Army being toward Rethel, and the left of the Fifth Army resting on La Fère. The Sixth French Army, comprising the Seventh Corps, the Cavalry Corps, 4 Reserve divisions, and possibly the Sixth Corps, had been ordered to fall back to the line Compiègne—Clèremont. General Joffre appeared to me to be anxious that I should keep the position which I am now occupying north of the line Compiègne—Soissons. I have let him know plainly that in the present position of my troops I shall be absolutely unable to remain in the front line as he has now begun his retirement. I have decided to begin my retirement to-morrow in the morning behind the Seine in a south-westerly direction west of Paris.

This means marching for some eight days without fatiguing the troops at a considerable distance from the enemy. It will be possible for us to commence our reorganisation on the road. My base is now in the neighbourhood of La Rochelle, and I am now forming an advance base at Le Mans. All that we need to refit and make good our deficiencies can be sent from this latter place up to meet us at points behind the Seine which I select and which will be quite safe under the outlying forts of Paris. I do not like General Joffre's plan. I should have liked to have assumed a vigorous offensive at once, and this has been represented to him, but he pleads in reply the present inability of the British Army to go forward as a reason for retirement and delay. Of course, in view of the advance of the Russians, he may be right. My intentions have been misunderstood by the I.G. I have no idea of making any prolonged and definite retreat.

A few hours after this ominous telegram had been deciphered the King's Messenger arrived with a gloomy letter: COMPIÈGNE, *August* 30, 1914.

MY DEAR LORD K.—This is the first day that we have been able to obtain any details as to casualties.

As you are aware, these returns should be sent to the War Office from the Line of Communications, but I have thought it advisable to send you a copy of the return which has been sent for my information to-night. It is accurate, and you will know best how to deal with it as regards the relatives and the public.

I think I may say that we are now free from any annoyance in our further daily marching, which I have arranged to be short in order that we may make progress every day towards re-establishing a normal state of affairs. Therefore I hope an amended return will be sent in to me every night, as missing men are found and the fate of others becomes decidedly known. I will forward copies of such returns direct to you.

The Line of Communications will, of course, furnish returns to the War Office, in accordance with regulations; but by means of these private communications I shall be able to put you in possession of the facts far more quickly than they would come officially.

I cannot say that I am happy in the outlook as to the further progress of the campaign in France. . . .

My confidence in the ability of the leaders of the French Army to carry this campaign to a successful conclusion is fast waning, and this is my real reason for the decision I have taken to move the British Forces so far back.

To-night a report has come in that the Fourth French Army has been driven back towards Rethel. This was the line which, as I explained to you in my wire this morning, was assigned to it in the new dispositions of General Joffre; and so the rumour that he was driven back may not be true, but still it is very disquieting.

I feel most strongly the absolute necessity for retaining in my hands complete independence of action and power to retire on my base when circumstances render it necessary.[1]

I have been pressed very hard to remain, even in my shattered condition, in the fighting line; but I have absolutely refused to do so, and I hope you will approve of the course I have taken. Not only is it in accordance with the spirit and letter of your instructions, but it is dictated by common sense.

Knowing what I do of the French soldiers' fighting capabilities and the immense amount of energy, skill, time, and trouble which for many years has been brought to bear upon their training and efficiency, I can attribute these constant failures to no other cause than defective higher leading. . . .

The bright spot in this dark picture is to be found in the proved certainty of the superiority of the British troops over the German. Our Cavalry do as they like with them. The German patrols simply fly before our horsemen until

---

[1] In his book *1914*, Lord French, quoting this letter, says "to retire towards my base should circumstances render it necessary." The difference is not without distinction in military parlance.

they are confronted by thrice their numbers. They will not face our infantry fire; and as regards our artillery they have never been opposed by less than three or four times their numbers, so it is impossible to judge of their relative superiority. But I firmly believe, with our splendid gun detachments, our magnificent artillery officers, our heavy 18-pounder shell and our five-inch heavy gun, they will hold their own with a superior German artillery in front of them.

I sent Seely up to Guise yesterday to ascertain the truth as to the French victory there on the 29th. He saw the Commanders of the Third and Twentieth French Corps (those engaged). It is perfectly true that they gave the Germans a real hard knock (Guard, Tenth, and a Reserve German Corps).—Yours, J. F.

CHAPTER XCVIII

KITCHENER regarded the proposals in this letter and in the telegram which arrived a few hours before as calamitous. For him—with his long view of the war and his sense of the country's stupendous commitment—the Expeditionary Force was the point of the spear which he was fashioning. He knew that he could make of the British Empire a great military power, but he must have time on his side, and meantime we must keep tight hold of the hand of our Allies; the mere appearance of deserting them when their troops were giving ground to the invader and Paris was threatened would be a disaster. From the first hours of the retirement his counsel was, "We are falling back in unison; so long as we keep together and forbid the enemy to separate us, even the loss of Paris can be repaired." His first thought on receiving the untoward messages from France was that an independent retreat of such magnitude as an eight days' march would be not only a violation of the spirit of the *Entente,* but a negation of the policy enjoined by the British Government.

In the original instructions issued to the Commander-in-Chief it was definitely laid down that the primary function of the force under his command was to support and co-operate with the French Army

CH. XCVIII THE DANGER OF CLEAVAGE 51

against our common enemies. Kitchener had cautioned Sir John against participating in forward movements in which large bodies of French troops would not be engaged. But here was no question of a forward movement. While Joffre had decided upon a general retreat, Sir John was proposing to withdraw from the Allied line altogether. Kitchener held that to take the British Army away would spell something even worse than disaster.

A question of policy being at issue, the Secretary for War asked the Prime Minister to summon the Cabinet at once, and telegraphed to the Commander-in-Chief:

> I am surprised at your decision to retire behind the Seine. Please let me know, if you can, all your reasons for this move. What will be the effect of this course upon your relations with the French Army and on the general military situation? Will your retirement leave a gap in the French line or cause them discouragement, of which the Germans might take advantage to carry out their first programme of first crushing the French and then being free to attack Russia? Thirty-two trains of German troops were yesterday reported moving from the Western field to meet the Russians. Have all your requirements been supplied by the Line of Communications and how has your reorganisation progressed?

Having sent this off, Kitchener took Sir John's telegram to the Cabinet, where it was regarded as of the utmost gravity. The War Minister, as their military adviser, represented to his colleagues the serious danger which must lie in any cleavage between the French and British troops. The retirement of the British Army to the indicated position behind the Seine, even for the purpose of refitting and reforming the troops, might mean nothing less than the loss of the war. He was heart and soul with the British Commander-in-Chief in the difficulties which beset him, but every other consideration must yield to the paramount necessity of his maintaining touch with Joffre.

The Prime Minister was no less insistent that the policy of the Government, as defined in Sir John's original instructions, must be followed, and Kitchener was asked to telegraph:

August 31.—Your telegram 162 submitted to the Cabinet. The Government are exceedingly anxious lest your force, at this stage of the campaign in particular, should, owing to your proposed retirement so far from the line, not be able to co-operate closely with our Allies and render them continual support. They expect that you will as far as possible conform to the plans of General Joffre for the conduct of the campaign. They are waiting for the answer which you will no doubt send to my telegram of this morning, and have all possible confidence in your troops and yourself.

Kitchener waited all the evening for Sir John's reply, and when it reached the War Office at midnight ordered it to be repeated to him word by word as deciphered. It ran:

August 31.—I have despatched by messenger who left early this morning a letter to you. I have explained in this at length the reasons for the course which I have taken. If the French go on with their present tactics, which are practically to fall back right and left of me, usually without notice, and to abandon all idea of offensive operations, of course then the gap in the French line will remain and the consequences must be borne by them. I can only state that it will be difficult for the force under my command to withstand successfully in its present condition a strong attack by even one German Army Corps, and in the event of a pause in my retirement I must expect two Army Corps at least, if not three. If owing to Russian pressure the withdrawal of the Germans turn out to be true, it will be easy for me to arrest my retirement and to refit north of Paris; but this I cannot do while my rearguards are still engaged, as it was to last night. An effective offensive movement now appears to be open to the French, which will probably close the gap by uniting their inner flanks. But as they will not take such an opportunity I do not see why I should be called upon again to run the risk of absolute disaster in order a second time to save them. I do not think you understand the shattered condition of the second Army Corps, and how it paralyses my power of offence. If I have time to refit the force in the proper manner when our further reinforcements arrive it will be a self-contained and efficient army capable of acting with telling effect. With reference to the progress of the reorganisation, the French retirements, which I am obliged to flank march, have made any progress quite impossible, though I have been able to obtain a certain amount of rest for the troops. My supply and L. of C. have been both excellent in every way. The difficulty in organisation is not behind but in front. I think you had better trust me to watch the situation, and act according to circumstances. Your second telegram to-day. If the French Armies are not driven south of their present situation I could engage not to go back further than a line drawn E. and W., through Nanteuil. I shall reach this position to-morrow, and will endeavour to refit there.

This telegram only reiterated the reasons for that independent movement which Kitchener dreaded. He quickly made up his mind. He must cross the Channel immediately and discuss the position and prospect orally with the Commander-in-Chief. He could do no more by telegraph, and to avert what might prove an irreparable ill, he must urge the views of the Cabinet personally. It was then one o'clock in the morning of September 1. Half-an-hour later Sir Edward Grey was startled from sleep by Kitchener's walking into his bedroom and telling him that, after consulting the Prime Minister, he had ordered a destroyer to be ready within three hours to take him to Le Havre. He then wired to Sir John:

Has a message from the President of the French Republic about leaving the line reached you yet? The result of this may be serious to the French Army, and we feel that you should call upon your troops for an effort. I am coming to see you this morning to talk over the situation, as I find it very difficult to judge. Please send a telegram to the Embassy at Paris stating where we can most conveniently meet.[1]

Kitchener had no misgivings as to his mission. As Secretary of State he must convey to the Commander-in-Chief in the field instructions as to the policy of the Government. He had no idea of interfering with the military execution of the policy,[2] but every intention of seeing that the policy was understood, and that the instructions would be fol-

---

[1] Before receiving this message, Sir John had sent a telegram which Kitchener did not receive until his return from Paris:

"I wish you to clearly understand that in my opinion the force under my command is not in its present condition able to render effective support to our Allies no matter what their position may be. I don't seem able to bring home to the Cabinet the shattered condition of 2 Divisions of my small force, and the necessity of rest and refitment for the remainder. . . .

"If you order it we will go up into the front line to-morrow and do our utmost, but I am convinced it would end in grave disaster to the French troops, for I could never extricate them as I did before. I am grateful to you for the confidence you express in me and my troops, and your words are a great encouragement to all of us."

[2] A week or two later, when the relief of Antwerp was in question, Sir John wrote to the War Minister:

"I never for a moment supposed you wished to interfere with my operations."

lowed. He travelled in uniform, which, like every other War Office official, he constantly wore, but nothing was further from his mind than to take any advantage of his being a senior Field-Marshal; and, fully aware of Sir John's anxieties and preoccupations, Kitchener was careful to leave to him the choice of the meeting-place, so as neither to pay an inconvenient visit to General Headquarters nor draw the Commander-in-Chief any distance away from them. The meeting was held at the British Embassy, the place selected by Sir John for that afternoon.

Even by then the situation had sensibly improved. Von Kluck, instead of following up the British in hot pursuit after the battle of Le Cateau, had switched off towards Amiens, and after driving back Maunoury's Army had swerved back again in an attempt to cross our front and cut off the French Fifth Army from the Marne. These movements took off pressure successively from ourselves and from Maunoury. Our men were quickly refreshed by a short rest and a few square meals, and the respite gave Maunoury's Army time to grow. In these happier conditions Sir John cordially undertook to do all that the Government had asked.

Immediately after the meeting Kitchener drafted a letter to Sir John to confirm the conclusions reached at their interview:

September 1, 7.30 P.M.

MY DEAR FRENCH—After thinking over our conversation to-day I think I am giving the sense of it in the following telegram to Government I have just sent:

"French's troops are now engaged in the fighting line, where he will remain conforming to the movements of the French Army, though at the same time acting with caution to avoid being in any way unsupported on his flanks."

I feel sure you will agree that the above represents the conclusions we came to; but in any case, until I can communicate with you further in answer to anything you may wish to tell me, please consider it as an instruction.

By being in the fighting line you of course understand I mean dispositions of your troops in contact with, though possibly behind, the French as they were to-day; of course you will judge as regards their position in this respect.

I was very pleased to meet you to-day and hope all will go well, and that Joffre and you will make the best plans possible for the future, which you will, I hope, communicate to me. I leave the first thing to-morrow morning.—Yours very truly, K.

I hope you will do your utmost to refit as soon as possible from the Lines of Communications, and put in men and horses necessary to refill units to their proper strength.

Thus happily ended an episode which Kitchener himself always looked back upon as one of the most pregnant of the war. In the succeeding twenty-two months he had many talks in many places with Sir John, but no conversation was more fraught with anxiety, or more fruitful in success, than the rapid exchange of views in Paris in the seemingly darkest hour when official Paris was betaking itself to Bordeaux. Our retirement continued, but without serious molestation. It was possible to give the troops much-needed sleep and rest; drafts to replace casualties came steadily up, and fresh equipments speedily repaired the ravages of the retreat from Mons.

On September 2 Sir John wired cheerfully that a further marked improvement had already taken place; and next day he could report that Joffre was planning a vigorous offensive in which he could bear his part.

On September 5 Joffre had given the signal.[1] Von Kluck had rashly crossed the Marne, leaving only one reserve corps to watch Maunoury, whose army, now assembled to the north of Paris, had reached formidable proportions. A new French army—the Ninth, under Foch—had been formed and brought in on the right of the French Fifth Army, in support of the Allied centre. On this day, September 5, Maunoury struck at the German force which was opposite to him west of the Ourcq, and so opened the fateful battle of the Marne. A day earlier Kitchener had wired to Sir John:

Am informed by the Ambassador that General Joffre now considers the strategical situation to be excellent, and has decided to employ all his troops on a most vigorous offensive. General Joffre considers it very essential that you should fully realise that it is most important that you should co-operate most vigorously with him. Please inform me when you can when this offensive movement will be taken, as the above message does not state this. Of course we can fully trust you to use your force to the best advan-

---

[1] Kitchener had telegraphed to Joffre:
Je me hâte de vous remercier du fond du cœur pour les mots que vous avez adressés à Sir John French et qu'il vient de me transmettre. Je suis surtout très sensible aux éloges que vous faites sur les travaux de nos soldats qui se trouvent rangés à côté des vôtres.

"Il paraît que nos Anglais ont subi ces jours-ci des attaques lancées par des corps allemands dont la supériorité numérique était formidable et je ne peux que regretter profondément les pertes sérieuses qui nous ont été imposées.

"J'espère que le soutiens solide que nous prêteront les troupes françaises parviendra à diminuer la pression écrasante que notre ennemi a exercée sur les troupes anglaises et que les soldats français et anglais s'appuieront constamment les uns sur les autres avec une entente militaire parfaite.

"Notre Gouvernement autant que moi ne doute pas un instant du succès final et triomphal qui attend nos armées et nous constatons que nos sacrifices auront leur pleine récompense lorsque l'ennemi sera mis en fuite.

"Je me suis battu avec l'armée français en 1870 et mon cœur est en plein accord avec le cœur français aujourd'hui. La prochaine bataille sera de la plus haute importance et je suis convaincu que chaque soldat de nos armées marchera jusqu' au bout vers une victoire éclatante et décisive."

tage in contributing to the success of this movement of General Joffre's.

By the time this message reached Sir John, our Army had already turned its face northwards with a joyous shout, and advanced to meet the enemy, and Sir John replied:

I have impressed upon General Joffre since the beginning of the war the need of a vigorous offensive, in which I have promised my entire co-operation. . . . Yesterday I had a personal interview of one hour with him, and—as we have always been—we were in complete accord. He has always acknowledged the indebtedness of France to the English soldiers, and he never expressed the least doubt personally to me. The offensive movement of which you wrote is now actually in progress, and in a few hours I expect my cavalry to be in close touch with the enemy's flank. (6.9.14.)

And a little later:

Although the serious congestion of the railways renders the process of refitting very slow, most of the reinforcements have now come up. I saw a great deal of our troops to-day and they are in excellent spirits.

Next day in the course of an inspiring telegram Sir John reported:

Our cavalry took part in a vigorous engagement on our front all day, and the enemy's cavalry have been driven back with heavy loss. The retreat of the enemy to the north-east continues.

This news was indeed exhilarating. A few days earlier the fall of Paris was so likely that the seat of Government had been transferred to Bordeaux. German troopers had passed through Chantilly, and appeared before the outer defences of the French capital: what would British feelings have been if an enemy advancing upon London had reached Hounslow Heath? The Allies' retirement had been proceeding *de die in diem,* and while it still seemed impossible to set any term to it the British Commander flashed home the message that it had given place to a resolute advance.

The relief was great after the days of intense strain and dark anxiety; but care for the present hour had not interrupted for a moment Kitchener's calm work of creating and preparing his armies for the stern prosecution of the war.

CHAPTER XCIX

THE story of the first battle of the Marne was in brief this. Von Kluck, following up the retirement of Sir John and de Lanrezac, had crossed the Marne with the bulk of his army, leaving only one reserve corps to guard his flank and rear north of the river. This reserve corps was attacked on September 5 by Maunoury, whose strength von Kluck appears to have altogether under-estimated. Faced by imminent danger the German General on the night of September 5-6 brought two corps which were opposite our front back across the Marne to attack Maunoury, a strong force of cavalry being ordered to delay our advance.

The particular story of the 6th, 7th, and 8th of September is that of a desperate encounter to the west of the Ourcq, in which Maunoury is more and more hardly pressed as the Germans opposed to him grow in strength, but is just able to hold his own with the help of reinforcements sent out to him by Gallieni from Paris. The British Army advancing in the meantime towards the Marne, and driving back von Kluck's cavalry in front of it, crosses successively the Grand Morin and the Petit Morin. The French Fifth Army on our right, now under the command of Franchet d'Espérey, makes good progress against

CHAP. XCIX BATTLE OF THE MARNE 61

von Kluck's left wing; but still further to the right, round about Vitry-le-François, Foch is engaged in a fierce struggle against the two German Armies which are trying to break through the French centre; and though he fights with his own indomitable spirit, he is compelled slowly to give ground.

Up to the evening of September 8 the question was whether the advance of the British Army would relieve the pressure upon Maunoury, and compel von Kluck to retire, before the Germans should succeed in breaking through the front held by Foch. On September 7 Sir John had written:

I am very sorry to seem to have allowed you to lack information in the previous two days, but the situation and the arrangements for our advance were so uncertain on Saturday [September 5] that I was afraid of misleading you. For instance, late on Friday night Joffre asked me to retire twelve miles in order to make room for his Fifth Army south of the Marne. I had half completed the movement when he determined to keep the Fifth Army north of the river, and asked me to retrace my steps and get into touch with that Army. I think this was unavoidable, and on the whole his conception and dispositions were really quite good. He tells me of the success in the advance of the Fifth Army yesterday on my right and adds, "This result is certainly due to the advance of the English forces towards the east. The continuance of your offensive will be of the greatest assistance to the attack of the Fifth Army during the movement to-morrow." He asked me to direct the march to-day a little more to the north, so as to be in closer touch with the 6th Army on the left. As regards this latter Army, they have in front of them the Fourth German Reserve Corps, which has retreated north of the Marne, and which they appear to be hammering pretty freely. . . . As I told you, we pushed back considerable detachments of the enemy yesterday, and hope to reach a much more forward line to-day. I have been a great deal amongst the men and I find them in excellent spirits and good heart. Most of our casualties have now been replaced. Thank you for all your trouble about the Sixth Division. I know very well you are doing all you possibly can. . . .

Besides replacing the heavy losses—amounting to nearly 20,000, incurred during the retreat from Mons Kitchener was providing a substantial reinforcement. At a Cabinet meeting held immediately on his return from Paris, he succeeded in persuading the Government to allow the Sixth Division to proceed as soon as transport was available, where it took its part in complete order in the battle of the Aisne. Kitchener always maintained that he had been able to despatch the four divisions which followed the original Expeditionary Force at the most appropriate times; the Fourth Division arriving to strengthen the Second Corps at the battle of Le Cateau, the Sixth Division coming up fresh and in fine fettle for the battle of the Aisne, the Seventh arriving in time for the first struggle round Ypres, while the Eighth appeared at the front just when the battle-weary troops needed new vigour and blood.

On September 8, after driving the Germans back from the Petit Morin, the British drew near to the south bank of the Marne, which was crossed at an early hour on the 9th. That day Sir John wired to Kitchener: "At daybreak advance continued. Yesterday the Sixth French Army on our left suffered heavily, but I hope to take pressure off them north of the Marne to-day." In this the British Commander-in-Chief completely succeeded.

VON KLUCK'S RETREAT

He had by now sent in his first despatch describing the retreat from Mons, and on September 9 Kitchener wired:

I have received your despatch and it will be published at once. It is to the energy and skill displayed by you, your generals, and your force that the favourable position of the Allied Armies is largely due. I hope that pressure on the Sixth French Army will be relieved by the operations you are undertaking, and that the Germans will be forced to retire further. I feel a little anxiety as to the French forces operating near Vitry-le-François and to the south of Châlons. Please, if you have an opportunity, congratulate General Joffre warmly on the success that has hitherto been attained. I hope a decisive victory may be the result of it.

Within a few hours of the despatch of this telegram the victory hoped for had been won. Early on the morning of September 9 von Kluck found the flank and rear of his troops fighting with Maunoury and threatened by the British advance across the Marne; and all his efforts to overcome the superb resistance of the French Sixth Army having failed, he threw up the sponge and ordered a retreat. Our troops had crossed the Marne in the nick of time, for Maunoury the day before had found his left flank in danger of envelopment by von Kluck's forces, and had thought it prudent to concert with Gallieni measures for a possible retirement on Paris. Kitchener had in his telegram indicated the point of danger, the French centre about Vitry-le-François; but here too on this fateful September 9 the tide turned in our favour. The successful advance of the French Fifth Army on our right enabled Joffre to send a timely reinforcement to Foch, whose unconquerable spirit was inspiring his exhausted troops to hold on.

Almost at the same time von Bülow, who was attacking Foch with the Second German Army, had to extend his right to the west to pull von Kluck out of his difficulties, and in so doing left a gap in his front between the marshes of St. Gond and Vitry-le-François. Foch leapt at the opportunity, made his famous counter-attack on the evening of the 9th, and transformed what might have been only a local success over von Kluck's Army into a victory which wrecked the first German plan of campaign.

But to the British Army fell the honour of showing the way across the Marne, and of compelling von Kluck to retreat several hours before Foch dealt with him. On the night of September 9 Sir John could tell Kitchener:

> To-day the enemy has been driven back all along the line. The First and Second Corps have reached a line about 8 miles north of the Marne, and to-night the Third Corps crosses the Marne at La Ferté. . . . The First Army Corps have taken 12 maxim guns and some prisoners, and have buried 200 German dead just in front of them. The Second Army Corps have captured a battery and some 300 prisoners. The enemy is retiring at all points except at Vitry. The French are being reinforced at Vitry and everything seems to be progressing favourably.

This telegram was sent off before the news of Foch's victory had reached the Commander-in-Chief. Our troops, flushed with success and hard on the enemy's heels, reached the Aisne on September 12 to force its passage. But the Germans, hurrying reinforcements southwards from Belgium and from Maubeuge—which had just fallen to them—were able to hold up our further progress and to launch a series of fierce assaults upon the first trench lines dug by the British Army.

To Kitchener and Sir John alike the heavy loss of officers was a subject of grievous anxiety. The reserve of officers consisted mainly of men who had retired from the higher ranks of the Army, and there were few captains and subalterns of experience available. Kitchener obtained authority for the Commander-in-Chief to promote non-commissioned officers on the field, and on the 16th wired to him:

> We have sent you, since the war began, 593 officers to fill vacancies, and at rate demands are coming in from the front we shall soon be unable to supply well-trained officers. Units will then have to work with reduced numbers and staffs, which in some cases are apparently rebundant and will have to be cut down. . . . I am trying to get well-trained officers everywhere, and hope to get a few more from India. Many of the officers sent home are only slightly wounded and sick, and will rejoin their units in a short time. I hope to be able to continue to send drafts with a due proportion of officers, but it seems to me that, unless we stop all preparations of larger forces to continue the war, forces which are now being trained with the smallest number possible of Regular, Reserve, and dug-out officers . . . we shall be forced to take steps I have indicated.

While the operations on the Aisne were settling down into a state of deadlock, Kitchener was doing his utmost to reinforce the Army in France. An Army Corps was on its way from India; the formation of the Seventh Division, made up from Regular battalions withdrawn from the colonies and overseas garrisons, was proceeding apace; and by the middle of September he could make an immediate promise to Sir John of a number of selected Territorial battalions. This cheerful annunciation and the improved situation on the Aisne induced Sir John to put forward an epoch-making proposal, which he unfolded in a letter to Kitchener on September 24. At that time General de Castelnau, who was in command of the French left, was preparing an attack upon the German right flank, and Sir John's scheme was contingent on the result of this manœuvre. In his letter he says:

> There is no change in the situation, but I have been closely watching for an opportunity to get forward. During the last two days the artillery fire has slackened a good deal, and there have been few attempts at counter-attack. Reconnaissances of every kind, however, show clearly that the enemy's trenches and positions are still strongly held. I sent Wilson this morning to General de Castelnau's Headquarters, and he has just come back and told me that the attack has commenced and seems to promise well, but his decisive movement to turn the German right cannot develop until to-morrow afternoon; so I do not expect the situation on our front to undergo any change until Saturday. If Castelnau's attack fails, or ends in stalemate, I should like to suggest to the Commander-in-Chief [*i.e.* Joffre] to place the British forces once more on the Allied left. With the two new Corps and fresh Cavalry divisions I feel quite confident we could get well in on the German flank and bring about decisive results; but I will write more fully on this later.

Such was the inception of the fine *démarche* which brought a British Army back to Flanders, where until the end of the war it was to fight, and in the end of the war was to prevail.

CHAPTER C

THE enemy was now beginning to expose his hand in his new design on the Western front. He was quite evidently preparing to pounce on Antwerp, which was held by the Belgian Army under the King, and was the seat of his Government. The information which reached Kitchener from Belgium as to Antwerp's peril was slow in arrival and scanty in detail. It is just thinkable that, with earlier and fuller intelligence, some means might have been contrived to ward off the blow. On October 2 Kitchener wired to Sir John:

> A serious situation has been created by the German attempt to besiege Antwerp, which has now culminated in placing Antwerp in very grave danger of falling in a short time. If this happens you can realise how extremely damaging it would be to our future campaign. . . . The German forces are, as far as we can calculate, about five divisions of not first-line troops. We are impressing on the French Government that, if Joffre cannot bring off decisive action in France in three or four days, we can hardly hope that Antwerp will hold out, unless he can send some Regular troops to act there in conjunction with all the Regular troops we can send, that is the Seventh Division and a division of cavalry. If you are disengaging from the line, would it not be possible to suggest to Joffre that, if he can send troops, you should join the Seventh Division and other troops from here, with whatever por-

tion of your force is considered necessary for the relief of Antwerp, while the remainder moves into its new position?

Sir John immediately replied that he would consult with Joffre and do all that was possible. From this it will be seen that the first conception in Kitchener's mind of the plan for the relief of Antwerp was a combined movement through Southern Belgium of a part of Sir John's Army, transferred from the Aisne, and of the Seventh Division and a Cavalry Division, which, under the command of Sir Henry Rawlinson, were to land on the Flanders coast, and to be handed over to the British Commander-in-Chief. This, in the light of the knowledge then available as to the enemy's strength, was a justifiable military operation; but the information available was far from complete, and the Germans had already fully prepared to spring their second great surprise.

The first surprise, which culminated at Mons, was consummated by the Germans bringing to the West a much larger force than we had anticipated. They then reaped the advantage of having, on mobilisation, created a number of Reserve Corps, which at once reinforced the Regular Army in the field. Thereupon was formed a number of entirely fresh Reserve Corps, which, by a marvel of organisation, stepped into the fighting line at the beginning of October. Thus, just when we were about to make our flank march through Belgium for the rescue of Antwerp, the Germans were again prepared to envelop our left. As an overture to this effort, the attack upon Antwerp was pressed with the utmost vigour, and before our last troops had slipped away from the Aisne to Flanders the Belgian fortress was in grave danger.

Events, indeed, moved far too rapidly to permit the accomplishment of Kitchener's hope to relieve Antwerp by a force under Sir John. The Government in their anxiety sent off the Seventh Division and the Third Cavalry Division to disembark at Ostend and Zeebrugge, and act at first as an independent corps under Sir Henry Rawlinson. The news from Antwerp grew daily worse, and Rawlinson could scarcely be in time. As a desperate attempt to save the place, the Government agreed to the despatch of the half-trained troops of the Naval Division, which, however, availed nothing to avert or delay the disaster; Antwerp fell on October 9, when Rawlinson's force was placed definitely under Sir John's orders.

Next day Kitchener wrote to Sir John:

The telegrams about Antwerp will make rather interesting reading. I am having them compiled and will send you a copy. I hope you do not think I was unduly interfering with your operations by not putting the special force it was proposed to send for the relief of Antwerp under your direct orders. My reasons for doing so were, in the first place, that the Cabinet would not allow the Seventh Division, etc., to leave the country for more than a rapid movement on Antwerp, with the intention of bringing it back here when the blow had been struck there. I only got this decision altered yesterday, and at once placed them under your orders; secondly, we were in such close touch by telegraph and telephone[1] with Ostend and Antwerp, while you were engaged in moving and more or less cut off. I think you will find the Seventh a first-rate division. I am sorry the 2nd Brigade of Cavalry was unduly hurried off, and there is still a regiment required to complete it; but I

---

[1] The telephone conversations were carried on with considerable difficulty from the Central Telegraph Office.

think I have been lucky hitherto in giving you reinforcements when they were most wanted, and I hope I shall be able to continue to do so. . . . I am doing all I can for you and for the sake of the main operations, which I never lose sight of.

Sir John answered pleasantly:

It is very kind of you to write as you do. I never for a moment supposed you wished to interfere with my operations, and I know perfectly well that I have your confidence, and that the same mutual understanding exists between us now as always. Don't think I forget South Africa so easily. So much for the personal side. As regards what actually happened, I know perfectly well that the condition of Antwerp came upon you as a bolt from the blue, and was as much a surprise to you as it was to me.

The attempt to relieve the beleaguered city, if directly a conspicuous failure, was indirectly a signal success. Kitchener was able to persuade the Government, who were the more perturbed about Home Defence by the enemy hammering at the gates of Antwerp, to send Rawlinson's Corps to Belgium. He at first—perhaps a little naïvely—recommended its despatch overseas as a temporary measure; then having gained their consent to it, he shortly after induced his colleagues to sanction the addition of this important reinforcement to Sir John's command —a timely support which just turned the scale in our favour at the first battle of Ypres. At that time every hour of delay to the Germans was of priceless value to us; every man we could put in was an obstacle in their maleficent path. Without the Corps which Kitchener so hardly squeezed from the Government, Ypres would almost certainly have fallen into the enemy's hands, Dunkirk must have been let go, and Calais itself could scarcely have been saved.

By October 12 the march from the Aisne to Flanders was in full swing, and the Second and Third Corps, advancing towards La Bassée and Lille, were in contact with the enemy. On October 14 Kitchener was greatly distressed to hear that General Hubert Hamilton, who had brought the Third Division out to France and commanded it at Mons and in all the subsequent fighting, had been killed in action near Neuve Chapelle. "Hammy," as he was familiarly known, had served on Kitchener's Staff in Egypt, and as his military secretary in both South Africa and India.[1] A high-souled soldier, a man of infinite tact and considerable ability, he was a close and trusted friend, on whose cool and sound judgement Kitchener was wont to rely.

Sir John's hope to reach Lille was frustrated by the new German movement against the Allied left flank. A fierce and fluctuating fight raged between La Bassée and Armentières, which finally faded into stagnation and led to the establishment of trench lines, while the scene of the vital struggle shifted to the north, towards Ypres and the Yser. On this front the opposing forces were converging from various directions. Haig with the First Corps and Allenby with the Cavalry were marching from the west towards Ypres and the Messines Ridge; Rawlinson from Ostend was moving towards the same goal from the north-east; the Belgian Army was falling back from the east upon the Yser, being reinforced by French troops brought up from the south, while

[1] Of Kitchener's Staff in South Africa and India, Col. Victor Brooke, V.C., was almost the first officer to fall in France. Col. Marker died of wounds in November 1914. Col. Learmonth was killed at Gallipoli in 1915. Col. Maxwell, V.C., fell in the battle of the Somme in July 1915.

the German masses were converging from the east and south-east for their attempt to drive through to Calais. Thus, in the last weeks of October, armed forces were moving from all points of the compass to the field of the last great battle of the campaign of 1914.

On October 22 Sir John wired to Kitchener:

More or less heavy fighting yesterday all along my front. Here and there we were slightly driven back; but our successes predominated, and everywhere the enemy suffered severe loss. Belgians continue to hold their ground splendidly on Canal north of Ypres, where the French Ninth Corps is moving up in support. Joffre and Foch are both up in the Belgian theatre of war and are intent on driving the Germans eastwards. In my opinion the enemy are vigorously playing their last card, and I am confident they will fail.

The grim struggle which followed was watched with deep anxiety by Kitchener, who realised the almost intolerable strain thrown upon our men. In former European wars battles had been incidents in a series of manœuvres and marches, and had rarely lasted for more than a day; now the fighting was almost continuous, and not only strained human endurance almost to snapping-point, but entailed an expenditure of ammunition beyond all calculation. Our own limitations were quickly evident. The Germans in the battle of Armentières, more than once, had all but exhausted their supply of gun ammunition, while the French were compelled at this time to limit strictly the number of rounds fired. Both French and Germans had in time of peace directed vast manufacturing resources to the output of munitions of war; we had not exercised the same prudence, and shells for the men to fire were looming almost as largely in Kitchener's mind as the men themselves.

On October 30 the Indian Corps, which he had sent to France, went into the line on the Neuve Chapelle front, and enabled Smith-Dorrien to lend a hand to reinforce Haig at Ypres. Kitchener, well satisfied with the smooth despatch of the Corps from east to west—for which his own organisation was so largely responsible—sent its Commander, Sir James Willcox, a telegram of welcome:

Am glad to hear the Indian troops are *Razi*[1] and have got what they want. Give them my salaams, and tell them I feel sure they will maintain their glorious record of the past when they meet the Germans.

On October 31, the vigil of the first battle of Ypres, he telegraphed three times to Sir John:

A good many of your men must be tired out by the hard fighting in which the troops are now engaged. I am therefore placing six more battalions of selected Territorials under orders to go out to you in addition to the eight ordered or sent already. Some time, as you know, will be required before the Eighth Division is ready to be fit.

The impossibility of accurate observation for artillery has led us to consider that it would be advantageous to have an aeroplane and its detachment with a gunner-flier attached exclusively to Artillery Generals in each division. I could organise and send these out, if you agree, in addition to all your flying corps.

Experiments in this direction had been carried out on a small scale on the Aisne; the proposal was

---

[1] "In fine fettle."

welcomed in France, and issued in the service of the Air Force as the eyes of the artillery.[1]

The other two telegrams related to ammunition:

The supply of ammunition gives me great anxiety. I telegraphed to you this morning what we have done. Do not think we are keeping any munitions back. All we can gather is being sent, but at the present rate of expenditure we are certain before long to run short, and then to produce more than a small daily allowance per gun will be impossible. I hope to increase the ammunition being sent to-day.

In my opinion our supply of field-gun ammunition ought to be represented to Joffre and Foch as a matter of urgency. Desperate efforts are undoubtedly being made by the Germans to break through, and they have massed large forces for that purpose. I consider that, for the next few days, the situation is critical, and that steps ought to be taken at once by Joffre with a view to increasing our combined resistance in the Northern section. He ought to send more French guns, with a plentiful supply of ammunition. Are more men, or anything that I can send, required by you?

[1] "I do not think any one will ever realise how much Lord Kitchener did for aviation in the early part of the war. From the very first he realised its enormous importance and its possibilities, and he was always urging me to push on, place more orders, and do more. He hardly realised the numerous difficulties we had to compete with at the beginning of the war owing to our unpreparedness in peace, and I well remember that when I was rejoicing over a very feeble output of partially trained pilots, he was telling me that they should be trained to fly in groups of 60 to 100 with a view to bombing Essen. I remember how one day he explained to me his ideas of how it should be done and what formations should be adopted.

"Of course at that time, although I absolutely believed in his ideas, I had to be obstructive, simply because neither men nor material were available, and the Expeditionary Force wanted everything we could give them.

"More than a year later I was temporarily commanding the Flying Corps in France when Lord Kitchener came and visited St. Omer aerodrome. Just as he got out of his car, about 12 aeroplanes in beautiful formation flew over his head. He smiled and turned to me saying, 'There you are! I told you to do that a year ago, and you said it couldn't be done!'

"The Royal Flying Corps owes a very great deal to Lord Kitchener for the assistance he gave in every possible way at the beginning of the war." (Gen. W. S. Brancker, Lecture before the Royal Aeronautic Society, 25.1.17.)

VISITS DUNKIRK

On November 1 Kitchener crossed by destroyer from Newhaven to Boulogne and proceeded to Dunkirk to meet the President of the Republic. At the French port he availed himself of the first opportunity of talking to wounded men before their arrival in the hospitals in England, which he often visited. A Red Cross train had just come in, and the men were eager to tell their exploits to the soldier whose name was a household word. They tried to make light of their sufferings, but Kitchener was not to be deceived—"The men are more worn and look even worse than I feared they would," he said sadly to his Staff officer, and the impression then made was never wiped away from his mind.

Sir John sent two of his Staff to Dunkirk, explaining that the critical state of affairs prevented his coming himself. "Please tell him," was the reply, "that I should have been unhappy if he had even thought of doing so. I would not interrupt him for any consideration."

That afternoon and evening were devoted to a conference between the President, M. Cambon the Ambassador, Joffre, Foch, and Kitchener. The definite promise of an immediate despatch of further Territorial troops was rapturously received by the French; and Kitchener's knowledge of their language enabled him, despite the intricacies of the discussion, to hold his own and carry his own points before crossing back the same night to Dover.

On November 2 the Commander-in-Chief was able to report that French reinforcements had arrived, that the French had relieved him, and that his danger was less acute:

The French have come into part of our lines during last night and this morning, and I have been considerably strengthened in consequence. On the whole, I am much less anxious to-day, for the enemy appear to be much less active along our front. Yesterday we evacuated Messines and retired to an entrenchment behind it.

A few days later the Germans began to withdraw troops from the West to parry the ponderous Russian advance on the Eastern front; but, even so, they made further efforts to break through to Ypres, culminating in the attack—and complete repulse [1]—of the Prussian Guards on November 11. Two days before Sir John had wired to Kitchener:

Foch told me on the 5th that Joffre expected that a German withdrawal had already begun and would proceed slowly to the extent of passing from twelve to fifteen Army Corps to the Eastern theatre. He expected, as a prelude to and cover for this withdrawal, that the enemy would make a powerful offensive movement against one or two places on the Allied line. These blows have since been struck and successfully parried, with great loss to the enemy. I do not expect that you can give me any more Regular troops at present. I have formed great hopes of the Territorials, from what I have seen of the London Scottish and other Territorial units.

---

[1] "700 dead, killed in yesterday's attack of the Prussian Guards, have been picked up by the First Army Corps in front of their trenches." (Sir John to Kitchener, 12,11.14.)

CHAPTER CI

THE last serious German attempt on Ypres in 1914 was made on November 17, when the whole Western front stagnated into dreary, but no less deathly, trench warfare. By this time Territorial troops had relieved the Regulars in India and other Overseas garrisons, and all trained soldiers who could be spared from foreign stations had arrived, or were arriving, in England. Besides the Seventh and Eighth Divisions, formed out of Regular troops abroad at the declaration of war, three more Regular Divisions, the Twenty-seventh, Twenty-eighth, and Twenty-ninth were now constituted and being trained. As with the Territorial and New Army Divisions, so with these; the delay in putting them into the field was due to the lack of the necessary equipment—a cause of grave anxiety to Kitchener, who was eager to reinforce Sir John at the earliest possible moment, and so arrest the transfer of German troops to the East.

The King's visit [Sir John wrote on December 4] has been very successful, and has certainly had the best possible effect in every way upon the troops. I think His Majesty has been pleased and interested. . . .

The weather has been very foggy and misty, making regular air reconnaissances difficult; but still during bright intervals the Flying Corps are very energetic and pushing, and we glean from their reports that a good deal of movement by rail has been going on during the last five or six days. By far the greater movement is from West to East, but a considerably smaller number of trains have been observed coming West.

I am pretty certain that a good deal of artillery has gone from our front and has been replaced by guns firing shells of inferior power and efficiency (many of them fail to burst) but about the same range. I think they have brought a good many guns here which they captured at Maubeuge.

I am sure the infantry in our front has been changed and I think very possibly reduced, if not in quantity, certainly in quality. We find dead men with one shoulder strap on their coats and another with a different number in their pockets. These and other indications show that the Germans are doing their best to prevent us from determining what corps have been withdrawn from our front, but I am pretty sure that the Seventh Corps has gone and also the Second. The Guards Division has also gone.

I feel sure there are still a considerable number of eight-inch howitzers in our front, as well as those heavy Austrian guns which they brought up some time ago.

Similar conditions are reported in front of the French on our right and left. I have had several talks with Foch as to our future plans, and also a long conversation with Joffre when he came up here on Tuesday to see the King. We have no reason to suppose that the forces in front of us are inferior as regards numbers, and they may possibly be slightly superior. They are certainly superior in heavy artillery, and they are very strongly entrenched all along the line. In fact we know that they have carefully prepared successive positions for many miles behind them.

Joffre, Foch, and I all agree that a vigorous offensive at the present moment would certainly entail very heavy loss; and even if we could make any headway at all we could not get very far in one effort.

Then there is the question of our immediate ammunition resources, which do not admit of the expenditure which offensive operations would entail.

Your letters and telegrams seem to express surprise that some forward movement is not undertaken or some effort made to prevent the enemy moving troops from West to East; but the situation being as I have described it, we are of opinion that it is impossible at the moment to do any more. Joffre tells me that he expects to have a considerable quantity of heavy artillery available in a week or two, and by that time we hope that German requirements in the Eastern theatre will have caused more withdrawals from our front in the West, and that we shall be thus enabled to batter down the enemy's trenches and make a vigorous advance. He gave me an outline of the plans he was evolving in his head, but he has not yet finally decided on the point where he will make his big push.

In the meantime we are doing all the reconnoitring we possibly can and securing points in our front wherever we see an opportunity.

The troops stood in urgent need of rest after the hard experiences of our last battle; and reinforcement, refitting, and reorganisation have been going on with enormous advantage to the efficiency of the forces generally.

I have inspected a great number of the troops lately and have been much struck by the appearance and condition of the drafts. I expect the last Indian Infantry Brigade, which landed from Egypt, to be up here in two or three days, and Rimington's Cavalry Corps to be formed and ready for service early next week.

The fact is that Krupp is our most formidable enemy at present, and we must find means to get on terms with the enemy's heavy artillery before any advance can be very speedy or vigorous. The 9·2″ howitzers and 6″ guns have been a great help.

I have, however, urged strongly on both Joffre and Foch the necessity for taking a vigorous offensive at the earliest possible moment, and pushing through a point in the enemy's line, which would have the most decisive results.

The end of the campaign of 1914 had extinguished the hope of the Germans that they would over-run France in a short and decisive contest. But though many—friends and foes—who had once flouted Kitchener's forecast of a prolonged struggle [1] were now disposed to back his opinion, few still believed that civilised nations could stand the wear and tear and financial burden of a three years' war.

It was anyhow patent to every observer that preparation must be made for the whole of the year 1915. The fighting about Ypres had led to a mix-up of the Allied forces. The French were on the coast near Nieuport, the Belgians stood next in order towards the south, then several French divisions held the Ypres sector, while the left of our Army was opposite Wytschaete and its right in the neighbourhood of La Bassée, south of which stood the bulk of the French Army. It was obviously desirable to draw the three Allied Armies together as much as possible.

A more thorny question was how to help Russia. Matters were going badly on the Eastern front. To keep our own Army supplied was difficult enough, but to supply Russia with rifles and ammunition was in every way, and in some very unsavoury ways,

---

[1] His surmise as to the duration of the war did not prevent him from taking into early consideration the future condition of the men taking part in it. "I hear," wrote Earl Grey to him in December 1914, "that you are already concerning yourself with regard to the future of your soldiers when they are disbanded after the war. I am not surprised. It is obvious that there will be thousands of men who will not be content to return to the humdrum conditions of their old life; and unless proper provision is made for their employment, they may constitute a social and political menace."

more harassing. Sir John, who was asked to take early counsel with Joffre, wrote on December 28:

In accordance with the wish of His Majesty's Government I had an interview of about two hours' duration with General Joffre at his Headquarters at Chantilly yesterday.

I told him that, from information received from the Foreign Office, the British Government had reason to consider the military situation in Russia (as it existed a week ago) serious. They apprehended a rapid advance by the Austro-German Forces on Warsaw, and a retirement of the whole Russian Army, possibly as far back as the River Bug. They attributed the failure of the Russians to continue the offensive to lack of artillery, ammunition, and rifles with which to equip their reserves, which were otherwise ready to come up and reinforce the first line. They feared that when this happened, Germany would be able to withdraw a sufficient force from the Eastern theatre of war to render her strong enough to break our Western line and eventually take Paris.

I told the General that His Majesty's Government was anxious to hear if he had formed any plans to meet such a contingency, and in what way he wished the British Forces to participate in such plans.

General Joffre replied that he had always been prepared to meet any possible break which might occur in our line by concentrating groups of reserves near the railway centres and strategic points, whence they could be moved by trains or 'buses to any threatened point in the line.

The French General Staff under his supervision had full plans to meet any situation which was likely to arise; but he did not think the present moment was opportune to enter into a discussion to meet a contingency which, in his opinion, had, since the conclusion of the battle of Ypres, become always remote; and was more so than ever in view of events in the Eastern theatre during the past week.

I thought it unnecessary to press him further on this

particular subject, and we fell to discussion of future plans to meet the situation as it now presents itself to us.

We agree in thinking that it is unlikely that the Germans will be able to detach any troops from the forces with which she now confronts the Russians for any purpose whatever, but we feel the necessity for pressing hard on this side in order to prevent any more troops being detached to the Eastern theatre, and to gradually drive the German forces out of France and Belgium.

The plan which I am about to describe to you was really commenced on the 14th instant, between which date and the 21st, you may remember, there was a good deal of activity all along our line and that of the French to the north of us.

This and some other minor operations at other parts of the Allied line were a kind of prelude to draw the attention of the Germans from the preparations which were being made at the main points of attack. These points lie at Arras on the western side of our line, and Rheims on the southern side. Joffre has massed a huge force of artillery (both heavy and light) opposite these points, and is massing all the troops he can get behind them. The push has already commenced at both points; many of the enemy's trenches have been captured and his line has been pushed back from four to six hundred yards opposite both places.

At other parts of the line the rôle is to be twofold:

1. To economise troops so far as is consistent with the safety of the line, and send every possible man to one of the two decisive points.

2. To maintain sufficient local reserves to engage the enemy and keep him employed to such an extent as to prevent his detaching troops to either of the two decisive points.

I have now got Joffre to agree to the wishes of His Majesty's Government and make such arrangements with me as will enable me to act on the extreme left of the line in conjunction with the Belgian Army and, so far as possible, with our own Fleet. He has arranged that I shall eventually take over the whole line between La Bassée and the sea, leaving the French troops between my present left and the Belgian right (which is really Bixschoote, the southern limit of the inundations), as fast as the successive reinforcements reaching me from you will permit. The French troops so relieved will be used at the decisive point, Arras. The sooner, therefore, that I can relieve them the more effective will the action be at the decisive point.

I sent for Bridges and had a long talk with him this morning. I have made certain suggestions to him with regard to the employment of the Belgian Army in conjunction with ourselves which he is going to put before the King. If they meet with the King's approval, and there is any chance of their being favourably considered, I think we shall be rendered much stronger on this flank.

From what I have said you will see that the progress of a vigorous offensive depends upon how fast I can get troops up here and release the French Forces (probably three Corps). If I could have the Canadians any earlier, or the Marine Contingent, or one or two divisions of Territorials, it would materially further all these plans.

Up to the present the strategical problems of the war had been stiff but simple. To stop the Germans and sustain the French had been the governing consideration to which all others had to yield. The forwardness of the Territorials to serve overseas had enabled Kitchener alike to provide for Imperial defence and to create from the Regular garrisons a number of divisions for service in France. He knew to a nicety the resources of the Indian Army, and he understood what risks could be taken. With the potent help of India, the Dominions, and the Crown Colonies, we could well take on Turkey and bring to book the German colonial forces. The Dominion of South Africa suppressed with energy the rebellion fostered by German agents, and undertook the eviction of the Germans from their South-West African colony. Australia, New Zealand, and Japan charged themselves with clearing the Pacific. Our forces in Nigeria and the Gold Coast secured Togoland, and prepared for the conquest of the Cameroons. India helped to make Egypt secure and sent a small expedition to Mesopotamia. None of these expeditions absorbed troops who would have been employed in the main theatre, and there was no clash of interests. But at the end of the year 1914 the main problem was no longer how to check the German campaign of conquest in France, but how best to win the war. The strategical horizon widened and discussions started which were to continue till the guns ceased to fire. So the already great burden borne by the Government's chief military adviser increased in weight.

CHAPTER CII

THE earliest hint of operations in other theatres of war was given to the Commander-in-Chief by Kitchener in a letter dated January 2:

> There does not appear to be much sign of the contemplated push through on the part of the French Army. Probably they find themselves up against the same problem all along the line as you do in your part, viz. trenches that render attack only a waste of men for a few yards gained of quite worthless ground. The feeling here is gaining ground that, although it is essential to defend the line we hold, troops over and above what is necessary for that service could be better employed elsewhere.
>
> I suppose we must now recognise that the French Army cannot make a sufficient break through the German lines of defence to cause a complete change of the situation and bring about the retreat of the German forces from Northern Belgium. If that is so, then the German lines in France may be looked upon as a fortress that cannot be carried by assault, and also cannot be completely invested—with the result that the lines can only be held by an investing force, while operations proceed elsewhere.
>
> The question of *where* anything effective can be accomplished opens a large field, and requires a good deal of study. What are the views of your Staff? Russia is hard pressed in the Caucasus, and can only just hold her own in Poland. Fresh forces are necessary to change the deadlock; Italy and Rumania seem the most likely providers; therefore some action that would help to bring these out seems attractive, though full of difficulties.

Sir John in a reasoned statement rejected the impossibility of piercing the enemy's lines. The thing, he thought, was feasible enough with an adequate supply of guns and high explosive shells; he argued that, even if a break-through in the West were denied us, the safety of France in general, and of the Channel ports in particular, was vital to Great Britain. Germany might conceivably put Russia *hors de combat,* and bring the bulk of her forces to the Western front. In so dire an event, the troops which Great Britain could throw into the field would provide no more than a margin of safety. After examining all alternative theatres of war for the appearance of British soldiers, he thought that an expedition to Serbia *via* Salonika was the least objectionable, although the difficulties of land communication would be very great. As to a descent on Gallipoli, he believed that any attack on Turkey would be barren of decisive result:

> In the most favourable circumstances it would only cause the relaxation of the pressure against Russia in the Caucasus, and enable her to transfer two or three corps to the West—a result quite incommensurate with the effort involved. To attack Turkey would be to play the German game, and to bring about the end which Germany had in mind when she induced Turkey to join in the war—namely, to draw off troops from the decisive spot, which is Germany herself.

Sir John had a plan of his own—to relieve the French troops in Flanders, who could then be sent south to back up Joffre's impending offensive, and to employ the British Army, with such help as the Belgians could give, in ousting the Germans from Ostend and Zeebrugge. This scheme, he was at pains to represent, would permit of our Fleet co-operating with our Army, and, if successful, would relieve the Admiralty of much anxiety as to submarine attack.

For such a campaign he asked for a reinforcement of fifty Territorial or New Army battalions, a copious supply of artillery ammunition of all kinds —but especially of high explosive—and a sufficient number of heavy guns; all these to supplement what had already been promised—the First Canadian Division and the last two Regular divisions, the Twenty-eighth and Twenty-ninth. With these fifty battalions Sir John proposed to swell his existing divisions; he thought the new soldiers would show to better advantage if shaken down with experienced fighters.

A well-considered campaign to clear the Belgian coast had been concocted between Sir John and Mr. Churchill while the battle of the Aisne was still swaying. The Admiralty may have viewed with something like dismay the establishment of the enemy on the flank of our cross-channel routes; the employment of our amphibious power was an attractive idea, and in transferring his troops to Flanders the British Commander had well in mind that he might be able to concert operations with the Fleet. The fierce struggle in which he finely foiled the German attempt to reach Calais had absorbed all Sir John's thoughts, but no sooner had he gained the upper hand than he re-addressed himself to the recovery of Ostend and Zeebrugge. Mr. Churchill, who at this time set scarcely any limit to the effect of naval guns on land defences, had written to Sir John on November 22: "If you push your left flank along the sand dunes of the shore to Ostend and Zeebrugge, we could give you 100 or 200 heavy guns from the sea in absolutely devastating support.''

Kitchener was no less anxious than Sir John and Mr. Churchill to see the British Army in definite charge of the Allied left flank, and for administrative reasons he coveted from the French the control of Dunkirk. Therefore, after a further visit of Mr. Churchill to Sir John, and agreeably with the wishes of the Cabinet, the War Secretary wrote to our Ambassador in France:

The military situation points to the advisability of shortly taking steps to prevent the Germans withdrawing their best first-line troops from the Western theatre for employment against Russia and replacing them by second-rate troops. As some forward movement to effect this may be decided on, I desire to bring to the serious attention of the French Government the very strong opinion held by His Majesty's Government that British troops should be so placed in the line as to advance along the coast in immediate co-operation with our Fleet, and thus enable us, if necessary, to land further forces at any critical juncture during the operation. To obtain this result a slight change in the present position of Sir John French's forces in the line would be necessary. The British troops would have to be moved to the left of the Allied line, being replaced in their present position by the French troops now on the left. They would thus be again taking up the position in the line they held after moving from Soissons.

I would point out to the French Government that the people of this country realise that the Belgian coastal positions are now held by Germany as a menace to Great Britain. They would, therefore, regard any losses entailed by an active offensive taken by our troops against these coastal positions as fully justified. British public opinion will even demand that the menace should be removed, for the forts on the coast of Belgium are being prepared as a base of operations by sea and air against Great Britain especially, and this may in time hamper the safe transport of fresh troops from England to France. Moreover, we feel sure that our co-operation with any contemplated French effort to drive the Germans back from their present position would be rendered much more effective, and lead to more decisive and far-reaching results, if this preliminary step in the redistribution of the troops were now taken and our troops subsequently used in the manner indicated. His Majesty's Government consider it most urgent and important that this step should be taken, and you should ask the French Government to agree to it and to arrange with General Joffre for carrying it out.

The French Government received the proposal with scant enthusiasm. Joffre feared an attack south of the Somme, directed upon Amiens; he knew that the Germans were creating fresh formations, and he thought that at any moment they might stay their vaunted march to Petrograd and rush back to the Western front. He desired with all his soul to build up his reserves in his centre for offence or defence as circumstances might dictate; he protested that it would be perilous to commit troops to an offensive campaign on the extreme left flank, where the country was no less intricate than defensible, at any rate until the direct lines of advance to Paris were absolutely secured.

Kitchener kept an open mind as to the Belgian coast scheme until the details were worked out. With all its glamour, he was not greatly attracted by it. No human effort, he felt, could supply the extra guns and munitions which would be required, nor was he disposed to perpetuate the piecemeal employment of the Territorial Force. When danger loomed large he had sent Territorial battalions to France as fast as they could be turned out, and these in the hour of utter need had rendered inestimable service in stemming the German onrush. But he had regarded this as an emergency measure, to be discontinued when the emergency was past. The war would be long, and he was looking far into the future. The proposed operations might achieve a considerable local advantage, but they must interfere seriously with the organisation of our fighting power, which he was painfully plodding to rear so as to touch culminating strength in 1917.

Up to January 2 Mr. Churchill highly approved a naval and military attack on the Belgian coast as recommended by Sir John, but between that date and January 7, when the War Council met to discuss future plans, his attention had been drawn elsewhere, and he desired to use his ships otherwise. The War Council gave full consideration to Sir John's memorandum, and did not lightly dismiss the benefits it held out. It was carefully weighed with other propositions just then brought forward, but on January 9 Kitchener was instructed to veto the plan of an offensive campaign in Flanders:

F.M. Sir John French—
The questions raised in your recent memorandum of January 3, 1915, and in your appreciation of the situation in the various theatres of war, were considered by a War Council, presided over by the Prime Minister, on Thursday, January 7, and Friday, January 8.

The principal questions discussed were:
1. The proposed advance to Zeebrugge.
2. The organisation of the New Armies.

3. The possibility of employing British forces in a different theatre from that in which they are now used.

1. With regard to *the proposed advance to Zeebrugge,* the First Lord's telegram No. 2623,[1] sent to you on January 2, explained the difficulties imposed on the Admiralty by the development of Zeebrugge as a base for submarines, and the War Council realised that one of your principal motives in suggesting an offensive to effect the capture of Ostend and Zeebrugge was to ease the naval position.

On a general review, however, of the whole situation, naval and military, the Council came to the conclusion that the advantages to be obtained from such an advance at the present moment would not be commensurate with the heavy losses involved, as well as the extension that would be thus caused to the lines of the Allies in Northern Flanders.

The Council was also influenced in this conclusion by the following considerations: (*a*) The first of these was that the reinforcements of 50 battalions of Territorial troops which you considered indispensable could only be supplied at a considerable dislocation of the organisation of the future reinforcements to be sent you. It must be borne in mind that the original organisation of the Territorial Force included no provision for drafts. Great difficulties have already been encountered in providing drafts for the 24 battalions already in your command, and although arrangements for the necessary machinery to create a special reserve for the Territorials are in hand, it would not at

---

[1] The battleship *Formidable* was sunk this morning by a submarine in the Channel. Information from all quarters shows that the Germans are steadily developing an important submarine base at Zeebrugge. Unless operations can be undertaken to clear the coast, and particularly to capture this place, it must be recognised that the whole transportation of troops across the Channel will be seriously and increasingly compromised. The Admiralty are of the opinion that it would be possible, under cover of warships, to land a large force at Zeebrugge in conjunction with any genuine forward movement along the shore to Ostend. They wish these views, which they have so frequently put forward, to be placed again before the French Commander, and hope they may receive the consideration which their urgency and importance require."

present be possible to supply 50 more battalions with drafts without an entire reorganisation of the forces allotted to Home Defence, and this would modify the programme for reinforcements to join your Army in the future.

(b) The second consideration was that it is impossible at the present time to maintain a sufficient supply of gun ammunition on the scale which you considered necessary for offensive operations. Every effort is being made in all parts of the world to obtain an unlimited supply of ammunition, but, as you are well aware, the result is still far from being sufficient to maintain the large number of guns which you now have under your command adequately supplied with ammunition for offensive purposes. You have pointed out that offensive operations, under the new conditions created by this war, require a vast expenditure of artillery ammunition, which may for even ten or twenty days necessitate the supply of 50 or 100 rounds per gun per day being available, and that unless the reserve can be accumulated to meet expenditure of this sort it is unwise to embark on extensive offensive operations against the enemy in trenches. It is, of course, almost impossible to calculate with any accuracy how long offensive operations, once undertaken, may last before the object is attained; but it is evident that the breaking-off of such operations before accomplishment, owing to the want of artillery ammunition, and not on account of a successful termination or a convenient pause in the operations having been reached, might lead to a serious reverse being sustained by our forces.

The abandonment of the Zeebrugge project does not prevent you from co-operating—to the utmost extent compatible with your present resources—with any offensive movement contemplated by General Joffre, and your previous instructions in this sense are in no way modified.

(c) The Council further thought that there were certain indications, which should not be neglected, of German reinforcements reaching their Armies in the Western theatre in the near future, which may lead German Commanders to undertake a fresh attempt to force the lines you and the French Army hold. If this movement should develop, it could probably be better met and defeated by holding your present lines of prepared positions than by extending the line to the Dutch Frontier and placing the Belgian Army in probably a more exposed position than they now occupy. You may rest assured that, as they become available, fresh troops will be sent to you, with the least possible delay, to strengthen your forces as far as is practicable. The Twenty-eighth Division have already received orders to leave for France on the 14th instant.

2. *The organisation of the New Armies.*—Careful consideration was given to your remarks on the best method of utilising the New Armies when they are ready for the field. Before this time arrives the whole question will have to be very carefully examined from every point of view, and it will be necessary to obtain the advice of competent General Officers, after personally making themselves acquainted with the condition and training of the new troops. It would be premature to arrive at any decision at the present moment, though this important question will not be lost sight of.

3. *The possibility of employing British forces in a different theatre from that in which they are now used.*—The Council considered carefully your remarks on this subject in reply to Lord Kitchener's letter, and came to the conclusion that, certainly for the present, the main theatre of operations for British forces should be alongside the French Army, and that this should continue as long as France was liable to successful invasion and required armed support. It was also realised that, should the offensive operations subsequently drive the Germans out of France and back to Germany, British troops should assist in such operations. It was thought that, after another failure by Germany to force the lines of defence held by the French Army and yours, the military situation in France and Flanders might conceivably develop into one of stalemate, in which it would be

impossible for German forces to break through into France, while at the same time the German defences would be impassable for offensive movements of the Allies without great loss of life and the expenditure of more ammunition than could be provided.

In these circumstances, it was considered desirable to find some other theatre where such obstructions to advance would be less pronounced, and from where operations against the enemy might lead to more decisive results.

For these reasons, the War Council decided that certain of the possible projects for pressing the war in other theatres should be carefully studied during the next few weeks, so that, as soon as the new forces are fit for action, plans may be ready to meet any eventuality that may be then deemed expedient, either from a political point of view, or to enable our forces to act with the best advantage in concert with the troops of other nations throwing in their lot with the Allies.

Sir John, who was probably not slow to recognise that Turkey in arms afforded ample reason for "pressing the war in other theatres," loyally resigned his Zeebrugge project, and solidly set himself to co-operate with Joffre.

CHAPTER CIII

On October 29, 1914, Turkish warships bombarded Odessa, Sebastopol, and Theodosia, and the next day the *Entente* Ambassadors at Constantinople demanded their passports. On November 2 Russia declared war upon Turkey, and on the 3rd a British and French squadron bombarded the entrance to the Dardanelles. The motive of this demonstration was to test the range of the Turkish guns in the Dardanelles forts; but, as it preceded, instead of followed, a determination of our naval and military policy towards Turkey, it served chiefly to put the Turks on the *qui vive*. On November 5 followed the formal declaration of war on Turkey by Great Britain and France.

Kitchener had always reckoned with the likelihood of an actively hostile Turkey, and had hardly entered the War Office before he planned his counter-measures. His military policy was to be safe in the East in order to be strong in the West, and he looked to Egypt as the key to our position in the East. His judgement was shared by the German General Staff, who openly said that the Suez Canal was the jugular vein of the British Empire; and from the moment when Turkey declared against us, her domineering Ally never ceased to hound her on to Egypt, which was over-run with German agents stealthily preparing the way for an attack.

At the end of August 1914 Sir John Maxwell, then employed as chief British liaison officer on Joffre's Staff, was sent by Kitchener to organise the defence of Egypt. Maxwell had spent nearly thirty years of his military life in Egypt, which to him was an open book; he was as familiar with local conditions as he was popular alike with soldiers, pashas, sheikhs, and fellahin. If military arrangements were to be smoothly and swiftly carried through, no better—probably no other—choice than Maxwell[1] could have been made.

While Turkey was making up her mind to act, there was no immediate anxiety about Egypt. Troops on their way to the Western front from India and Australasia found Egypt an excellent half-way house, where in case of emergency they could stay until an adequate garrison was provided. To obtain such garrison, Kitchener asked the East Lancashire Territorial Division to go to Egypt, and arranged with the Government of India to despatch thither eight battalions of Indian Infantry and the Camel Corps which the Maharaja of Bikanir had handsomely lent us on the outbreak of war. These new defenders had arrived by the middle of October —a fortnight before the Sultan finally put his hand into the fist of the Kaiser.

On October 16 Maxwell wrote:

There is rather more nervousness in Egypt, but everything is quiet. It is part of the German propaganda that a revolution in Egypt is imminent, and that there are agents all over the country fomenting the natives against the British. We can find very little evidence in support of

---

[1] In April 1916 Kitchener despatched Maxwell to Ireland to deal with the German-engineered rebellion there.

this. There are, however, far too many able-bodied reservists, German and Austrian, all over Egypt. I have just finished a general registration, and though I have not yet the exact figures there must be at least 600, and there must be another 200 from the crews of captured ships. This is a danger. I have wired you asking to have them all interned at Malta. They can do no harm there. On Monday I am trying before a Military Court an undoubted spy of Enver's. He is a German and an officer in the Alexandria Police, and he had on him when arrested a secret code, maps of the Suez Canal, and two boxes of detonators. The Turks are getting at our Sinai Bedawin with robes of honour, bakshish, and promises of arms, and they are also trying to get at the Senussi. I think we ought to do something ourselves to try and keep as many as possible loyal with money, and promise that we will look after them when these very difficult times are over. I do not know what the policy of the Foreign Office is, but I think the Arabs about Mecca and the Yemen ought to be approached and set against the Turks.

As we are not going to attempt to hold our Sinai frontier and will destroy as many wells as possible, I expect all the Bedawin will join the Turks if they come over. As I cannot send out patrols I do not know much about what is going on on the frontier lines. I expect there will be raids before long. The Turks seem to be doing a lot of work in road-making, building forts, etc., all over Palestine and Syria, which looks as if they expected attack from us, but their tendency is to move south, and this can only mean attack upon Egypt. With the eight battalions from India, two mountain batteries, the Bikanir Camel Corps and the Coast Guard, the Canal ought to be safe. I am putting all these at Ismailieh, Port Said, and Suez. The Territorials are coming on splendidly. They get on very well and are keen. I hope nothing will interfere with the passage of the Indian contingent to Marseilles. By the time they are here we ought to know one way or the other what the Turks mean to do. The desert and Canal are tough obstacles, the nature of which the German officers advising the Turk may not realise.

Thus, when Turkey entered the lists, our first defensive measures were in good trim. They were further improved when in December there disembarked in Egypt the first troops of the Australian and New Zealand contingents, the nucleus of the splendid Anzac Corps, to command which Kitchener brought Sir William Birdwood from India.

The Government of India had meanwhile sent its force to the head of the Persian Gulf to encourage the friendly Arab tribes in Southern Mesopotamia, and to protect the pipe line of the Anglo-Persian oil-fields. This expedition landed near the mouth of the Shatt-el-Arab and captured Fao. Meeting with little opposition on November 23 it occupied Basra, the port which receives the traffic of the Tigris and the Euphrates. At two vital points the Turks had been forestalled.

Towards the end of November the extension of the war to the East demanded a change in the control of our war policy. Hitherto this had been vested in the whole Cabinet of twenty-two members, with the assistance of the Committee of Imperial Defence. The size of the Cabinet not only hindered business but imperilled the secrecy indispensable to the success of a war-plan. The Prime Minister, therefore, extracted from the Cabinet a War Council on which served only those Ministers immediately concerned with the conduct of the war. At its first meeting on November 25 the Near East was the main theme. Mr. Churchill contended that the best way to defend Egypt was to land on some part of the coast of

Asiatic Turkey, and he counselled an attack on the Gallipoli Peninsula. If this were happily accomplished the Fleet would sail through the Dardanelles to Constantinople, where we might hope to dictate terms to the Turks. The First Lord intimated, however, that to ensure success large forces would be necessary, but Kitchener—who would equally have liked to cut up the Turkish communications— had no military means available. He himself preferred a plan, which he had already discussed in general terms with Maxwell, for effecting a landing in the Gulf of Eskandroon at Alexandretta, a short distance from the main line of the Baghdad railway —joined a little farther south, near Aleppo, by the Syria-Arabia branch line. But as, at the moment, there were neither men nor material for such an enterprise, the matter had to rest, although the defence of Egypt from without by carrying war into the enemy's country was perpetually in his thoughts.

On December 4 Maxwell wrote:

If any diversion is contemplated, I think the easiest, safest, and most fruitful in results would be one at Alexandretta. There, if we do not impinge on Russian spheres, we strike a vital blow at their railways and also hit German interests very hard. I am assured that round about Alexandretta the Armenians would join any European landing expedition, and that they are all good fighting men, but would want arms and ammunition. An expedition to cut the line at Maan would not produce much result. It would be difficult in regard to water. Any damage done could be easily repaired, and it is too near the Holy Places for our Mohammedan troops. Alexandretta would not want a very large force. All other places—Raafa, Jaffa, Acre, Beyrut —are too far from the Turkish lines of communications.

These were the earliest of many proposals which simmered during the subsequent weeks. With the failure of the Germans to reach Calais had begun our session in the trenches to which no term could be foreseen, and German troops were being transferred from the Western front as fast as the railways could take them to reinforce Hindenburg against Russia.

Certain members of the War Council were excogitating some cheaper and quicker way of winning the war than by storming defences bristling with barbed wire and manned by Germans who outnumbered and outgunned us. At the same time the dispositions in Central and South-eastern Europe called loudly for attention and action. Italy was still neutral and would probably require a special inducement to throw in her lot with us; Serbia was isolated and was haughtily threatened with castigation by Austria; Rumania, though sympathetic, was afraid to move while large Austrian armies were near her frontiers, the more so as she could see no direct assistance coming from the Entente Powers; Greece was facing both ways; Bulgaria was openly coquetting with the Central Powers. Our Foreign Office, which had a fine field open to it for benevolent action, protested the helplessness of diplomacy unbacked by military achievement. The eyes of statesmen were being drawn more and more towards the Middle East.

The discussions in the War Council moved Kitchener to write his letter to Sir John of January 2, and on that same day our Ambassador at Petrograd telegraphed that the Turks were pressing the Russians hard in the Caucasus, and that the Russian Government, to relieve this pressure, begged for a demonstration against the Turks on some other quarter. The Russians had chivalrously come forward at the time of our retreat from Mons, and by invading East Prussia had drawn off considerable weight from us. This inroad into Germany had cost them two heavy disasters in which they had lost a vast quantity of precious war material. Kitchener felt that Russia's appeal must be met, and he telegraphed, promising a demonstration against the Turks, but expressing a fear that no action we could take would assure the withdrawal of enemy troops from the Caucasus. He then wrote to Mr. Churchill:

I do not see that we can do anything that will seriously help the Russians in the Caucasus. The Turks have evidently withdrawn most of their troops from Adrianople and are using them to reinforce their forces against Russia, probably sending them across the Black Sea. We have no troops to land anywhere. The only place where a demonstration might have some effect in stopping reinforcements going East would be the Dardanelles. We shall not be ready for anything big for some months.

CHAPTER CIV

THERE now began to be voiced the ideas of those who advocated campaigns in the East to safeguard our interests there, to influence potential Allies, and to strike an easier path to victory than through the German trenches. Mr. Lloyd George was convinced that any attempt to force the German lines in the West must fail unless we had a superiority in men of at least three to one—a superiority hopeless of attainment. He thought that the country would hereafter be wroth if the superb army then in the making were thrown away on "futile enterprises such as we have witnessed during the last few weeks." His proposal was to establish a considerable reserve in England from which France could be helped if hard pressed—a certain number of men being stationed at Boulogne in case of emergency—and to transfer the whole of the British Army in France—bag and baggage, lock, stock, and barrel—and to dedicate the new forces to the Balkans. He sought thus to reinforce Serbia, attract Italy and Greece to our side, overawe Bulgaria, and possibly persuade Rumania to join us. Such a movement would, he argued, isolate Turkey and enable us to attack Austria, the weakest of our enemies, in overwhelming force. The Chancellor of the Exchequer also thought, as a secondary operation, to defend Egypt by landing 100,000 men on the coast of Syria; he hoped thus to cut off the Turkish forces assembling in the Sinai Desert for an attack on the Canal, and by carrying the war into the enemy's country to win a dramatic victory which would hearten the people at home. He said that, short of some such project, he had little hope of achieving any signal success, and saw rather a prospect of perpetual stalemate.

Mr. Churchill had become more and more enamoured of the Gallipoli scheme, which he wished to take shape as a combined military and naval attack upon Constantinople. Lord Fisher offered a third alternative in naval and military operations against the coast of Schleswig-Holstein. Sir John was still bent on clearing the Belgian coast, and his Staff were satirically suggesting that the Germans would gladly furnish transports to carry British troops to the Dardanelles. Joffre abided resolutely by his Anglo-French offensive.

For the guidance of the Government a very careful and exhaustive examination by highly-trained naval and military General Staffs was requisite. But the Admiralty had no real General Staff, and that credited to the War Office was attenuated to a shadow. After Sir Charles Douglas's death Kitchener, loath to deprive Sir John of any one valuable to him, had appointed Sir James Wolfe-Murray as *ad interim* Chief of the Staff, but had not taken out letters-patent appointing him a Member of the Army Council. Circumstances and the Cabinet alike assigned to Kitchener every military problem, and his calculations were rendered the more intricate by considerations of foreign and domestic politics. One thing was painfully clear—he had no troops ready for extraneous military enterprises.

This was the position when the War Council met

on January 7 and 8 to consider the various plans of campaign; the only decision reached was that the British Army in France should be left to co-operate with Joffre, and Kitchener's Memorandum of January 9 was the outcome. Long and lively discussions took place as to whether and where new theatres of war should be opened up. A week later, on January 13, Kitchener absolutely refused to weaken our front in France or to take troops away from Egypt, and for this amongst other reasons Mr. Lloyd George's proposal for a grand expedition to the Balkans fell to the ground.¹ Kitchener explained that he could not for some time be ready for a serious naval and military attack upon the Dardanelles, and he estimated the military force necessary for this purpose at 150,000 men. There was to his mind a very marked difference between a naval demonstration, which could *à la rigueur* be broken off, and a great combined assault, which must suffer no final rebuff. His wide knowledge of the East compelled the belief that any serious adventure against the Turks, once begun, must be carried right through. In India he had denounced the policy of "Hit and Scuttle" as dangerous, futile, and wasteful; he was persuaded that here it would be open to the same objection in an enhanced degree. He believed in—but was not yet ready for—his Alexandretta scheme, and was still corresponding with Maxwell as to its feasibility. Meanwhile a definite promise for a demonstration against the Turk had been given to Russia.

---

[1] Difficulties of communication figured in the military opposition to Mr. Lloyd George's plan. From Salonika to Nish there was only a single-line railway, poor in rolling-stock. Further on there lay on one flank of the line a doubtful neutral Greece and on the other a probably hostile Bulgaria.

Since the appeal from Russia arrived on January 2 Mr. Churchill had come to the conclusion, after conference with our Admirals in the Eastern Mediterranean, that an attack upon the Dardanelles by the Fleet promised substantial success. He favoured a combined naval and military expedition to Constantinople, but, accepting Kitchener's dictum as to the impossibility of finding troops, he devoted himself to purely naval operations. The First Lord had been deeply impressed by the effect of the German and Austrian heavy howitzers upon the forts of Namur and Liége, which had been overcome with amazing ease and rapidity. It had been a well-established principle—and one which Kitchener in an immediate protest emphatically asserted—that an attack by ships upon equipped forts is, without military co-operation, rarely productive of results. But Mr. Churchill, fortified by his naval advisers, held that this war itself had shown that the principle required entire modification; we had, he urged, in our new battle-cruiser *Queen Elizabeth* guns of similar calibre to that of the howitzers which had in a short time knocked the Belgian forts to pieces, and he believed that the fire of *Queen Elizabeth's* guns would be no whit less effective. Here was a highly technical and up-to-date *ex cathedra* naval opinion which the Secretary for War did not feel himself competent to over-ride. Mr. Churchill's argument was weighty. The weapon he proposed to wield might well ward off the blow of which Russia was in dire dread. The War Council decided that the Admiralty should prepare for a naval expedition in February to bombard and seize the Gallipoli Peninsula with Constantinople as its objective.

The Government then received information which pointed to German and Austrian preparation on a large scale for the invasion of Serbia, and Mr. Lloyd George returned to the charge, emphasising our obligation to aid a weak Ally. Notes were addressed to Greece and to Rumania pressing them to co-operate actively with Serbia, and Grece replied on the 20th agreeing to come in on certain conditions—chiefly, that she should receive direct military assistance from the Entente, and that Bulgaria should be actively friendly, or at least a benevolent neutral. On receipt of this encouraging news Mr. Lloyd George persuaded Kitchener to agree provisionally to the despatch of the Twenty-ninth Division to the Balkans. This was the last of the divisions of Regulars made up by him from troops of the Old Army withdrawn from the East, and was now being trained in England. It remained to enlist the aid of the French Government, and while negotiations were proceeding the War Council, on January 28, definitely decided to make a purely naval attack on the Dardanelles. There was then no question of landing troops, the Twenty-ninth Division being ear-marked for an entirely distinct campaign. The next day Mr. Lloyd George, anxious to lose no opportunity of impressing upon the War Secretary the urgency of his Serbian proposals, wrote:

MY DEAR LORD KITCHENER—You will, I am sure, have seen telegram No. 14 in last night's sections—from Sophia. It is so obviously the German interest to crush Serbia in order to detach Bulgaria from the Triple Entente and to free a way to Constantinople that it is risky to doubt the accuracy of this telegram. The French delayed assistance to Antwerp until it was too late. This time the responsibility is ours and we shall not be held blameless if a catastrophe occurs.—Ever sincerely, D. LLOYD GEORGE.

At this time the Turks had already begun the last stage of their advance across the Sinai Desert to attack the Suez Canal.* The first fight on the Suez Canal began on February 2 and ended on the 4th with the flight of the enemy.

Maxwell wrote on February 15:

I am very sorry we are so hampered in getting information, but it is exceedingly difficult to obtain, for the Turks effectively prevent our agents from getting in. Hydroplanes with floats are very tricky machines for land reconnaissance. It is very dangerous, and those the French have are not of the best and they are always having engine trouble. Our aeroplanes have not range enough. Though they are going back to Beersheba and perhaps further north, I feel the Turks must come on again after all their talk about a Holy War.

We gave them a nasty knock, killing and wounding a great many more than I have reported, for every day bodies in hastily-dug graves are discovered; also many more were drowned in the Canal than we knew of. Yet they got away with their guns in fairly good order. As we knew that there was the Eighth Corps and part of the Third, Fourth, and Fifth Corps against us, and they only showed about 20,000 men, I did not think it safe to go out and meet them, for it was quite possible they were laying a trap for us, and I felt that anything in the nature of a reverse, or even a check, would have fatal results in Egypt, for there is no doubt that the feeling here is pro-Turk and anti-English. It is odd, but nothing that we do or say is believed, whereas every Turkish or German lie is sucked in.

It is satisfactory that our Moslems, both Indian and Egyptian, showed no disinclination to kill their co-religionists when they had the chance.

CHAPTER CV

WHILE Kitchener's measures and Maxwell's means had averted a danger from Egypt, there were ugly messages from the Balkans and the Russian front. Italy was still wavering; Rumania had decided not to intervene; and the Bulgarian Government had negotiated a loan of £3,000,000 with Germany, who did not lend her money without consideration. The Serbs had repelled the first Austrian invasion of their country and had re-occupied Belgrade, but their enemies were mustering against them with added strength. The Russian Armies were woefully short of munitions, and their military operations were poor of promise.

In no wise discouraged by these events Mr. Lloyd George travelled to Paris as the representative of the War Council to arrange for the co-operation of French military forces in the Balkan enterprise, and returned on February 6[1] with M. Delcassé, who guaranteed that the French Government would send a division to Salonika if we would do the same.

---

[1] "Lloyd George and Montagu were here to-day on their way back from Paris. I understand there is still question of sending troops to the Balkans. I find it very difficult to understand why the appearance of British and French soldiers in that part of the world should have so great an influence, and, unless something very decisive in that way will be gained by such a move, it appears to me to be a strategical mistake." (Sir John French to Kitchener, 6.2.15.)

Kitchener agreed that this was a cheap price to pay for the assistance of Greece and very possibly of Rumania, and went as far as to propose to add a Territorial Division to the Twenty-ninth Division. These discussions were still proceeding when Mr. Lloyd George and the advocates of the great adventure to the Balkans received a severe shock in Greece's categorical refusal to come in. The Kaiser had evidently been hectoring King Constantine, and the German Great General Staff was in touch with the corresponding organisation at Athens. The idea of a Balkan campaign was thus ruled out, but it had its sequel. Kitchener had offered troops to help to win over Greece, and as Greece would not be won over, they might serve for the Dardanelles. Mr. Churchill and his friends began to see visions of the concerted naval and military operations for which they thirsted.

The Turks, after their failure on the Canal, were reported to be withdrawing their troops from Palestine towards Constantinople, and at least a part of the garrison of Egypt might be available for the Dardanelles. Mr. Churchill had ready a considerable body of Marines and also the Royal Naval Division, which was in process of being refitted—or rather, fitted—at the Crystal Palace after its trip to Belgium. He continued negotiations with the French, who favoured the naval attack and were prepared to lend a division for the land operations. The outlook had somewhat changed; when it was decided to utilise the Fleet alone no troops were available, whereas now a military force of appreciable importance might be forthcoming.

Despite the altered conditions the orders to the

Fleet were not countermanded. Mr. Churchill continued to exert his influence to obtain troops, but without arresting or modifying his purely naval plan, and Kitchener, relying on his assurances, was still unwilling to embark with his exiguous resources on any considerable military enterprise. He saw, however, that some military force might well be necessary to confirm the success of the Fleet, and he was prepared to substitute military action at Gallipoli for his own Alexandretta project, remembering that the Turks would scarcely venture on Egypt while we were hammering at the western gates of Constantinople.

On February 9 the Secretary for War stated to his colleagues that if at a later stage the Navy should still call upon the land forces for assistance, such assistance would be forthcoming, and he clearly had in his mind the possibility of employing the surplus troops in Egypt, particularly Birdwood and his Anzacs. In the week which followed Mr. Churchill was exerting his great powers of persuasion on behalf of the policy of increasing the military force, and at a meeting of Ministers on February 16 it was decided—the Salonika project having evaporated—that the Twenty-ninth Division should be sent as soon as possible to Mudros, that preparations should be made for a force to be despatched from Egypt, and that the Admiralty should make arrangements for providing the transport and for collecting in the Levant the lighter tugs and horse-boats required for landing. Lord Kitchener momentarily gave his consent to despatch the Twenty-ninth Division, but quickly withdrew it.

The reason for this sudden change was the receipt of bad news from the Russian front. The Austrians —hitherto unable by themselves to cope with the Russians—had with German help assumed the offensive in the Bukovina, and captured Czernowitz, while almost simultaneously our Moscovite Allies suffered a severe set-back on the other flank of their long line in North Poland.

Kitchener was under no illusion as to the prospect of obtaining an early victory on the Western front, and did not share Sir John's optimism; rather he shared Joffre's apprehensions that the Germans would, after driving the Russians back sufficiently far to make their Eastern frontier safe, withdraw large numbers of troops to France and attack again in the West. In fact he feared that the enemy might in 1915, before our new armies were ready to take the field, and before we were adequately equipped with munitions, bring off the same sort of coup in which he so nearly succeeded in the spring of 1918. Where Kitchener differed fundamentally from Mr. Churchill and Mr. Lloyd George was in regarding the Western theatre as the front vital to us; he would embark on Eastern enterprises only on the twofold condition that they were purely subsidiary to what he considered to be the main issue, and that their success would ensure us security in the East and attract the adhesion of new Allies.

His two colleagues, on the other hand, both protested that we had larger forces on the Western front than were necessary for safety, provided we and the French adopted a strictly defensive attitude and improved our trenches; and they were convinced that the war could be won most quickly and most easily in the East if we planted our arms and imposed our will there.

Kitchener, nevertheless, by no means blinked the consideration that the political situation in the Balkans required something more than a demonstration at the Dardanelles. The German authorities had begun energetic propaganda in their own country in favour of the *Drang nach Osten,* and the War Secretary began to think it probable that the defeat of the enemy on the Marne had caused him to change the basis of his war policy, that he might be looking to the establishment of a great German Eastern Empire to compensate him for the failure of his initial plans of conquest in the West.

The whole situation required very careful watching, for Germany's central position allowed her to change rapidly from one policy to the other, while once we were committed in the East it would take us a very long time to bring troops back to France if the Western front were threatened.

Despite, therefore, angry protests from the advocates of the Eastern campaign at the delay in des patching the Twenty-ninth Division, Kitchener refused to allow himself to be rushed. At the same time he thought it prudent to prepare for military support to the Fleet, for he now felt that the attack on the Dardanelles having started, it could not be discontinued until we had obtained such a measure of success as would safeguard our prestige in Asia. He was still hopeful that the Navy would suffice for this. The bombardment of the outer forts at the Dardanelles had begun on the 19th, and the results obtained were promising; but he was determined that military support should not be lacking if it were needed.

On February 20 he telegraphed to Maxwell:

A naval squadron is proceeding to the bombardment of the Dardanelles, and during the first day they have silenced one fort and severely damaged another. In order to assist the Navy a force is being concentrated in Lemnos Island to occupy any captured forts. At present 2000 marines are on the island, to be followed about March 18 by 8000 more. You should have a force of approximately 30,000 of the Australian and New Zealand contingents under Birdwood prepared for this service. We shall send transports from here to convey these troops to Lemnos, and they should arrive at Alexandria about March 9. You should, however, communicate with the Navy through Admiral Carden, commanding at the Dardanelles, as he may require a considerable force before that date, so that you may be able to send him what he most requires.

You should not therefore wait until transports arrive from here, but should take up any transports you can obtain and despatch units to Lemnos immediately.

On the 23rd Maxwell answered:

I have sent the following to Carden: "In anticipation of embarking a large force from here, I am ordered to communicate with you as to your immediate requirements. I can have ready at short notice a mixed brigade of infantry, engineers, and artillery. In what order would you like these sent? It would greatly help me if you could send me some plan of disembarkation."

Carden replies: "I have been directed to prepare for landing a force of 10,000, if such a step is found necessary. At present my instructions go no further. If such a force is sent, I would propose landing at Sedd-el-Bahr, with the object of occupying the Gallipoli Peninsula as far east as the line Suandere River—Chanalvasi."

The same day Kitchener telegraphed to Birdwood:

By the earliest possible opportunity you should proceed to meet Admiral Carden, to consult him on the spot as to the combined naval and military operations which the forcing of the Dardanelles is to involve. The result should be reported to me. It is important that you should learn from local observation and information the strength of the Turkish garrison on the Gallipoli Peninsula, and what their composition is; whether the Admiral thinks troops should be employed to take the forts, and if so what force will be wanted; whether a landing force will be required of the troops to take the forts in reverse, and generally in what manner it is proposed to employ them.

The next day's telegram to Maxwell showed what was passing through Kitchener's mind:

It is clearly essential that Birdwood should consult Carden on the spot. In considering operations he should be guided by the following considerations—the object in forcing the Dardanelles is to gain the entrance to the Sea of Marmora and ultimately to gain possession of the Bosphorus and overawe Constantinople. The operation is to be effected mainly by naval means, and when successful will doubtless cause the retirement of the Gallipoli garrison. According to our information it would not be a sound military undertaking to attempt a landing in force on the Gallipoli Peninsula, whose garrison is reported to be 40,000 strong, until naval operations for the reduction of the forts have been successful and the passage has been forced.

The entrance of the Fleet into the Sea of Marmora would probably render the Turkish position in the Peninsula untenable, and would enable a force to occupy the forts if necessary; but to land 10,000 men in face of 40,000 Turks while the naval operation is still incomplete seems extremely hazardous. If it can be carried out without seriously compromising the troops landed, there would be no objection to the employment of a military force to secure hold of the forts or positions already dominated by naval fire, so as to prevent re-occupation or repair by the enemy.

What he said in this telegram he emphasised in a message to Birdwood sent off on the 26th:

> Navy undertakes the forcing of the Dardanelles. The task of your troops at present seems to be limited to minor operations pending the actual forcing of the passage, such as the final destruction of batteries already silenced by the ships. Possibly, however, howitzer batteries may be concealed in land, and it may be beyond the power of the ships to cope with these effectively. You might, if called upon by Admiral Carden, have to undertake special minor operations from within the Straits in order to deal with such batteries. Remember, however, that large enemy forces are stationed on both sides of the Straits, and you should not commit yourself to any such enterprise without aerial reconnaissance and assurance of ample covering fire from the fleet.

Evidently Kitchener still regarded any landing as subsidiary to the action of the Fleet, and in his mind the *raison d'être* of the whole operation was the probability that the Fleet alone would be able unaided to overcome the Dardanelles forts. He told his colleagues in the Cabinet that, from his knowledge of Constantinople and of the East, he was quite sure that the conditions in Constantinople would entirely change the moment the Fleet had secured a passage through the Dardanelles, and that we could judge matters accurately so soon as the defences at the Narrows should totter.

Mr. Churchill, on the other hand, pleaded with all his fiery and suasive energy for the Dardanelles Campaign as our main offensive effort during 1915, vehemently appealing for the immediate despatch of the Twenty-ninth Division; and he recorded his dissent from any retention of the Division in this country and his disclaimer of responsibility for any disaster in Turkey due to insufficiency of troops.

So the pair of policies were pulling against each other. The First Lord of the Admiralty, who had persuaded Kitchener to agree to the Dardanelles enterprise on the explicit pronouncement that the ships would be able to overcome the forts and force the Straits, was pressing for the employment of large military forces; while the Secretary of State for War, who had in the first instance made it clear that he had no large military forces to spare, was relying upon the Fleet to perform what it had undertaken. The cardinal error of procedure had been an over-sanguine estimate of the power of the ships' guns. This estimate had set the feet of the Government on a path from which it was dangerous to draw back, but which—*via dolorosa* though it proved to be—was not trodden in vain.

CHAPTER CVI

A ROYAL Commission was appointed in mid-war to report on the Dardanelles Campaign. In their Majority Report they specially addressed themselves to the temporary holding-back of the Twenty-ninth Division:

The favourable moment for action was allowed to lapse. Time was given to the Turks, with the help of German officers, to strengthen their position, so that eventually the opposition to be encountered became of a far more formidable character than was originally to have been anticipated.

The Commissioners [1] were not at the pains to note Joffre's remarkable declaration—which the French Ambassador on the morning of February 21 called at Sir Edward Grey's private residence to communicate to him—that unless the Twenty-ninth Division were available for the next few critical days he would not guarantee the immunity of the line. The signatories—secure in the fact that Death had removed rebutting evidence—seemed somehow anxious

[1] When the Commission was about to sit, the Prime Minister, believing the Government to be in a sense the trustees of Lord Kitchener's memory, asked that Sir Frederick Smith—then Attorney-General and later Lord Chancellor—a personal friend and colleague of the late War Secretary, should attend the meetings and reply so far as possible to any points criticising his judgement. The suggestion was not accepted.

It may be remembered that Lord Cromer was compelled by ill-health to absent himself from many of the sittings of the Commission.

to score any point against Kitchener; they admitted, however, that, if they had been able to hear him, they might have modified their views—or rather, the views they accepted from Mr. Churchill—as to the War Minister's judgement in withholding the Twenty-ninth Division. But, even with this reservation, it is not easy to follow them in their affirmation that in the third week of February occurred the moment favourable for the despatch of the Twenty-ninth Division.

Kitchener was well aware that the Turks had large military forces hovering near Constantinople, which could reach the Peninsula long before we could be ready with a landing force. Maxwell had wired to him on February 24 that the Turks could easily concentrate 40,000 men west and 30,000 east of the Straits, and that the Peninsula was so prepared for defence as to be practically a fortress; to advance against it from any quarter without heavy guns must be highly hazardous.

On February 28 Maxwell wrote:

> I am very much in the dark as to the intentions and objects of the Fleet in forcing the Dardanelles, and await Birdwood's report with great interest. As I write, I hear the Fleet have forced the entrance, but they have the difficult part before them. There are seven lines of mines, the great part worked by electricity from the shore; the first line is just south of Kilid Bahr—Chanak, the entrance to the Narrows. This mine-field is well protected by a series of strong forts on both sides of the Straits. There are also two mine-laying boats at Nagara whose mission is to let loose mines to float down with the current. The Admiralty seem to me to be oversanguine as to the capacity of the Fleet to force the passage without an expeditionary force. The

Gallipoli Peninsula is very strongly organised for defence—all the bays on the northern littoral are defended, and from Maitos to Gallipoli it is an entrenched fort. Apparently there are any number of 15 c.m. howitzers in prepared positions.

There was therefore no reason to suppose in February that the Turks would be unprepared to defend the Gallipoli Peninsula against a landing. Kitchener believed and said that the Turks would abandon the Peninsula if the Fleet forced the Dardanelles; in such event troops would be required only to complete and crown the success of the Navy, for which purpose he could well draw on Egypt. If success were denied to the Fleet, extensive naval and military operations would become necessary, and would demand elaborate preparations. The delay of a week or two at the end of February in the despatch of the Twenty-ninth Division could not be presumed to affect the situation in the Dardanelles; while a weighty reason arose for keeping the Division back. The favourable hour for military action was that in which the Navy attacked, but for the Twenty-ninth Division to have co-operated with the Fleet on February 19 it should have left England early in January, when it was neither formed nor fit. The guns of the Fleet warned the Turks, who could no longer be taken by surprise. The fact that the first landing-parties from the ships were weakly opposed is no proof that a military landing in force would not have been strenuously resisted by the time the Twenty-ninth Division arrived; the Turks could not have been blind to the assembly of the transports and other arrangements for landing, and they easily could, and certainly would, have brought up troops to defend the Peninsula.

The first bombardment of the Dardanelles forts had reverberated throughout Europe. Bulgaria began to trim her sails, and on March 4 Italy put out a tentative hand to the Allies, while the next day M. Venizelos offered the Greek Fleet and troops to help in the attack on the Gallipoli Peninsula. The King of the Hellenes immediately repudiated this offer and M. Venizelos resigned, but the fact of its having been made showed that there was a strong party in Greece ready to go all the way with the Entente. Russia heard with delight of the attack on the Straits, and promised to provide an Army Corps for the move on Constantinople—so fondly anticipated; she was just then easier as to her own battle-front; she had retaken Przemysl and saw the Austrians pulled up short in the Bukovina.

Events strengthened the case for vigorous pressure on the Dardanelles; an assemblage of troops outside the gateway might well be the preface to an entry into Constantinople. On March 4 Kitchener wired to Birdwood and Maxwell:

> Unless the Navy are convinced that they cannot silence the guns in the Straits without military co-operation on a large scale—in which case further orders will be issued—there is no intention of using troops to take the Gallipoli Peninsula. In such a case even more troops would be required to force the Turkish positions, and you would have to wait for further reinforcements from here. In the meantime only small bodies of troops will be required for subsidiary operations while the Fleet are successfully silencing the forts. The concentration of troops at the entrance to the Dardanelles is not so much for operations on the Galli-

THE DIVISION RELEASED

poli Peninsula as for operations subsequently to be undertaken in the neighbourhood of Constantinople. In these operations the co-operation of a Russian Corps of 40,000 men is contemplated.

Evidently Kitchener must prepare himself for military action, either to supplement the success of the Fleet or to redeem its failure, and three distinct courses were in his thoughts—the landing of small forces under Birdwood to complete the work of the Navy; the employment of a considerable expedition in co-operation with the Russians, after the Dardanelles had been forced; a military attack upon the Gallipoli Peninsula if the Navy should be foiled. This last would require more troops and a complete recasting of plans. On the 5th Birdwood telegraphed:

> I am very doubtful if the Navy can force the passage unassisted. In any event the forcing of the passage must take a considerable time; the forts that have been taken up to the present have been visible and very easy, as the ships could stand off and shoot from anywhere; but inside the Straits the ships are bothered by fire from unknown sources. No troops could be landed in the present bad weather.

And next day:

> I have already informed you that I consider the Admiral's forecast as too sanguine, and though we may have a better estimate by March 12, I doubt his ability to force the passage unaided.

On March 10 the War Secretary told his colleagues that the Twenty-ninth Division might start for the East. He had waited till then in order to have Birdwood's reports and to hear how Sir John had fared at Neuve Chapelle. Sir John's first information synchronised with improved accounts from Russia, and Kitchener felt that he could release the Division without prejudice to the battle-line in France. The Dardanelles operations must not be permitted to languish, and a great military attack might be indispensable. He still hoped that this would not be the case, and was still strengthened by Mr. Churchill's renewed assurance that the Admiralty adhered to their belief in the ability of the Navy to force the Straits unaided. Kitchener's mind is shown in the instructions to General Sir Ian Hamilton, who, early in March, was selected to command the troops being mustered in the neighbourhood of the Dardanelles.

1. The Fleet have undertaken to force the passage of the Dardanelles. The employment of military forces on any large scale for land operations at this juncture is only contemplated in the event of the Fleet failing to get through after every effort has been exhausted.

2. Before any serious undertaking is carried out in the Gallipoli Peninsula all the British Military forces detailed for the expedition should be assembled, so that their full weight can be thrown in.

3. Having entered on the project of forcing the Straits there can be no idea of abandoning the scheme. It will require time, patience, and methodical plans of co-operation between the naval and military commanders. The essential point is to avoid a check, which will jeopardise our chances of strategical and political success.

4. This does not preclude the probability of minor operations being engaged upon to clear areas occupied by the Turks with guns annoying the Fleet, or for the demolition of forts already silenced by the Fleet. But such minor operations should be as much as possible restricted to the forces necessary to achieve the object in view, and should

as far as practicable not entail permanent occupation of positions on the Gallipoli Peninsula.

5. Owing to the lack of any definite information we must presume that the Gallipoli Peninsula is held in strength and that the Kilid Bahr plateau has been fortified and armed for a determined resistance. In fact, we must presuppose that the Turks have taken every measure for the defence of the plateau, which is the key to the Western front at the Narrows, until such time as reconnaissance has proved otherwise.

6. Under present conditions it seems undesirable to land any permanent garrison or hold any lines on the Gallipoli Peninsula. Probably an entrenched force will be required to retain the Turkish forces in the Peninsula and prevent reinforcements arriving at Bulair, and this force would naturally be supported on both flanks by gun-fire from the Fleet. Troops employed on the minor operations mentioned above (paragraph 4) should be withdrawn as soon as their mission is fulfilled.

7. In order not to reduce forces advancing on Constantinople, the security of the Dardanelles passage, once it has been forced, is a matter for the Fleet, except as in paragraph 6 with regard to Bulair.

The occupation of the Asiatic side of military forces is to be strongly deprecated.

8. When the advance through the Sea of Marmora is undertaken, and the Turkish Fleet has been destroyed, the opening of the Bosphorus for the passage of Russian forces will be proceeded with. During this period, the employment of the British and French troops, which will probably have been brought up to the neighbourhood of Constantinople, should be conducted with caution. As soon as the Russian corps has joined up with our troops, combined plans of operations against the Turkish Army (if it still remains in European Turkey) will be undertaken with a view to obtaining its defeat or surrender. Until this is achieved,

landing in the town of Constantinople, which may entail street fighting, should be avoided.

9. As it is impossible now to foretell what action the Turkish military authorities may decide upon as regards holding their European territories, the plan of operations for the landing of the troops and their employment must be left for subsequent decision. It is, however, important that as soon as possible after the arrival of the Fleet at Constantinople, all communication from the West to the East across the Bosphorus, including telegraph cables, should be stopped. Assuming that the main portion of the Turkish Army is prepared to defend European Turkish territory, it may be necessary to land parties to hold entrenched positions on the East side of the Bosphorus, and thus assist the Fleet in preventing all communication across the Bosphorus.

10. Should the Turkish Army have retired to the East side of the Bosphorus, the occupation of Constantinople and the Western territories of Turkey may be proceeded with.

11. As, in certain contingencies, it may be important to be able to withdraw our troops from this theatre at an early date, the Allied troops working in conjunction with us should be placed in those positions which need to be garrisoned, and our troops might with advantage be employed principally in holding the railway line until a decision is come to as to future operations.

The instructions bear date of March 13, and three days earlier Kitchener had informed his colleagues that the forces to operate against Constantinople would consist of the Royal Naval Division, the Anzac Corps, the Twenty-ninth Division, a French Division, and a Russian Army Corps—their strength being about 127,000 men and 298 guns.

On March 18 the Navy made their last attempt to force the Dardanelles, and failed with the loss of one French and two British battleships.

CHAPTER CVII

In the meantime Ian Hamilton had arrived, and after a close reconnaissance of the Peninsula reported on the 19th:

> Yesterday we steamed close along the whole western shore of the Gallipoli Peninsula. There are landing-places here and there, but except at Cape Helles all are commanded by elaborate networks of trenches. We were so near as to see clearly the barbed wire defences covering the trenches. Afterwards we entered the Straits, but before we had gone a mile we were shelled by field-guns and were then signalled to stand by H.M.S. *Inflexible* on our way back to Tenedos. I have not yet received any report on the naval action, but from what I saw of the extraordinarily gallant attempt made yesterday, I am being most reluctantly driven to the conclusion that the Dardanelles are less likely to be forced by battleships than at one time seemed probable, and that if the army is to participate, its operations will not assume the subsidiary form anticipated.
>
> The army's share will not be a case of landing-parties for the destruction of forts, but rather a case of a deliberate and progressive military operation carried out in force in order to make good a passage for the Navy.

This report shows the Turks fully prepared to resist a landing, and that the Twenty-ninth Division, if despatched at the end of February, would have found itself in the teeth of the same difficulties it encountered on April 25.

On hearing of the failure of the Fleet and Ian Hamilton's opinion, Kitchener wired to him:

> You know my views—that the passage of the Dardanelles must be forced, and that large military operations by the Army on the Peninsula are necessary to clear the way; those operations must be undertaken after careful consideration of the local defences, and they must be carried through.

Admiral De Robeck, who had succeeded Admiral Carden, at first hoped to renew the effort to push through; but the mine menace was serious, and time was required to cope with it. The Admiral thought that a decisive operation three weeks later would be better than taking a big risk for what might be only half-measures.

Kitchener, somewhat perturbed on hearing through the Admiralty of this delay, telegraphed:

> I hear you consider April 14 as about the date for the commencement of the military operations, if the Dardanelles has not been forced by the Fleet before that date. I think you had better know at once that I regard any such postponement as far too long.[1]

Ian Hamilton explained:

> Admiral and myself are agreed in the conviction that to enable Fleet effectively to force Dardanelles, co-operation of the whole military force will be necessary.
>
> The strength of the enemy is estimated at 40,000, with a reserve of 30,000 west of Rodosto. The unsettled March weather is a dangerous incalculable factor in handling a large force in face of certain opposition. The April weather should be more settled, and I am sanguine of success then for a simple straightforward scheme based on your broad principles. I have already worked this out in the

---

[1] This information came from the Admiralty; Sir Ian Hamilton had not fixed any such date.

main features, and can communicate it if thought safe to do so. Practically the whole force will be required to effect what has been planned, and on the thoroughness with which the preparations are to be made, of which proper allocation of troops to transports is not the least important, the success of plans will largely depend. This is one of the principal reasons why importance has been attached to proper organisation of the expedition at a convenient place like Alexandria. The Turks will meanwhile be kept busy by the Admiral.

Kitchener promptly assured him:

I have not changed my original views, but your fixing a date rather upset me. I can, I know, implicitly trust you not to waste time, but I have no wish in any way to rush the situation so long as it is being pushed by you and the Admiral to a final successful conclusion. You ought to be careful in naming any definite date for the commencement of operations, as in my opinion the weather would be much more a governing factor in determining the date than our preparations.

The Dardanelles Commissioners in their first report quoted Kitchener's telegram of March 23, but suppressed that of March 25, and in referring to the telegrams of March 19 and March 23 they say:

These telegrams are conclusive proof that Lord Kitchener had by that time wholly abandoned the idea of a purely naval operation, and realised the fact that military operations on a large scale were necessary. The telegrams also prove that Lord Kitchener in contemplating military action had no clear idea of when a landing could be made.

It is quite true that Kitchener had by then abandoned the idea of a purely naval operation, but he had done so only when convinced that the hopes persistently held out by Mr. Churchill could not be realised. His somewhat impatient telegram of March 23 was clearly due to the report from the Admiralty that the date for the military attack had been fixed for the middle of April, while he had not then received from the military commander on the spot any reasons which he could give to his anxious colleagues as to why that date was selected. His message of March 25 to Ian Hamilton absolves him of any wish to interfere with the discretion of the man on the spot.

So the die was definitely cast, and at Alexandria the military heads were put together to prepare for the complicated operation of landing on an open beach in face of an entrenched enemy. The Admiralty's assurances—continually reiterated from the time when a naval demonstration was first mooted up to the moment of this weighty decision—that the Fleet could force the Dardanelles weighed heavily on Kitchener's mind. He had from the first shown no desire whatever to embark upon a second great military campaign when he was well aware that we had not, and for many months to come would not have, the men, munitions, or equipment needed for the effective prosecution of the big job already on our hands. None the less, he was fully alive to the great political advantages to be obtained from successful action at the Dardanelles; he was ready to welcome the proposal for a naval attack and to give it such military support as he considered necessary, once he was assured by the Admiralty that there was a good prospect of the Fleet succeeding in its mission. It was only when Birdwood's reports made him fear that the naval forecast was oversanguine that he addressed himself altogether to a serious attack by land forces. The failure of the Navy compelled him to a military effort, less because he hoped—like some of his colleagues—thus to win the war, than because it was the only way to secure our position in the East, and safety in the East was a main plank of his military policy. If any error of judgement can arguably be attributed to him, it was that he accepted the view of the First Lord of the Admiralty as to the power and effect of the naval ordnance. But even if reliance on the Navy to force the Straits is to be accounted an initial miscalculation, every subsequent step was consequently right and had to be taken.

CHAPTER CVIII

THE concentration and the organisation in Egypt of the troops for the landing proceeded smoothly, and on April 7 Ian Hamilton was able to return to his advanced base at Mudros, from whence he wrote to Kitchener on April 10 outlining his plans:

I arrived here this morning and I have just cabled you a brief account of my discussion with the Vice-Admiral, and of his full agreement with our scheme.

The more I ponder over the map and consider the character, numbers, and position of the enemy, the more I am convinced that the very essence of success must lie in upsetting the equilibrium of the Turk by the most rapid deployment of force possible over a fairly wide extent of country, combined with feints where troops and launches cannot be spared for an actual serious landing.

My main reliance will be on the Twenty-ninth Division, the covering force of which will be landed at dawn at Seddel-Bahr, Cape Helles, and, D.V., in Morto Bay. I put in a special "D.V." to the Morto Bay project because the transports will be there under fire from the other side, and whether they can stick it or not is rather a question. Still, they must try. Also, no doubt, they will be under long-range fire from field-guns and perhaps howitzers from behind Achibabi. To help these fellows along, subsidiary landings in boats will be made along the coast in small groups from Tekke Barnu up to opposite Crithia. Even a few men able to scramble up these cliffs should shake the first line of defence which stretches from Old Castle northwards to the coast. The Australians meanwhile will make

a strong feint which will, I hope, develop into a serious landing operation north of Kaba Tepe. Braithwaite has marked out a good circular holding position, stretching from about Fisherman's Hut round to Gaba Tebe, and if they can maintain themselves there, I should hope later on they may be able to make a push forward for Koja Dere. Whatever this does, it will tend to raise anxieties in the minds of the men opposesd to the Twenty-ninth Division, and will prevent the plateau being reinforced. I fear we must expect casualties from guns in concealed positions, both on the sea and whilst this is being done. But that is part of the hardness of the nut.

Meanwhile the Naval Division will move up and make a simultaneous feint somewhere opposite Bulair, which will keep the Gallipoli people on tenterhooks at least for a time.

These are my plans in broad outline. I do not want to talk about the difficulties, for I try to keep my mind fixed on my own objective, feeling sure that if I can stick to that and carry it through with vigour, the enemy will not be able to do all the wonderful things which theorists might expect.

Kitchener was equally sure that the success of the operation depended largely upon the result of the first attack, which he wished to see made in the greatest possible strength. He had wired to Maxwell on the 6th: "You should supply any troops in Egypt that can be spared, or even selected officers and men whom Sir Ian Hamilton may want for Gallipoli."

On the 17th Ian Hamilton reported to Kitchener the only untoward incident of the voyage of the Twenty-ninth Division:

At 10 A.M. the transport *Maniton* arrived here having on board the 147th Brigade R.F.A. and 50 infantry details. The Officer Commanding troops reports that at 10 A.M.

yesterday the transport was stopped by a torpedo boat, thought to be one of ours, which turned out to be an enemy boat. The *Maniton* was given three minutes to abandon the vessel, but on appeal this was increased to ten minutes. The troops got into boats and extemporised rafts. The torpedo fired three torpedoes at the *Maniton* after eight minutes at 300 yards' range, and on our destroyers appearing the enemy steamed off. Headed off by others of our destroyers the enemy boat beached herself. There are 24 identified deaths from drowning, and 27 missing, feared to be drowned. These casualties were caused mainly by the boats upsetting during the hurried disembarkation. Although at first too many men entered the boats and had to be got out there seems to have been no panic. For example, after two torpedoes had been fired the sergeant on duty came up and saluted, and reported to his major that all horses had been duly watered and fed.

While the last touches were being put to the preparations for the new venture, our troops in Mesopotamia won a signal victory over the Turks in the battle of Shiva near Basra, and gave us possession of Southern Mesopotamia. On the 19th Kitchener wired to Ian Hamilton giving him the experiences of this battle:

The Turks are brave, well trained, and well disciplined. Their trenches were admirably sited, part at 110 yards and part at 800 yards, at the foot of a slope leading from us down to them. Their machine-guns were effectively concealed and well used. They had no idea of being shot out of their trenches, and had to be turned out by a charge of the whole line with the bayonet.

If our force had not been handled with initiative and decision, and if the pluck of our troops, British and Indian, had not been of the sternest, the battle would not have been won. The trenches were so well concealed that the brunt of taking them fell on the infantry. The Turks were so

THE LANDING EFFECTED

severely handled that they retired 19 miles during the night, and later information indicates that they continued their retirement next day.

All was ready by the 23rd, though bad weather imposed a delay of two more days. On the 23rd Kitchener telegraphed:

Convey to the Admiral my best wishes for all success for the Fleet. The Army know it can rely on their energetic and effective co-operation while dealing with the land forces of the enemy.

Assure General d'Amade and the French troops of our entire confidence that their courage and skill will result in the triumph of their arms.

My best wishes to you and all your troops in carrying to a successful conclusion the operations you have before you, which will undoubtedly have a momentous effect on the war. The task they have to perform will need all the grit Britishers have never failed to show, and I am confident that your troops will victoriously clear the way for the Fleet to advance on Constantinople. When operations commence all my thoughts will be with you.

The landing took place on the 25th; hearts beat high, and Ian Hamilton could announce:

Thanks to God who calmed the seas and to the Royal Navy who rowed our fellows ashore as coolly as if at a regatta; thanks also to the dauntless spirit shown by all ranks of both Services. we have landed 29,000 upon six beaches in the face of desperate resistance from strong Turkish Infantry forces well backed by Artillery. Enemy are entrenched, line upon line, behind wire entanglements—sometimes 50 yards wide—spread to catch us wherever we may try to concentrate for an advance.

Birdwood gave a vivid description of the landing of the Anzac Corps:

May 4, 1915.—You will, I know, like to hear of the first doings of my Australian and New Zealand Army Corps in the field. We effected a landing as you know on the morning of the 25th. The day before we transferred 500 men each to the warships *Queen, London,* and *Prince of Wales,* where all were given a good square meal before midnight. When we got about four miles from land, these men were transferred to the ships' boats. You will, I know, be glad to hear how extraordinarily enthusiastic the Naval Officers were at their behaviour on board. It took under ten minutes to transfer the whole of these men to their boats, and when this had been completed the Flag Captain said to me: "Your men are not quiet, they are absolutely silent." These 1500 men then pushed off in tows of picket boats to the shore, and, as they disappeared in the distance without a sound of any sort, I had every hope that we had succeeded in effecting the surprise we wanted. These hopes, however, were shortly dispelled, as, before the troops touched the beach, a heavy fusillade broke out against them. Some of the boats, I am sorry to say, suffered severely in this, but nothing daunted our men for a second, and they just dashed ashore and, once there, raced for the hills as fast as they could. I think I told you there had been some intention at first to have done our landing by day after the Navy had thoroughly bombarded the place. I was, however, averse to this, as I felt that the bombardment would do more harm than good, in that it would advertise our intention of landing, while I felt sure that our great chance was surprise—partial if not complete. I also made up my mind that, having landed, it would be essential for us to hurl ourselves at the position we had to take without a moment's hesitation, and on as broad a front as possible. The results, I think, fully justified this, as, had we attempted landing in full daylight after any hesitation or delay, I think it is more than doubtful if we should ever have been able to get a footing.

It would have done your heart good to see the way the men went. Nothing would stop them, and I cannot say how deeply I regret their necessarily heavy losses. Normally, of course, regiments would regularly form up before an attack, but in the present instance this was impossible, as with all the bombardment that was going on at the transports and beach it was not possible to land in exactly the order planned, and consequently when a tow reached the land, the officers commanding had to take the men off to where they were most required. This naturally resulted in the splitting up of regiments very much, and small sections of different regiments found themselves together chasing the Turks off the hills. In their zeal, some went too far to the flanks, while the enemy still held the centre of this large hill in strength, and I fear that some of these detachments were cut off and unable to rejoin, though we have not yet been able to get all details. We might say that the men really started fighting at about 3.30 A.M., and were continuously at it until dark, and even during the whole night; in fact they really had no respite for over 36 hours. On the evening of the day of landing they were, however, naturally terribly exhausted, as they had to get over some very severe hill climbing, carrying heavy weights all the time they were fighting. With exhaustion came the consequent reaction, and when I went round all their trenches (or rather the places where their trenches should have been, had there been time for digging) I found a good many men very much done up. Several small detachments of 20 men or so, when I spoke to them, told me they were the only remaining survivors of their battalion, the whole of the rest having been cut up! Of course I was always able to cheer them up by telling them they only had to go round the corner to find at least another 500 on duty there. It took us, however, two or three days to try and collect together these scattered groups, and even now all are not accounted for. Could you see the position we are now occupying, you would realise what the work has been. The hillside everywhere is honeycombed with most cleverly-made trenches, which are thoroughly concealed, while the "going" is extraordinarily difficult, and in many places the country is quite precipitous. However, as I say, nothing stopped the men, and whatever further actions we may have to fight, this must always stand out to their great credit.

That we have enormous difficulties still before us there can I think be no doubt, and I think it will take a long time to fight our way through, as we mean to do. Khalid Bahr plateau in front of us is a regular Gibraltar, which we shall have to tackle, unless we can sufficiently dispirit the Turks before then so as to make them leave it.

Ever since landing on the 25th we have not had a moment's respite from fighting. Day and night we have been attacked, and yesterday 250 shrapnel burst over one corner of this camp in ten minutes. All have, however, I hope, now fully realised the necessity of digging by which alone they can hope to escape heavy casualties, and it is rather nice to see what old soldiers a great many of the men have become during the week, and how little respect they now show to the enemy's shrapnel. The waste of ammunition at first was terrible, as was perhaps very natural in an army practically composed of young soldiers. The whole of the hill on which we are living is covered with dense scrub about four feet high, and it is certainly rather trying to men's nerves to have an enemy all round them hidden in this stuff, and never knowing when and in what strength the attack may be made. By constantly going round the trenches and talking to them all, I hope we have now been able to induce them to hold their fire until the attack actually approaches them, and then to pour in rapid fire and use the bayonet. Whenever this has been done the Turks have been completely routed, and I think we have accounted for a great number of them.

My losses on 25th were roughly 500 killed, 2500 wounded, and 2000 missing. Since then they have totalled up to about 8000.

Early hopes were, however, soon damped. On the 28th the first battle of Krithia was fought, and the Peninsula was evidently not to be rushed. Kitchener, burning to strengthen Ian Hamilton, had arranged with the French to despatch a second division to Gallipoli, and he did not hesitate to draw on Egypt to the bare margin of security, remembering that while we threatened Constantinople the Turks would keep their hands off the Canal. But Ian Hamilton was still unable to get on. The second battle of Krithia was fought on May 6 and ended on the 8th much where it had begun. On May 9 Kitchener telegraphed to Ian Hamilton:

I had hoped the naval artillery would be more effective than it is apparently on the enemy's fixed positions. The whole situation naturally gives me some anxiety, particularly as our transport service is much hampered by want of ships. More ammunition is coming to you *via* Marseilles.

Ian Hamilton wrote on May 10:

The success of the actual landing was due to the very careful organisation worked out beforehand by Braithwaite and his officers. Certainly, although I say it, the feat was remarkable, and I think too that the double movement north of Kaba Tepe, combined with the southern movement on Sedd-el-Bahr, was, in its conception, essentially sound. Some of the Australians in the first rush got very nearly across to Maidos. Had they had a regular brigade with them to steady them, they might really almost have made the thing good in one tremendous dash. Even as it is they have held off at least 20,000 Turks, have killed and wounded many thousands more, and still maintain themselves like a thorn in the enemy's side through, I am afraid to think now how many days and nights of continuous fighting they have had.

Here the troops are very, very tired. Our British fellows are, all of them, in good spirits, barring that extreme fatigue. If I can pull through this night, then to-morrow, D.V., I shall be able to replace the whole of the front line with the East Lancs Territorial Division and give the others a rest to enable them to reorganise themselves, for, during that last fight, battalions, and even companies, have got very mixed up, and, under the constant sniping fire of the Turks, any rearrangement in the trenches is a sheer impossibility. Moreover, the trenches themselves must be consolidated and worked on to before we make another advance. At present it is a sort of Victoria Cross business getting food and water over to the first line, as there are no proper communication trenches.

I got a most charming epistle from Fitz [1] this morning. His letters bring home to me more vividly than ever how disappointed you must feel we have not been able to carry through to the Narrows with a rush. It is too bad after such a dashing opening to find oneself collared by superior numbers as we are at present. Not only the numbers of the Turks, but the fact that they are really fine, bold troops has put a stopper on us. Also, as I have already indicated in my telegrams, these inventions of the devil, wire entanglements and machine-guns. Cleverly placed, such obstacles give a ten to one chance to the defence. Well, it may be worth while for the gain of some particular point to sacrifice on occasion ten Englishmen or Frenchmen for one German, but I must say I grudge such high rates of payment where our enemy is the Turk.

Water is another great worry, as I foresaw it would be. The Sedd-el-Bahr and Cape Helles wells are all drying up, and I shall have to sink wells on towards the front line and pump the water back to the beach.

Getting on a mile or two further would solve this difficulty together with many others. For instance, if the Turks were to get a powerful artillery on to Achi Baba they could take such toll of us working on the beaches as to render the whole position precarious. So you may rely on my pushing forward the very moment I feel the condition of my troops and my entrenchments warrant it.

I fear I have been parading my difficulties before you. Still I have not made them—they exist. Also, they were made to be surmounted, and, tired though the troops are,

---

[1] Lieut.-Col. FitzGerald, Lord Kitchener's personal military secretary.

their bravery and the skill of my Staff will, I am confident, tell in our favour decisively in the long run however many fresh troops the Turks may send down against us.

May I, in conclusion, be permitted to say what a help it has been to me to receive such comprehending and sympathetic telegrams as those which you have been good enough, from time to time, to despatch.

This news was depressing. We were faced on another front with the deadlock of trench warfare, while still unable to cope with the requirements of Sir John French.

Ian Hamilton had asked for an additional Army Corps, and the respective champions of the Eastern and Western theatres pleaded their causes strenuously. Joffre had begun to plan his summer campaign, and Sir John French was therefore pressing for all possible reinforcements.

Mr. Churchill, despite the failure of the Fleet, remained an enthusiast for the Near Eastern venture, and urged that we should concentrate our offensive power to carry the Gallipoli campaign to a triumphant issue. That campaign had already made a big mark. Italy had denounced the Triple Alliance on May 3 and had decided to join us. She declared war against Austria on the 23rd, and the next day her troops crossed the frontier. This further heartened the Ministers imbued with Eastern tendencies, who painted with new colours the advantages of attracting Greece, Rumania, and Bulgaria, of opening further communications with Russia, and closing to the Germans the door of Constantinople. There was high debate on these matters in the War Council, and on May 14 Kitchener telegraphed to Hamilton:

The War Council would like to know what force you consider would be necessary to carry through your present operations to success. You should base this estimate on the supposition that I have adequate forces to place at your disposal.

On the one hand [was the reply], there are at present on the Peninsula as many troops as the available space and water-supply can accommodate.

On the other hand, to break through the strong opposition on my front will require more troops. I am, therefore, in a quandary, because although more troops are wanted there is at present no room for them. Moreover, the difficulty in answering your question is accentuated by the fact that my answer must depend on whether Turkey will continue to be left undisturbed in other parts and therefore free to make good the undoubtedly heavy losses incurred here by sending troops from Adrianople, Keshan, Constantinople, and Asia; we now have direct evidence that the latter has been the case.

If the present condition of affairs in this respect were changed by the entry into the struggle of Bulgaria or Greece or by the landing of the Russians, my present force, kept up to strength by the necessary drafts, plus the Army Corps asked for in my No. M.F. 216 of the 10th May, would probably suffice to finish my task. If, however, the present situation remains unchanged and the Turks are still able to devote so much exclusive attention to us, I shall want an additional Army Corps, that is, two Army Corps additional in all.

I could not land these reinforcements on the Peninsula until I can advance another 1000 yards and so free the beaches from the shelling to which they are subjected from the western side and gain more space; but I could land them on the adjacent islands of Tenedos, Imbros, and Lemnos, and take them over later to the Peninsula, for battle. This plan would surmount the difficulties of water and space on the Peninsula, and would, perhaps, enable me to effect a surprise with the fresh divisions.

I believe I could advance with half the loss of life that is now being reckoned upon, if I had a liberal supply of gun ammunition, especially of high explosive.

CHAPTER CIX

THE Russian co-operation upon which Ian Hamilton was counting faded into the distance. Hindenburg's offensive on the Eastern front was in full swing; the Russians, worsted in the Baltic Provinces, were being pressed in Poland; the Austrians with German help were again approaching Przemysl—a chapter of accidents causing the withdrawal of the Russian Corps destined to join us in an attack on the Bosphorus after the Dardanelles had been forced. This was really a double disaster: a large reinforcement was denied us, and Turkish divisions were released which had hitherto been retained to protect Constantinople.

The War Council had decided to send out the Fifty-second Lowland Territorial Division to reinforce Ian Hamilton, and to follow this with the despatch of two more Territorial Divisions, the Fifty-third Welsh Division and the Fifty-fourth East Anglian Division, but the destination of the New Army Divisions was still debated. On May 18 Kitchener telegraphed to Ian Hamilton:

> You will fully realise my serious disappointment that preconceived views as to the conquest of positions necessary to dominate the forts on the Straits, with naval artillery to support our troops on land, and with active help of naval bombardment, were miscalculated. A serious position is

created by the present check, and by the call for men and munitions we can ill spare from France. From the standpoint of an early solution of our difficulties your views are not encouraging. The question whether we can long support two fields of operations draining on our resources requires grave consideration. I can only rely on you to do your utmost to bring the present state of affairs in the Dardanelles to as early a conclusion as possible, so that any consideration of withdrawal—with all its dangers in the East —may not enter the field of possible solution.

Three days later Ian Hamilton wrote:

I have tried to make my cables as clear and descriptive as I could, feeling that I should thus enable you to weigh the situation and to decide for or against any applications for material aid I might make to you.

Birdwood has now, I think, knocked most of the fighting edge off Liman von Sanders's two newly arrived divisions. Anyway they did not really come on with the bayonet last night (to my great disappointment), but contented themselves mainly with a heavy and continuous fire of artillery and musketry.

At the end, namely at 4 A.M., we drove them right back by half-an-hour's heavy bombardment. Words won't make shells, but I think if you could come and see us for a day or two you would realise that, except on such occasions as this, the fighting troops are themselves frightened of running out and that they are responding to our appeal for economy. We now only allow two rounds per gun per diem unless in case of repelling an attack.

The Turks too have seemed to have absolutely no stint. It was reckoned that in one 24 hours, a week ago, they fired a million rounds of small arms ammunition at Anzac, independently of what they showered upon us in the south. Admiral Thursby counted 240 shells in ten minutes falling on Birdwood's trenches. On the 18th fifty heavy shell, including nine 12-inch and 14-inch, dropped inside his position. On the other hand it has been noticed that their field-guns are beginning to use lead-driving bands.

Birdwood and his Australians are depressed at the departure of Admiral Thursby. They looked on him as their guardian angel, and he certainly was always willing to take any trouble and run any risks towards backing them up. Under this new arrangement I fear it is most unlikely we shall get another like him.

The Reuter more than hinting at Cabinet changes has arrived this morning, and has left us all gasping with surprise. With the selfishness inherent in humanity every one is inclined to look at the question from the point of view of the Gallipoli Peninsula, and wonder how such a transformation will affect our efforts. Personally I don't worry, for I know that as long as you remain at the War Office no one will be allowed to harm us out here.

Good-bye for the present. Could you not take a run out and see us? If once you saw and realised with your own eyes what the troops are doing I would never need to praise them again. Travelling in the *Phaeton* you would be here in three days, and you would see some wonderful things and the men would be tremendously bucked up. The spirit of all ranks rises above trials and losses, and is confident of the present and cheery about the future. My best love to Fitz.

P.S.—When I began this letter an hour ago I was under the impression that it was our turn now to press on with the offensive, but a message just received from that gallant General, Gouraud,[1] puts rather a different complexion on the situation of the moment, and shows the Turks in front of this section have still plenty of fight left in them. At 4 this morning the French carried a couple of trenches by assault at an important tactical point, well to the north of their present line. After a heavy bombardment with field-guns, 6-inch howitzers, and 4·5-inch guns, the Turks coun-

---

[1] General d'Amade had through illness been obliged to give place to General Gouraud.

ter-attacked and drove our Allies out. Gouraud quietly adds he is now making arrangements to re-attack the trenches, and will make sure this time that they are held. He adds that the Turks are massing in great strength opposite our right and left, and that he thinks that we ought to stand prepared for a general attack. So we pass without intermission from one violent conflict into another. But I must say, anxious work though it may be, I am glad when the enemy elect to attack, for it gives us a real opportunity to punish them.

The Cabinet changes to which Ian Hamilton referred were incidental to the formation of the first Coalition Government, and the new Ministers asked for a little breathing time, as well as further information, before deciding on reinforcements. Kitchener telegraphed on June 3:

Owing to the restricted nature of the ground you occupy and of the experience we have had in Flanders, I have some doubt of an early decisive result being obtained by increasing the forces at your disposal. But I should like your views as soon as you can. Are you convinced that with immediate reinforcements to the extent you mention you could force the Kilid Bahr position and thus finish off the Dardanelles operations? You mentioned that you intend to keep reinforcements on the islands. Is this your intention with regard to the Lowland Division now on its way to you?

This telegram caught Ian Hamilton on the eve of the third battle of Krithia, of which he could only say:

On the morning of the 4th we made a general attack upon the Turkish trenches in the south of the peninsula, after a heavy bombardment by all guns, including the battleships, the cruisers, and destroyers. The troops then rushed forward with the bayonet and were immediately successful along the whole line, except in one spot where the wire entanglement had not been destroyed. The Sixth Gurkhas on the extreme left made a fine advance and took two lines of trenches, but were compelled to retire because the regiment on their right was held up by wire. The Territorials and the Twenty-Ninth Division did brilliantly and made good progress but were compelled by exposed flanks to retire. The Naval Division took a line of trenches but were enfiladed after a French retirement and had also to come back. To sum up, a good advance of 500 yards, including two lines of enemy trenches, has been made along a front of three miles in the centre of our southern section, but we are back in our original lines on our right and left. The Turkish position was very strong.

Slow progress might spell something much worse than disappointment, for the year was advanced and autumn weather might well forbid a landing of troops and stores. The new War Council saw the situation with very serious eyes, and on the morrow of Krithia Kitchener telegraphed:

Your difficulties are fully recognised by the Cabinet, who are fully determined to support you. Sending you three divisions of the New Army, one at the end of this week and two more as transport is available.

Thus Ian Hamilton was to receive three Territorial and three New Army Divisions instead of the two Army Corps of four Divisions for which he had asked.

Much fighting [he wrote on the 8th] has taken place and many lives have been lost since last I wrote you, but the matter which has perhaps weighed on my mind most of all during that interval has been the responsibility of answering your cable regarding reinforcements. To weigh the probabilities of taking Kilid Bahr, *i.e.* of positive success, where so many of the factors are indeterminate (submarines, aeroplanes, enemy's force, water supply, politics, plus the whole glorious uncertainty of war), is in any case very, very hard. But to convey a complete picture of what is in my mind within the narrow limits of a cable is practically impossible. Here on paper I have more scope, and I submit one or two of the more salient considerations which underlay the telegram I sent you last night.

We are becoming tied up—knotted up I might say—into this cursed trench warfare just as much as British and Germans appear to be tied hand and foot by it in France. Every day I see the growth of the system. Machine-guns; barbed wire; redoubts. Only, there is this notable difference that, good as the Turks undoubtedly are, they are not fighting for any cause they clearly understand. Nor have they as powerful an artillery as the Germans. Hence their resistance, though most formidable, is not yet equal to that of the Germans. On the other hand, in France, splendid lines of railways connect the battle front with the heart of the United Kingdom. Here our roots run down into that most precarious element, the sea.

Had the conditions between us and the Turks been at all equal we should long ago have got them on the run. But, so far, the conditions have not been equal. That is to say, the Turks are holding previously skilfully laid out lines of fortification whilst they have been able to redress any inequality in the moral of their troops by replacing demoralised or worn-out units by fresh formations. Our troops, with all their officers up to the rank of corps commander, have been, in a greater or less degree, under fire night and day for the past six weeks. The Turks we have been fighting the last two days were quite fresh. Our men may be withdrawn for comparative rest from the first lines into reserve, but such rest is only comparative, for shelling goes on, whether at Anzac or Cape Helles, right to the beach.

Consequently the troops get very tired. This emphasises the absolute necessity of a fresh division being sent out to these parts quite irrespective of questions of taking Kilid Bahr in a comparatively short time.

The way I would use this division would be to relieve a worn-out division for a week, while with the fresh troops I made a good effort to deal a telling stroke at the enemy. How far such a stroke would carry one is another question. For the whole face of war seems to me to be changed. There is no strategy, no tactics; all that is wanted is a high courage, a quick eye for probable points of attack or defence, and a clear determination not to let loss of life stand in the way of gaining a few yards of ground. Still, just at the present moment, the particular way our trenches seem to lie with those of the Turks give me a certain opportunity of cutting off a good number of their men whilst straightening my line. And if I do not so use this configuration of our trenches, it is possible that the enemy may make use of the same feature against me. With the help of the brigade of the new Lowland Division I may be able to do this. But anything like a general advance and general attack cannot be entertained at present, as, apart from munitions, the men are not equal to it.

P.S.—Officers here who have fought in France say that the *individual* Turkish infantry soldier is braver and more of a warrior than the individual German.

CHAPTER CX

WITH the reinforcements which he was to receive, Ian Hamilton's force would be increased to eleven British and two French Divisions, and some additional troops—such as Cox's Indian Brigade and Peyton's dismounted Yeomanry, which had been under Maxwell's hand, but at Ian Hamilton's call. The thick-and-thin champions of the Western front have represented that these Divisions at the battle of Loos would have doubled the vigour of Sir John's hand and might have secured for him the success he so ardently sought. But provision for the safety of Egypt must inevitably have detached the larger part of these troops from France. If no landing had taken place at Gallipoli, and the Turks had been free to approach the Nile in 1915, we should have required at least eight Divisions to protect Egypt, at any rate until we could proceed—as we did later—to occupy the wells in the Desert, the Turks' only possible source of water-supply. This *démarche* involved the construction of a broad-gauge railway and the laying of a pipe-line with pumping-stations to bring fresh water from Egypt to our troops, whose digestion violently resented the brackish water of the wells which the Turk absorbs with impunity. Troops for the defence of Egypt would have been as

CHAP. CX EFFECTS OF A WITHDRAWAL 149

necessary in 1915 as they were in 1916, and not more than three, or at most four, Divisions could have been spared for France if the Dardanelles Expedition had been rejected or abandoned.

Underlying all considerations of withdrawing British troops was the burning question as to the effect in the East of a British failure to accomplish a set purpose.

When the evacuation took place—without injury to life or limb—there was surprisingly little stir among the vast masses of the Sovereign's Eastern subjects, but the calm—so Kitchener maintained—might well prove deceptive, and disquiet and disruption might be the direct sequel of the denial of success to our arms, even if postponed until the event itself had receded into history.

It seemed therefore that, so long as any reasonable prospect of victory presented itself, nothing should be left undone which could by any means be done to back up the famous efforts of the Gallipoli fighters and prevent any tarnish to our prestige. The Government asked the Commander-in-Chief on the spot what he needed in fresh troops to ensure success, and managed to provide a margin. Nor did Kitchener overlook a possible extension of front. On June 11 he wired to Ian Hamilton:

> Have you considered advantage of landing troops on the Bulair Isthmus, thus cutting the Peninsula completely from the Mainland? This would besides enable us to supply our submarines in the Sea of Marmora overland. What force would be needed for this operation? Will the troops landed be liable to serious attack? Could they be adequately protected by the guns of the Fleet? I presume the Bulair lines could not be captured without very severe fighting?

Ian Hamilton had not neglected, but had mentally rejected, the proposition:

The Bulair project has been an attractive one and seldom if ever out of my thoughts, but except near Enos all possible landing-places are entrenched and heavily entangled. Even if a landing were effected the Fleet's guns could not give adequate protection to the troops. Also the troops could not be maintained there, partly owing to the submarine danger and partly because the Navy is already fully occupied with keeping our forces supplied and has neither men nor small craft sufficient to maintain a third detachment. I am afraid the project must be ruled out till the submarine danger is removed, or a large increase in small craft is sent from England.

The plan of the Suvla Bay landing was already maturing in Ian Hamilton's mind, but he was naturally unwilling even to hint at it at this early stage. "It is vitally important," he telegraphed on June 12, "that future developments should be kept absolutely secret. I mention this because, although the date of our original landing was known to hardly any one before the ships sailed, yet the date was telegraphed to the Turks from Vienna."

One way of cutting off the Turks being ruled out, there still remained an alternative, and the Commander-in-Chief was asked his opinion "as to diversions on the Asiatic side of the Dardanelles when your operations commence."

Ian Hamilton's reply ran:

I have always been attracted by the advantages of a diversion on the Asiatic shore. We might thus reduce the enemy's strength on the Peninsula, free our trenches and beaches from troublesome enfilade fire, and repay the Turks in likewise securing obvious tactical and strategical advantages, against which one must set difficulties which are practically insurmountable. The landing would be costly. Once we had landed re-embarkation would be absolutely impossible. For any serious advance large forces would be necessary. You may rely upon me to jump at any opportunity that offers.

A week later he telegraphed:

As the Cabinet are anxious to consider my situation in all its bearings, it is necessary that I should open to you all my mind. . . . To summarise, I think I have reasonable prospect of eventual success with three Divisions, with four the risks of miscalculation would be minimised, and with five, even if the fifth Division had little or no gun ammunition, I think it would be a much simpler matter to clear the Asiatic shore subsequently of big guns, etc. Kilid Bahr would be captured at an earlier date and success generally would be assured.

While this correspondence had been going on the Turks, reinforced by the troops no longer needed for Constantinople, had been fighting fiercely, and on June 19 Ian Hamilton reported:

Between 7 P.M. and 8 P.M. yesterday evening Turks expended 450 H.E. shell on South Wales Borderers' trenches and were seen massing for attack. Trenches and men suffered considerably, but enemy's hearts failed them and attack degenerated into fire action. At 7.30 P.M. the 125th Brigade attacked Turkish trench but were unsuccessful, and Turks in counter-attack effected lodgment in their line at awkward salient captured by us on 4th instant. The 125th Brigade were unable to recover lost trench when the 5th Bn. Royal Scots, assisted by one company of the Worcestershire Regiment, came to their help. This attack was ably organised and brilliantly carried out to a successful issue by Lieut.-Colonel Wilson, who displayed fine initiative and bold leading and whose troops followed him with great gallantry and determination. I have, under the powers granted me, given Colonel Wilson the D.S.O. If Lord Kitchener could tell the Lord Provost of Edinburgh how well the 5th Bn. Royal Scots have done the whole of this force would be pleased. A small party of the Royal Naval Division made successful attack at 2.30 A.M. on another Turkish trench, beating back a heavy counter-attack which attempted its recapture with heavy loss to Turks, principally by enfilade machine-gun fire. Captured trench held till 9.45 A.M. when Turkish enfilade shrapnel and bombing fire from both flanks forced them to retire to their own trenches. Prisoners state Turks expected their bombardment with high explosives would have cleared us out altogether and were much disappointed at so little impression being made, though trenches much damaged. Turkish dead estimated at 300 in front of 87th Brigade alone, and I think 1000 in all parts a low estimate. I have had no report yet of our casualties. Heavier shelling to-day from Asiatic batteries, from which it appears Turks have received a fresh consignment of high explosive, as over 220 shells of that nature fired from Asia during course of day.

CHAPTER CXI

WHILE the troop-ships were threading their way to the Dardanelles, it was becoming daily more evident that enmity with Turkey was plunging us up to the neck in the East. Mesopotamia, so far, presented no cause of anxiety; General Gorringe, one of Kitchener's lieutenants in South Africa, had led a column up the Euphrates from Basra, and on July 25 had so punished the Turks at Nazarieh as to give us the same control over the lower Euphrates we had already obtained over the lower Tigris. But in Mesopotamia, about Aden, and in Egypt, we were directly in touch with Arab tribes, and every day it became more necessary to enlist and enjoy their aid.

When Turkey drew the sword there was revived in Kitchener's mind a long-cherished idea of founding an independent Arab State in Arabia and Syria.[1] From the hour he set foot in the Holy Land until the last hour of his life the Near East, in its manifold aspects, allured his interest, and at times almost absorbed his thoughts. He marvelled how seldom people remembered the greatness of England not only as a Christian but as a Mohammedan Power. He would immerse himself agreeably in such subjects as the interplay between the Sunnis and Shiah sects,

---

[1] The Government of India just then received a message from an important sheikh: "Following for Lord Kitchener. 'Remember our conversation at ——. The day has come.'"

or the place of the Sultan of Turkey *vis-à-vis* the Sherif of Mecca as religious hierarch of Islam. His personal influence with the Sherif of Mecca and the Arabs generally had been an asset on which he had not hesitated to rely in the preparation of his plans, and as early as November 1914 he gave the Sherif a positive pledge of British support should he essay to throw off the Turkish yoke. In any negotiating with the Sherif it behoved him to walk delicately, as intricate religious questions were involved, affecting all Islam. He could not affront millions of the Sovereign's Mohammedan subjects even to attract the Arabs, and in considering an independent Arabia which would embrace two of the most sacred of the Mohammedan cities he had to remember that the Moslem overlord at Constantinople was in arms against us. His tact and Eastern sympathies were happily matched in handling a religious question which was solved for the time by the Sherif's willingness to disclaim publicly any pretensions to the Caliphate.

The political web was as intricate as the religious. The claims of the French in Syria, of the Russians in Northern Mesopotamia, of the Zionists in Palestine, and the rights of the Arabs themselves, reared their several heads, and had to be carefully regarded by Kitchener no less than by the Foreign Office. After consultation with the Sirdar, Kitchener sent Sir Mark Sykes, who thoroughly understood his part, to the East, and there resulted in October an agreement with the Sherif formulating the promise of the previous November. We undertook, if the Arabs shook off Turkish supremacy, to support them with cash, comestibles, and cartridges, and to recognise

Arab independence south of latitude 37°, except in the provinces of Basra and Baghdad, where British interests require peculiar measures of administration, and in any locality where England was not free to act without prejudice to France. This agreement rendered the so-called "Arab movement" practicable, and brought about the final revolt of the Arabs against the Turks on the very eve of the tragedy of the *Hampshire*.

Far more difficult to deal with was another religious chief, whose influence stretched along the western frontier of Egypt. Quite early in 1915 Maxwell was aware that the Turks were coquetting with the Senussi.

I am much concerned [he wrote to Kitchener on June 24] about the Senussi; we have done all we can to keep him quiet; but there is no doubt that his claims to temporal power are daily becoming more pronounced; one day we will have to reckon with him. As you know, we have always treated him as a religious sheikh of very considerable importance, but since the Tripolitan War and his undoubted successes over the Italians his status has changed considerably. There is no doubt that if he declared against us we would have an infinity of trouble, and no one can foresee where it would end. All our coast guards, Bedouins of the West, right up to Darfur, would be, if not actively *for* him, at any rate certainly not against him. He would have a large following in Egypt too, and all this on account of the religious veneration in which he is held. Moreover, there is also the fact that he has considerable stocks of mountain guns, machine-guns, rifles, and ammunition, all taken from the Italians, and augmented by smuggling from Turkey, it is said; but I am not sure of the latter, as there seems little object in this, when he gets so much from the Italians. He is now camped close to Sollum with about 1500 men, who are all well trained, and he demands as a right that his emissaries should freely enter Egypt; he sends in men to collect supplies and taxes from his Zaweas in our territory. His own "territory" is closely guarded, as is also his camp; his adherents are daily becoming more and more convinced that he is a great power. He even hints at the possibility of a war with England, though he confesses he does not want it. He has latterly been talking rather big about Free Trade between him and Egypt, and wishes all his supplies duty- and custom- (also search-) free. We have humoured him to the full, and the question now comes whether this should go on until the war is over, or whether we should pull him up and take the consequences. Of course he takes the line that Islam knows no frontier, and he has a right to do what he likes with his brethren in Egypt. I do not think there is the least doubt that there are two parties in his camp, one urging him on to break with us, the other trying to maintain peace. He is a shrewd man, but with no great knowledge of our world; yet he seems to have a clear idea that he is in a strong position. Nuri Bey and others are with him, nominally in confinement, but they exercise pressure on Senussi, and in my opinion persuade him to ask for concessions from us which they think we will refuse, and thus, by making him angry, push him to break with us. He latterly recently captured several motor cars from the Italians, and now wants petrol to work them. I don't think there is any doubt he received considerable sums of money from Turkey, for he seems to have plenty to spend.

I think it right that you should know all this, and I think you will agree that, whatever the future may bring forth, we must keep the Senussi quiet and with us, even at the risk of appearing weak and afraid of him. We cannot afford an outbreak of Islamism just now; this is what the Germans are trying for, and I see that little arch-spy, ——, is off to Persia to make trouble. . . .

I telegraphed you details of a scheme to use the Hasheesh

smugglers to get at the submarines, and their depots; as you will know, they have a very efficient organisation, but we would only pay by results, big money for big results! I think the Germans are using this organisation, so it would be a question of the highest bidder!

Maxwell said truly that the day of reckoning with the Senussi was at hand, and in 1916 the actual garrison of Egypt had to be strengthened to make a clearance of the western frontiers and bring the Senussi to reason.

Towards the end of June 1915 there were indications of trouble in the neighbourhood of Perim and Aden. The Turks had sat down at Sheikh-Sayed opposite Perim and shelled the island. It was suggested that General Younghusband might take a brigade from Egypt and dispose of them. Kitchener, however, did not smile on the project; he thought the Turks at Sheikh-Sayed could do no serious damage, and remembering how much that was vital needed protection, he had set his face against all but unavoidable enterprises. On the 22nd he telegraphed to Maxwell:

> It is highly probable that the Turks will have strengthened their positions and we should have to attack entrenchments strengthened with barbed wire. This needs considerable superiority in the attacking force. Could we in a week capture the Turkish works and destroy the guns which shell Perim? Could we withdraw our force when landed? We don't want to fritter away forces and diminish the strength of Egypt. Information regarding the enemy's strength seems undefined, and unless success is tolerably certain it is undesirable to undertake operations which would only have a temporary effect. Could adequate results be obtained by naval means alone? We await the views of the naval authorities.

The expedition was consequently held in abeyance. And fortunately so, for a few days later a more pressing emergency arose. On July 4 Turkish forces attacked, and the next day took, Lahej, within the frontier of the Aden Protectorate. Aden must be secured against all risk, and Maxwell was told to send there Younghusband's brigade and two batteries of artillery. These troops arrived in time to obviate any danger, but the difficulties of the country forbade any attack upon Lahej, and Younghusband was committed to a long bout of guerilla warfare under rather cruel climatic conditions. Such were some of the minor difficulties which studded the main difficulty of the Dardanelles.

Early in July the Turks, strongly reinforced, had made a series of heavy but ineffectual attacks upon our lines. On the 5th Ian Hamilton reported that Enver was known to have issued specific orders that the Australians were to be driven into the sea; he had also heard that their officers had been told to use their revolvers upon any Turkish disinclined to go forward. On the other hand, the enemy had considerably strengthened his artillery on the Asiatic shore, where his galling fire was daily more and more effective. General Gouraud, when handing over his command, had, in a parting message, represented to Ian Hamilton that the French troops were smarting under the gun-fire from Asia.[1]

Very soon official complaints reached Kitchener from Paris of the effect of the enfilade fire upon the

---

[1] "From the point of view of *moral* one man killed by a shell from Asia is equivalent to ten men killed in action. It is difficult to expect warships constantly to expose themselves to submarine risks in order to keep the Asiatic guns under. Our provisioning operations were often thus hampered. Later southerly gales will render Morto Bay untenable under Asiatic fire." (Ian Hamilton to Kitchener.)

French troops, and on the 21st he wired to Ian Hamilton:

> The French state that the fire from the Asiatic side allows them no rest. The landing of necessary stores is already difficult, and this trouble must increase with the advance of the season. They propose secondary operations on the Asiatic side to deal with the enemy's artillery there and suggest the employment of 20,000 British troops assisted by French '75s. What do you and De Robeck think? Could the guns near Kun Kale be silenced by monitors? Would the main scheme of our operations be jeopardised by thus detaching a considerable force which may find itself engaged by hostile forces of unknown strength?

Ian Hamilton perhaps knew that the only real solution was to obtain two more Divisions and land troops on the Asiatic shore. He told Kitchener that such a landing might be forced upon him, but that any such diversion of troops must be made at his own time and must not prejudice his well-matured main move. The Commander-in-Chief was speeding up his preparations for another landing, being determined to forestall autumn winds and waves, and Kitchener was somewhat perturbed to hear suddenly that the last two Territorial divisions to leave England would scarcely be in time to take their part in it.

In a telegram of July 30 the War Secretary told the Commander-in-Chief that he was not precisely informed as to plans and dates, but was quite willing that these should be kept back till the last moment, and Ian Hamilton answered, "You have done everything for us that man can do."

Kitchener had certainly spared neither means, nor pains, for the grand effort to throw the Turks out of the Peninsula, and must possess his soul in patience for the result. The new landing took place on August 6, and the battles of Sari Bair and Suvla began. As before, the early reports were encouraging, and on the 9th Kitchener telegraphed:

Glad to hear that your operations have started so well. I am sure you will push all you can to obtain command of the Marmora Shore without being held up by trenches. Your forces have all our best wishes. Use the Egyptian troops if you want them.

Then came the news of checks and delays.

CHAPTER CXII

THE divisions of the New Army at the Dardanelles were denied one precious advantage enjoyed by troops making their début in France. Neither time nor terrain availed for them to receive the special training in trench-warfare to be acquired in presence of an active enemy, though, before being thrown into actual battle. Valuable opportunities were probably thus lost and never recovered. On August 11 Ian Hamilton in a letter clothed with flesh the dry bones of a series of telegrams:

> Heartfelt thanks for your cable expressing satisfaction with our work. Truly, Lord K., I am deeply touched with your action in sending me this most kind message. I think you really must be (what I have always half suspected) a Superman. For you must have had the balance of mind to be able to take pleasure in our gains without fretting too much over the decisive victory we have missed (for the moment) by the skin of our teeth.
>
> As for myself, I believe a General never feels so depressed as when he has won a good stake and then realises that with one ounce more energy, push, intuition, or luck—call it what you will—he would have swept the entire board.
>
> Well, you know our story, and I won't trouble here to put it into strict chronological shape. Broadly, all my plans (more correctly Braithwaite's and the General Staff's) came off quite marvellously—better a great deal than I could reasonably have hoped.
>
> First, Anzacs. Into their little bay we had managed to smuggle no less than 19,000 men, with a lot of guns and ammunition, during the previous week, without the Turks

knowing anything at all about it. This itself was a pretty tall order, I think.

Next, when the Australians, New Zealanders, and Indian Brigade swept out to the northward and then round up and eastward on to the high dominating ridges, it looked as if we had got fairly astride the peninsula, which would have meant absolute security from the south for Suvla Bay and also the dominating of Maidos and most of the roads of the peninsula.

Lastly, during this eventful night 13,000 troops of the New Armies had been landed at Suvla Bay without serious opposition. There was a terrible chance that the Turks might have smelt a rat and might, at the last moment, have had a regiment or even a brigade down along the coast to oppose the landing. Had that been the case, we should have had the most dreadful casualties, and I doubt very much, from what I have seen since, if we would have got the men ashore at all. This, therefore, was worth a king's ransom. We had 13,000 troops on shore; there were plenty more to follow, and only a very few hundred Turks stood between us and the ridge running between Ejelmer Bay and Kuchuk Anafarta. From that ridge we should have been able, I think (I have not had a section made yet), to see the Straits, and certainly to see the roads running northwards.

Now, up to this point nothing could have been more perfect. But here things began to go wrong. One of those horrible incidents which sometimes happens lost us actually the top of Sari Bair—a monitor chucking some heavy shell into the columns just as they reached the top. Two of the New Army regiments (the North Lancs and Wilts), who had relieved the New Zealanders on Chunuk Bair, were suddenly attacked in overwhelming numbers by the Turks, and were driven off by sheer weight, so Birdwood tells me. We did not fall back more than 150 or 200 yards, and still hold the same area, but we cannot look over the ridge or deny that unrivalled observation post to our enemy's artillery commanders. However, we've got to do it somehow or another, and do it we will yet with the help of Providence.

But the real awful worry has lain in the impossibility of getting a proper move on to the Ninth Corps, viz. in this case the Tenth and Eleventh Divisions. The vital importance of time has been impressed over and over again on the higher command. I could not go on to the ground the first day myself until quite late, namely 5 P.M. All this most critical fighting was going on at Anzacs and at Helles, and I was not sure what was going to happen, and I held the small reserve in my own hand. Therefore I had to stay at Imbros. When I got to Suvla Bay about 5 o'clock, I found most of the troops strolling about as if it was a holiday. The Eleventh Division was extended on a broad front about two and a half miles to the east, and Mahon, with five battalions, was held up by a party of five or six hundred Turkish Gendarmerie at the capital letter T of Kiretch Tepe Sirt. I found that it was intended to do nothing that day (during most of which the men had been resting), but that an advance was to be made on the hills either side of Anafarta Sagir at dawn next morning. I was horrified at this, and ordered Stopford to get a move on at once. The Turks always make use of the night to bring up reinforcements, entrench, etc., and I knew it might make all the difference in the world whether we started at once or next morning. I then went across myself in a steam launch to see Hammersley and tried to urge him on. He put forward all the usual strong reasons for delay, want of water, want of artillery, etc., etc. Moreover, he said his troops were so extended it would be quite impossible to organise an advance for the whole division before daylight. I found, however, he could move one Brigade, the Yorkshire Brigade, and I did extort from him a distinct promise they would move on the hills to the right of Anafarta Sagir. Soon after nightfall the Brigade, preceded by one battalion, made good

---

1 Before this letter came to hand his cables had made it clear that only a company, not a full battalion, had effected a lodgment on 280. When writing, Ian Hamilton still thought his order had been carried out, and was not yet aware that this Brigade, instead of starting "soon after nightfall," did not actually get off till 4 A.M.

its footing on the ridge numbered 280 immediately north of and dominating Anafarta Sagir.¹ The thing was practically done. The other three battalions which were to support this advanced battalion seem, however, to have remained a long way back. There being a certain amount of sniping, the advanced battalion got worried, and fell back on the other three. Naturally as this fell back the snipers grew bold and they lost heavily. I slept there, and next morning witnessed the set attack. The men seemed quite untrained at that open South African advance, which was the only method of doing the trick here. They bunched together in little clusters, and when this big force was counter-attacked they fell back to the position they had been in in the morning, and, indeed, somewhat behind it.

Since I began this letter I have good news about the Tenth and Eleventh Divisions. My General Staff, who have been there, say they are pulling themselves together and regaining their cohesion. I fancy they were upset and tired by landing at night, and then thought they had done such a tremendous big thing advancing a couple of miles or so into the country that they might then rest on their oars. It is a fearful dilemma to know whether to give men more rest at the expense of seeing the numbers of the enemy double and treble during the period. A General has just to strike a balance and steer clear of overstraining his troops whilst, at the same time, preventing the enemy from getting himself too thoroughly into a state of preparation for attack or defence.—Yours very sincerely,

IAN HAMILTON.

P.S.—We have killed an enormous number of Turks, but they always seem able to replace them. Our men have been quite splendid.

August 12, 1915.

I quite agree with Stopford it is a million pities we cannot bring on these new troops quietly by mixing them up in the trenches with war veterans. But to do this sort of thing would be to bring altogether too great a strain on the Navy. It is just all they can do to keep us supplied with water, food, and ammunition, and if we ask them, in addition, to take a Division out of Helles and put in a Territorial Division in their place, their arrangements for vital necessities would break down. I am going on to make my attack with the Essex on these three Spion Kops all the same. If we do not push on, the Turks will. If only they were a Division of Gurkhas [1] my mind would be perfectly and absolutely at ease, but the worrying thing to me in this particular move is that the whole of the flattish plain east of Suvla Bay is covered with thick trees up high above your head, small and big dongas, long grass, etc., etc. In these a very considerable number of Turkish snipers are concealed, sometimes up in the trees, sometimes down in hollows amongst the grass. Quite close to the beach and a mile behind our troops I am told there are some still undiscovered. Supposing, then, the Essex make good their footing on the high hills north of Anafarta, there will always remain the problem of getting their mule convoys through this dense bush without being too much harried, or losing too many mules. Still there it is. I am borrowing from Birdwood a few Gurkhas and Australian scouts so that the Essex may have at least a few experienced individuals with them.

As you may well think, I have not time to weigh my words or calculate my thoughts. Do not please, then, view this letter of mine in any critical spirit. I am merely pouring out to you what is in my mind just as it comes, for I think that will give you a better idea of how things are going than anything else. On reading all that I have said over once more, I think I have allowed myself to be a little too much depressed by failure to get as much as I had hoped out of our good arrangements, and that I have been, like every bad workman, finding too much fault with my tools. This was

---

[1] The Gurkhas possess special aptitudes for work in broken, jungly country.

not my real intention, but I have not time to rewrite my letter and must leave it as it stands.[1]

---

[1] On August 10 Birdwood wrote to FitzGerald a luminous story of the battle of Sari Bair:

"AUSTRALIAN AND NEW ZEALAND ARMY CORPS,
MEDITERRANEAN EXPEDITIONARY FORCE,
August 10, 1915.

"I write in the midst of a most desperate battle about which I am most anxious, but as I have done all that is possible up to the present, I can write.

"As you know, our big move was started on the evening of the 6th, when I attacked the big Turkish work and labyrinth of trenches known as 'Lone Pine' on my right front. I put an Australian Brigade at it, who dashed forward in the most gallant style possible, and, though under a very heavy rifle and shrapnel fire, went clean across and fought their way through from trench to trench completely expelling and routing the Turks. Ever since then the Turks have been counter-attacking, and our boys have held on for all they are worth, and have accounted for a really enormous number of Turks. I am sorry to say, though, that our own losses have been heavy, and I have lost two of my best commanding officers. The Australian Division under Walker carried on the whole operation most excellently and with the very greatest gallantry.

"This attack to the right front was purposely made to let the Turks think we meant to make a big advance from there, and I think it had the desired result, as they at once moved down all their local reserves for their counter-attacks.

"As soon as it was dark I launched out the New Zealand and Australian Division, supported by Shaw's Division of the New Army—all under Godley—marching them round the left flank and along the shore as far as Aghil Dere. From there they wheeled to their right and made a night attack on the Sari Bair range. The country we had to go through was far worse than anything we had to negotiate the day we effected our landing, and must be seen to be realised. It is a mass of most broken country with practically precipitous islands joined by necks of land to each other running through it everywhere, and finishing up with most difficult spurs and precipices leading to the high ground, the whole being covered with scrub. As, however, I told my troops before starting, it was the very difficulties of the country which we must regard as our best friends, for had the country not been so broken the Turks would have had continuous lines of trenches to meet us everywhere, as indeed they have on every side but this.

"The first obstacle met was a very strongly entrenched but rather isolated hill. Having made up my mind a good month ago that we should attack over this particular country, we started a ruse which I am glad to say proved most successful. I made a destroyer regularly shell this position every night for about ten minutes, then cease firing but keeping her search-light upon it, and again a second heavy burst of shelling for another ten minutes. The Turks had got quite accustomed to this, and I knew used either to lie down at the bottom of the trenches or vacate them when shelling commenced.

"On the night of the attack we carried out the exact ordinary programme, and during the half-hour the search-light was on the Turkish post my men were creeping up all round it, and the second the light was off they were able to make a rush for it and seize the whole place almost without opposition. As there were some 500 Turks in it, and the place was very carefully entrenched and prepared, this was, I think, a capital performance.

"The next obstacle met was a flat tabletop, which the Turks had also entrenched very carefully. We had carried out the same programme with the destroyer on this, but I quite realised it would be impossible to effect a surprise after our capture of the first post, so we had had that registered and well pounded by 5-in. howitzers while we advanced up to it, and the New Zealand Mounted Rifles again stormed it with comparatively speaking small loss.

"I had given orders that the whole attack was to be on as broad a front as possible, men scattering up every spur, and if any particular company found themselves stopped by trenches or precipices, those on the right and left were to keep shoving forward, as I knew if once men got in rear of any trench the Turks would vacate it. This is exactly what happened, and throughout the night the small columns continued to make progress through the ravines and along the steep spurs.

"I had every hope that we would have been able to reach the crest line of the Sari Bairridge, which was our objective, and I cannot even yet get over my grief at the fact that they failed to do so. I am wrong in saying that they failed to do so, as one Brigade—the New Zealand Infantry—did get up and make a lodgment on the southernmost part of the crest. The Brigades on the left had, however, further to go, and rather more difficult country, and dawn found them still at the foot of the main ridge, even though we had made our start immediately it was dark enough to do so. Such a lot of the country had to be traversed in single file that columns naturally spread out, hence the delay.

"All I know did their real best, for I had told them all just before we started how absolutely important it was to shove along and let nothing stop us. By daylight the Turks, of course, had manned the crest line and made further movement then almost impossible, though the troops gradually moved forward to better positions on some of the lower spurs. At dawn the following day was ordered an attack on the main ridge, the other Brigades pivoting on the New Zealand Infantry, who still held the southern crest.

"Here again I am sorry to say it was a case of 'so near and yet so far.' We had a tremendous military and naval bombardment of the whole of the crest from 4.30 A.M. to 5.15 A.M. when the assault was to be made. At this time the leading regiments of two Brigades were just creeping up to the positions we wanted, and we had every hope that in a few moments we would have got the crest, and that the leading regiments would have been supported in time by the rest of their Brigades 'to make it good.' Most unfortunately, however, it proved to be a very cloudy morning (about the only one we have had), and it was very hard for the heavy guns who were doing a big bombardment to see exactly where troops had reached, and by the worst of luck big shells happened to fall in right among both regiments as they were nearing the crest, and I fear temporarily demoralised them, though whether these were our own or Turk shells we do not know—most probably the latter; with the result that the Turks rushed in and drove them down the hill.

"Again it was a case of trying to consolidate ourselves before a further advance. The New Zealand Infantry were much exhausted and were relieved by two battalions of the New Army, who have all been doing excellently. In the early morning the Turks apparently attacked these battalions in very great strength, and, as they say, by sheer numbers drove them down the hill.

"It was impossible to put a stronger force than that on the hill, as the amount of ground they held did not permit of it, but you can imagine how deeply regretful I am that we should not have been able to hold on. We have now had to withdraw to the lower spurs, and the troops have to rest, as they have been continuously fighting for nearly four days without a breather. I am in a real tight corner for water and can only just hold on on account of the scarcity. It has only been possible to get water to them in small quantities with the greatest difficulty, and I am sorry to say casualties have been very heavy—in all, I suppose, about 10,000 men, but I am glad to say this includes a large number of slightly wounded. At the same time I have lost a great many really valuable officers, whom I hardly know how to replace, and we are now consolidating the position, and trying to reorganise regiments who have got much split up. When this is done I hope we may be able to get together a good fighting force again to make another determined attack on the ridge, the capture of which is, I feel, essential to ensure the safety of any base in Suvla Bay. General Godley [who had been chosen by Kitchener in 1910 to organise and command the New Zealand force] has done excellently well with his force of two Divisions, and done everything to ensure success. The New Zealanders have fought magnificently—in fact all have—and were better than our old Indian comrades.

"Up to the one small point of failing to get the crest I feel we really were meeting with success, for from every direction reports come to me of the enormous number of Turks who have been killed, and from all I can hear I think they must amount to several thousands—but they seem to have a marvellous way of replacing them. We have captured 700 prisoners, two new German trench mortars, one Nordenfeldt, and nine maxims, as well, of course, as a great many rifles and a large amount of ammunition.

"We have 'made good' a lot of new country, but, alas, I feel that none of this is of any great value unless we can also get the crest line on the hill and look down on the Dardanelles.

"Shaw commanding Thirteenth Division, who arrived long after all plans were made, told me he had tried to pick holes in them, to see if any others could better have assured success, and he said he couldn't see where we could have improved on what we did, which is satisfactory, but all the more vexatious to have just failed.

"All the boys are, however, I am glad to say, in capital spirits, and as I told them we are still going to knock these Turks out, and if it comes to a case of which of us is going to see the other through and stick it out longest there can be no doubt that it will be us, and they must remember that for every one of us they have killed, we have got half-a-dozen Turks.

"On our left the Ninth Corps, I fear, have not made the progress I had so much hoped for.

"When Stopford came to see me some little time ago, I told him his one chance was to follow our tactics on landing, viz. to hurl people forward as fast as he possibly could throughout the night disregarding all minor operations near the landing place, and at once go for the range of hills north of Anafarta. We knew there would be no great opposition there, and the support of the troops following would see him through everything. There was, however, I fancy, some delay which was probably unavoidable, with the consequence that we had not got anywhere near making good any of the hills commanding the bay, and now I fear there will be terrible difficulty in taking them, as, of course, the Turks have rushed up reinforcements.

"However, there it is! We have both got to take our bits, and I am sure the Chief knows we will do our best to see it through.

"My anxieties about water have been almost as great as about successful fighting—nearly all wells have dried up, pumps keep going wrong, and water-boats do not arrive or get holed, and on 5th I was almost on point of wiring to say not only could I not receive reinforcements, but must contemplate sending off some of my troops. There is one thing the Australian will *not* do, and that is fight without water, and I have been warned more than once by Bridges and many senior officers that if we failed to get water up to the trenches or fighting line in reasonable time, there were many men who, in spite of all orders, would just break off and come down to the beach for a drink! Fortunately I haven't had to deal with such a situation yet. But I had to send a brigade into action with only 400 gallons between them for twenty-four hours. It really has been and is a perfect nightmare to me, for the danger is by no means over, though I hope it may be soon, as I am hourly urging the sappers to dig in the new country we now hold, and which is much more promising than anything here, and we have already found small quantities—but even now a complete breakdown of my pumps for twelve hours and I'd be in Queer Street!—a rotten old boiler, too, got from Egypt. You can imagine it is not an easy time. W. R. B.

"*P.S.*—I fear I have not done justice in this to the Lone Pine fighting. Every hour brings further evidence as to its severity. Turkish reinforcements to the extent of several regiments were thrown in in succession, and eventually we had nearly all Walker's Australian Division involved in the hardest real hand-to-hand fighting we have ever experienced—in this, as you may be sure, the Australians excelled themselves and fought with the most dauntless courage."

CHAPTER CXIII

KITCHENER, on hearing of the set-back at Suvla Bay, immediately intervened to replace, without reproaching, those Generals who had not been successful.

If you should deem it necessary [he telegraphed on August 14] to replace Stopford, Mahon, and Hammersley, have you any competent Generals to take their place? This is a young man's war, and we must have Commanding Officers who will take full advantage of opportunities, which come but seldom. If, therefore, any Generals fail, do not hesitate to act promptly. I think that Peyton will be useful to you as a good fighter. If you wish him to take the Corps in the place of Stopford, I will give him Lieutenant-General's rank. As I am asking French to supply one Corps Commander and two Divisional Generals, real fighters, we had better not act definitely until we hear what he can do. I am suggesting to him the names of Byng, Horne, and Kavanagh, all good fighting men.

The next day he could say that Byng was being sent out to take command of the Ninth Corps, with Generals Fanshawe and Maude to lead the Divisions. Ian Hamilton telegraphed on the 14th: "Your anticipation of our wishes and difficulties in this way is very gratifying. Byng, Kavanagh, and Horne are all fliers"; and two days later: "I am enchanted to hear that Byng, Maude, and Fanshawe are coming— I could wish for no better men."

On August 17 Ian Hamilton telegraphed:

I hope you will realise how nearly this operation was a success complete beyond anticipation. The surprise was complete, and the army was thrown ashore in record time, practically without loss, and a little more push on the part of the Ninth Corps would have relieved the pressure on Anzac, facilitated the retention of Chunuk Bair, secured Suvla Bay as a port, and threatened the enemy's right in a way that should have enabled Anzac to turn a success into a great victory.

Now we are up against the Turkish Army, which is well commanded and fighting bravely.

The Commander quoted 110,000 enemy rifles as against his own 95,000, and asked for large reinforcements. The demand was referred to the Cabinet, of whom Kitchener alone seemed to remember that, although Ian Hamilton had received more cadres than he had expected, the actual numbers of men had been under his calculations to secure the success which had been denied him. True, the success had only just eluded his grasp, and no doubt was cast on his opinion that a heavier push on the part of the Ninth Corps might have meant "a great victory." But it was unhappily true also that the Turks were now fully posted as to our procedure and plans: that they were in superior strength and could call on potential reinforcements. It was therefore more than debatable whether a fresh influx of British troops would compel a decision favourable to British arms. The season for landing operations was drawing to a close, and for any good purpose troops must be sent forthwith, and could only be sent at the expense of the New Army in France, where we were committed to support Joffre's autumn offensive. Two campaigns had to be fought without the adequate means for either.

It had not been burnt into the Cabinet that the failure at Suvla Bay had marred the fair promise of the Expedition. Something, it was thought, might and should be done to repair the mischief. A success somewhere, and of some magnitude, was the need of the hour. The Germans were scoring rapidly in Poland, and the Russians were so short of munitions that no good thing could be expected from them.

The Bulgarian Government had on August 6 concluded a loan of 400,000,000 francs with the Austro-German banks, and the cash was obviously the prelude to a convention.

The only possible course was taken. Ian Hamilton must be told to fight on for all he was worth, but must learn that large reinforcements were unprocurable.

Kitchener telegraphed to him on August 30:

> It is very desirable, owing to the general situation, to score a success either in France or at Gallipoli. We look to you to do whatever is possible without incurring undue risk of a serious set-back or heavy losses. When your troops have been pulled together and you have been joined by any reinforcements obtainable from Egypt, we greatly hope that you will find it in your power to carry out the operations you have in hand. You must understand that in the circumstances no large divisional units can be diverted from the main theatre in France. We feel confident that you will do your utmost, as we are doing ours to support you. In case of failure you will have to remain for some considerable time on the defensive.

Ian Hamilton replied:

> I will do my best with the forces at my disposal and quite

REINFORCEMENTS PROMISED

understand why reinforcements are not sent. I thank you for putting it so plainly. I do not wish to paint a gloomy picture, it is simply a problem of arithmetic and measurement. With normal wastage and present scale of drafts, the total fighting strength by mid-December will, with the French, be only 60,000. Of these a certain percentage must rest off the Peninsula. The remainder will only suffice to hold Cape Helles and the Anzac line unless the enemy collapses. Till now the Turks have replaced their casualties promptly. Sickness may abate, but with the weariness of the bulk of the force, I am doubtful if it is wise to reckon on this.

This telegram was more than disconcerting. The Government had scarcely realised that the Suvla operation had so much of a neck-or-nothing character, and that, in default of reinforcements, Ian Hamilton might have to reduce considerably his newly-acquired holding of Suvla territory. By close calculations Kitchener found that within six weeks it would be possible to despatch 29,000 men to the Dardanelles. He advised Ian Hamilton immediately of this, and, at the request of the Government, telegraphed to him on August 27:

Though still maintaining the decision to send no complete divisional units, it is desirable to have all possible materials upon which to form a judgement from time to time. Therefore will you please telegraph me your opinion, from the point of view of the military and strategical situation now existing of the Peninsula, as to the prospects there are, after the experience you have recently had, of our achieving our main objective of turning the Turks out, and what force you consider would be required to do this?

Ian Hamilton answered on September 2:

I am sure the Turkish Commander-in-Chief is in equal trouble. The *moral* of our fresh troops is not what had been hoped for, but there has been some improvement through commanders encouraging initiative, and teaching them their superiority man for man. The old troops much need rest, many being literally worried out of mind and body. The plan depended on surprise, which was attained, and on rapidity, which was lacking. The failure was due, not to lack of numbers, but to moral considerations. We shall now be confronted with a network of trenches and machine-guns sighted and manned often by Germans, who shoot better now. They outnumber us by three to two. Naval opinion forbids a fresh landing. Therefore we must make fresh efforts at the narrow neck of the Peninsula. The 29,000 reinforcements, of which 12,000 are drafts, will not reduce the present deficit of 55,000, which will be 63,000 by the time the reinforcements arrive if the rate of wastage continues. The launching of a grand new attack would need new formations up to 50,000, besides sufficient drafts to bring my divisions up to establishment.

Ian Hamilton therefore required at least 100,000 fresh men to initiate a new offensive, and 100,000 men were not to be found.

Just at this moment an unexpected offer of help came from France. The French Government asked General Sarrail—whom Joffre had just relieved of his command on the Western front—to advise them as to the operations in the East, and Sarrail worked out a plan for a landing on the Asiatic shore of the Dardanelles. Thereupon to effect this the French Government offered four divisions with Sarrail to lead them.

Kitchener hurried to Paris to find that the offer had been made without consulting Joffre, who protested hotly against it.

I have just returned from France [he wired to Ian Hamilton] and have found that the decision was taken by the

French Government without reference to their military advisers. The outcome of the meeting with Millerand, Joffre, and Sarrail was that the four French divisions ear-marked for the Dardanelles cannot leave until the result of the approaching offensive in France is determined. If it be successful the Dardanelles position will naturally be affected favourably. It is hoped the issue will be clear in the first days of October, and, if the result is indecisive, that by October 10, two of our divisions may be at Marseilles closely followed by the four French. By about mid-November all should be ready. Meantime reinforcements and drafts are coming as drafts and transport become available. Sarrail, backed by General Bailloud, is greatly in favour of the French Expedition being employed independently on the Asiatic shore. Joffre greatly doubts the wisdom of this course, and Millerand requested me to ask you to state fully and confidentially your opinion for his information on this matter. Joffre's objections appear to be that a landing in Asia opens up a very wide field if the force be not immediately successful, in which case more troops, munitions, and drafts would be required than could be spared with due regard to the safety of France. Secondly, he is not very confident of Sarrail's leadership, particularly as the plans Sarrail has made seem to be worthless. Joffre is having careful plans worked out by his staff for the Expedition on the Asiatic shore, which, he says, though unfinished, do not look promising.

Unity of command was a subject which had dwelt in Kitchener's mind from the beginning of the war, and he was glad to receive the suggestion from Ian Hamilton:

If the French were employed at Suvla, they would have to fight side by side with the British—a situation which, with co-equal commanders, would be a military absurdity. Were that course decided upon, I would ask the Allied Governments to make up their minds which General had most daring, brains, and experience, and if it were the Frenchman I would serve under him loyally.

Before any joint plan could be further worked out the events in the Balkans consigned it to the limbo of the impracticable. On September 6 Bulgaria had agreed with Turkey as to their common frontier. A fortnight later the ineffable Czar Ferdinand had ordered a partial mobilisation, quickly followed by a general mobilisation, while preparations from Austro-German attack upon Serbia were well advanced. On September 21 M. Venizelos asked for a guarantee of 150,000 troops from England and France as the condition of Greek intervention, and three days later the French and British Governments intimated that the troops would be sent. The eyes of the Entente Governments were then turned to Salonika. On September 21 Ian Hamilton enumerated the difficulties of renewing offensive operations:

Day succeeds day, never without incident, but rarely now with any action of sufficient importance to warrant me cabling. I feel quite burnt up with a desperate impatience to get on, and, my own sensations being such, I very well understand how keen your eagerness must be. The fact of the matter is, I *can't* force the pace. Progress continues to be made at Suvla, as I told you in my last, but whereas Fanshawe thought he would carry the north-east corner of the ridge "within a few days," he does not see his way to doing the trick till the end of this week at the earliest. Moreover, in discussing the matter Byng now declares he must have lots and lots of ammunition. All these fellows from France come here with this idea. Byng would like to have four days' successive bombardment for an hour, and then attack, and speaks of one High Explosive shell per yard as pat as if they were shells we could pick up on the sea-shore. I assured him it is "no earthly"; that he shall have his share, and more than his share, of what I have got, but that stuff for a bombardment is simply not in existence.

The Yeomen in their section have certainly made a definite advance, and have now joined the heads of their saps, thus actually consolidating a distinct gain of a hundred yards or so. But I am boiling to have one more try with them at a dashing assault before we subside definitely into this ghastly trench warfare. Byng has now agreed to make use of the waning moon in a few days' time to try such a bayonet with the Yeomen. He will carry it out in the dark, and then hopes, if successful, to have the waning moonlight to help him in consolidation before the Turkish shrapnel and High Explosive get to work with daylight.

Personally, I am getting rather dubious about the sovereign efficacy of these bombardments now that the Germans have taught the Turks how to be cunning, and make deep dug-outs behind the front line. I should put more faith myself in what is being strongly recommended me by the Australian Engineers here. Had we but the pumps, they say, we could use hydraulic pressure to throw jets of sea water, seven and nine inches in diameter, against Turkish trenches, which would go through the earth as a knife cuts through cheese and sweep our enemies, together with the debris of their works, down the *khud*. Several of the Australian Engineers are actually engaged, in civil life, in a sort of alluvial mining, when they wash away whole sides of mountains. These fellows declare that, at certain points, the whole network of Turkish trenches could be thus destroyed as you flush out a wasp's nest.[1]

Well, that is the situation. Within a week from now we shall have had, D.V., a partial "go in" or two at the enemy. Both Birdwood and Davies declare they can do nothing more—nothing like a general attack—without lots of ammunition. As to Byng, I feel sure I am doing right in not putting too much pressure on him. Doubtless Hunter

---

[1] C. G. S. is having this inquired into by the responsible people.

Weston, in his place, would have a dart of some sort or another by now, but it by no means follows that Hunter Weston would have been right. Byng's troops have been highly tried, and the Turks in front of him are very strong. He is determined, he says, to make a success of his first spring. Certainly, as far as I can see at present, he could not have keener, better fellows under him—no, not if he had the pick of the whole British Army—than he has in De Lisle, Maude, Fanshawe, and Peyton.

Just off to Anzacs to go up to Rhododendron Spur and Hill 60 with Birdie. . . .

Now that bombs have become a regular London amusement it isn't much use writing you about them. You won't be impressed. Anyway, we have within the last few minutes had ten, or, to be precise, ten bursts and one blind, into this tiny little camp of five hundred souls. The miraculous thing is—only one man wounded.

I yesterday went all over Birdie's left and saw some of the new Australian Division—splendid fellows. Things are still quite lively up there and the country, including the places they have stormed, simply amazing. Little Table-Top hill, for instance, is a plateau of about one acre jutting right up into the sky in a most peculiar formation (such as one sees in Saxon Switzerland) with apparently sheer sandstone cliffs on all sides. Such a tangled, confused country you never saw, and, even map in hand, it is extremely difficult to say what parts are held by Turks and what by ourselves.

Birdie is in precisely the same frame of mind as Byng. He cannot, for the life of him, see his way to make anything like a general attack, at least so long as he has a brigade out resting at Mudros. But he is going to take something big and serious in hand at once which, if successful, will give us a point of capital importance.[1]

P.S.—Just heard of Bulgarian mobilisation, and hope to live to see Ferdinand transfixed by an Australian bayonet.

---

1 [The reference was to a huge mine which the Australians were tunnelling.]

CHAPTER CXIV

On September 23 Kitchener wired to Ian Hamilton giving the first hint that it might be necessary to withdraw troops from the Dardanelles for the Salonika Expedition, and invited his opinion upon this. Ian Hamilton foresaw a probable grave loss of men and prestige, and a certain surrender of a vast quantity of valuable stores. Matters were, however, brought to a head on the 27th by an order from the French Government to General Bailloud to concentrate one of the two French divisions in the Dardanelles at Mudros, in readiness for despatch to Salonika; and on the 28th Kitchener, on instructions from the Cabinet, directed Ian Hamilton to concentrate two divisions for the same purpose. Ian Hamilton pleaded that he could not spare all these troops:

I write to you in the middle of my arrangements for the movement elsewhere. In the cables which have passed between us, I have found it anything but an easy business to strike the happy mean between executing your wishes promptly and cheerfully on the one hand, and, on the other, giving you a faithful impression of how we shall stand here once your orders have been carried out.

If I make too little of the dangers which surround me, then you might be encouraged to weaken me still further, thereby jeopardising the whole of this enterprise. But if I allow my anxieties to get too much the upper hand, why then I may be ruining some larger enterprise, the true bearing of which I have no means of gauging.

You will understand, then, the principles which have been my guide in drafting, with the assistance of the level-headed Braithwaite, my various cables to you in connection with this latest development. It is especially in cabling that these difficulties arise, as it is impossible to be explanatory or full.

Now that I am writing to you it is another matter. At the present moment the Tenth Division and one brigade of the French are under orders. In my cables I have shown that (at a real pinch such as I understand this to be) I can spare either one more brigade of French or the Fifty-third Division.

But our position when these troops are gone will be such as to cause me myself the most serious concern pending the arrival of reinforcements, and there is no use blinking the fact that until that time the general situation of the Dardanelles Expedition will be dangerous. It is not only that a large proportion of my troops are of second-line quality, but that the very best of them, *i.e.* the Australians and the Twenty-ninth Division, are, as they put it themselves, "not the men they were." I have a medical report in my hands stating that 50 per cent of the old troops examined at Anzac from seven battalions have a rapid, feeble heart with shortness of breath, and that 78 per cent of these have diarrhœa, and 64 per cent sores on skin. Amongst an equal number of men examined from people who had only been at Anzac a week, there were no feeble hearts, no shortness of breath, only 8 per cent of sores on skin, and 14 per cent diarrhœa. This is a result of having been in the trenches under continuous shell and musketry fire for eighteen to twenty weeks. Therefore, in a physical sense, my first-class troops can no longer be regarded as first-class. Anywhere else, I suppose, these men would be in convalescent homes, but here they *must* carry on, and, God be praised, their spirit and *moral* are unshaken.

Consider for a moment what these troops have to do. Not only must they continously be under fire—for the rest trenches are harried and shelled just as much as the front line—but the whole of the men in reserve have to spend the night in getting up stores to the front, and in making communications. Fatigue parties of soldiers have to go out to the vessels and unload the stuff out of the hold into the lighters. They then have to bring the heavy cases in the lighters on to the shore and unload them. Thus there is precious little rest for any one anywhere. Thus also it becomes easy to understand our enormous sick evacuations, which amounted, during last week, to 1310 for Helles, 1483 for Anzac, and 1949 for Suvla; the wounded for these same three places during that period were 28, 328, and 285. What would help us a great deal would be some thousands of men at each place who, though enlisted soldiers, and therefore bound to go under fire or do whatever they were ordered to do, need not necessarily be beyond the recruit stage in training. It is not necessary, therefore, that all the drafts for this force should consist of highly trained men.

I hope what I have dictated to-day may make you understand that after sending these troops we shall be struggling along without any margin at all. The Turks will very promptly hear of this movement, and there can be no reasonable doubt that the Germans, who advise them, will press them to make heavy attacks along our line everywhere.

In the small hours of the morning, before I have had my matutinal cup of tea, the immediate outlook gives me a feeling of cold feet in a more aggravated form than I have ever hitherto experienced. The whole plan of the French Asiatic subsidiary operation has gone for the meantime by the board. For even England and France between them cannot find men enough, I should think, to send considerable forces to Asia as well as run an entirely new show elsewhere. Indeed, Naval requirements alone would seem entirely to forbid it.

But I must not worry you any more with these surmises. After all, nothing great in this world was ever easily accomplished. Never has there been such an example of that as in the Dardanelles Expedition. How many times has success seemed to be on the point of crowning our efforts, and yet, on each occasion, just as we are beginning to see light through the tangle of obstacles, preparing for an assault, or whatever it may be, something occurs to upset the apple-cart.

None the less we do advance, and we will succeed in the end. I feel I am playing it rather low down inflicting on you the outline of my own troubles at a moment when your own must be infinitely greater. (29.9.15.)

P.S.—Reading over this letter, which I have not now time to re-write or correct, it strikes me that in concentrating my mind purely on the Dardanelles I may have given a wrong impression of my general attitude towards your latest demands. No one can realise, I believe, more clearly than I do that the Dardanelles operations themselves hinge for their success to a very large extent upon the maintenance of a barrier between the Central Powers and Constantinople. As far as reinforcements of men to the enemy in the field is concerned, such inter-communication would not be so fatal as might perhaps be imagined. The Gallipoli Peninsula is a limited area, and if the Germans had a million men at Constantinople they could not, under present conditions, add many, if any, to the numbers already opposed to us. But the free transit of coal, flour, ammunition, and big guns might well put us all in the cart—the cart being, in this instance, the sea.

Further, ever since both sides in France and Flanders began to dig in, I have consistently maintained that the real home-thrust at the German Empire cannot be delivered from the West, but must be directed either via Constantinople or via Salonika.

So please remember that I grudge nothing, and think no danger too great, to further such an enterprise, provided always the effort does not leave me locally too weak to hold up the Turkish Army.

The French Government had now set itself to a mighty effort to save Serbia, and the British Government had agreed to co-operate. Since Ian Hamilton's telegram of August 23 Kitchener had given up hope of forcing a way through the Turkish lines in the Gallipoli Peninsula, and though he was far from certain that the Salonika enterprise would be strong enough, or in time, to achieve its purpose, he felt bound to reciprocate the loyal help the French had lent us in the Dardanelles. From this time onwards the question of evacuating the Peninsula altogether was anxiously discussed in the Cabinet, who called Sir William Robertson from France to advise them. He unhesitatingly pronounced for cutting our losses in the Peninsula, and believed evacuation to be quite feasible. On October 11 Kitchener telegraphed to Ian Hamilton inviting his views if a withdrawal were decided upon.

Losses would depend [Ian Hamilton replied the next day] on various uncertain factors—the enemy's action, the weather, and the reliability of the covering troops. The question is also a Naval one. A consultation which I once had with Gouraud yielded the conclusion that at Cape Helles we must sacrifice two divisions out of a total of six, Cape Helles being the easiest of the three places to get away from. My present opinion is that we cannot reckon on getting out of Gallipoli with less loss than half the total force and the guns (which must be used to the last), stores, railway plant, and horses. . . . Twenty-five per cent might get off easily, then trouble would begin; by great good luck the loss might be less, but with raw troops at Suvla and Senegalese at Cape Helles there might be a veritable catastrophe.

As Ian Hamilton would not hear of calling off his heroic men from the ground they had so hardly and so gloriously won, the Cabinet determined to call in other advice. Ian Hamilton was asked to tour the Near East and report on conditions prevailing and likely to prevail. To Sir Charles Monro was committed the command of the Mediterranean Expeditionary Force. A few days later Kitchener was asked by the Cabinet to set out at once for the Dardanelles and give a final decision whether or not the positions should be held.

CHAPTER CXV

It was confessedly with a heavy heart that Kitchener left London. He was highly sensitive as to British prestige in the East, and deeply disturbed as to the probable cost in life which retirement would entail. He would not shrink from putting down the price of victory, but a fruitless sacrifice of soldiers was abhorrent to him, and he had been advised that a third of the force might be lost in withdrawal. The gallantry of the Gallipoli fighters had won Kitchener's almost startled admiration, and he felt in his very soul his responsibility for these brave men. "I pace my room at night," he told the Prime Minister, "and see the boats fired at and capsizing, and the drowning men." Candid friends had, moreover, hinted to him that some of his Ministerial colleagues would be content to see his chair empty or otherwise filled, and would rejoice in any incident—or accident—which might prolong or perpetuate his absence. "Perhaps, if I have to lose a lot of men over there, I shall not want to come back," was his remark when the Cabinet approved a mission fraught with grave responsibility and capable of indefinite extension.

On the morrow of Kitchener's departure the air was thick with rumours of his supersession. The story—a rather expensive luxury to the newspaper which invented it—of the War Secretary's visit to the Sovereign in order to surrender the seals of office was an example of ingenious inference from a quite simple fact. He had sent word to the Palace that he felt he had nothing to say of sufficient importance to justify his asking an audience of the King, then only slowly recovering from an accident sustained in France. The reply was an invitation to spend half-an-hour in the sick-room: the King simply wished to hear his Minister's latest opinion as to the retention of Gallipoli, and no question of his term of office was ever suggested.

Kitchener was obliged to stay two days in Paris; at a long interview at Chantilly he discussed anxiously with Joffre the recalcitrance of Greece, and learnt that the abandonment of Gallipoli would be to the French High Command a subject of "poignant regret." "The French Government," he wrote, "are more anxious about the numbers going out to Salonika than about their quality," and he suggested therefore that men unsuitable for attacking purposes should be put in at the Greek port in lieu of the two hard-fighting divisions, the Twenty-seventh and Twenty-eighth. From Marseilles he telegraphed that he found the available transport there should be more expeditiously filled up; and just before sailing he was diverted from Alexandria, and asked to go direct to Mudros, where McMahon, Maxwell, Monro, and Birdwood had been ordered to meet him.

On the morning of November 7 the party embarked on the *Dartmouth,* and from some rough notes made on the voyage there may be gathered Kitchener's general prepossessions. Attack, he thought, was impossible for us at present; but Gallipoli could be held even if the Turks received considerably more ammunition. It would, however, be untenable against German troops. Therefore "we must evacuate when we are certain that the Germans are about to employ their own troops against us." To do so with the minimum of loss in men and material "the withdrawal must be started in good time, must be gradual, and must be kept secret, as many guns as possible being removed and the remainder destroyed. The enemy should be 'bluffed' by increased scale of fire, change of position, and other devices. The final garrison will remain as long as possible, destroy material, and then surrender. This would mean a defeat, but not disaster." Withdrawal would, of course, create an immediate problem in the defence of Egypt. "If we remain in Gallipoli, an attack on Egypt is always possible; if we withdraw, it may be certain." Ten divisions at least, it was estimated, would be necessary for the defence of Egypt, and these must come from France, any reduction in the force in Gallipoli being used either to reinforce Salonika or to garrison Egypt. With regard to the Balkans, the Entente detachments at Salonika were too small and had arrived too late to prevent the destruction of the Serbian Army; but they might suffice to stop Greece and Rumania joining the Central Powers. The motto for the Entente Powers during the winter must be:

"Offensive-defensive in France and Russia and Italy, defensive in Egypt, and conditional defensive in Gallipoli."

Purely military considerations apart, Kitchener was an opponent of immediate evacuation. He thought, too, there was still room for further assistance, and before leaving London had even urged Mr.

Balfour to consider the possibility of another enterprise by the Navy to force the Straits. Vigorous proposals in this direction had been laid before the Admiralty by Commander Keyes, who had been permitted by Admiral De Robeck to come from the Mediterranean and speak for himself. The Admiralty, however, was not to be charmed; it was not eager to "wet its feet" again, as Kitchener expressed it; and, by some unexplained delay, Keyes, who would have accompanied Kitchener to the Mediterranean and continued to press his suit, failed to get his instructions in time. It was not until two weeks later that he was able to meet Kitchener at Salonika, when he urged on him that the Admiralty were not averse to a naval assault, and that to bring it about he had only to put in the weight of his own counsel. The soldier could only tell this splendid naval enthusiast that three urgent applications had failed to stir the Admiralty, and Keyes ruefully saw his plan folded away.

Kitchener anchored at Mudros on November 10, and spent the next few days and nights in close inspection of the positions and long conferences on board the *Lord Nelson,* to which he was transshipped for a few days. He told the 2nd Australian Infantry Brigade that the fame of the Anzac Corps had echoed throughout the whole Empire. He dwelt on their tenacity in defence, their dash in attack, their consummate ingenuity in the construction of trenches, and reminded them that if the British forces had been unable to conquer the Peninsula, they had at any rate contained and destroyed great numbers of Turks who would have been capable of terrible mischief elsewhere. Helles drew from him expressions of genuine surprise that its seizure could have been effected in the teeth of strong opposition. It presented possibilities of successful defence greater than the maps had indicated to him. Sadly he recalled his own warnings to Mr. Churchill that the Straits could scarcely be forced by an unsupported Navy.

On November 13 the Anzac position was thoroughly overhauled, and Kitchener was rapturously received by the Australians and New Zealanders, to whom he gave messages of congratulations from the King and nation. His methodical inspection persuaded him that evacuation need not be so costly as he had been led to fear, especially if certain precautions—which he indicated in some detail—were closely observed. His telegram to the Prime Minister of November 11 expressed his wonderment at the "most remarkable feat of arms" in securing ground far more forbidding than he had imagined:

> The lack of proper lines of communication is the main difficulty in carrying out successful operations on the Peninsula. The landings are precarious and often impossible through rough sea and want of harbours, and the enemy's positions are peculiarly suitable for making our communications more dangerous and difficult. The base at Mudros is too far detached from our forces in the field, and the proper co-ordination of the administrative services of a line of communication is prevented by distance and sea voyage, dependent on the weather. This state of things in my judgement is the main cause of our troops not having been able to do better and to attain really strategic points on the Peninsula which would have turned Kilid Bahr.

He was confident that the present position could be held against the Turks; officers and men were sure of themselves, though "somewhat depressed at not being able to get through."

I consider, however [he went on to say], that if Germany sent a German force to attack, the lines are not deep enough to allow for proper arrangements for supports, and if the front-line trenches were taken these difficulties would increase.

Our occupation of the Peninsula immobilises about 125,000 Turks and causes them considerable loss; and until the recent German operations in Serbia opened communication with Turkey and changed the situation, practically the whole Turkish Army had to be held in readiness to defend the capital if we succeeded on the Peninsula. In present circumstances the *raison d'être* of our forces on the Gallipoli Peninsula is no longer as important as it has hitherto been; if another position in the neighbourhood of Alexandretta were occupied, where Turkish movements eastwards could be effectively stopped, the realisation of the German objective against Egypt and the East would be prevented.

The evacuation of the Peninsula is being carefully and secretly prepared for. If undertaken, it will be an operation of extreme military difficulty and danger; but I have hopes that, given time and weather, which may be expected to be suitable until about the end of December, the troops will carry out this task with less loss than was previously estimated. My reason for this is that the distance that they have to go to embark, and the contraction of the lines of defence to be held by a smaller force, gives them a better chance than I previously thought.

Two days later he added: "I think it will be easier to evacuate Suvla and Anzac fronts first, whatever may be decided as to Helles afterwards."

The dominant thought of the military conclave at

Mudros was that, if the Peninsula must be left to the Turk, a resounding blow must be dealt him elsewhere. The first consideration was to defend Egypt, which would at once be threatened by the liberation of the troops contained at Gallipoli. The next was to counteract a disastrous effect which might well be produced on the Mohammedan and Arab world. For this twofold purpose Kitchener, strongly backed by the other Generals, proposed a landing at Ayas Bay, in the Gulf of Alexandretta, with a view to "cut and hold the railway between Amanus and Taurus at Missis, preventing the Turks moving east, and thus protecting Egypt and Baghdad." Ten months earlier a landing near Alexandretta had been considered by Kitchener, but had been set aside as altogether too costly then in troops and transport. The present plan was more modest in its dimensions, and there were now the means to put it into effect; for the present he need only call upon two more first-class divisions from France.

This plan the General Staff viewed "with grave concern." The locality, they alleged, was favourable for the Turks; the perimeter to be finally held—which appeared to be fifty miles—would take about 160,000 infantry; the forces would probably be tied for the remainder of the war, re-embarkation being little if any less difficult than the evacuation of Gallipoli; the strain on available military resource would be excessive, and there would be a "most dangerous dissemination of both Naval and Military forces"; the defence of Egypt could be better conducted on the Suez Canal line. To these objections Kitchener replied categorically within an hour of receiving the message, reminding the Prime Minister that the exponents of the scheme were in the nature of experts:

There is nothing in the objections raised in your telegram that was not foreseen and discussed here before sending my telegram.

The political situation in the East in our opinion so seriously affects purely military considerations as to outweigh those military disadvantages which might otherwise carry weight. The effect in the East of the Turkish Army being allowed to carry out unopposed and unmolested the declared intentions of Germany combined with a possible evacuation of our positions in Gallipoli (which would be equivalent to a serious defeat) will be enormous, and will have far-reaching results by throwing the Arabs into German hands and thus uniting them against us, endangering French as well as British possessions.

McMahon, Maxwell, and myself must be admitted to know the difficulties of defence in Egypt, and we are unanimously of opinion that your plan for carrying this out on the Canal is doomed to failure, while involving much greater commitments in men and resources than the plan we advocate. In Egypt we should have to face certain hostility all along the western frontier, which would extend to Tunis, Algiers, and Morocco; serious unrest and disturbances throughout Egypt and the Sudan endangering our internal communications as well as the closing of the Canal for a prolonged period. Reliance on the defence of Egypt in Egypt foreshadows, in our opinion, a withdrawal from it and the Sudan within a measurable time, with results so far-reaching both for ourselves and France as possibly to allow the Germans to attain their object and thus jeopardise the campaign in Europe by the withdrawal of larger forces than can be afforded.

The Admiral will telegraph on the Naval question, which does not seem to us and to him to be insuperable.

The telegram then set out the replies of General Monro and the Staff to the military objections raised by the War Office. The Intelligence had calculated that the Turks could not make available a greater force than 150,000 men, and that the maintenance of that number would involve very considerable transport difficulties. It was estimated also that the first opposing force would probably not exceed 5000 men, unless the Turks had received timely information. The perimeter to be held might approximate to fifty miles, but much of this consisted of marsh and mountain, while two-thirds of the position was covered by an unfordable river under fairly close fire of defence. The War Office calculation of men per yard throughout the whole length was hardly applicable, and the difficulties of re-embarkation would be far less than at Gallipoli, because the Bay is well protected from weather and defensible against submarines:

I would ask the General Staff to consider if it is recognised that the defence of Egypt on the Canal is unsound; and if we cannot maintain our present position in Gallipoli against possible attack by German forces, or force the Dardanelles by Naval action, what other alternative to that proposed they would suggest to meet the Germano-Turkish menace in the East. I would point out that very valuable time is being lost and that a decision on our future action is urgent.

"French susceptibilities" being hinted at in further messages, Kitchener suggested that the British Government should "follow the precedent of Constantinople being awarded to Russia, and allot Syria, with suitable boundaries, to France after the war. We might then be allowed to operate in future

French territory for our own protection against present dangers against which they are unable to guard us." In another telegram he reiterated the necessity of prompt decision, and suggested that any suspicion between the Allies "only plays into the hands of Germany."

The delay in drawing a definite reply from the Home Government was embarrassing, and not a little exasperating. On November 15 Kitchener telegraphs that the rejection of the scheme

> enables the Germans to carry out their announced object [against Egypt and the East] unless we can thwart them by bringing the utmost pressure to bear on the Bulgarians and Turks through Salonika. . . . Unless a far greater number of troops, up to a possible total of 400,000, are available for action in the Salonika theatre, we do not think our object would be attained.

He insisted that the defences of Egypt must be greatly strengthened, but was certain that Egypt could best be defended by external offensive: "It is a matter for grave reconsideration whether they [the forces required for the purpose] could not be far more effectively employed outside Egypt in the vicinity of Ayas." No reply was received, and Kitchener, remembering the limitations of Russia [1] and our liabilities in the East, telegraphed once more on November 16:

> The decision about to be come to appears to me to have such a momentous effect on the future of the war that I should like to place my opinion on record, as it may, I think, be the turning-point leading to the loss of the war by the Allies.

---

[1] He was by now very anxious as to the social condition of Russia.

Owing to limited communications, natural causes, and the approach of winter, the pressure we can exert in Serbia will probably be ineffectual and can easily be held off by our enemies from reaching the railway. Meanwhile the German-announced plans for raising the East against us will proceed without opposition, culminating in the spring. With the East then in a blaze the combined vigorous offensive of the Allied Powers, which was being arranged for early next year, will be very greatly weakened, and if the war has to go on through the winter of 1916–1917 without in the meantime any decision or our positions being considerably improved, I greatly fear some of our Allies if not ourselves will be unable to stand the strain.

The "decision" was referred to and rejected by a Conference at Paris, but had not been received by Kitchener when he had to leave Mudros for Salonika, whither he was called to confront another chapter of difficulties.

CHAPTER CXVI

THE decisive successes of the Bulgarian Army, to which German and Austrian troops largely contributed, had not only eliminated Serbia as a serious fighting force, but had gravely compromised the French and British contingents which had been despatched in haste to her relief. Greece, bound to Serbia by treaty, had declared a "benevolent neutrality," but early in November her Prime Minister induced a situation of acute tension by a solemn pronouncement—afterwards largely modified—that it would be her duty to disarm Allied troops falling back on Greek territory. The King of the Hellenes, inclined by natural sympathy, and compelled by peculiar circumstances—military, dynastic, domestic, and financial—to lean heavily on his Imperial brother-in-law, had shaken off the guiding hand of M. Venizelos, and was now served—and nerved—by Ministers notoriously well affected to Germany. The aged Prime Minister, M. Skouloudis, was a mere figurehead, and the politician who had the ear of the King was M. Gounaris, a confirmed pro-German. Pressure of some sort had to be applied to Greece, if not to compel fulfilment of her treaty obligations to Serbia, at any rate to prevent her acting directly in the interests of the Central Powers. There was no time to be lost, yet precipitate action might issue in just what it was highly desirable to avoid. Greece was between two fears: out of one eye she saw the German and Bulgarian Armies; out of the other the British Fleet. On the one side hovered the threat of subjugation, on the other that of blockade. Fortunately for the Entente, Athens was to a peculiar degree dependent on sea-borne trade, and from Mudros Kitchener had given the Cabinet a broad hint as to putting the City of the Violet Crown on short rations if the Ministry were persistently inimical. "McMahon," he telegraphed on November 11, "tells me 7500 tons of wheat are being allowed to go from Egypt to Greece. I think all such shipments should be stopped for the present. McMahon has still time to stop this wheat. Shall he do so?" The reply was that all supplies in money and kind were being held up until the situation cleared.

The situation did not clear. By November 14 it was so overhung that the British Minister at Athens, Sir Francis Elliott, begged Kitchener to go from Salonika and see the King. This, the diplomatist urged, would have an excellent effect. "I hear," he added, "on the best authority that the King much wishes to see you." "I think," telegraphs Kitchener to Mr. Asquith, "that, after visiting Salonika, I might possibly be able to do good at Athens. But I should not leave here till I can see the situation [regarding Ayas Bay and the arrangements dependent on it] clear."

The next day, however, Elliott himself repaired to Mudros, and so represented Greek affairs that Kitchener told the Prime Minister:

He [Elliott] thinks I should go to Salonika and thence to Athens, where I might have some influence on the King, and by bringing home to him the wrong impressions he holds as regards the future result of the war induce him to carry out the views of the Allies without our having to resort to the coercive measures contemplated. With regard to this view I greatly doubt my being able to do much good, as matters have, I think, gone too far, and Germany is apparently in complete control. But Salonika is different, and I think I ought to go there at once and see Sarrail and our officers.

Before he started there arrived a messenger bearing the opinion of senior officers newly arrived at Salonika. They held that if the Greeks took up a hostile attitude to the retiring Franco-British troops the whole Allied force, including those at Salonika, would be "at their mercy." Salonika was described as "chock-a-block" with Greek troops, refugees, and Franco-British troops; food and accommodation at famine prices; Greeks obstructive rather than friendly: "Franco-British camps scattered around town with Greek camps interposed gives us no chance of organised defence."

Kitchener arrived at Salonika on November 17, and General Sarrail, commanding the Allied forces, hurried on board to impress on him the need of taking strong measures with the Greeks.

I have seen General Sarrail [Kitchener telegraphed to Downing Street], and the following are his views on the situation. As regards the position of Salonika, our troops, as well as the French, are at the mercy of the Greek Army Corps, who are either in or in close proximity to Salonika; we do not hold any defensible posts or camps, as the Greeks do not allow us to occupy defensible positions or create defended camps. If the Greeks became hostile the Allied Armies could not hold out, and the gun-fire from the Fleet would not enable them to embark. General Sarrail is of opinion that it would require 300,000 men to hold Salonika.

I explained to General Sarrail the arrival of our troops to complete 150,000 men, but he declared that he requires double that number to deal satisfactorily with the military situation. He strongly urged that further French reinforcements should be sent him immediately. With his present number of troops in the field he does not consider that he can hold on long enough to the positions he now occupies, and although he can retire a short distance to the other side of the river Carna, he cannot retire further without the loss of all his guns, as there are no roads by which the artillery can move back.

At the front there are now 60,000 French and British troops, and there are 150,000 Greeks between them and Salonika, and either no roads or very bad ones to retire along. Moreover, the train service is very defective and entirely managed by the Greeks. The military situation is therefore very grave.

General Sarrail is of opinion that the naval demonstration at Athens should be proceeded with at once, so that the situation may be cleared up once for all, as it will only apparently get worse if left in the present unsatisfactory state. He thinks the Greeks ought to be asked either to join us or to demobilise, returning to peace garrison stations and leaving Salonika to us, or to take their troops entirely away from the theatre in which we are operating; he thinks they might be tempted by being asked to occupy Monastir. He considers it essential that the German officers now in Greece should be sent away and Germanophile Greek staff officers dismissed.

I have also seen General Mahon, who is of a similar opinion. If under these circumstances the result of the naval demonstration is that the Greeks declare themselves against us, there seems to be little probability of our getting many troops re-embarked at Salonika. The ships of the Twenty-sixth and Twenty-eighth Divisions are expected almost immediately.

I do not believe that the Greeks will dare to attempt

acts of hostility against our troops at Salonika, whatever they may do with regard to those that have crossed the Serbian frontier; all possible precautionary measures will be taken.

Sarrail, however, on second thoughts, prompted by nervousness as to the safety of his troops outside Salonika, deprecated definitely hostile action by the Navy, even if Greece should turn down the Allied terms. Other considerations just then inclined the Allied Governments to season any coercive vigour with a good deal of caution. The King, while firmly resolved not to put himself *à tort* with the German Emperor, who plied him with thinly-veiled threats, had privately repudiated any intention of disarming Allied troops, and pleaded that coercion would drive the Greeks into the arms of the Central Powers. His military training in Berlin had served to persuade him that, even if Germany did not win the war hands down, the utmost the Allies could look for would be stalemate, and he wished Greece to pose at the eventual Peace Conference as everybody's friend.

Kitchener was not so sure as Elliott that he would be able to impair King Constantine's faith in the German star. "I am afraid," he telegraphs on November 19, as soon as he had returned to Mudros, "I shall not be able to do much with the King of Greece, who has evidently made up his mind. Please let me know what line you want me to take with him." The "line" indicated was simple enough. Constantine was to be told that the disarmament or internment of Allied troops would be construed as an act of war; but that there was no question of forcing Greece into an unwilling alliance. Kitchener could intimate—no one better—that Germany's present triumph was illusory, and her final humiliation only a matter of time; that the Allies were but at the beginning of their efforts, that their will was unbending and their resources unbounded.

Just before leaving for Athens Kitchener received the "decision" for which he had waited so long. The French Government, as already stated, had early frowned on Ayas Bay. "Susceptibilities" apart, the military and naval advisers condemned it as leading to a "new dispersal of the Allied forces." On the urgent representations from Mudros, Mr. Asquith had arranged for further consultation between the British and French General Staffs, to be followed by a meeting of representatives of the two Governments. This took place on the morning of November 19 in Paris.[1] Ayas Bay was definitely ruled out, and Kitchener was immediately asked for his considered opinion as to—in other words, to accept responsibility for—the evacuation of the Gallipoli Peninsula "in whole or in part." Kitchener had set his heart on the plan by which he thought to assure the safety of Egypt and recover any possible loss of British fame in the East. He had awaited with scarcely concealed impatience the decision of the Government, and on the eve of its arrival he had spoken of "going home at once." When, however, the answer— acutely disappointing to him—was put into his hand, he accepted it with his usual philosophic loyalty, and set out for Athens unconvinced, but serenely pondering the issues immediately ahead. At the Piraeus,

---

[1] This conference recorded the impossibility of undertaking any new military effort "at any other point whatever in the Eastern theatre of war." Important military and diplomatic decisions with regard to the Balkan situation were taken. Consideration of the evacuation of Gallipoli was deferred until Lord Kitchener and Colonel Girodin had reported.

in the early morning of November 20, he was met by two officers of the Greek General Staff, both ardent Germanophile, who had been considerately attached to him; and at noon he was received in audience by the King. Kitchener, very firm, but very courteous, always giving the impression of meaning a little more than he said, was precisely the emissary to bring the shifty and unbalanced Constantine to his bearings. So far that unhappy Prince had grounded his faith in the omniscience of the German Emperor and the omnipotence of the German arms, and had thought lightly of defying the Entente Powers. Now he was to hear another story told in very plain words. The conversation between the straightforward, far-seeing Minister and the intriguing, time-serving Monarch lasted an hour and a half, and culminated in the querulous interrogatory, "What am I to do when Germany threatens me with a million men?" "Remember the four millions England will have in the field next year," was the quick retort. Behind the perfect correctitude and proper deference of Kitchener's manner there was a grim determination which went to persuade Constantine that, if he would observe the orders of his Imperial brother-in-law, it must be by guile and not by force.

After luncheon at the Legation, from which the Greek Ministers of War and Marine somewhat clumsily tried to excuse themselves, Kitchener called on the Prime Minister, the aged M. Skouloudis, and there elicited the opinion of the Chief of the General Staff.

I have seen the King and Prime Minister [he wrote to Mr. Asquith]; they both seem very determined to stick to their neutrality, but the King gave me his word that the

Allied troops in Serbia would not be interned or disarmed on returning through Greek territory. If a fight took place while our troops were crossing the frontier the situation would become very difficult, for if Greek troops intervened against Bulgarians the Germans had told him it would be considered an act of war against them, and he did not see how his troops could stand on one side and allow the Bulgarians to cross the frontier following up our troops. I was able to tell him all you wired me and I think it had some effect. He was very angry with Venizelos, and said that the latter had not given the Allied troops an invitation to come, in which I assured him that he was wrong. He was full of complaints about the way he and Greece were being treated; he vowed he was an anti-German at heart, but certainly would not allow his country to go to war with the Central Powers, though later they would fight the Bulgarians when they could do so without risk of being compromised with Germany. The Prime Minister said he was very friendly to us and would do all he could at Salonika; he recognised that the situation there was a difficult one, but said that this state of things was not his fault. If we would formulate our demands he would accede to them if it was possible to do so. He complained about hostile treatment by England, but I pointed out that he had given cause for it by suggesting that our troops should be disarmed and interned. I told him that I feared the position of Greece on the fence would give rise to constant similar difficulties as long as the war lasted. He begged us to cease to be suspicious of Greece, and to allow them to obtain foodstuffs and other commercial facilities. . . .

I had some talk with the Greek Chief of the Staff and Colonel Metaxas, of whom the King had spoken to me very highly; they were evidently well primed with German ideas about the war, but were not able to argue that the strain of a prolongation of the war could be sustained by Germany. They were evidently much concerned about the Germano-Turkish attack on Egypt and the East, which they looked upon as very serious and for which preparations in heavy guns and munitions were, they said, being made at Constantinople. They curiously enough pressed upon me a concentration of our troops in the Eastern theatre almost exactly the same as detailed in my telegrams [with reference to Ayas Bay] and based their conclusions on the same argument almost word for word. They emphatically stated that there was no other way of preventing the accomplishment of the German project. I, of course, pretended to have never thought of such a scheme and to doubt its possibility; they seemed to be repeating a German phrase when stating "the war would end in Egypt."

I think they are quite sincerely with us about Egypt as there are very large Greek interests involved there.

They promised me to give us any information they could get on the subject. Their idea about the operations in Serbia is that we cannot accomplish much owing to want of equipment and the approach of winter.

Colonel Metaxas spoke a good deal about a possible peace, and appeared to think that Germany's demands would be very moderate.

The visit had its effect on Constantine's future demeanour and on his outlook on the war. His conduct was afterwards always tempered by his reflections on the strength and substance of the Allies in general and of the chief maritime Power in particular.

CHAPTER CXVII

ARRIVED once more at Mudros, after a boisterous passage, his cabin flooded with several inches of water, Kitchener was immediately in conference with the general officers on the now crucial question of evacuation and on the suggestion from Downing Street that he should himself go on to Egypt.

Our offensive on the Peninsula [he telegraphed to the Prime Minister] has up to the present held up the Turkish Army, but with German assistance which is now practically available our positions there cannot be maintained and evacuation seems inevitable. If our forces on the Peninsula withdraw to the islands of Imbros, Tenedos, and Mitylene, they can there refit, and will whilst there threaten Turkish communications eastwards, retaining considerable Turkish forces in Asia Minor. The evacuation of Suvla and Anzac should be proceeded with, while Cape Helles could at all events be held for the present. This will enable the Navy to maintain the advantages already gained and still threaten the Straits, and also give greater facilities for the evacuation of Suvla and Anzac.

By retaining Helles, the Admiral points out, the mounting of heavy guns at the entrance of the Dardanelles, thus entirely closing the Straits to the Fleet, would be prevented. If given up, it would enable them to establish a submarine base and utilise their torpedo craft in the Aegean. By keeping the forces for the present on the islands we should prevent the serious effect that would be created in Egypt if all the troops after withdrawal at once returned there. The Australians will feel deeply giving up the positions they have gained at so much cost; they have already represented this through General Birdwood. I presume you will inform Russia of our intended withdrawal. As all our efforts will have to be concentrated on the defence of Egypt from Egypt, I propose to send General Horne there to study the situation with McMahon and Maxwell, with whom I have already discussed the steps it will be necessary to take. I think it is essential that I should return to England at once to give you full information of the situation out here, and to make the necessary arrangements to carry out the policy decided upon. I personally can do no good in Egypt. The above is the considered opinion of the Admiral, McMahon, Maxwell, Monro, and Birdwood. On receipt of your reply I shall at once leave for Brindisi.[1]

---

[1] Then followed a detailed statement of the steps considered necessary to secure Egypt:

"We consider that the defence of the Canal should not be of a passive nature. Active operations should be commenced at once to destroy as far as possible all enemy's preparations in the desert and be increased as more troops become available.

"Local arrangements for camel transport to be provided. A light railway to be constructed to Katia along the inundation, and a defensive post created there to guard the left flank and Port Said. The main lines of defence to be laid out about 12,000 yards from the Canal; native labour can be provided. Following will be required. Royal Engineers with material, wire for defences, telephonic and cable communications for a front of 87 miles. Water arrangements for troops holding these lines will have to be made locally by pumping stations along the sweet-water canal and syphon connection across the Canal with piping to the front. Transport by tugs, barges, and armed craft to be arranged on the Canal. Heavy gun positions on west bank to be selected and connected by railway. With regard to Royal Engineers, not less than 15 companies in addition to those available from Medforce will be required. Aeroplane establishment proportionate to the force should be sent. Two Divisions of Indian Cavalry from France to be sent to Egypt at once and be followed by British Infantry, Artillery to complete. All troops of Medforce to be collected in Egypt. Heavy guns at three-quarter the scale of present allotment per mile in Flanders and ammunition at full scale in order to form a reserve should be provided. Severely wounded and sick not likely to recover in six weeks to be evacuated to England. We consider that in view of the new conditions in Syria and Arabia created by the evacuation of the Peninsula and an uninterrupted advance of the Turkish army under German control the forces which may be brought to bear against our positions in Egypt have been under-estimated. Also the dangers to Egypt from the western frontier had not apparently been considered."

On the 23rd the Prime Minister telegraphed that the Army Council approved evacuation "including Helles," but "stages and method of evacuation must be left, of course, to the judgement of the commander on the spot." In view of the shock which evacuation must produce, and its possible development, it was again suggested that Lord Kitchener should be in Egypt "when the moral effect was being felt."

The Army Council's "approval" was, of course, a purely military pronouncement, and the final decision was only reached after the presentation of Kitchener's report to the Cabinet. Indeed, at this time there was distinct divergence of opinion in the Cabinet, and Lord Curzon, in a vigorous memorandum, was emphasising the lamentable losses and grave political conditions, which he believed to be irreparable, from evacuation.

Kitchener's answer was prompt and precise:

According to the plans for evacuation [he said], it will be a fortnight at least before definite evacuation is proceeding on the Peninsula. I feel very strongly that I should be back in England, as time is passing and I can do no good here. I have arranged with McMahon to quiet the effect in Egypt as far as possible. If necessary, I could go out again. My presence here calls attention to what is going on.

Again urging, in another telegram, that every possible step should be taken to send troops to Egypt over and above those detailed to Salonika—"there will be little or no time to spare"—Kitchener announced his intention of leaving at once for England *via* Marseilles, "as time is pressing," and on Wednesday, November 24, the *Dartmouth* sailed.

The same afternoon a wireless message was received that the King of Italy was most anxious to see

Lord Kitchener, and that the British Government wished him to accept the invitation. The journey was therefore broken at Naples; at Rome Kitchener invested General Porro, Chief of the Italian General Staff, with the G.C.M.G., and calls were paid on Signor Salandra, the Prime Minister, and other notabilities. Arrived at Udine, he presented General Cadorna, the Italian Commander-in-Chief, with the G.C.B.; the battle-field round Gorizia was visited; and in the evening Kitchener, in a little roadside villa, dined *tête-à-tête* with the King of Italy, who decorated him with the Grand Cordon of St. Maurice and St. Lazarus. On November 30 he arrived in London, signed the register at the wedding of the Prime Minister's daughter, tendered his resignation to her father, which was promptly and even peremptorily refused, and resumed his seat at the War Office.

He had now to advise the Cabinet finally as to whether we should retain or relinquish our foothold in the Dardanelles. At the outset he himself had to enter his protest against the Dardanelles Expedition, because all military experience went to discourage any hope of successful naval action unsupported by military troops, and he had then no troops to offer. Nor had he been easily convinced by Mr. Churchill's testimony as to the capacities of the *Queen Elizabeth,* one of a class of battleships then lately completed, and possessed of unprecedented and unheard-of fighting powers. It would seem that the *Queen Elizabeth* had but to let off her guns for the walls of the Gallipoli Jericho to fall down flat. He was assured by those who ought to know that a project which seemed doomed to failure on all previous calculation was under new conditions quite practicable.

The certified potentialities of the great new battleship overrode conclusions dictated by history. If this naval puissance were admitted, Mr. Churchill's scheme was not only highly opportune, but could claim all political merit. Kitchener, once committed to grips with an Oriental enemy, was exceedingly unwilling to be called off from his hold. When Keyes's proposal—backed though it was by Admiral Wemyss, who succeeded Admiral De Robeck in November—was shelved, he pressed for the Ayas Bay project as a means at once of punishing the Turks, defending Egypt, and impressing the Moslem world. After the adverse decision of the two Governments he was convinced that military consideration offered no choice other than evacuation, and his bitter draught was only sweetened by the belief that the losses would be very much lighter than he had been led, before personal inspection, to expect. To remain at Gallipoli, he told the Cabinet, was to play a game of chance with the opponents holding all the high cards. If, on political grounds, it was still considered necessary to prolong this every soldier would bring to it all the energy and skill at command. But as a soldier he could adduce no military justification for such persistence, and, reluctantly, framed his lips to give the only advice he could honestly tender.

Evacuation having been decided on, the precise method and dates [1] were confided only to the officers

---

[1] In April 1915 Kitchener had to complain to the Cabinet that two of his colleagues had, at one of the meetings of the Munitions Committee, stated the numbers of men then at the front and calculated to be there by August. He urged the vital importance of keeping such information absolutely secret, and feared he would be unable to continue his responsibility if figures were allowed to leak out. The Cabinet then agreed that any figures given to them by Kitchener should never be made known even to confidential committees.

immediately responsible. Discretion does not always lodge with the wives of high political officials as it did with Mrs. Bucket in fiction or Mrs. Gladstone in fact, and absolute secrecy was the only key to even comparative safety. To secrecy, scarcely less than to consummate skill on the spot, was due the astounding success and immunity from hurt which attended the exodus from Gallipoli. Kitchener was at Broome, where he had gone for a few hours, when the message arrived: "Second operation even more successful than the first." He spoke no word as the telegram was handed him, but his eyes were eloquent of a great content. In truth he had occasion for relief. There was overpast the nightmare of a great sacrifice or surrender of noble lives, and the miracle of withdrawal with scarcely a bruise would—at any rate for a time—impress Turkey and the Eastern world as well as any bare success in arms. Nor—now that all was over—did he forget that the adventure to the Dardanelles, politically well conceived, would be far from barren of eventual effect. He saw from the first that a blow at Turkey's heart —even if not immediately fatal—must weaken and might paralyse her activities in the East. He did not live to gauge how far Gallipoli cleared the road to Jerusalem, but he could recognise the real worth of Ian Hamilton's work, and knew that the heroes of the Dardanelles Expedition, thwarted in their main object, had still, like an iron rod, broken the spine of Turkish military power.

APPENDIX TO CHAPTER CXVII

HEADQUARTERS,
DARDANELLES ARMY, M.E.F.
December 20, 1915.

MY DEAR OLD CHIEF—

I wrote to you last week in a natural state of considerable anxiety about our evacuation, but I said that I felt confident of being able to carry it off successfully provided the weather did not play me false, and the Navy could produce the necessary small craft. I never, however, dared to hope that we could possibly meet with the success we did, and none of us can ever be sufficiently grateful to Providence for seeing us through as was done. The weather was absolutely perfect. Two perfectly quiet, calm nights, with no wind, and I am thankful to say a certain amount of cloud to dim the strong moon. This saved the Navy from all anxiety as regards their boats being knocked about, hence we were able to work with complete confidence of success.

The first night of my final stage was of course no trouble, for though we got rid of 10,000 men in each Corps that night, it left us with 10,000 in each to hold the respective areas for the remaining twenty-four hours. What I most feared was a big storm coming on when we were short of strength, so you can imagine how thankful I now feel. I carried out exactly the programme I had always intended, spending the last day but one in making all final arrangements at Suvla—cruising up and down the coast that night in a destroyer—spending my very last day on the peninsula at my beloved ''Anzac,'' and going round for the last time the trenches made by the Division which first landed with us—then the final night on board the *Chatham* with Wemyss.

My last day there was, as I am sure you will believe, really a trying one, as I very much felt leaving the place, and I could see that a great many men did the same, though when I explained it was only to enable us to put in more useful work against the enemy elsewhere, they were I hope satisfied.

You can imagine how anxious we all were on the very last night. Things at Suvla were quiet practically throughout the night, but I was a little disturbed when there was a good deal of firing off and on at "Anzac," at one time almost threatening an attack, but I was thankful that there was very little shelling. The Naval arrangements I may mention were absolutely perfect, and without any hitch of any sort. Boats all came in at the appointed times at their proper places. The last big lot, holding the front trenches all round from the right of "Anzac" to the left of Suvla, were divided into three sections, who gradually withdrew through each other in turn, until very small parties were left covering the actual piers, and they, too, got quickly down on board and left. At times, constant heavy firing kept breaking out round the "Anzac" front, which naturally made me anxious up to the end, as it was impossible to tell how much of this was being opened from the Turks' trenches, or how much the Turks had found out and were following on.

You will probably remember that some months ago I started making several really big tunnels under the enemy's positions, with the idea of sapping forward and having some very big blow-ups under more than one of their main trenches. We had caused a tunnel under the most important of these, viz. Russell's Top, to be pushed on rapidly during the last fortnight, and this we charged with several hundred pounds of ammonal in three separate mines, which were ordered to be exploded at intervals of two minutes. When the rear party were well away, these were fired with complete success, a volcanic eruption being seen for miles around, and quite competing on a small scale with Vesuvius! The result was wonderful, in that the whole of the Turks, evidently anticipating a big attack, lined their trenches, and for about an hour continued to fire away as fast as they could possibly load; meanwhile our men were well down on their way to the beach in comfort.

The results of this and many other ruses which were tried were so satisfactory that it is hard to believe that we got away the two Army Corps with only two men wounded! It really is almost incredible, for the Turks must have observed us for a week beforehand making preparations, for though we naturally tried all we could to conceal these, yet the nights were fairly light, and it was impossible to hide everything. I must say the men were perfectly wonderful, and no praise can be too high for the way they entered into it as an adventure quite after their own hearts, and this not only applies to my Australians and New Zealanders, but I know that the troops on my left were just the same. There was an absolute struggle with the men insisting to be with the final rearguard party, and they were most indignant on being told that they must get on, and that the rearguard was following, as each man seemed to claim that it was his special right to be with it to the very end. With a spirit like this, you will realise how easy matters were.

We wrapped up all the men's feet in old sacking and blankets, so that there was not a sound made as they left the trenches. In a few places most cunning devices had been made by fastening a rifle on to the parapet, and firing it by a weight arranged with a tin full of water and a hole bored in it, which could be timed to drop and pull the trigger at any given number of minutes after the trenches had been vacated. Several other dodges of the same sort were devised, such as candles burning for an inch or so, and then reaching a firework which exploded with a loud report. The results of them all were evidently satisfactory, for the Turks never seemed to discover that we were off. When the mine was fired, they kept up their continuous fire on our trenches for a good hour after we had actually left the shore, which the last man did at about 4.30 A.M. Later on still they began to bombard our whole (now deserted) position, and at nine o'clock in the morning they seemed to turn every gun they possessed on to the trenches, so it is at all events some satisfaction to know that they have got through and wasted a great deal of ammunition. Our mine must have accounted for a really large number of them, as it spread right into the middle of one of their positions covering two or three trenches.

During the preliminary stage of about a week, we had dribbled off nearly everything of value we possessed, and the last day I went round I could find practically no ordnance or engineer stores left, while we evacuated nearly the whole of our animals, leaving I think fifty only at "Anzac" out of a total of some 6000 between the two Corps. Guns had of course been dribbled off gradually, every battery being reduced, first to a section, and then to a single gun with lots of ammunition for it, and finally single guns were dribbled off. We had 200 guns originally, and of these Suvla got off the whole of their 90, while "Anzac" evacuated 100 of their total of 107, the seven remaining being completely blown to pieces.

I am bound to confess that Suvla managed their evacuation in *material* better than we did at "Anzac," though, as you will remember, their facilities were very much greater, for they have more piers, and their transports could stand right in close to the piers in Suvla Bay, while at "Anzac" the lighters have to go a long way out to sea. Also, I must confess that Suvla got a real flying start! You will remember that we had orders to commence evacuating, when both Corps started making preliminary arrangements—then came an idea of the possibility of our not going, when I had to tell both Corps to sit tight for a bit, and in fact to put in more supplies for themselves. Suvla was not able to take much action on this, having got rid of much stuff, and as it so happens this has turned out all right. Byng organised the destruction of the stores he left behind very well indeed, and it was a wonderful sight to see at the last moment, as if by a wave of the magician's wand, the whole of his surplus stores suddenly bursting into flame, and forming huge bonfires. At "Anzac," I am sorry to say, this had not been done to the same extent, and the enemy must have got a certain amount of food, though nothing that would last them for more than a few days, and of course not of any great value.

Yesterday afternoon, to take the Turks' attention off the Northern zone, I asked Davies to organise a fairly big attack on the Turks' trenches at Helles, where we had a tremendous bombardment by the Navy, which I think created a most successful diversion, for three or four monitors and two cruisers were down there, hammering in as hard as they were worth with their big guns, and attracting the whole attention of the peninsula to them. The attacks made were quite successful, and Davies took two or three Turkish trenches.

It may be that we got away just about the right time, for when I was going round "Anzac" yesterday, the Turks suddenly opened on us with new, very big howitzers, firing some excellently-made, clean-cut, steel shells of about ten inches in diameter. It is quite possible that these were the Austrian howitzers which we had heard about, and that they were just registering our positions before starting a big bombardment. In the course of about an hour they put in fifty of these big shells along the trenches, and though I believe no one was hurt, yet they seemed to fall all round, and I got covered with mud from one that came a bit nearer than usual.

To show how little the Turks suspected our going, deserters came in even up to the very night before we left, and the tremendous shelling they gave directly we had gone looked as if they could hardly believe we had cleared out. When you come to think that in a great many places our trenches are not more than twenty-five yards apart, it certainly is a wonderful credit to the men that they should have been able to slip away as they did, and I think shows a very high state of discipline which is altogether praiseworthy. You can imagine what a weight seems to have rolled off my shoulders, when I got back here early this morning, and realised the astoundingly good fortune we had had, when a piece of bad fortune might have resulted in terribly heavy losses.

It is not, too, as if the Turks had reduced their numbers in front of us, for we calculate that in the trenches facing the "Anzac" and Suvla Corps, with their supports and purely local reserves, there were approximately 80,000 Turks and a great many guns of all calibres, and I should imagine the higher German officers on the spot will come in for some well-deserved abuse when it is known that they have allowed us to slip away from such a difficult position through what one might call the narrowest possible of bottle-necks (viz. one or two temporary piers) without being able to do us any damage. It was extraordinary, too, that they had not the enterprise to push forward at once to find out the situation themselves, instead of allowing the whole of their heavy and light artillery to carry out a continuous, organised bombardment as they did on our evacuated position.

Our intentions, too, should have been obvious to them, looking down as they do from the hills around on practically all our movements. As you know, not a single lighter can leave our beaches without being seen, and though we of course confined movements to the night as much as possible, yet a certain amount of craft was necessarily seen moving about in the daytime. Curiously enough, they seem all along to have anticipated that we were making arrangements for an attack, and not a retirement. The attack we did carry out on their position at Helles, about eight hours before we commenced the withdrawal from the other areas, may perhaps have deceived them more than I thought probable, as we know that they at once reinforced down there when the attack began.

You know how I have all along hated the idea of leaving "Anzac," and all the wonderful work done there by my men, but it is at all events some consolation to realise we have been able to do this without any loss whatever, while we certainly must have inflicted a considerable amount on the Turks, even if only in the explosion of the mines at Russell's Top, which as I have said were right under several of their trenches, which were evidently fully manned at the time, as immediately to right and left rolls of musketry fire were opened from men apparently at quite close intervals, so it is reasonable to suppose that they were manned like this throughout.

Then, again, I have just had reports that late this afternoon large numbers of Turks came swarming over, seeing I suppose what loot they could get hold of that had been left behind, when the cruisers and destroyers, who had of course remained off the coast, put heavy fire into them, and say they accounted for large numbers.

Now I feel that the only thing I want at the present moment is a really long sleep, as I have not had more than an hour in the last forty-eight.

Before closing, I should just like to mention that the whole of the success of this operation is due entirely to the Corps Commanders—Byng and Godley—and their staffs, and very much to Wemyss and the Navy, who made all arrangements most excellently, and left me really little or nothing to do beyond perhaps a suggestion here or a word of encouragement there during my practically daily visits to their positions, while the co-operation of Davies in his attack from Helles was as whole-hearted as you would expect.

Aspinall, who has practically represented my General Staff throughout all this, and MacMunn, who is now my D.A. and Q.M.G., have both played up capitally, and have done magnificently, relieving me of all worry.

Though I was, as you know, determined to do my very best to see this thing through successfully for its own sake and that of my troops, yet I have also felt very much indeed about you all the time, my dear old Chief. I quite realised that had we made a failure of it, and had there been anything like some sensational losses, there would have been a great outcry at Home, and I feared there might be people who would have begun to abuse even you for the Dardanelles policy, and I was determined that this should not be the case as far as lay in my power.

Monro has been very good in giving me an absolutely free hand—indeed I feel he has shown his confidence in me —which I very much appreciate—by the generous way in which he has allowed me to run my own show without interference.

I do not know what policy will eventually be decided on about Helles. I have reinforced there by three howitzer batteries and two Naval 4-inch guns, and if they will only really dig like my men will, I think they can ensure being all right, but the ground there is not nearly so easy as I had at "Anzac," and they do not seem to get at it in the same way.

I asked Monro to send you a telegram, which I hope you will have received yesterday, suggesting that the Australian and New Zealand Governments should be at once informed of the details regarding our withdrawal here, as otherwise I was so afraid that the German wireless would at once produce some sensational story that we have been driven into the sea, which would alarm people out there horribly, unless they knew the truth.

P.S. (21*st*).—More than ever do I realise how entirely we have to thank Providence for evacuating successfully as we have done. A real south-westerly gale sprang up at about 1 A.M. to-day. Had this been 24 hours earlier, it would probably have caught us with some six to eight thousand men still ashore, when getting off would have been extremely difficult. I had given orders that once embarkation had actually started on the final night, it was to be continued whatever happened, the men if necessary having to wade out up to their necks to be hauled into boats, but this would of course have entailed not only considerable loss at the time, but so much delay that we could not possibly have got through everything before daylight, when we should have come in for a bad time of it. (It is indeed wonderful to look back on, and I trust I am sufficiently thankful.)

To emphasise this, I may mention that my original plans were to have had the final night of evacuation on 20th/21st, and it was only about ten days ago that I found the Navy could manage to guarantee the collection of the necessary small craft 24 hours earlier than we originally thought, when I put forward the date by one day, which as you see has been of such wonderful and unforeseen consequence—though of course the putting it forward was entirely in view of taking advantage of the weather, which we know must necessarily get worse daily at this time of the year.

Where I got hit on the head in May last has been rather bothering me lately, but as I have not had the time to have it looked to, I left it alone. Now, however, that we are clear for a bit, I have got the doctor to have a dig at it, with the result that he has extracted a long piece of the casing of a bullet, which it is just as well to have got rid of, and I am sure it will not give me any more trouble now.

W. R. B.

CHAPTER CXVIII

SUCH were Kitchener's cares through 1915 in the East. To return to Sir John French on the Western front: an immediate consideration in the early spring was the entrance into his line of the Kitchener Armies. Kitchener had disfavoured the thrusting of Territorial battalions into Regular divisions, and his objection was even more deeply rooted with respect to the New Armies. He had been assured that any important alteration in the size of the divisions would lead to serious difficulties, and he felt that their diffusion in the cadres of the Standing Army might not give fair play to the quality of the men who had flocked to the Colours, and whose *esprit de corps* was already a property to conjure with. Kitchener alone among soldiers had believed it possible to create in war time—from the manhood of an unmilitary nation—large bodies of new troops fit to meet and beat the finest combatants of the Continent. He backed his own opinion with complete faith in his own judgement, and the Armies with which his name will be always identified more than justified his confidence. Under his instructions an official intimation—covered by a friendly letter—was sent to Sir John that the New Armies would be incorporated by divisions in the Armies in France. The Commander-in-Chief wrote in no less friendly terms on January 23:

> GENERAL HEADQUARTERS,
> BRITISH ARMY IN THE FIELD,
> *January 23, 1915.*
>
> MY DEAR KITCHENER— I have been away at French Headquarters arranging plans with Joffre, and received your letter of January 20 when I returned last night. The "official" came at the same time under separate cover.
>
> I think we can arrange the organisation of the Army in the Field on the lines laid down by the Army Council, and I will do all I can to give effect to their views.
>
> I am very glad that official sanction has been given in this letter to a defined method of amalgamating the New with the existing Army in the Field, and I think there ought to be no difficulty in carrying it into effect.
>
> I have agreed with Joffre—
>
> 1. To relieve his Ninth and Twentieth Corps[1] as soon as reinforcements from home permit me to do so, and he on his part has agreed then to take over the line from La Bassée to the north, now occupied by the First Corps.
>
> 2. That he will sanction my making any arrangement I can with the King of the Belgians for the co-operation of the Belgian Army with the British Forces.
>
> 3. That after the above reliefs have taken place he will still leave one Active and one Territorial Division, as well as those troops now at Nieuport, to assist in the northern operations, whether in attack or defence.
>
> I will send an official answer to the War Office letter of January 20 to-morrow, and I will add a request that I may be given some idea at what date I may expect to receive the first troops of the New Army. This is not because I want to press for them, but that, in forming plans for the future,

---

[1] The French Ninth and Twentieth Corps had remained on the Ypres front ever since they relieved our troops at the end of the first battle near that town of ill omen. This movement was part of the process of sorting out the armies which has already been mentioned as necessary.

I may have some distinct idea as to when I may expect to receive fresh reinforcements.

My telegrams will have informed you of the good work which has been done by our aeroplanes lately. They have also been very active in reconnaissance in the last two days, as the weather has been fairly bright and favourable.

There is no particular development in our front, but I think all the enemy's units have been strengthened by the influx of the 1914 Class. Prisoners are unanimous in saying that the strength of their companies has been raised, and is now from 180 to 200.

This would bring the Corps up to about what I thought, viz. from 75 to 80 per cent of their war establishment. All reports indicate a lack of officers.

The country is under water again, but colder and harder weather seems to be setting in to-night.

A kind of epidemic of influenza seems to have set in. A number of my Staff are down with it, including Murray, Lambton, Brooke, and Huguet.

The epidemic of influenza necessitated a change in Sir John's Headquarters Staff. Sir Archibald Murray's strength had been overtaxed during the retreat from Mons, and his health temporarily gave way. A little later he was able to join the General Staff at the War Office, and his place as Chief of the Staff in France was filled by Sir William Robertson, whose energy in supplying the troops in the hectic days of August and September 1914 had won for him their complete confidence—and something more.

Of greater importance was a change in the constitution of the Army itself. The reinforcements which Kitchener was steadily pouring in had rendered necessary a recasting of the Higher Commands, and to Sir Douglas Haig and Sir Horace Smith-Dorrien were assigned the leadership of the First and Second Armies now formed in the field.

On February 1 Sir John wired to Kitchener: "All very quiet. Signs of a possible concentration on this part of the line. Sincerely hope that there will be no alteration in the arrangements for troops coming out, as this would upset Joffre's and my plans."

Kitchener, who saw with Sir John's eyes the paramount importance of the Western front, answered the same day:

I have had a talk with Churchill. If the orders for the movement of troops to France are in any way altered, I will let you know immediately, and unless therefore you hear from me to the contrary you may take it that existing arrangements stand. I have been unable to see the Prime Minister this morning, but I do not intend to make any change in the arrangements made with you. You are aware that we are sending the First Canadian Division on the 8th, and that other troops follow, of which details later. You refer to your joint plans with Joffre, and I am rather puzzled as to what these plans exactly are. I gather that Joffre will relieve only one of your corps on your right, which is now holding about 6½ miles of front from Guinchy to Neuve Chapelle, and that on relief of this corps you intend to take over all the trenches from Wytschaete to Old Fort near Dixmude. If this is your plan, your new line will be about 40 miles long, and on such a long line—including the rather dangerous salient of Ypres—will you not be rather extended? Please let me know whether I have correctly stated your plan; also please say when the projected changes take place, and how soon you expect them to be completed.

This telegram did not exactly represent Sir John's mental evolutions, but he was anxious—and Kitchener cordially agreed to his wish—to lock up his secret for the moment. Joffre was eager to take all advantage of the temporary transfer of large enemy forces from West to East. The Germans were in possession of large stretches of French territory:[1] no soldier of France, with superior forces in hand, could passively accept such insult. Russia, too, was being hard pressed and was appealing to the French Commander-in-Chief to do all—and more than all— he could to draw the Germans away from the East. In the lurid light of bitter experience of attacks upon entrenched positions, it were easy to preach the wisdom of waiting until more troops, more guns, and more shells had been accumulated. But trench warfare was foreign to the Western military world, and until every weapon had been tried Joffre could not fold his hands and stand still while the heart of his country was exposed to a deadly blow, while an Ally was being sorely bruised, and while his compatriots in thousands were at the mercy of a brutal enemy.

The French General was determined to be up and doing. He proposed that the British should relieve most of his troops in Flanders; that Foch, who commanded the French Armies in the north, should use these troops to reinforce the French on our right—between La Bassée Canal and Arras— and aim for the important Vimy Ridge; the British troops were to attack concurrently north of La Bassée Canal, and another French inroad was to be made in Champagne to the east of Rheims.

Joffre was *de facto* Generalissimo on the Western

[1] Near Noyon, as M. Clemenceau lost no opportunity of impressing upon his countrymen, they were within sixty miles of Paris. A comparatively short advance by the enemy on this part of the front might jeopardise the whole Allied position in the West.

front. It was he who formulated the Allied plans, on broad lines, and Sir John, agreeably with his early instructions, lent him all possible support. The exact extent of front which the latter was to take over depended upon the arrival of reinforcements from England. When the relief of the French was effected, they handsomely retained the northern half of the Ypres salient, and Kitchener's fears as to an undue prolongation of our line were allayed.

By the middle of February Sir John had made his arrangements for a purely British and local manœuvre to precede the concerted attacks. His Army, except when he led it from the Marne to the Aisne, had been thrown on the defensive, with little experience of assaulting entrenched lines. The Commander thought, and thought wisely, that while he was awaiting the incoming divisions, he would give the troops in the field an opportunity for which they were hungering, and a close insight into the grim realities of the new warfare. Sir Douglas Haig was therefore instructed to prepare for the battle of Neuve Chapelle. Every gun which could be spared from the remainder of the front, and every round of accumulated ammunition, was put in his hand. Although the provision of ammunition for Neuve Chapelle exceeded the total expended in South Africa, it was less a question of inflicting any decisive defeat than of gaining valuable elbow-room for later battles. Again, it were easy now to mock at the notion that an attack on a front of some 2000 yards might result in the perforation of a line which extended from the North Sea to Switzerland. But the public remembered how the tables had been turned at the battle of the Marne, and hopes ran high that a spring offensive would drive the Germans from France and Belgium, and out of the war. The first news of Neuve Chapelle therefore aroused unwarranted optimism, and the later knowledge of the meagre results actually attained induced corresponding depression. On March 10 the village and some 2000 yards of German trenches were carried by assault, but the enemy's counter-attacks soon arrested further progress, and on the third day lack of gun ammunition brought the operations to a too speedy close.

CHAPTER CXIX

At Neuve Chapelle was first essayed the system of intense bombardment followed by infantry assault which for the next three years marked the battles on the Western front. The French were much impressed by it; they thought now that, given an adequate number of guns and an ample supply of shells, much would be possible that had hitherto seemed impossible, and they modelled their great autumn campaign of 1915 upon our experiences in this battle.

Neuve Chapelle was very costly in men, but the Twenty-eighth Regular Division and the First Canadian Division were by now afoot, and our front could be gradually extended northwards into the Ypres salient. On March 10—the day of Neuve Chapelle—Kitchener wired to Sir John:

> A very satisfactory report of the entraining and departure of the North Midland Division has been received, and credit attaches to the troops concerned. Please express the gratification which this report has given me, and say I have no doubt that the reputation with which it started will be maintained by the division which is the first of the Territorial divisions to go to France as a complete unit.

Two days later he could say that the number of Territorial battalions sent out separately would be increased to twenty-three; but he must break to Sir John that the Twenty-ninth Division would be earmarked for service in the Near East. Sir John was naturally heartened by the arrival, actual and prospective, of reinforcements. He refused to be depressed by the abrupt term which he had to set to the battle of Neuve Chapelle, and with fine optimism he took a rose-coloured view of a further attack, the details of which he was weaving with Joffre, and which he wished to discuss orally with Kitchener. He wrote on April 8:

> I am sending another despatch by the Prince of Wales, which includes a report on Neuve Chapelle and Saint Eloi —and other operations. I sent Maxwell home to you two days ago, and he has no doubt told you all about the . . . guns and their ammunition, and has talked to you about Calais, Dunkirk, etc. . . . Our joint plans will be fully matured by the end of this week. May I appear at your breakfast-table at 8.30 A.M. on Wednesday the 14th? I can get over late on Tuesday. I am telling the Prince of Wales to tell the King I can go to see him on Wednesday if he wishes to see me, but I have asked him to tell no one that I am coming, and I am sure you will also keep my secret. I don't want the P.M., or Winston, or any one but you and the King to know I am in London. I will bring maps and copious notes and tell you everything, but I don't want to have anything in writing. I am in strong hopes of a great advance. I hope you agree in all this. A wire in answer will do: put "Yes" or "No."

Kitchener's answer was a cordial "Yes," and after a long conversation preceded by a *tête-à-tête* breakfast the War Secretary was able to tell the Prime Minister that the Commander-in-Chief would have sufficient ammunition for the next forward movement in which his troops would be engaged.[1]

[1] Four and a half years later Lord French professed himself unable to reconcile this message with a conversation in which, as he suggested, there was no reference to the subject of ammunition. The difficulty in Lord French's mind may have been due to a confusion of dates—he alluded in his

Sir John returned to France and proceeded apace with his preparations for supporting Foch, who was moving the troops relieved by us on the Ypres front southwards to Arras. To divert the enemy's attentions from the French General, as well as for strategic purpose, Sir John sought to secure Hill 60, one of the dominant features on the southern side of the Ypres salient.

On April 19 he telegraphed: "Successful action begun on the evening of the 17th by the Fifth Division of the Second Army culminated last night in the capture and occupation of Hill 60. Hill 60 was lost by the French in December, and dominates the country to the north and north-west." The next day's message was as happy: "The Second Army Commander thinks hold on Hill 60 quite secure. Situation there was normal. Spirit of the troops magnificent, including 9th London Regiment Territorials. Casualties, 50 officers, 1500 rank and file. German losses, 2500 to 3000."

The news was unexpectedly good and public hopes unduly soared. The War Minister voiced the general feeling in telegraphing to the Commander-in-Chief: "This brilliant feat of arms clearly shows what our men are made of. I congratulate heartily

---

book to a conference at York House on March 31 when he came over somewhat unexpectedly—or to an omission in his Diary on which he based himself for his recollection. Otherwise it would seem unlikely that during a conversation in which he wished to tell Kitchener "everything" the momentous matter of ammunition should not have been mentioned. And, referring to the meeting of the 31st, Sir John wrote to Kitchener three days later:

"It was a great comfort and help to me to have a quiet talk with you like our meeting on Wednesday morning. I have always been most anxious to keep you in close touch with everything; but writing is so difficult and unsatisfactory when dealing with a big business like this, and telegraphing is worse. I can always run over to London for a few hours, so long as things are quiet; in about ten or twelve days our joint plans—self, Foch, and Joffre—and arrangements should be complete, and I should like to lay them all before you one morning *early* (whilst we are fresh!), without any one knowing—just like last Wednesday."

all concerned." But the public—unlike Kitchener—had not yet adjusted its mind to the proportion of a world-war, and could not yet regard as a mere enterprise an action as expensive in casualties as the battle of Paardeberg. The armchair critics were counting upon the rolling-up of the whole German position in the Ypres salient when untoward news arrived, and on the 21st Sir John reported: "Violent and continual counter-attacks on Hill 60 have caused us much further loss." Much confused fighting followed, and the position on the Hill was for some days shrouded in uncertainty; and when the veil lifted and disclosed the Germans again in possession, there was much indignation at the alleged concealment of bad news. The Press made scant allowance for the egregious difficulty of ascertaining the precise circumstances of our troops when those circumstances were hourly shifting. The communication trenches were few, and such as had been dug were little better than channels for the liquid mud of Flanders. Shellfire constantly barred all approach to the front line in daylight, and continually broke telephone communication. Kitchener knew nothing more, and the Commander-in-Chief in France very little more, about the happenings on Hill 70 than was communicated to the public.

CHAPTER CXX

But public resentment at the supposed suppression of news was quickly silenced in anxiety as to a still graver matter. The Germans ever since Neuve Chapelle had flung accusations against us of using asphyxiating gases. The sole basis for this astounding lie was the temporarily stupefying effect of our lyddite fumes, an effect perfectly well known before the war; but the Germans seized upon this fact to justify before the world the wholesale employment of poison gas which they had for long been sedulously compounding. On April 22 they discharged great waves of the poisonous stuff from cylinders, mainly against the Northern or French portion of the Allied position in the Ypres salient. The French troops in this quarter had been recently weakened by withdrawals—in accordance with Joffre's plans—for an offensive farther south, and those upon whom this barbarous attack fell were to a large extent coloured troops, who were horror-struck by the sight and overwhelmed by the fumes of the great rolling greenish clouds of mephitic vapour which spread death and torture in their ranks. The flank of the First Canadian Division, which had just gone up into the line—on the immediate right of the French—was completely exposed, and that a great disaster was averted is due to the splendid gallantry of the soldiers of Canada, under unthinkably hideous conditions. Sir John on April 24 described to Kitchener the opening events of this, the second battle of Ypres:

As my telegrams have told you, the situation north-east of Ypres has become very troublesome. At 9 P.M. on Thursday the 22nd I got a message from Smith-Dorrien to say that the left flank of the Canadian Division had become exposed, as the French troops between Steenstraate and Langemarck had been driven out of their trenches, which the Germans had occupied. The various accounts which we received were much involved by all kinds of contradictory reports; but it subsequently transpired that the Germans had devised a means of blowing asphyxiating gas into the French trenches, which had the effect of scaring and stupefying their whole line. Whatever the cause may have been they appeared to have abandoned their trenches and bolted, carrying the gunners with them, and leaving some thirty field and heavy guns and four of our own 4·7 guns (which were in rear of their right flank) in the hands of the Germans.

The Canadians held their ground until the morning, although subjected to a heavy enfilade fire during the night from the Germans who had occupied the abandoned French trenches. In the morning they threw back their left, although they would have remained it they had been allowed to do so.

During the night of the 22nd-23rd one of the Canadian brigades which had been in support was moved to a flank, recaptured the four guns which had been lost, got touch with the men holding the trenches on their right, and, after great difficulty, established connection with some French Zouaves on their left, who, in their turn, carried on the line west to the Canal. All the other French troops had taken shelter on the west side of the Canal, which they were lining from the left of the Zouaves as far as Lizerne; but the Germans, who had seized and held the bridge at Steenstraate, turned them out of Lizerne, and they formed a line with the Belgian right to the west of that place.

Handwritten note at top: Six months previous - British secret service men in Germany reported the manufacture of this gas - and how they would use it. The W.O in London did nothing!

Handwritten note in left margin: 40,000 ...... of them hospital gas cases. / 16,000 " " deaths from gas. / 5,000 "

POISON GAS

During yesterday, the 23rd, Smith-Dorrien put in some battalions of the Fifth Corps between the Canadians and the Zouaves, and the whole line succeeded in driving the Germans back about three-quarters of a mile; but, as the French did nothing all day yesterday to support this movement from the west of the Canal, very little progress could be made towards regaining the old line of trenches.

During yesterday Foch ordered down 3 batteries of artillery and 2 battalions from Nieuport, and a fresh division from St. Pól (west of Arras). These troops only arrived in support of the French to the west of the Canal about noon to-day; and Foch tells me this afternoon that they have turned the Germans out of Lizerne, and are now attacking Steenstraate and along the Canal to the south of it. Foch has ordered another division up from west of Arras which arrives at daybreak to-morrow to support the French troops on the Canal. I have also got all the First Cavalry Corps out in that area, to be ready to support them if necessary, and have sent reserves from other parts of the line to help Smith-Dorrien, who has not been able to make any progress to speak of to-day.

The Canadians also felt the effect of this asphyxiating gas, but stood their ground. They have behaved splendidly throughout.

Although the gas, no doubt, had something to do with the panic, this would never have happened if the French had not weakened their line a great deal too much; and it was in the fear of something of this kind that I was so averse to relieving their Ninth and Twentieth Corps until I was stronger.

I am afraid this will delay what I told you about by several days.

The most authentic account of how these gases are used is as follows:

"A prisoner of the 233rd R. Rgt., taken to-day, states that the gas is contained in metal cylinders, about 4 feet long, which are sunk in the earth at the bottom of a trench.

When required for use, pipes are attached to the cylinders, and the nozzles project over the parapet. At a given signal the taps are turned on, and the gas, which is of a yellowish colour (probably chlorine), drifts in clouds down the wind over the opposite trenches. The operators, who attend to the apparatus, wear rubber garments with special respirators. The rest of the troops are provided with cotton mouth-pads which are wetted with a certain solution (probably bicarbonate of soda)."

Further reports tell me that this attack was intended for the 20th but postponed to the 22nd as the wind was wrong before.

My latest news this evening is that the French have retaken the village and bridge of Steenstraate.—Yours truly,

(Signed) J. W. FRENCH.

If things quiet down I should like to go over again for a few hours about Wednesday or Thursday, and have breakfast with you. But I won't propose it now, as until things are more settled I can't get away for a moment.

Kitchener at once telegraphed to congratulate the Canadians on their dauntless bravery, and added to Sir John:

The use of asphyxiating gases is, as you are aware, contrary to the rules and usages of war. Before, therefore, we fall to the level of the degraded Germans I must submit the matter to the Government, and in the meanwhile should be glad if you could send any specimen or diagnosis of the material used; and I am also having the matter fully gone into in our laboratories and by experts in this country. These methods show to what depth of infamy our enemies will go in order to supplement their want of courage in facing our troops.

Our most eminent chemist was immediately invited to devise an antidote to the German poison, and within thirty-six hours Kitchener had sent Mr. John

Haldane and Professor Baker to investigate the outrage on the spot. Sir John, backed by Joffre, declared that, if he was to preserve the *moral* of our troops, there was no alternative but to turn the enemy's lethal weapon against himself. Kitchener was emphatic that Sir John's judgement must be upheld; and the Government—regretfully but instantly—gave orders for the manufacture of poison gas. At this second battle of Ypres the enemy so far scored as to catch both British and French unprepared for his evil stratagem, and thereout sucked no small advantage. But in the end he had good reason to regret his recourse to a devilish device, for eventually the British beat him hollow both in the effective use of gas in the attack, and in the efficacy of self-protective measures; whereupon, with sublime cynicism, the Germans pronounced for the abolition of gas as a weapon of war.

It was many days before the crisis at Ypres was over; many troops intended for the major operations and a large slice of our store of shell had to be enlisted to close the road to Calais, which the Germans once more threatened. While the battle was swaying, Sir Horace Smith-Dorrien was replaced in the command of the Second Army by Sir Herbert Plumer; and it became necessary to postpone and somewhat to modify the Anglo-French offensive which Sir John and Foch had contemplated for early May. On May 2 Sir John wrote:

> I was at Ypres with Plumer for some time yesterday: a great deal of shelling was going on, but the enemy has not attempted any other form of attack since April 29. I discussed the whole situation with him. . . . It has become necessary to retire our forward line. This operation is

now in progress, and the new line will have the effect of retiring the East end of the salient about two thousand five hundred yards to the West. Otherwise all our trenches remain as before. . . . No other course is possible for us. Although they [the French] moved three divisions up here from Arras, they have done very little with them beyond reestablishing the line North of Ypres and West of the canal and pushing the enemy back about a mile to the North on the East of the canal. I think when their troops lost their trenches in the first instance they did not know the British troops would be able to make so firm a stand. . . . The only consolation we have lies in the enormous losses the enemy have suffered. All reports go to confirm this, and my opinion is that their offensive in this part of the theatre has now been abandoned. Of course we cannot be certain of anything, but this is what I think. I was with Foch some time this morning, and am now making all arrangements for the *big* operation. But I have spoken very seriously to him about recent events, and have warned him that if his part of the line to the North of us is in my opinion not yet sufficiently strong (with a good deal to spare in view of possible gas annoyances), I shall abandon my support of him in the big business and reinforce my left. . . .

I would rather say nothing to you now about the big business, but if things remain quiet I suggest going over as late as I can on Wednesday, and going to breakfast with you on *Thursday morning at 8.30*, when I can tell you everything. I can then be back here by five that afternoon, which will do quite well.

If you agree please wire "Yes" as before on receipt of this. And please keep it secret from every one. . . . Secrecy is of the utmost importance. The ammunition will be all right.

P.S.—There are many other things it is very necessary I should see you personally about. . . . It has been necessary to make a good many changes in our plans owing to what has happened. There will be very little delay, however.

CHAPTER CXXI

SIR JOHN, undeterred by the drain on his resources during his recent struggle, was determined to adhere, on its broad lines, to his main plan. "The ammunition will be all right," he had told Kitchener on May 2; he knew his men to be in as high fettle as ever; he was assured as to the safety of his left flank. He was with Kitchener in London on the eve of the engagement, returning to his Headquarters just in time for the actual fight. In the early morning of May 9 Sir John opened fire at Festubert, while Foch attacked on the La Bassée—Arras front. It was quickly and unhappily evident that Sir John would be unable to make good the substantial support he had so manfully intended to lend. He could do little except employ and destroy a considerable number of Germans, and capture—at sad cost to himself— some not very important trenches. If Sir John was disappointed at Festubert, Foch was baulked of his ardent desire to rush the Vimy Ridge, and his movements were as costly and as devoid of immediate material advantage.

Sir John, for once despondent in spirits, descended from the Church tower whence he had watched the abortive move at Festubert and returned to his Headquarters, where he found a telegram which still further depressed his mentality. He was asked to "hold in readiness for despatch to the Dardanelles *via* Marseilles by quickest route 20,000 rounds 18-pounder ammunition and 2000 rounds 4·5-inch howitzer ammunition." He immediately, and very reasonably, telegraphed:

> This morning I commenced an important attack, and the battle is likely to last several days. I am warding off a heavy attack East of Ypres at the same time. In these circumstances I cannot possibly accept the responsibility of reducing the stock of ammunition unless it be immediately replaced from home.

Kitchener at once answered:

> The state of affairs in the Dardanelles renders it absolutely essential that the ammunition which has been ordered should be sent off at once. I will see that it is replaced.

Sir John then sought further relief for his feelings by confiding his necessities to the representative of the *Times* newspaper, and by deputing two members of his personal staff to call on certain gentlemen—within and without the Government—in London and enunciate his requirements. In his book *1914*—a work which he seems to have compiled during his tenure of the command of the Home Forces—the author gave his readers to understand that the shortage of ammunition at Festubert and the order to send the rounds to the Dardanelles spurred him to action which drove the Government of the day from power, leaving only the Prime Minister and the War Secretary in possession of their offices.

The story of the 20,000 rounds is the constantly recurring story of a sudden emergency. It was absolutely necessary that 20,000 rounds of 18-pounder ammunition should reach Ian Hamilton in time for an operation which could not be postponed.

The ammunition was in England, but if started from there would be hopelessly belated. Sir John was therefore asked to give the amount from his reserves, and was assured it would at once be made good. The amount was replaced within twenty-four hours of its being despatched to the Near East; and the replacement was not allowed to interfere by so much as a single round with the quota daily shipped to France.

The failure of Sir John's cherished plan could excite nothing but sympathetic regret, even if it were a little difficult to square it with his lately expressed strong hopes of an advance. But, apart from his own suggestion, it is not easy to trace to the shortage of high explosives, and the momentary displacement on May 10 of some reserve ammunition, the cause of Mr. Asquith's inviting his colleagues a week later to place their portfolios at his disposal.

While Festubert was being fought the first two divisions of the first New Army reached France, and Sir John asked for another division, the Fourteenth, to follow on their heels.

It is essential [he telegraphed on May 15] that pressure on the enemy should be continuous until his line collapses. The present plan now in execution was prepared in conjunction with the French—on the assumption that the first New Army would be sent as promised. The whole Allied plan will be seriously affected if it is held back, and an opportunity missed for important results not likely to recur. Our relations with the French will also be strained.

Sir John was still animated by the hope that the Allies might before midsummer cross the German trenches. Kitchener's reflections were far more chastened; and until the requirements of the Dardanelles campaign could be more definitely formulated, and the training of the first and second New Armies more advanced, he was reluctant to exhaust his reserve without a substantial prospect of a decisive success on the Western front.

I promised [he wrote to Sir John on May 16] that, if the German lines were really broken through, I would send the first New Army to carry on the advance which would then be possible. There is up to the present no certainty that this result will be achieved by the operations now in progress, and until I am assured of it I cannot send the only reserve we have. Moreover, your reports about both gun and rifle ammunition, and our capability of production, show that further troops now sent to the front could not be supplied with all you require, and the ammunition question will be imperilled. The Fourteenth Division have not yet got their gun or rifle ammunition, as in order to meet your requirements we are sending all the ammunition available.

Sir John answered quickly:

Of course, if His Majesty's Government so decide, I have nothing further to say. It is unfortunate that I received official notification that the Fourteenth Division would be despatched on May 18. It was on that understanding that I entered into engagements with the French Commander-in-Chief which may possibly make my position very difficult.

This telegram put the matter in a new light. Kitchener was always scrupulously exact as to the fulfilment of any engagement entered into with our Allies, and he telegraphed:

As you appear to have entered into some arrangement with Joffre regarding the Fourteenth Division, this Division will be sent to you to-morrow, May 18.

CHAPTER CXXII

From this time onwards the New Army Divisions were no sooner trained and equipped than they were shipped to France, a very modest reserve remaining at home to supply, as and when necessary, effective help elsewhere.

By June the Field Force in France had now so grown as to claim the formation of a Third Army, which was entrusted to Sir Charles Monro. Joffre hungered for this New Army [1] to relieve one of his own; he was already counting on the British troops

---

[1] "République Française.

"Armées de l'Est.

Le Commandant en Chef.

"Au Grand Quartier Général,
le   mai 1915.

"Note du Général Joffre, Commandant en Chef les Armées Françaises, pour Son Excellence, Lord Kitchener, Ministre de la Guerre.

"L'entière communauté de vues qui a toujours animé les Alliés fait un devoir au Général Joffre de communiquer à Son Excellence Lord Kitchener son opinion sur la situation militaire actuelle et la solution des problèmes qu'elle a créés.

"Le recul de l'Armée russe, consécutif à l'échec momentané de son offensive, va permettre sans doute aux Austro-Allemands de récupérer, au moins temporairement, un certain nombre de Corps d'Armée qu'ils pourront appliquer sur un autre front; mais il est vraisemblable, que la majeure partie de ces disponibilités sera absorbée par la riposte nécessaire à l'entrée en action de l'Italie.

"La situation des Russes, impuissants d'ici quelque temps à réaliser une offensive décisive, les difficultés de terrain qu'offre le théâtre italien tant que l'Armée italienne n'aura pas pu déboucher dans la plaine, montrent

now streaming into France to carry out an even bolder offensive than he was originally minded to launch. Sir John was no less eager to be astir again, and wrote to Kitchener on June 11:

Sir Arthur Paget has arrived at my Headquarters and has, on your behalf, asked for my views on certain questions regarding future operations. These views I have given to him verbally, and I now inform you in writing what I have said to him.

clairement que, pour l'instant, l'effort principal des Alliés doit être fait en France.

"Les événements d'Arras ont prouvé que, tactiquement, on peut rompre le front allemand, mais qu'il faut pour cela un effort plus puissant encore que celui que nous avons fourni, et qu'il est nécessaire d'attaquer simultanément sur plusieurs points.

"La France, qui a actuellement engagé 2,200,000 hommes sur son front Nord-Est, est à la limite de ses possibilités en hommes. Elle peut maintenir ses Armées à leur chiffre actuel, elle ne peut plus les augmenter.

"La solution de la question est donc entre les mains de l'Angleterre. Si elle nous envoie de nouvelles Armées, nous nous trouverons en situation de faire non seulement un effort anglais et un effort français, mais un effort anglais et deux efforts français simultanés, dans le moment le plus favorable à notre offensive commune, avec de grands moyens.

"Les forces britanniques en France, réinforcées des armées nouvelles, recevront des zones d'opérations en rapport avec leurs effectifs. Elles conserveront d'une part, leur zone actuelle en élargissant leur front sur leurs deux ailes au Nord d'Ypres et au Sud du canal de La Bassee; elles prendraient d'autre part à leur compte la zone au Sud d'Arras jusque vers la Somme. Elles encadreraient ainsi la Xe Armée française qui conserverait le terrain d'attaque qu'elle a organisé.

"L'alternance des troupes britanniques et françaises a d'ailleurs toujours donné les meilleurs résultats.

"L'effort principal des Armées anglaises se porterait entre la gauche de la Xe Armée et le Canal de La Bassee et plus au Nord; il se lierait ainsi à l'attaque française d'Arras.

"Bien entendu, si les Allemands étaient contraints à se replier avant le moment où toutes les forces anglaises se trouveraient en ligne, toutes leurs disponibilités seraient consacrées à l'exploitation du succès, en direction générale d'Anvers et de Bruxelles.

"Nous nous devons à nous-mêmes et nous devons à nos alliés de faire maintenant un grand effort.

"Il est en conséquence, à l'heure présente, de la plus haute importance que l'envoi des Armées nouvelles britanniques se fasse dans le plus court delai, à des dates et dans des conditions déterminées qui permettent l'établissement de Projets d'opérations définitifs, d'accord entre les Commandants des Armées.

"Par la combinaison de nos actions et par leur concordance, j'ai la ferme conviction que notre action sera décisive."

You will have learned from my letter of the 17th ultimo that I am in agreement with General Joffre as to the supreme importance of taking the offensive on the Western front with the maximum available forces at the earliest possible date. Germany has now reduced her forces on the Western front to what she probably considers to be the minimum compatible with reasonable safety, in order to obtain a decision in the Eastern theatre. It is obvious that a defensive attitude on the part of the Allies in the West at the present time will allow Germany to take full advantage of her central position, may conceivably lead to the defeat of the Allies in detail, and must in any case postpone indefinitely a favourable decision of the war. A considerable success in the next few weeks would almost certainly force Germany to put in piecemeal such troops as could be spared from the Russian front; while to await passively the return of enemy reinforcements to the West would allow her to choose her own time and place for striking an effective blow.

The latter course can only be justified if it is proved that it is impossible to break through the enemy's lines. As I have informed you in my letter of the 17th ultimo and on other occasions, the experiences of our own and the French attacks have convinced me that this is not the case, and here again my views are in complete agreement with those of General Joffre. To obtain a decisive success it is necessary to have sufficient men and sufficient ammunition to be able to attack at more than one point and to keep on attacking for a prolonged period. We have not yet had a sufficiency of ammunition for such an operation, and the French have never yet had a sufficient superiority in numbers. In my opinion it rests with us to establish the necessary superiority on the Western front, since the French Army has reached its maximum numerical development, and this superiority should be established at the earliest possible moment.

With regard to the suggestion that I should relieve the six divisions of General Castelnau's Army now between Hebuterne and Chaulnes, I would point out that this front of 35 kilometres is very extended for a force of six divisions. It is possible for the French to hold portions of their front to the south of the British Army very thinly because the whole of their forces and the whole of the communications south of the British area are under one control. They can therefore reinforce rapidly any part of their line which is threatened. I should not be in the same position with regard to the British troops east of Amiens, and it would be necessary for me to provide a reserve of at least two divisions for that part of the front or rely upon the French for reinforcement. By adopting a purely passive attitude I could at most set free four divisions in all as against the eight required for the purpose of taking over the line, and even this would involve considerable risks since I understand that no further reinforcements are likely to arrive for at least a month. Six Territorial divisions are now in the line and some thirty-six Territorial battalions are incorporated in Regular Brigades. Until an adequate system of drafts has been arranged to replace wastage in these formations, it is necessary for me to be prepared to shorten the line they now hold.

Further, I am of opinion that if the necessary additional troops were forthcoming for taking over the line in question, it would be an extravagant and unsound distribution of force to lock up reserves for one section of the front only, in such a way as would be required if British troops held the line East of Amiens. Reserves can only be regarded as satisfactorily disposed when they are readily available for employment wherever needed either for offence or defence. It is equally objectionable to rely for reinforcements upon the French. It would be problematical whether they would be forthcoming when and where required, and if they were, their employment in the midst of British troops must lead to difficulties with regard to command and administration.

In connection with the policy of holding a line thinly which is separated from our main force, I would remind you of the critical situation which arose at Ypres at a time when

RÔLE OF THE BRITISH ARMY

General Joffre had denuded his line on my left in order to obtain troops for his attack at Arras. Since then the French detachments on my left and at Nieuport have been self-supporting as regards reserves.

I understand that it has been suggested that in order to obtain the requisite troops for the relief of General Castelnau's Army we should withdraw from the Ypres salient. I am very strongly opposed to such a withdrawal. It would involve the abandonment of our line as far as the south-west of St. Eloi, and a greater extent of ground than has ever been voluntarily resigned to the enemy. The moral effect upon our own troops and upon the Belgians would be very bad; it would shorten the German line more than our own and thus set free hostile forces for an offensive which would almost certainly follow our withdrawal, and thus make it extremely doubtful whether any troops could be released. Lastly, there is, in my opinion, nothing in the present military situation at Ypres to render this withdrawal necessary. The salient is now hardly more pronounced than that occupied by us at Armentières or by the Germans at Wytschaete. The enemy appears to have adopted a defensive attitude for the time being at Ypres, his artillery is less active, and the losses suffered by our troops are not excessive.

In conclusion, I would urge most strongly that it is very inadvisable that the rôle of the British Army in the Field should be one of passive defence. Such a course can only have a disastrous effect upon the moral and offensive spirit of our troops. The prestige of the British Army must suffer if we remain inactive and watch our French comrades attacking day after day. I would also point out that if I denude myself of reserves and pass to the defensive, I cannot undertake to defend the Channel ports should the need arise. I regard this responsibility as the most weighty which can fall upon any British Commander placed in my position. The only course which in my judgement is compatible both with the requirements of the military situation and the honour of British Arms is that I should co-operate in the proposed French offensive in July with all the resources which His Majesty's Government can place at my disposal.

Kitchener, wishing to be certified as far as possible as to dates, wrote on June 15:

With regard to Paget seeing Joffre, I said if you agreed I had no objection and he might give him my salaams.

I read your letter and explained your points to the Prime Minister.

There is one point of some importance. You will remember when we last met I asked you how long Joffre intended the present offensive at Arras to continue, you told me it would be over about the end of June and that we could then consider the policy of the campaign before taking further steps. At the end of your letter you say, "I should co-operate in the proposed French offensive in July with all the resources H.M. Government can place at my disposal."

Would you explain this, as it is rather upsetting to my calculations?

Sir John, two days later, answering the question, spoke of Foch's attempt on the Vimy Ridge:

My conversation with you referred altogether to the operations which are now proceeding. I then said that if we attained our object, and broke up the German line of defence in front of us, the military situation thus created would decide our future movements. But that if these June operations failed in their object or only partially succeeded then it would be necessary to consider the further policy of the campaign. I told you that I thought if the Vimy heights were not taken and the line broken by the end of June we ought to consider other plans.

My letter of June 11 given to you by Paget did not refer to the present operations, but to certain proposals for action *in July* which Joffre had never communicated to me at all and about which I was entirely in the dark—except certain gossip—until Paget brought me your message.

The big French attack—all along their line—commenced yesterday. They were, as usual, delayed by mist and fog, and I had to start our attack before them as we couldn't delay after the wire was cut.

The French certainly made a good deal of progress yesterday, and the attack of our First Army warded off and contained a big counter-attack which the Germans were directing against their left flank near Loos.

I never like to anticipate anything in this war, but I am not without hope that before the end of the month affairs may wear a different aspect here.

Whatever happens, I propose then—if I can possibly be away for 48 hours—to go over and see you quietly as usual and tell you exactly how we think of proceeding, and discuss the situation.

CHAPTER CXXIII

FIVE days afterwards Sir John made it clear that Foch, however successful he might be towards Vimy, would still be faced by serried German lines, and that therefore they must address themselves to a new campaign. On June 22 he wrote to Kitchener:

Although we have not yet reached the limit of time we gave the French to "break through," I think it is very unlikely that they will succeed in doing so as a result of the present effort. I have seen Foch and know all he thinks, and it is highly probable the French will be in complete possession of the "Vimy Heights" within a week from now; but the Germans have had time to prepare a line farther East.

I have discussed the situation fully with Foch, and we have agreed upon a joint plan of combined action at a later date. I believe this plan has Joffre's concurrence, but I have not yet been told so definitely.

I have therefore ceased offensive operations—except in the case of one or two small pushes to be made at Ypres—for the moment in order to save up ammunition and prepare for the next operation. I think we have a more complete mutual understanding now, and have arrived at the best method of proceeding with a combined offensive.

I am making all arrangements on the existing numerical basis, but I need not say that another three divisions would be of the greatest help.

In order that you may have some official statement to put before the Cabinet, if you so desire, I am sending a letter

CHAP. CXXIII   MR. CHURCHILL'S NOTE   249

generally describing the situation, without going into any detail or giving away plans.

If nothing happens to stop me I propose to breakfast with you on Thursday morning, July 1, and tell you everything.

Please wire one word "Yes" if you agree.

P.S.—Joffre agrees in my proposed method of operation in the new plan—I am going to see him to-morrow.

Here was adumbrated the autumn campaign in which Joffre made himself so powerfully felt in Champagne, when Foch threw himself once more against the Vimy Ridge, and Haig fought the battle of Loos. But while this triple plan was being elaborated, there were heard again high voices insisting that our military effort in 1915 should be made in the East. In the middle of June Mr. Churchill, who was now charged with the care of the Duchy of Lancaster, put out a paper in which he urged in trenchant terms that we should, and must, concentrate our force of arms on the Dardanelles campaign.

There can be no doubt that we now possess the means and the power [so ran his peroration] to take Constantinople before the end of the summer if we act with decision and with a due sense of proportion. The striking down of one of the hostile Empires against which we are contending, and the fall to our arms of one of the most famous capitals in the world, with the results which must flow therefrom, will—conjoined with our other advantages—confer upon us a far-reaching influence among the Allies, and enable us to ensure their indispensable co-operation. Most of all it will react on Russia. It will give the encouragement so sorely needed. It will give the reward so long desired. It will render a service to an Ally unparalleled in the history of nations. It will multiply the resources and open the channel for the re-equipment of the Russian Armies. It will dominate the Balkan situation and cover Italy. It will resound through Asia. Here is the prize and the only prize which lies within reach this year. It can certainly be won without unreasonable expense, and within a comparatively short time. But we must act now, and on a scale which makes speedy success certain.

Sir John had all the courage of his opinion as to Eastern ventures, which he expressed with little circumlocution. To embrace any other military creed than that of mastering the Germans between Switzerland and the sea was, to Sir John, sheer and damnable heresy.

My dear Kitchener [he wrote on June 25]—I have just received your letter enclosing Churchill's Note. I have read it very carefully and will return it to you with my notes and comments. This is only one line to tell you at once that I know him to be wrong and inaccurate in many of his facts, and I regard his conclusion as misleading and unsound.[1]

Joffre was scarcely less definite than Sir John. He apprehended that, any time after the middle of July, the Germans might return exultant from Galicia and put the whole weight of their shoulder against the Western front. If their push—as was not unlikely—were to be made at a point near Paris, any German success would mean a real French disaster. Joffre laid it down as imperative to force the German line farther back, lest so sinister a thing should happen.

The Cabinet had decided to let Ian Hamilton have as many divisions as he calculated necessary to smash the Turks at Gallipoli; Sir John was to have the remaining Territorial and New Army divisions

[1] "The whole proposal is based on 'ifs,'" he wrote in his notes; "no consideration is given to what may happen if the gamble does not come off."

CXXIII REINFORCING EAST AND WEST

as fast as they became ready. This was a compromise, and in war the best compromises work only moderately well. But a commitment to two concurrent campaigns rendered compromise inevitable: Ian Hamilton must not be denied the timely support which he believed would bring him to the brink of victory; Joffre's heart-searching appeals could not be disregarded.

In France, therefore, Monro took over some 17 miles of front—on ground soon to earn an immortal name as the Somme battle-field; and Joffre, turning to account the troops thus relieved, laid himself out for his Champagne operations, with which a joint attack in Artois engineered by Foch and Sir John was to synchronise.

Kitchener, for his part, was not satisfied with replacing the losses in the existing divisions and despatching the divisions of the New Armies the moment they were ready. He must strengthen the force in France by forming into divisions the Territorial battalions already given to Sir John during the critical days of 1914, and by constituting a Guards' Division, a magnificent unit now rendered possible by the creation of the Regiment of Welsh Guards and by adding battalions to the famous "Brigade."

He had always considered the despatch of the Territorials in battalions to France as an expedient necessary under emergency, but unsatisfactory in organisation. No pre-war provision had been made for depots for the Territorial Force from which men could be drafted to feed the Territorial units in the field. To furnish drafts it had been at first necessary to call for volunteers from Territorials at home.

This arrangement was very reasonably resented by Commanding Officers, who ruefully regarded both their depleted units and their own diminishing chances of taking their battalions to the front. By the end of June Kitchener had turned out a satisfactory system to secure the even flow of drafts for the Territorial Force and to reorganise divisions which had been temporarily broken up, and by mid-July he could pronounce on the Guards' Division:

The King has approved of the formation of a Guards' Division to be commanded by the Earl of Cavan. To do this I propose to send you 4 battalions of Guards and 4 battalions of the Army Troops of the First and Second Army. You have the 19th Brigade still outside your divisional formations which might replace the Guards' Brigade of the Second Division, while 2 battalions of the 4 I am sending you would replace the Guards in the First and Seventh Divisions respectively. I will send you the Artillery and divisional troops to complete the Division. Perhaps you may wish to mix these up with earlier formations so as to give the Guards a certain number of older units with those I can send. If you will let me know that you like this idea I will go on with it and arrange about getting men ready.

P.S.—The Guards' Division would have no number as in other armies.

The Guards' Division stood complete in time for the autumn fighting in France, and with the last two of the New Army divisions to arrive, the Twenty-first and Twenty-fourth, was formed into the Eleventh Corps under General Haking. Normally divisions arriving from home in France were given a period of practical training in trench warfare before they were employed in battle, but in the case of the Twenty-first and Twenty-fourth Divisions there was no time to do this before the battle of Loos began. Joffre, who built great hopes on the outcome of his campaign, was insistent that we should make use of every available man, and the new Eleventh Corps was sent forward and placed in General Reserve under Sir John's own orders. To the First Army under Sir Douglas Haig was assigned the attack on the enemy's lines between Lens and La Bassée. Foch at the same moment was to assault the Vimy Ridge, and it was fondly hoped that an advance upon both sides of the intricate mining area of Lens would compel the Germans to evacuate that hideous but vitally important industrial centre, and that Haig and Foch would then step out to Douai.

The Anglo-French programme was to rush the enemy's trench line before his redoubtable reserves could come up; and success would lie largely in prompt support being given by troops in reserve to troops in the line of fire.

CHAPTER CXXIV

THE battle of Loos opened on September 25, and there was just sufficient breeze in the right direction to facilitate our first discharge of gas.[1] The gas unquestionably made its mark on the Germans—although here and there the fumes came back upon and overcame some of our own men—and the infantry, storming forward behind the vaporous yellow clouds, made short work of carrying the town of Loos, and pressed on beyond it. Then the unhappy happened: the reserves on whom Haig depended to complete and confirm his fine initial success were belated, or withheld,[2] and he must see his leading companies driven back by weighty German counter-assaults, while he heard that the French on his right were unable to make anything like full headway.

Apart from the sharp controversy which arose as to the non-arrival of Haig's reserves, students of the battle of Loos will always remember that the British attack was only a fraction of a combined movement. If Foch, who was to sweep forward on a much

---

[1] The French did not use gas on this occasion.

[2] The two divisions in reserve were kept under Sir John's orders and were only directed to join Haig when the success of the First Army became known at G.H.Q. Though the two divisions then came on as fast as they could, their leading troops did not cross our former front line until 6 P.M., that is, twelve hours after the taking of Loos. Haig had asked for the reserve divisions to be placed under his orders before the commencement of the battle, in order that they might be so disposed as to be available immediately Loos had fallen, and before the enemy had had time to reinforce his second line.

broader front, was held up, Haig was helpless to increase or even make permanent his own advantages.

On September 30 Sir John wrote what he thought of the battle in general and of the service of gas in particular:

I enclose a report which Foulkes sent me about the gas. It will probably give you the information you ask for in the best form.

My own opinion is that the gas has helped us enormously, and I hope we shall continue to be supplied with it.

As regards the operations, you probably know as much as I can tell you in a letter like this.

I am quite satisfied with the results so far attained. Of course, nothing ever happens in war exactly as one wishes. I think the French Tenth Army on our right were too slow in starting their attack so long after ours had begun. We were already on the southern slopes of Hill 70 when their attack began at one o'clock in the day! And their progress was very slow.

Had they been able to keep anything like abreast of us we should certainly have completely broken the line on the 26th or 27th.

On the 27th I sent a special messenger to Joffre to say that, if he wished me to get on, he really must bring up the French Tenth Army, as my right flank was becoming dangerously exposed and weakened.

On the morning of the 28th he sent Foch to ask me what I wished the Tenth Army to do. I told him that, if they could not get on, they must take over some of the positions on our right and thus free troops to enable me to push through.

He at once agreed to send the Hundred and Fifty-second Division to take over the "Double Crassier," which was seized and is being held by the Forty-seventh Division on our present right. Next morning (29th) he came to see me again, and proposed to send the whole of the Ninth Corps (to which the Hundred and Fifty-second Division belongs) to take over all our ground up to and including Hill 70. This relief is now taking place, and I am organising a new attack on the enemy's third and (we believe) last line on the early morning of October 2. The attacking troops will be in considerable depth and should succeed.

There is no doubt the French Tenth Army, like ourselves, was heavily opposed. In fact we know that they had the whole of the Second German Guard Corps (which we know has just been brought over from Russia) in front of them. They have since got on well and have captured Vimy Ridge.

When our attack gets forward the French will be able to get heavy artillery on to Hill 70 and, in conjunction with guns on the Vimy Ridge, they will be able to direct effective cross-fire on the plain to the east of Vimy.

The news from Champagne was very good last night. They say they have pierced the enemy's last line of trenches south of St. Marie-a-Py, and that they have put three fresh divisions through this gap, besides some cavalry.

Various documents which have been found amongst the prisoners make it clear that the Germans intended to make a big attack on us during October. We have therefore timed our offensive well.

Since Friday last my Personal Headquarters have been at Lillers, where I am in close touch with the main attack. I have a special telephone to Robertson's room at St. Omer.

I have managed to see and talk to a good many of the troops which have been engaged, particularly the Ninth and Fifteenth Divisions, which have both done splendidly.

. . . . .

Since dictating this this morning I find that the French will have to make more ground to the East before they can put guns on the Ridge.

Sir John erred a little on the side of optimism. The taking of Hill 70 by the superb Fifteenth (Scottish) Division stands to its undying credit, and was a foretaste of the contribution which the "Kitchener Armies" would make to eventual victory. Lack of support alone prevented their retaining the points they had so hardly won, and they had much ado to establish a line on the forward slopes of the Hill.

Foch's Tenth Army made its way some steps up the Vimy Ridge, but could never grip the crest; and the German reserves arrived in fury and force to bar Joffre's road in Champagne.

But Joffre, Sir John, and Foch had not laboured in vain. Their autumn campaign had given the German High Command cause for genuine anxiety, and General Ludendorff in his reminiscences [1] admits that nothing but the arrival of strong bodies of troops from the Russian zone averted a serious setback in France.

The Germans hastily availed themselves of their refreshed strength to institute a series of sharp counter-attacks, culminating on October 8 in an assault to which the Allied leaders so retorted as to give the German front the appearance of a shambles.

The German attack [Sir John wrote to Kitchener on October 10] made on the afternoon of the 8th upon our line south of the Canal—the right being now taken over by the French—consisted of 28 battalions in first line. The French say they have some 4000 dead in front of their line, and there are from 5000 to 6000 dead (at least) lying in heaps and piles near our trenches. There must have been a German loss of 20,000. Our casualties were under 6000. I think you would like to hear this.

Further fighting for a week swayed to and fro, chiefly round the Hohenzollern Redoubt, and on

---

[1] *My War Memories, 1914–1918*, i. 172.

October 15 a term was set to the battle of Loos. Neither French nor English had reason to be dissatisfied with their performances, and this perhaps made easier the question of detaching Allied troops from the Western front for Salonika—a course which Joffre came himself to London to press upon the British Government. The French War Minister, M. Millerand, was at the same moment arguing with warmth that British troops ought further to relieve the French by taking over a longer stretch of line on the Western front—a point which remained for long a bone of contention. Both sides could claim a very strong case—each from its own point of view. Judged as a matter of mere mileage the French plea was convincing—they were holding a far longer line, in proportion to their numbers, than we were. The British rejoinder took account of the strength rather than the length of the line: the French front was in many places held so weakly, both by themselves and by the enemy, that from these "quiet sectors" they could afford to give ground without imperilling any vital point.

On the other hand, the British in Flanders—of whom a large proportion were new troops—were wedged in so tightly between their front line and the Channel ports that they could yield no inch of ground to an enemy who always kept himself at full strength in the North.

Sir John was reasonably accommodating as to the despatch of troops for Salonika, but rightly adamant in resisting any further extension of his front.[1]

[1] "*Le* 13 *octobre* 1915.
"Cher M. Millerand—
  "J'espère que vous aurez la bonté de communiquer le suivant au Général Joffre. Je me permets de le lui faire parvenir par votre intermédiaire afin que vous soyez parfaitement au courant du contenu.

The non-achievement of victory at Gallipoli impelled the Government to seek an offset in some striking and spectacular *coup* in the East. In the nick of time General Townshend on September 28 hit the Turks hard at Kut-el-Amara and hurled them back on Baghdad. To have and to hold the ancient seat of the Caliphate became a prime point of policy: it would be an opportune rehabilitation of the British name throughout the Orient. But to do this it was imperative to send fresh troops to the Tigris. Kitchener, who had been greatly concerned at the sufferings of the Indian infantry in France during the previous winter, had for some time been contemplating their transfer to some other theatre before the next winter should set in. The advent of an instalment of the New Armies had now made this possible, and the two Indian Infantry Divisions went joyfully to the assistance of Townshend.

As soon as he had wound up the accounts of the

"Je suis bien reconnaissant au Général Joffre pour son appréciation par écrit de la situation dans l'Est, qui d'ailleurs s'accordait exactement avec les vues qu'il m'a exprimées à notre dernière rencontre.

"J'ai aussi reçu le mot urgent qu'il m'a envoyé et qui m'a fait comprendre combien il espérait qu'aucune démarche ne serait faite pour retirer des troupes du commandement de Sir John French jusqu'à ce que les opérations en cours ne soient terminées.

"Étant donné décision qu'il m'a communiquée relative à l'impossibilité de pousser plus loin l'offensive en Champagne (qui aurait été tant à désirer à ce moment ou l'Allemagne disperse ses forces et se trouve aux abois pour maintenir sa position en Champagne et Artois), et aussi en vue du fait que la France expédie rapidement des divisions à l'Est, il nous paraît nécessaire d'y envoyer des troupes britanniques le plus tôt possible.

"J'ai soumis à Sir John French la question de tournir ces troupes mais je ne voie pas le moyen de retirer de notre front les divisions qui devraient partir de suite à moins que le Généralissimo ne consente à relever—avec des divisions français—le front tenu à présent par les 2 divisions au plus sud de l'armée du Général Monro.

"Quant à la répartition ultérieure de notre front, nous aurions alors le temps d'examiner avec Sir John French comment mieux les autres divisions pourraient être relevées.

"Tout à vous

"KITCHENER."

battle of Loos, Sir John paid one of his rapid visits to London to consult Kitchener and the Home authorities as to the despatch of British divisions to Salonika and of Indian divisions to Mesopotamia. Before returning to St. Omer he went to see Joffre at Chantilly, and on October 18 wrote:

I am enclosing copy of an official letter I am sending to W.O.—partly in reply to their letter to us as to possibilities of sending divisions away from here to the East, and partly contesting the memo.—which George Arthur sent me to-day —laying down M. Millerand's views as to the relative shares of defensive work undertaken by the French and ourselves. . . .

I came direct to Chantilly from London and saw Joffre this morning. We had a long conference, and he dwelt strongly on the necessity of getting troops under weigh for Salonika as speedily as possible. I also feel this myself, and, as I told you, I am ready to do anything I possibly can to expedite matters and help you in this serious dilemma.

I am therefore sending the Twenty-eighth Division first. They begin entraining for Marseilles on Thursday 21st. Joffre is relieving two divisions of the Third Army— Twenty-second first. This relief will be completed in time to enable the Twenty-second to follow the Twenty-eighth without delay. The despatch of the two Indian divisions and four others must be dependent upon the arrival of the divisions of the Fourth Army to relieve them. I am doing all I can to arrange to help you with battalion officers, and in other possible ways to make these divisions available.

I can go over and see you again when the King leaves (29th according to present arrangements) and discuss these questions.

To the Twenty-eighth and Twenty-second British Divisions destined for Salonika it was decided to add the Twenty-seventh, and these, with the Indian

Force, were embarking for the East just when Kitchener himself started on his mission. From Paris he wrote to the Prime Minister:

I have had my interview with Briand and Gallieni. As regards Salonika it is very difficult to get in a word; they were both full of the necessity of pushing in troops, and would not think of coming out. They simply sweep all military difficulties and dangers aside, and go on political lines—such as saving a remnant of Serbs, bringing Greece in, and inducing Rumania to join. I could get no idea from them as to when the troops could come out; they only said they must watch events.

As regards Gallipoli, they both said it would be a disaster if we abandon our position there and allow the Turks to go free. I said, if we found it necessary to maintain our position, we might have to use the Twenty-eighth Division on the Peninsula, relieving some of the tired troops there that could go to Salonika without loss of time. They rather agreed to this, and I said we would let them know before we diverted troops.

As regards the Arab movement, they quite agreed in pushing it on, but had no troops to help it forward. They spoke of maintaining French sentimental rights in Syria, but not with any view of stopping an Arab movement there. They quite saw that there would be no chance of any such movement if Gallipoli was evacuated.

As regards a greater *entente* between the General Staffs, they were in entire agreement, but wanted a combined War Council to decide on the policy of the war—with executive powers. Briand said this was being taken up officially. I pressed on them that in the meantime the Staffs should get into closer touch and discuss together, and Gallieni promised to let us have an *officier de liaison*, and to consider the matter carefully; but it is very difficult to pin them down to any actual fact. I shall see him again and try and get this arranged before I go.

They were fully alive to the dangers in Egypt.

The better co-ordination of the Allies' strategy was a subject seldom absent from his thoughts. Earnestly, if so far only informally, he had sought to represent both to his chief colleagues and to the French Ministers the vital need of a closer *entente* between the Allied General Staffs. The French Premier favoured setting up a body akin to Mr. Lloyd George's Versailles War Council of two years later. Kitchener was dead against arming an international council with executive powers. He saw many objections, and, above all, he set his face like a flint against vesting any council, however constituted, with actual control over military plans and operations—such an arrangement would ask for trouble in drawn-out discussions, delay, and compromise. Unification of military control was to him an object of even eager desire, but he saw the certain difficulty of finding the right man and of devising the best machinery. Eventually his suggestion was to bear fruit in consultations held under Joffre's presidency at regular intervals between the supreme military authorities of the chief Allies. The earliest of these conferences for the co-ordination of military plans met in December 1915, and marked the first real step towards unity of command.

CHAPTER CXXV

SUPPLIES to the armies in being and to be were a scarcely less weighty subject than the armies themselves, but the one relief from anxious care which Kitchener enjoyed was in the matter of food, clothing, and comforts for the Field Forces. So shrewd was the providence and so fruitful were the efforts of Sir John Cowans, the Quartermaster-General, that as regards his department the Secretary of State had to apply no spur—scarcely to make a suggestion.[1] "Carry on, and consult me if you are in difficulties," he had but to say to his inestimably efficient subordinate; "only let me be sure the men, who must be exposed to hurt and risk of life, have everything that wit can devise or money buy for their comfort and health."

It is not to belittle the department of the Quartermaster-General, which continued through five years of a world-wide war to supply to the edge of profusion and with startling rapidity every article of necessity, comfort, and almost of luxury, to say that the department of the Master-General of the Ordnance was at once and always in the thick of far greater, because more highly technical, difficulties. Kitchener knew as well as any one the fine fighting

---

[1] He sent the Quartermaster-General to France on more than one occasion to impress on the Commanders-in-Chief the importance of constructing light railways.

character of Sir John French; he knew better—because certainly earlier—than Sir John could do the requirements of ever-increasing forces for prolonged fighting; and he saw that on himself devolved the charge of forging every possible weapon to strengthen the arm of the Commander-in-Chief for the blows he must rain on a hulking foe.

There stood out three great needs—guns, ammunition, and labour; and of these the greatest and most baffling was labour.

The problem, too, was of creation, and not, as in the case of Continental armies, adaptation. Just as Kitchener had found the War Office administration wholly inadequate to the waging of a great war, so he was forced to evolve, instead of merely operate, machinery for the supply of munitions of war. He knew that even the Expeditionary Force was sparsely provided with medium artillery and wholly unprovided with heavy artillery, and that it must be compelled to an expenditure of ammunition which would outrun supplies immediately available. He could not but foresee that for many a long month munitions would multiply less quickly than the men he was planning to put in the field.

The economical pre-war policy of the Government —enjoined on them by the electorate—necessarily forbade any generous provision of war material; and the real root of any and all deficiency was that the nation plunged into Armageddon without armaments. There was but a tenuous store of guns, rifles, and ammunition; there was no reserve of machine-guns other than those for the Expeditionary Force. The lack of preparation for real war was only to be realised by those whose business it was to make it good. Woolwich Arsenal had been reduced to meagre proportions to meet financial exigencies, and could not be expected to do more than supply the first seven Divisions. The starved ordnance firms, whose eyes waited almost entirely on the Lords of the Admiralty for orders, were, with little plant and less material, impotent to meet sudden and staggering demands.

Kitchener, when he found the cupboard bare, complained less of the lack of munitions than of the absence of all machinery for producing them.[1] Each belligerent had miscalculated his requirements; every army in the field after a few months' fighting was confronted with shortage. But whereas the other Powers had to expand their means, Great Britain had to improvise hers. Kitchener's difficulties at the beginning of the war were analogous to those of a *chef* who, to produce an omelette, must first establish a poultry farm. He had simultaneously to meet the immediate necessities of the Divisions following one another to France and—while his colleagues in Council and the Commander-in-Chief in the Field were prattling of the war being a matter of months—to make provision for that army of millions, the vision of which, as the real gatherer of victory, had dawned on his mind alone. With means just sufficient to keep Sir John on his feet and with no potentialities for immediate expansion, he must provide for a long and bitter and far-flung tussle with a powerful enemy who for half a century had devoted himself to purposeful preparation.

[1] "Did they remember, when they went headlong into a war like this, that they were without an army, and without any preparation to equip one?" was the cry wrung from him once when the day's work had been specially wearing.

The retreat from Mons and the hard pounding on the Aisne demonstrated the absolute need of guns and howitzers of a heavier calibre than had previously been used, and not a moment was lost in ordering sixteen 9·2-inch howitzers, and hurried steps were taken towards acquiring as many 6-inch howitzers as could be collected. A Committee of artillery experts was formed to work out the possible requirements for siege operations on a large scale; and on their advice sixteen more 9·2-inch howitzers were put in hand, and thirty-two 12-inch howitzers; while some 6-inch guns were provided with travelling carriages and other 6-inch guns were converted into 8-inch howitzers.[1] With the promise of thirty-two 9·2-inch and thirty-two 12-inch howitzers which Kitchener was able to make him in January Sir John expressed himself as more than content.

It was not until eight or nine months later that Sir John had the 8-inch and 9·2-inch howitzers in any number in batteries. He quickly recognised their great value, and, as he found the pattern of the latter wholly suitable for service conditions, the provision of a larger quantity was taken up forthwith. At the Secretary of State's suggestion, Sir John, at Midsummer 1915, put forward his recommendations, which were at once approved, and demands for

[1] On September 15 he wrote to Lord Roberts, whom he kept closely informed: "We have already taken steps to provide a large number of 6-inch howitzers carrying a hundred-pound shell, both lyddite and shrapnel. We have also made arrangements for 6-inch guns on mobile carriages to go over there." Sir John wrote to Kitchener on September 24, 1914: "We have had the new howitzers in action to-day with splendid results. The Old Fort of Condé, just above the village of that name, has been full of Germans for the last week. A few rounds from these big guns sent hundreds of them flying out of the Fort over the plateau in the rear. The field-guns then got at them with shrapnel and did good execution. I am very grateful to you for sending them so promptly and feel sure they will have great effect."

sufficient guns and howitzers on the scale agreed on were then passed on to the Ministry of Munitions.

The total sum of guns prescribed for the Expeditionary Force was 484, and, when the Ministry of Munitions was formed, Kitchener was able to say that, with India's contribution of her spare pieces, he had put in hand tenfold that number, after replacing captured, damaged, or worn-out guns.

On October 12, 1914, the War Secretary presided over the first meeting of the Cabinet Committee on Munitions, instituted by the Prime Minister, and consisting of Lord Haldane, Mr. Lloyd George, Mr. Winston Churchill, Mr. McKenna, Mr. Runciman, and Lord Lucas.[1] They set themselves to organise all trade resources, and decided not to do so centrally from the War Office direct, but rather through a system of decentralisation, main orders being placed with the Ordnance Factories and large armament firms, who would themselves expand and sub-contract in default of existing buildings and machinery.[2]

Every nerve was strained, every suggestion considered, every possibility explored, for attaining the maximum output of really reliable material within the minimum period of time; but what was realised was usually short of what was promised.

The expenditure of gun and howitzer ammunition, starting on an unexampled scale, went up by leaps

[1] The War Office believed that by June 1915 it would be possible to turn out 864 18-pounders; the contractors, more sanguine, hoped (though they could not guarantee) to supply as many as 2148 by July 1; the Cabinet Committee, more sanguine still, ordered further increase. But it is one thing to order and quite another to secure delivery, and on July 1, 1915, the manufacturers had delivered only 803 18-pounder guns, 165 4.5-inch howitzers, and 37 60-pounders. They had envisaged the possibility of producing 2148, 530, and 96 respectively.

[2] In July 1915 the Munitions Advisory Council, presided over by the Minister, adopted the self-same course.

and bounds. The million and a half rounds sent out in the first six months swelled to four and a quarter millions by the end of the next six months, while another four months raised the total to eight millions. The thirty-three months of the South African war saw 273,000 rounds fired. During the first six months of the Great War the total fired was a million rounds. In the next three months the same figure was recorded—an increase of 100 per cent; while from April 26, 1915, to May 27 [1] the expenditure topped 775,000 rounds.

The figures illustrating the progressive manufacture of 18-pounder ammunition are even more striking, if it is remembered that the machinery and tools had to be of a special type to provide a quick rate of output. In 1914, the monthly pre-war average of 3000 rounds was raised in August and September to 10,000; in October and November to 45,000; in December to 78,000; in January 1915 to 93,000; in February to 128,000; in March to 194,000; in April to 225,000; in May to 400,000. By the following October the figure reached 1,014,812.[2] The total supply of gun ammunition of every nature during January 1915 amounted to 179,300 rounds, and in May the figures reached 483,630.

During the fifteen months covering the period in which supplies reached the Army under War Office orders, 7,000,000 rounds and 3317 guns (208 60-pounders and upwards) were sent out. By March 1, 1915, the figures were 1,900,000 rounds and 1100 guns. Such figures pale into insignificance as com-

[1] For the four weeks ending November 5, 1916, the consumption approximated to 1,120,000 per week.
[2] Of course no portion of these supplies represent any deliveries on orders placed by the Ministry of Munitions.

pared to the vast volume of projectiles with which Haig was later to beat into dust the accursed system of Prussianism; but, starting from zero and with every obstacle to breast and overcome, they suggest as fine an output of material as was made from end to end of the war.

CHAPTER CXXVI

BEFORE the war the value and use of machine-gun fire had been keenly debated in England and Germany, who were at one in adopting the proportion of only two machine-guns per thousand men. Active service at once revealed the true worth of the arm, and the Germans immediately—and by virtue of their immense war factories quite easily—increased the number of guns per battalion. But what Germany could do England could not.

The weapon adopted before the war was patented here by Messrs. Vickers, who alone were competent to make it. Without waiting for any mandate from Sir John, 1792 machine-guns were ordered—a number far in excess of any requirements then thought possible, and regarded by the believers in a short sharp war as a gamble in futures. In January 1915 Vickers were given *carte blanche* to supply every piece they could turn out. The Lewis gun, of which one firm enjoyed the monopoly of manufacture, had only been tried and approved early in 1914, but before the end of the year everything they could turn out was requisitioned. The number of machine-guns of all patterns ordered by Kitchener before May 1915 for delivery up to the end of 1916, including some from America, exceeded 27,000.

America was at once laid under contribution, though here zeal had to be tempered with discretion.[1] The War Office, for instance, was charged in Parliament with refusing to accept an offer with quick delivery for 10,000 Colt guns. The reason for the refusal was that, apart from the impossibility of adapting the Colt gun to our purposes, the manufacture was to vest, not in the Colt Company itself, but in some other party in the background, of whose very existence—to say nothing of experience and capacity—little could be gleaned. It was a question whether this shadowy—if not shady—entity had any knowledge of the craft, and inquiry engendered a suspicion that the offer lacked *bona fides,* and suggested that a snare might have been set for the country by a couple of German agents.

A very different story was when, early in October 1914, the Bethlehem Steel Corporation offered a few hours' option on a million complete rounds of field-gun ammunition—for that time an enormous quantity—to be delivered in twelve months. Within four hours the offer was accepted, and Mr. Schwab, the master spirit of the Corporation, crossed the Atlantic to see Kitchener. "This war," Kitchener said to him, "is not going to be a short one. I foresee five years of it at least. I want you to pledge that the control of the Bethlehem Steel Corporation will not be sold by you and your associates under five years from now." The agreement was made on the spot, and the immense capacities of the firm secured for the Allies for the rest of the war.

As regards rifles, the production of which takes

---

[1] America at this time was full of "hot-air artists," a term applied to would-be contractors who had a stock phrase that they could turn out any amount of anything in ninety days.

longer to organise than any other article in the soldier's equipment, the provision with which we entered the lists against the greatest military power of the world was 750,000, with a weekly output of 6000—barely sufficient to make up wastage. Machinery for making rifles and their ammunition was at once set up to cope with hitherto undreamed of requirements, and orders were placed—outside our usual peace-time factories—for 3,860,000 rifles, in addition to those already in hand. As many as two millions were ordered in America, delivery to begin in July 1915, but not until May 1916 did any consignment make its appearance. Moreover, the losses in rifles in the early hard fighting against desperately heavy odds were beyond all surmise, and the re-arming of combatants and the arming of the men in training to take their place in the firing line were one of Kitchener's most carking cares.[1] A friend who in the early weeks of the war noted in him signs of strain asked him if he were sleeping well. "I shall never have a good night's rest," he answered, "until I have two million rifles and their ammunition, and that cannot be yet."

The peg on which many critics hung an indictment was the allegation that full victory to our arms in Flanders was denied us because of a lamentable—and, as was suggested, avoidable—failure to supply high explosive shells, and the subject was destined

[1] Kitchener was taken to task for saying, in March 1915, that "rifles were not by any means our greatest need" and that "shells and fuzes were more important." The purport of the dictum was that the prospective rifle supply was adequate to an army numbering two millions, the maximum admitted by the Government at that time, and that to arrange for a larger output was to divert labour from more immediate necessary effort. The moment the three million standard of men was adopted, he at once ordered 1,500,000 more rifles.

for several months to become the theme of acute controversy.

The adoption of this projectile for field artillery had been often discussed on the Continent, and the French used it sparsely in Morocco. Kitchener had fired high explosive shell from his field howitzers at Omdurman, and again in South Africa; and it was employed seriously during the Balkan campaigns of 1912, but perhaps with insufficient effect to attract the approval, or at any rate to earn the recommendation, of the then Chief of Staff at the War Office.

The first proposal to use high explosive shell in field-guns [1] proceeded, not from Sir John to Kitchener, but from the War Office to General Headquarters in France. Before the war was a week old the Master-General of the Ordnance was inquiring whether some high explosive shell would not be welcome for horse and field artillery. The hesitating reply from the G.O.C.R.A. was, "This is really a big question. Consensus of opinion among gunners seems so far to be that high explosive from the German field-guns is terrible in its moral effect, but that the actual result is not very great. . . . As an advance opinion I should say that, if you really have safe explosive for field-guns, by all means proceed to manufacture. Our gunners would certainly like to be in possession of it, and I suppose money is but little object, and it will take considerable time to supply, will it not?"

A further inquiry from London elicited on Sep-

---

[1] High explosive shells had for long constituted the major part of the equipment of all our artillery, excepting only the light field-guns—13-pr. and 18-pr. Q.F.—and it had been deliberately left out of their equipment after extended pre-war trials.

tember 7 an answer that the matter had not yet been submitted to the Commander-in-Chief, but that the Chief of the Staff thought high explosive "would be welcome in the long run." A rider was added that there was not quite enough data to go upon, that "the moral effect of the stuff is no doubt high, though the actual effect does not seem to come up to statements." The next day the Master-General of the Ordnance was asked to write again on the subject, and a week later a telegram was received stating that the subject of high explosive had been brought before the Commander-in-Chief, who concurred in the request that the War Office should supply it as soon as possible. On October 19 the first 1000 18-pr. H.E. shell were sent out to France for trial;[1] three weeks later a favourable report was received, and the War Office was asked to send in future, as soon as procurable, 50 per cent H.E. and 50 per cent shrapnel for the 18-pr. and 13-pr. guns. A week later the Headquarters in France asked that the proportion of high explosive should be dropped to 25 per cent, and a fortnight later confirmed the diminution.

Kitchener decided that high explosive should have a department to itself, and in November 1914 Lord Moulton, a Lord of Appeal and well known as a great lawyer and scientist, was called in to take charge. He told Lord Moulton that the war would be of far longer duration than he could yet persuade any one to believe, and that large and largely increasing quantities of high explosive would be required. The reply was that the only way in which this could be

[1] It has often been stated that without H.E. shell for field-guns wire entanglements could not be cleared; but trials carried out in Flanders in January 1915 proved that rather more effect was obtained with 18-pr. shrapnel than with H.E. shell.

effected was "by widening the programme of manufacture." Pure Trinitrotoluol must—so the War Secretary was assured—fall hopelessly short of the immense quantities required, and it was an absolute necessity to use it in small quantities and in mixture with Nitrate of Ammonia. Kitchener could not at once secure for this suggestion the favour of the experts, who very reasonably urged lack of experience in war and difficulties with regard to the fuzes to be employed. But he would reject no advice tending towards a larger output of this explosive, and gave Lord Moulton a free hand to proceed with the manufacture of such admixtures, one of which, "Amatol," was multiplied to the end of the war in overwhelming quantities, to the confusion of the German armies. Parallel endeavours were made to obtain fuzes different in pattern from those used for shrapnel shells, and which offered much more trouble than the manufacture of the shell body. The Germans must have squirmed to hear that Kitchener, through Lord Moulton, had succeeded in acquiring and transferring to England while war was raging a factory for producing the Toluol needed for T.N.T. set up by them in Rotterdam, and furthermore had annexed in conjunction with France the whole production of a great Nitrate Factory in Norway which must otherwise have been employed on behalf of the enemy.

At the end of 1914 Army Headquarters in France made up their minds that 50 per cent of H.E. for horse and field guns was what they really required. The Army Council had to consider whether machinery, now being employed to produce the 18-pounder shrapnel so urgently required, should be diverted to the production of H.E. shell—it being a known factor in the problem that no H.E. shell could be turned out for at least ten weeks. The result would have been that during this period the supply of absolutely necessary field-gun ammunition would be seriously jeopardised, and this at the moment when the Commander-in Chief in the field was pressing for every round. Kitchener, without arresting his shrapnel orders, urged the experienced armament firms to make still further and supreme efforts to provide H.E. shell; he enlisted the services of other establishments previously engaged on other manufactures, and pressed Canada and America into this in addition to their other work. He secured positive promises of nearly half a million H.E. shells to be delivered by the middle of May, and any disappointment was due to uncompleted machinery and buildings and to paucity of labour.

It was at one time murmured that the Army Council had turned an unwilling ear to Sir John's urgent requests—that they had stonily declined to work up to more than 20 rounds a gun a day, and had refused his request for 50 per cent of H.E. The reply issued from the War Office bore no such complexion:

> The Council desire to emphasise the fact that the orders for manufacture are not being limited to what they think it necessary to supply, but are entirely conditioned by the highest possible output of the ordnance factories throughout the Empire and the trade of England and the allied and neutral countries of the world.
>
> In connection with the above proposed supply of 50 rounds a gun a day the Council wish to invite your attention

to enclosed letter [1] giving the opinion of the French War Office, from which it will be seen that, according to the experience of the French Army, based on a much larger number of troops and guns over a much longer line than that occupied by the British Army, a figure of 20 rounds a gun has been accepted by them as being sufficient to meet our requirements.

It is understood that the French, after arduous work, have secured a manufacturing output of 40,000 rounds a day, and that they hope to increase this in the near future up to 20 rounds a gun a day; and although the Council are unaware of the German output, they think it incredible that the Germans will be able to manufacture, or find the material for, an output of above the 400,000 rounds a day or more which would be required to supply them on the scale regarded by you as necessary for this war.

The Army Council will, however, continue their endeavours to augment the output of gun ammunition, and if and when the figure of 20 rounds a day for every gun in the field is attained, they will not relax their efforts in the direction of further increases if experience proves this allowance to be inadequate.

The Council would point out that although in the present operations in trenches the employment of a great number of

---

[1] The French Military Attaché had been deputed to write to Kitchener:
"Le Ministre de la Guerre de France, répondant à la question que vous m'avez prié de lui poser, me prie de faire connaître à Votre Excellence ce qui suit:

"1. Le chiffre de 20 coups par pièce et par jour a été admis pour assurer le coéfficient indispensable, en se basant sur la consommation atteinte pendant plusieurs mois, et notamment en *Flandre* où les corps engagés ont tiré du 25 octobre au 23 novembre, 33 coups par pièce et par jour en moyenne.

"2. Il estime cependant que l'armée anglaise pourrait se contenter d'un chiffre moindre, car elle a, dans l'offensive, des procédés un peu différents des nôtres, et garde toujours des forces importantes en seconde ligne, pour les besoins de la relève.

"3. Il est exact que le tir des batteries allemandes (batteries de campagne surtout) s'est ralenti. L'économie des munitions a été recommandée dans certaines circonstances. Les allemands utilisent tous leurs canons d'ancien modèle, les canons français pris à Maubeuge. Ils se servent de projectiles en fonte et de fusées très défectueuses, qui indique une fabrication hâtive."

H.E. shells may be found necessary for the field-guns, they cannot help thinking that the nature of the operations may again alter as they have done in the past, when the shrapnel shell will be found more effective on the enemy, and, therefore, though doing all in their power to increase the number of H.E. shell, they hesitate to make any sudden change which would interrupt the present output, but at the same time they will gradually work up to the increased percentage asked for.

Kitchener's anxieties were thick on him at this moment; for, while he was striving to meet Sir John's requirements *in esse* and *in posse*, he was painfully aware—through the Supplies to Allies Committee which he had instituted—that the Commander-in-Chief's anxious demands were echoed loudly from France and Russia, and, working hand-in-hand—as he constantly was—with the French Commander, one of his worst moments was when, early in February, the news reached him that a certain shell on which Joffre was relying for his future operations had caused premature explosions of a deadly and disastrous character.

Criticism sometimes sought a target in the person of Sir Stanley von Donop, the Master-General of the Ordnance. He was alleged to be hyper-conservative, to refuse offers made to him, to miss opportunities of securing material. That he did not accept open-mouthed all that was dangled in front of him was happily true. In September 1914 General Deville arrived from France to discuss the whole question of high explosive, and produced the design of a shell which he said could be manufactured with a good economy of time, since the component parts were at hand. With the exception of von Donop, everybody, the War Secretary included, was impressed; the Master-General of the Ordnance steadfastly refused approval. Kitchener told a friend that immediately after the conference he asked his subordinate rather testily why he had been so "stuffy" about the design, and received the pithy reply, "Because in my opinion it is unsafe." It is significant that four months later came the bursting of 800 guns and the derangement of Joffre's contemplated offensive. Kitchener told Mr. Asquith bluntly that if the same fiasco had happened in England the Prime Minister and the War Minister would have been hanged on the gallows of public opinion, and that our immunity from defective guns was due to the restraining advice of the M.G.O. He told von Donop that he was prepared to defend him openly in the House of Lords, but it was eventually arranged that he should write to the Prime Minister:

> I wish to place on record the complete confidence which I and the Army Council have in Major-General Sir S. B. von Donop, Master-General of the Ordnance.
> He has worked hard to supply the Army with the guns and ammunition needed in these days of enormous expansion, and has the complete confidence of every member of his Department.
> Above all, he has by the application of technical knowledge of the highest order secured that the guns and ammunition supplied are of a quality to ensure adequate safety, and he has enabled us to avoid the dangers—from which we know some of our Allies have suffered—arising from the use of material which has been hastily constructed and allowed to fall too far below the accepted standards. Wherever his experience has satisfied him that the interests of efficiency would not be damaged, he has been ready to advise relaxations from rigidly drawn specifications.

I have to-day seen General du Cane, and he informs me that the Army in France have complete confidence in General von Donop and consider him by far the most qualified technical adviser of suitable rank that could be obtained from the Regiment of Artillery.

In January the French War Minister, M. Millerand, came to London to consult Kitchener as to what England's future contribution of men and munitions would be. M. Millerand was taken to Aldershot and saw for himself the first of the New Armies in training, and was told, confidentially, when they and the next two Armies would be ready for the field. He was deeply impressed with the magnitude and merits of the force which Great Britain was proposing to contribute, but deeply anxious as to the matter of munitions of war. On the 14th Kitchener had an interview—the first of many—with a delegate[1] from the French Minister, from whom he did not conceal

[1] The Marquis de Chasseloup Laubat, a great French authority on explosive, who wrote:

"Tout d'abord Lord Kitchener examine à nouveau la question des explosifs qui, à ce moment-là, présente une gravité et une acuité exceptionnelles pour les Alliés en général et la France en particulier. Il n'est pas content. Il s'étonne que le Ministre de la Guerre en France n'ait pas encore ratifié officiellement la convention que, le lundi précédent 11 janvier, il a acceptée sur ma demande au nom de la Grande Bretagne, après une discussion qui dure de midi à 1¾h. pendant la première séance du 'Supplies to Allies Committee.' Il ne comprend pas pourquoi l'Administration de Bordeaux n'a pas accepté séance tenante un arrangement aussi avantageux pour les Alliés: les 50,000 fusils japonais et les 40,000,000 de cartouches japonais que doit oéder la France à la Grande Bretagne vont accroître le nombre de soldats anglais en Flandres et par conséquent diminuer le trop lourd fardeaue des soldats de la République; les 2,300 tonnes de benzol anglais tout venant que la Grande Bretagne remettra à la France chaque mois jusqu'à la fin des hostilités—et que l'on nespeut se procurer actuellement qu'en Angleterre—permettront aux Services techniques du Ministre de la Guerre de créer la fabrication d'un tonnage quotidien de mélinite suffisant pour repousser les attaques de l'ennemi.

"Il rappelle avec amertume que, afin d'imposer lundi dernier mon projet de convention et l'octroi du permis d'exportation, il a dû briser les réticences, les tergiversations, et les résistances de gens qui, ignorant sans doute certains éléments essentiels de leur service, et les dangers de l'heure présente.

his anxiety as to some methods which seemed unlikely to fulfil Joffre's requirements, nor his apprehensions that labour in England was far from keeping step with the stern necessities of war.

paraissent préoccupés non point de vaincre l'ennemi, mais bien de ne pas se compromettre et de ne pas assumer des responsabilités. Il se demande pourquoi, en France, le Ministre de la Guerre n'a pas lui aussi imposé sa volonté. Il termine en déclarant que, dans les graves circonstances actuelles, les chefs doivent savoir se décider rapidement, agir sans tarder, payer de leur personne, et assumer les responsabilités devant lesquelles se dérobent trop souvent les hauts fonctionnaires."

CHAPTER CXXVII

UNDERLYING deep and broad all Munitions trouble was Labour, or rather the lack of it. How little the onlooker knew what was involved in the mere laying down of plant for manufacture. For shell-making there were required furnaces—which needed weeks to build and days to heat; hydraulic forges; steam-boilers; lathes, great and small; tools, fine in quality, innumerable in quantity, and of infinite variety; complex chemical apparatus, demanding the utmost caution in handling—whence were these to be obtained, whither transported, how erected and set going? Then, how were the veteran workmen, scattered two years ago, to be found and brought back—men absolutely indispensable for training new hands in the various crafts of munition-making? Where was the labour to be obtained for building and making ready the new war factories? Men were wanted—not in hundreds or thousands, but in hundreds of thousands. The War Secretary pressed other Government Departments to help him. The Board of Trade agreed to find men of business capacity and push, with local knowledge of particular districts, to beat up labour. This was done at once, and workmen and mechanics were torn from their jobs and handed over to the armament firms; but yet in the course of a few weeks the numbers of men were in seriously decreasing proportion to the calls of the contractors.

The Home Office was asked to utilise the Police for unearthing fitters, mill-wrights, machine-hands, and skilled or unskilled labour, and the Police themselves were requested to release any likely men in their own ranks. The Board of Education helped to obtain expert workers from technological institutes, and the Local Government Board induced local authorities to spare their eligible employees for armament work. Kitchener wrote to the Minister of Education:

> I am, as you know, trying to augment our supply of fitters, mill-wrights, and skilled or unskilled labour, for use in increasing the output of munitions.
>
> Do you think that the technical school authorities have any such persons in their employ who could be taken from them for the vital necessities of our armament manufactories? I do not wish to leave anything undone in my search for workmen, and should, therefore, be glad if you would kindly see whether any assistance is likely to be forthcoming from this source.

Many employers stated that the volume of output could be largely increased if the Amalgamated Society of Engineers would waive some of their restrictions. Kitchener asked Sir George Askwith [1] to convene a Committee to inquire as to production in Engineering establishments engaged on Government work, and this Committee advised measures to secure for workmen stable piece-rates, and thus remove one bar to production. They emphasised specially that no stoppage, by strike or lock-out, should take

[1] Later Lord Askwith.

place upon Government work, and that female labour should be far more largely employed.[1] Kitchener accordingly asked for additional powers under the Defence of the Realm Act, and urged that clauses should be incorporated in a Bill then being drafted to penalise employers who should cause a lock-out, or workmen employed on the production of war materials who should strike, or any person who should incite either employer or employed to any act prejudicial to a maximum output.

These valuable clauses were—curiously enough—struck out of a measure designed to facilitate War Office requirements, though they were included in scarcely varied form in the Munitions Act passed five months later.

Throughout February 1915 Kitchener was more and more distracted by insufficiency of labour, distressed by slackness and unpunctuality among some —if only some—of the workers, and restless under the still heavy hand of the Trades Unions.[2] He

[1] "Get women into the factories; get them in thousands," Kitchener told General Mahon, an artillery expert deputed to inspect the manufactories.

[2] "With regard to the Chancellor of the Exchequer's practical suggestions, I am glad to see that there are more factories available for the output of war material in this country. The real crux of the situation is, in my opinion, the organisation of the skilled labour required to work the machinery, and, if the Chancellor of the Exchequer could help us in this and in the many labour difficulties with which we are confronted, I have little doubt that in time an increased number of men, up to a total of 3,000,000, may be recruited and trained fit to take the field.

"In the efforts we are now making to raise, arm, and equip 2,000,000 men we are faced with grave difficulties, not the least of which is that, constantly, our manufacturers find themselves unable, owing to shortage of skilled labour, to keep their promises of delivery of arms, ammunition, etc. This shortage could be very much lessened by the employment of unskilled together with skilled labour on the same machines, but trade union rules do not admit of this. One of the first essentials, therefore, is to secure the requisite modifications of those rules.

"A committee is sitting, on which Sir George Gibb represents the War Office, for the purpose of organising labour. I understand that they have been more or less successful in some of their efforts to induce trades unions to agree to modify the restrictive regulations which they now impose on labour; but, if the Chancellor of the Exchequer could use his great powers

knew that from March onwards Sir John would be active; and although the reserve of ammunition available would be large,[1] he was determined that workmen and workwomen should learn the stern need of putting in every ounce of energy and every moment of time, if operations—of which perhaps he alone saw the future range—were to enjoy success.

Hardly had the guns at Neuve Chapelle ceased firing when, on March 15 in the House of Lords—with a frankness carried to the verge of discretion—he spoke the plain truth as to the shortage of equipment and material, and the reasons for it:

The work of supplying and equipping new armies depends largely on our ability to obtain the war material required. Our demands on the industries concerned with the manufacture of munitions of war in this country have naturally been very great, and have necessitated that they and their ancillary trades should work at the highest possible pressure. The armament firms have promptly responded to our appeal, and have undertaken orders of vast magnitude. The great majority also of the employees have loyally risen to the occasion and have worked and are working overtime and on night-shifts in all the various workshops and factories in the country. Notwithstanding these efforts to meet our requirements, we have unfortunately found that the output is not only not equal to our necessities but does not fulfil our expectations, for a very large number of our orders have not been completed by the dates on which they were promised.

The progress in equipping our new Armies and also in supplying the necessary war material for our forces in the

---

to persuade the trades unions to deal with this matter at once, he would be doing a great deal to help us in preparing an army of the dimensions he regards as necessary." (Extract from Note by Kitchener of February 25, 1915.)

[1] There was as much ammunition fired at Neuve Chapelle as in the South African War.

field have been seriously hampered by the failure to obtain sufficient labour and by delays in the production of the necessary plant, largely due to the enormous demands not only of ourselves but of our Allies. While the workmen generally, as I have said, have worked loyally and well, there have, I regret to say, been instances where absence, irregular time-keeping, and slack work have led to a marked diminution in the output of our factories. In some cases the temptations of drink account for this failure to work up to the high standard expected. It has been brought to my notice on more than one occasion that the restrictions of trades unions have undoubtedly added to our difficulties, not so much in obtaining sufficient labour as in making the best use of that labour. I am convinced that the seriousness of the position as regards our supplies has only to be mentioned and all concerned will agree to waive for the period of the war any of those restrictions which prevent in the very slightest degree our utilising all the labour available to the fullest extent that is possible.

I cannot too earnestly point out that unless the whole nation works with us and for us, not only in supplying the manhood of the country to serve in our ranks, but also in supplying the necessary arms, ammunition, and equipment, successful operations in the various parts of the world in which we are engaged will be very seriously hampered and delayed. I have heard rumours that the workmen in some factories have an idea that the war is going so well that there is no necessity for them to work their hardest.

I can only say that the supply of war material at the present moment and for the next two or three months is causing me very serious anxiety; and I wish all those engaged in the manufacture and supply of those stores to realise that it is absolutely essential, not only that the arrears in the deliveries of our munitions of war should be wiped off, but that the output of every round of ammunition is of the utmost importance and has a large influence on our operations in the field.

MUNITIONS COMMITTEE

On April 8 the Prime Minister superseded the Cabinet Committee by a special Munitions Committee under the Chairmanship of Mr. Lloyd George, the Minister of Munitions elect. The functions of the Committee were to ensure the promptest and most efficient application of all the productive resources of the country to the manufacture and supply of Munitions of War for the Navy and the Army, and it was authorised to do all that was necessary for that purpose. This Committee was the germ of the Ministry of Munitions which blossomed forth a few weeks later, towards which Kitchener disposed himself in loyal co-operation, and with which—as he testified—he could recall no single instance of friction. A few days after the Ministry was formed he sent for the M.G.O. and the chief officers who had worked under him, and said he knew they would extend the same devoted service to Mr. Lloyd George that he himself had enjoyed at their hands.

The new Department crowned itself with such well-deserved honour that its panegyrists[1] might well have been content to laud the achievements indisputably its own, instead of inviting the country to assume that the great production of ammunition in the autumn of 1915[2] was born of the energy of the Ministry; whereas that office was just then largely an agency for the distribution of munitions supplied agreeably to the orders of its predecessor. It was curiously unhappy to claim for the Ministry the sole

---

[1] It was laid down on June 5, 1915, that "the duties of the new department with regard to the supply of each kind of ammunition will begin when the requirements of the War Office have been made known to it as regards the kind, quantity, and quality of such munitions, and they will end when the delivery of such munitions has been made to the War Office."

[2] During October the production reached 1,200,000 rounds; not one represented or was due in any way to orders from the Ministry.

credit for the increased supply of high explosive shells, which, though it followed, was in no way due to the transfer of munition output from one Government establishment to another. The rights of the matter can best be understood by adducing a concrete fact. The Ministry of Munitions was set up during the first week in June 1915. It was not until the end of October 1915 that a single component of ammunition worth speaking of was delivered from Ministry of Munitions' factories or orders, and not until April 1916 that the first complete round, made and filled under the orders and arrangements of the Ministry, was delivered to the Army authorities. In other words, the Army, for a period of more than eighteen months, was furnished with continually increasing supplies under the arrangements made by the War Office.[1]

It was no less unhappy than unnecessary that the whole public debate on the supply of munitions, instead of being lifted to the platform of patriotic effort, was too often lowered to the arena of partisan polemics. There were not wanting men and groups of men who, in their desire to heap honours on the Ministry of Munitions, pursued the War Office with cries of contumely and reproach. Their praise of the one establishment was the precise measure of their condemnation of the other. The truth was that the praise to the one was as rightly due as the blame to the other was unjustly levelled. The Minis-

[1] At the end of May 1916 Commander Bellairs stated in Parliament that quite recently he, with the Member for Devizes and others, went to one of the Munition Centres and were taken over the great works of Messrs. Kynoch. Although they had gone under the auspices of the Minister of Munitions, the first assurance of the Manager of the Works to them was that, up to a fortnight before, which would place the date about the middle of March 1916, not a single thing turned out by that great firm had been under the order of the Ministry of Munitions.

try, fired, and sustained for a year, by the genius of Mr. Lloyd George, made gloriously possible the mighty efforts which Haig put forth in the last two and a half years of the war. But Minister and Ministry would alike agree that they reaped much of what others had sown; that the experience so painfully gained was theirs to enjoy; that labour which had sought to master the War Office was forced to be their servant; and that the machinery for making not only an army, but all that an army requires, which Kitchener so bitterly missed when he entered the War Office, was just ready for the fine use to which they put it.

Embedded in the story of the supply of Munitions is the unhappy occasion when from the battle of Festubert the Commander-in-Chief sent an extra aide-de-camp and a secretary to London, with the double design of effecting a minor *coup d'état* and inflaming public opinion against the War Secretary, the man to whom he wrote, "Thank God you are there, and I mean it." The Commander's care for his soldiers, which constantly endeared him to them, and his mental chagrin and confusion when he saw success denied to their gallantry, must be his perpetual plea for a step which soldiers might otherwise find hard to condone. His embassy, whatever favour it found in Downing Street or Fleet Street, failed to shake by a hair-breadth the rock of public confidence on which Kitchener stood to, and beyond, his last hour. Messages and other testimonies of goodwill poured in to him from camps at home and overseas, and from every class and community and corner of England. A month later he received—on his way to and from the Guildhall—one of the greatest ovations of his life—and the Order of the Garter. He himself was always, and altogether, silent on the matter, but those who were close to him saw that he had been wounded, and, as he himself felt it, wounded in the House of a Friend.

APPENDIX TO CHAPTER CXXVII

August 21, 1915.

MY DEAR FRENCH—I will now answer the points you noted. I have just come back from the Admiralty, where I think they have done us very well. With regard to observation balloons, we shall get one in a week, and, it is hoped, though this is very doubtful, that we shall get one a week later. With regard to the 3-inch anti-aircraft guns, I have got a promise of the first three that become available, it is hoped this month, and four in September and four in October; these latter will, of course, be subject to further consideration.

The 12-inch gun ought to be ready in the middle of September, but next week I hope to get eight 6-inch guns that can fire at an elevation of 35 degrees and carry approximately 20,000 yards; the 12-inch ought to carry 25,000 yards.

So much for the Admiralty.

Of telescopic sights we have sent you 395, and hope to send you 20 to 30 a week. It would help us very much if your Headquarters would say whether the lens sight, such as the Mettay, is wanted, as larger numbers of these could be supplied. We have not yet received a report on it.

The two Labour Battalions are now going over to you, and I have hurried up the future production of more. I think there must have been some delay in getting these Battalions ready to start through organising them on probably a too elaborate official basis of officers, etc. Would you send me a report when you see the first Battalion, and say whether we could not send out labourers without so much organisation?

With regard to ammunition, we hope to see an improvement in 9.2 shell; the 6-inch howitzer and 60-pdr. ammunition are delayed at present for want of tubes, which we hope will be forthcoming in about ten days.

The letter of the 15th August about the heads of 4·7 shells coming off cannot be traced, but I am taking up the question of the strength of the attachment of the head in the Mark V. shell.

We are not sending you any more B small arms ammunition until it is got right. Apparently the metal used in its manufacture was faulty.

We are having samples of all the H.E. shells tested by hydraulic pressure for flaws. I hope the gaines will soon be put right.

I think this answers all the points raised.

I thoroughly enjoyed my visit to you, and I hope to repeat it some day.

August 23, 1915.

MY DEAR KITCHENER—Thank you for your letter of the 21st August.

The three 3-inch anti-aircraft guns which are to come during this month will be an enormous help to us. We are badly in need of them. Please hurry up the others as much as possible—it is really most important in view of coming operations.

They are sending the required information regarding telescopic sights to the War Office at once.

Hadden has just left us. I hope he has found a satisfactory solution of the difficulty with the high explosive 18-pounder shells.

Immediately I got your wire on Friday I made arrangements to meet Joffre and Foch.

As I wired you last night, we have expedited matters as much as we possibly can. It is far more a question of ammunition than anything else, and I feel sure you will do your utmost to help us in this direction.

You may rest assured that we realise as fully as any one, either in England or Russia, the vital importance of striking at the very earliest possible moment.

I shall go over to you about the middle of next week (3rd or 4th September) and tell you exactly how we stand and our full intentions and plans.

We were all delighted to see you here last week.

CHAPTER CXXVIII

On Kitchener's return from the Dardanelles he found that the Government had decided to relieve Sir John French of his command in the field. The war had already far outgrown, both in duration and dimensions, the proportions which the latter had anticipated. The strain on a Commander-in-Chief had been severe, and would be sure to increase. Other important duties awaited Sir John at home, and it had been decided that with the end of the year should come the end of his leadership in the field.

The Government sought a soldier who would add to Sir John's fine military qualities an even temper, a cool judgement, a broad outlook—and an aloofness from politics. Such a man was to their hand in the person of Sir Douglas Haig, and in him the command of the Army on the Western front was vested.

To the official instructions laid on the new Commander-in-Chief Kitchener joined an earnest personal request that he would to the utmost of his power, and almost at any cost, renew and retain the most cordial relations with our French Allies.

On New Year's Day 1916—just seven weeks before the inception of the great attack on Verdun—Haig wrote to Kitchener:

I must send you a few lines to wish you many Happy New Years, and to hope that the one on which we are now entering may bring you nothing but good fortune and the successes which your great labours have *earned*.

As directed by you I have done my best to start on friendly terms with the French. I think I have made a good beginning. I visited Chantilly about ten days ago on the first occasion, and got on so well with Joffre that he invited me to a sort of family gathering with his three Army Group Commanders and the President, General Gallieni, and M. Briand.

This meeting came off last Wednesday—we parted great friends!

The chief question under discussion was the defence against a German attack.

I stated that I was satisfied with our existing defences, but there was no finality in such matters, and that we kept on improving our system of defence from week to week.

I am aiming (when drier weather comes) to hold our front trenches with fewer troops so as to have a larger Reserve for counter-attack. At present the Strategical Reserve only consists of one Division per Army. It ought to be at least two Corps (of six good Divisions) under a commander.

There are indications of the enemy preparing to attack in the direction of Roye—Montdidier. The Xth Army say they think on south of Arras also. Also against the Ypres salient. Joffre thinks Toye is the most likely direction. I expect his view is correct, and that the other preparations are only feints intended to mislead us and to absorb our Reserves.

This letter was the first in a correspondence which the new Commander-in-Chief constantly kept up with the War Secretary, whom he pressed to visit the troops in France and Flanders as frequently as he possibly could: "I shall always have a room for you whenever you can spare time to visit the Army. I need not add that you will find, as always, the most friendly welcome awaiting you from the Army" (20.1.16).

Sir John French, on resigning his command, was raised to the peerage under the very appropriate title of Viscount French of Ypres; his great reputation and long service had recommended him for the responsible command of the Home Forces, and Kitchener was instrumental in securing full scope for his future authority.

From the beginning Kitchener had asked Sir John to keep him closely informed as to plans and movements, and to write to him fully and freely on any point where he might be helpful. The injunction had been well observed. Correspondence between the two had been close, and the interchange of visits frequent.[1] After the end of 1914 Sir John came over very often to London, although at his own request his visits were kept secret, and he never entered the War Office. His habit was to breakfast early with the War Secretary at St. James's Palace and to remain with him during the morning. His letters to Kitchener bear sincerity on their surface, and even on a day of great stress he could write:

I have just received your wire and want to add a word in answer to the last part of it. If my remarks as to strength and losses in the wire to which yours was a reply were rather pressing, they were intended to convey to the Cabinet, not to you, the necessity of reinforcing men. We all feel here that we are absolutely safe in your hands, and we

[1] Lord Esher—one of the select band of Kitchener's constant correspondents—as a close and trusted friend of both the War Secretary and the Commander-in-Chief, was a frequent means of confidential communication between them.

have the most unbounded trust in your support and help. I repeat what I have said before, "Thank God you are there," and I mean it. You are the one man I have always looked up to and believed in as a soldier, and I rejoice to be serving under you again. I am deeply touched by the kind tone of your telegram to me—it reminds me of all your kindness and friendly attitude in the vicissitudes of South Africa.

The Commander-in-Chief seemed to wish also that Kitchener should think his own feelings were shared by his Staff: "Arthur sent me Grey's letter, and at the same time told me that it was your wish that I should destroy it. I have done so. I do not believe the Germans can ever get to Calais, but we are ready for all eventualities. I well know how worried you must be by all the work you have to do, and the people who bother you. You have nothing but old friends here who sympathise and want to help you. We are all grateful to you for having done so much for us" (26.11.14). Nor was Sir John sparing in his expressions of gratitude for Kitchener's present as well as past help. "I cannot tell you," he wrote during the first battle of Ypres, "how much I feel your kindness and help in meeting my constant requests"; and a little later (November 4): "I have often had reason to wonder how the drafts were supplied and the casualties made good so quickly, and so I feel sure you have done all you possibly can for us"; and on November 15: "It is very good of you to have taken so much trouble about pay and allowances. I am very pleased with the Territorials and feel sure they will form a valuable help to us, and we can do with as many as you care to send. Our munition stores are having a bit of a rest and I am not so anxious about that now. I am lost in admiration at the punctual and efficient supply of the drafts you send." Such letters, which were many, happily linked the old friendship in South Africa with the new relations between the Secretary of State and the Commander-in-Chief of the Home Forces.

The multiplication of theatres of war had vastly increased the ever-present need of a highly trained General Staff, and Kitchener had long determined on the man who should be at the head. The officer of his desire was Sir William Robertson, then Chief of the General Staff in France, a strong, shrewd, honest, and exceptionally able soldier, to whose marked powers of administration the War Secretary wanted to give full play in his office. He had waited for Robertson about as many weary months as Jacob waited years for Rachel; he would not deprive Sir John of so important a subordinate, but he knew that this self-denying ordinance would not be perpetual. After the battle of Loos it was understood that a change in the command in France was more than a likelihood, but Kitchener set his face sternly—and spoke his mind in high quarters—against any word or hint which might tend to impair the prestige or undermine the authority of the Commander-in-Chief. But so soon as a term was set to Sir John's command he seized the opportunity offered by changes at the front, and by the revelation of new talent, to bring new blood into the War Office without crippling the Armies in the field. With the Prime Minister's willing consent, he paid one of his many visits to General Headquarters early in December, and there discussed the future with Robertson, and asked him to put on paper the suggestions he had to make. In a document which was really a covering ground for both men, Robertson postulated as conditions normally essential to the successful conduct of military operations: "There must be a supreme directing authority to formulate policy, to determine the theatres of war and their relative importance, to choose the men to execute its plans; promptitude of decision being essential, its power must be absolute; it must be an executive, and not merely an advisory body"; the War Council should be capable of performing the functions of the supreme authority, provided it is relieved of responsibility to the Cabinet as a whole as regards the conduct of military operations; advice regarding military operations emanating from members of the Cabinet, or of the War Council, in their individual capacity, or from any other individual, should be examined and presented, if necessary with reasoned conclusions, to the War Council by the Chief of the Imperial General Staff before it is accepted by the War Council. The Chief of the Staff elect also said that, if all communications with the Commander-in-Chief in the field regarding military operations were issued and received by him, it would greatly expedite the despatch of business, and make for greater secrecy than had prevailed. Finally, he proposed some changes which would fortify the Imperial General Staff. A long conversation between Kitchener and Robertson took place in Paris early in December, some modifications of Robertson's proposals were adopted, and arrangements for future war-work wholly agreeable to both were decided upon.[1]

[1] Robertson, after a few months' experience at the War Office, said that had he known how easy and sympathetic the War Secretary was to work with, he would never have asked for extension of the powers of his office.

Gossip was, of course, busy with the new appointment. It was whispered that the Government, willing but not daring to be rid of Kitchener, had cunningly neutralised his authority by clothing the new C.I.G.S. with powers which would effectively limit those of the Secretary of State for War; these "feathers plucked from Caesar's wing" would "make him fly an ordinary pitch." The absurdity of any such suggestion was patent to any one who knew with any intimacy either of the men. Robertson, who would shudder at the bare thought of any political intrigue, had simply made soldierly representations for the better success of British arms, and for securing to the War Council fuller knowledge and responsible advice. Kitchener welcomed Robertson's extended powers scarcely less than his personality for very many reasons, not the least of which was his desire for leisure to devote himself to the many and multiform international questions—racial, historical, and geographical—which would force their way to the front whenever and however the war should end. "I think," he often said, "I shall be of some real use when peace comes. I have little fear as to our final victory, but many fears as to our making a good peace."

His relations with the new Chief of the Staff were just those he had enjoyed with other members of the Army Council. The Dardanelles Commissioners, with their strange *penchant* for pecking at the reputation of a soldier who had just laid down his life for his country, chose to hold up Kitchener as habitually neglecting to consult his subordinates, and as frequently giving orders over the heads of the Chiefs of Departments. They glibly committed themselves to this assertion without the formality of consulting any of these officers—except Sir James Wolfe Murray, whose special abilities and merits had proved unsuitable for the position he temporarily held, and Sir Henry Sclater, whose answers ran contrary to any such idea. When the Commission sat again, the members of the Army Council severally put on record their declaration that the Secretary of State had never failed to consult them, had almost invariably accepted their advice on matters concerned with their respective Departments and had never given orders over the Heads of these.[1]

In fine, Kitchener was always ready to use men if they were usable, and was obsessed by no avarice of power for the mere pleasure of exercising it. He knew and trusted Robertson, and remembered that he would be a most valuable buffer against plans of campaign emanating from individual Ministers who might exercise highly trained faculties of persuasive rhetoric to commend to the authorities the children of their too fecund imaginations.

[1] The Chief of the Imperial General Staff wrote:
"I have publicly stated and will always be willing to repeat that in all my dealings with Lord Kitchener, before and after I became Chief of the Imperial General Staff, he never showed any tendency to deprive himself of Staff advice."
Sir David Henderson went so far as to say:
"I laughed when I read the Dardanelles Commission's Report and the accusation that Lord Kitchener did not take his military Staff into his confidence. I have never dealt with a Senior Officer who took me so much into his confidence and gave me his opinion so frankly as Lord Kitchener."

CHAPTER CXXIX

THE situation which the War Secretary and the Chief of the Staff had to consider at the close of 1915 was none too rosy. In October the War Committee —called at that time the Dardanelles Committee— inspired by the India Office, had decided that General Nixon should be ordered to march on Baghdad with the force at his disposal, two divisions being promised him as soon as possible. Kitchener dissented, decidedly but vainly, from this mandate; he even repaired to the Secretary of State for India and warned him that he considered the advance, without further preparation and a large force, to be fraught with danger; urging that anyhow it could be made with less risk, less cost, and equal value later on. Lord Curzon was wholly of the same opinion, and even negatived a suggestion of Kitchener's that a raid might be made on Baghdad to secure any valuable military stores there without permanent military occupation. The Committee, however, after consulting the Viceroy, over-ruled the main joint objection of the two members who had first-hand and first-rate knowledge of the East.

On November 22, after winning some initial success, General Townshend, at Ctesiphon, had encountered large Turkish reinforcements, and had been obliged to beat a hurried retreat. Early in December he was shut up in Kut-el-Amara, and how to relieve him became another grave preoccupation. At Salonika we held a perimeter covering the town and harbour, with strong hostile forces on our front, and an uncertain neutral on our flank. In Italy, Cadorna was finding in the hills beyond the Isonzo an obstacle of forbidding dimensions. The Russian armies, with scanty munitions, were sadly inert. In the East the storm-clouds hung ominously. Kitchener, however relieved to find that the retreat from Gallipoli had given no immediate encouragement to the Turks, was by no means sure that future trouble might not arise from it in the form of unrest in India and Egypt. German agents were trying to find their way across Persia Afghanistan, and there were rumblings of revolt in India itself. The Germans, loudly trumpeting the *Drang nach Osten,* were preparing to support the Turks in an attack on Egypt from the East. On the West the Senussi showed increasing truculence, and there appeared a certainty of simultaneous attack on both frontiers, while portents of trouble were not wanting in the Sudan, where the Sultan of Darfur had been approached by Turkish agents. In East Africa, von Lettow Vorbeck, who had been left at leisure after the failure of the first important enterprise, had organised considerable native forces and was threatening to invade Uganda. In Mesopotamia our arms were faring badly.

There was no difficulty in providing reinforcements. Maude's[1] Thirteenth Division, withdrawn from Suvla, was sent to that theatre of war, while

---

[1] Sir Stanley Maude, who subsequently commanded with consummate skill the troops in Mesopotamia, where he laid down his life.

the Indian Corps left France at the end of December for the Persian Gulf. But so little had been done to improve a long and difficult line of communications that it was found impossible to get the troops to the front, and, after the failure of four gallant relief efforts, Townshend was forced to capitulate on April 29.

Robertson, fresh from St. Omer, was assumed to be an uncompromising "Westerner," a popular conception which Kitchener knew to be far from correct. The two men were in complete accord that safety in the East must go hand in hand with strength in the West, and the wide knowledge and experience of the one helped the other in the detailed work of reconstructing our Eastern military security. The first step was to advise the Government that the control of the Mesopotamian operations should be transferred from the Commander-in-Chief in India to the General Staff at the War Office, and a few weeks later, on Kitchener's proposal, the War Office took over control, both administrative and operative. Time was required to collect the necessary fleet of river steamers, to build the railways, and to provide the means of maintaining the troops in even moderate comfort and health; it was too late now to save Townshend's little band, but from the fall of Kut-el-Amara onwards there was no check to our steady progress; and Maude first, General Marshall later, went from victory to victory.

Kitchener found Robertson entirely of his mind as to the defence of Egypt's eastern frontier. A mere tenure of the long line of the Suez Canal, while the people of the Delta were waiting to back the winning side, would be extravagant of troops and dubious of success. During the spring of 1916 was initiated the slow conquest of the Sinai Desert; the construction of a broad gauge railway and a huge water-main to convey fresh water from Egypt, which Kitchener had arranged for the previous year, did much to further this, as also to facilitate the eventual entry into Jerusalem and to bring about the throttling of Turkey's military power. Vigorous operations were taken on the western front against the Senussi, who at the end of December were severely handled at Mersa Matruh, an even heavier blow being bestowed on them early in January by British, Australian, and New Zealand troops under General Wallace.

It was in this little campaign that Kitchener tried the value of armoured motor-cars, which he thought would be equally suitable to the surface of the ground and the character of the enemy. A squadron of these—found wholly unfitted for the fray in Flanders—was sent to Egypt under the Duke of Westminster, and played quite a forward part in reducing the Senussi to their senses.[1]

During Kitchener's absence in the Near East an expedition had been planned for East Africa on a scale which he declared to be unnecessarily large,

[1] "It was known," Maxwell wrote in a despatch of April 9, "that somewhere in Cyrenaica the Senussi held some ninety-five British prisoners, survivors from the *Tara* and *Morrina* which had been torpedoed in November. After a thorough examination of the prisoners taken on March 14, 1916, Captain Royle came to the conclusion that these prisoners could be found at a place some seventy-five miles west of Sollum. It was decided to make the attempt, and, as has already been reported, it was a complete success. The task was entrusted to the light armoured car battery under Major the Duke of Westminster, accompanied by the Motor Ambulances. The distance travelled was 120 miles, and the fact that the rescue was effected without any loss of life does not, in my opinion, detract in any way from the brilliance of the exploit. To lead his cars through perfectly unknown desert country against an enemy of unknown strength was a feat which demanded great resolution, and which should not be forgotten even in this war where deeds of rare daring are of daily occurrence."

and which he insisted on being reduced to reasonable proportions. Smith-Dorrien, who was to have commanded it, was taken ill before the start and handed over his charge to General Smuts, who could report early successes in the country where Kitchener first took the measure of Germany's power for evil.

Meanwhile there had been stormy days in the West. On February 21 the Crown Prince set his teeth and swore to take the great French fortress of Verdun. Four days later Fort Douaumont was in his hands, and the safety of a main pivot of the Allied line trembled in the balance. The French Government at once appealed to Kitchener for aid, and he was proud to be able to assure them that we were not only willing but ready to give it. On February 2 he telegraphed to Haig:

> On a matter which should be arranged between yourself and Joffre it is of course impossible for me to ask the War Committee to issue instructions, but you will realise, I am sure, the importance of giving him all the assistance in your power, and of nursing and encouraging the French in view of the state of their reserves. Our information points to no serious enemy concentration elsewhere than in the Verdun area. Only yourself and Joffre can decide whether you can best assist by taking over additional front, or by offensive action across your own front. As you know, public feeling in France is at the moment none too stable; and it might have a serious effect if we remain inactive while the French are heavily attacked. I have telegraphed to Joffre that I have represented to you the importance of giving all possible help in the forthcoming battle, and that arrangements should be made between you and him.

The number of New Army Divisions now at Haig's disposal enabled him to agree quickly with Joffre as to relieving the French Army which held the front upon either side of Arras, and to make the British line continuous from Ypres to the Somme. With this reinforcement at his disposal Joffre was able to hold off all the attacks of the German Crown Prince upon Verdun, while Haig prepared to strike back when the French Commander-in-Chief gave the word.

Kitchener did not live to see his new levies tested in the maelstrom of the Somme, but he died knowing that the Armies which he had created had been the providential means of saving our Allies in one of the great crises of the war.

CHAPTER CXXX

On August 6, 1914, the day he entered the War Office, Kitchener made up his mind that England could and should put 70 divisions of Infantry into the field, and in January 1916 he was able to say that 67 were afoot and 3 were in the making. His creed was not that 70 divisions would suffice to ensure victory for the Entente Powers; they seemed to him what England [1] was in honour and duty bound to furnish, and they were arguably the maximum force which could be raised and trained during the war. Calculated on the basis of German military organisation, England's man-power could issue in 105 divisions, and Kitchener admitted that 100 divisions constituted his ideal. But he fixed the lower figure largely because he recognised the demands to be levied on British manhood for services scarcely less immediate than contact with the enemy on the battle-field.

The War Secretary found little in the way of facts or figures in the pigeon-holes of the War Office to provide solid ground on which he must immediately draw his big plan, and he must decide on the spot to what extent our military resources should be pledged. He dismissed the prevalent and pernicious

---

[1] A year later Kitchener told the War Policy Cabinet Committee: "If we do not maintain 70 divisions we shall fall short of our duty."

idea that the war would be a matter of months, and settled himself on the rock conviction that hostilities would last three, and possibly five, years, and that it behoved Great Britain, by progressive steps and within a definite period, to put out an Army of Continental proportions.

The material to his hand for erecting the new force was entirely inadequate in quantity and somewhat uneven in quality. There was the Regular Army administered by the War Office; it possessed reserves of all ranks; it had century-old traditions behind it; and connected with it by the tie of association were large numbers of experienced officers and non-commissioned officers whose liability for service had expired, but who could be counted on to answer an urgent call to re-engage. And there was the Territorial Force, only partially under War Office direction and administration, and largely in the hands of local associations in which the civilian element predominated, and in which local influences prevailed and would be sure to assert themselves. The force was not liable for oversea service, it was very much under strength, it had no reserves, it was not equipped to take the field, and its training for war was incomplete. The Territorials had been specially designed for Home Defence, and as, at the moment, the possibility of invasion had to be reckoned with,[1] any action which ruled out their defensive rôle might affect the public temper.

For these among many other reasons the War Minister preferred not to rear his New Armies on the base of the Territorial Associations. The decision

[1] Kitchener shared neither the alarmist views of some of his colleagues in the Cabinet, nor the irresponsible assertions that an enemy landing need not be considered.

to build a new fabric on a new foundation was freely criticised; but that the creation itself fulfilled to the uttermost the supreme purpose for which it was brought into being has never been challenged. Kitchener was thinking in terms of millions of men,[1] trained and equipped and commanded up to the highest and most modern standards. The whole man-power and all the resources of the Empire must be laid under contribution and expanded to their full value—a task which might well be too weighty to impose on the Territorial Associations. Kitchener felt there must be no hesitancy, no half-measures, and that peace-loving, go-as-you-please Great Britain must be transformed into an organised military nation on uniform military lines. He found it also immediately necessary to control, without quenching, the patriotic ardour of amateur soldiers who sought to raise units in their own way without due regard to considerations of military discipline and requirements. He was beset with tempting offers to raise special corps or units—sometimes at individual expense—with specially qualified men; but he realised that, if differential treatment were admitted, difficulties would abound. He had no wish or word to belittle the value of such efforts, but he knew that they would tend to favouritism, to overlapping and confusion, unless brought under the set plan of a central and purely military authority. Practical offers of help were never refused, but the rigid condition was always imposed that no special privi-

[1] At no time did Kitchener agree with military experts who pronounced that in a war between France and Germany decisive battles would be fought within a fortnight, or that our Expeditionary Force would ensure the success of the Allies. It is on record that, about the time of the Agadir incident, he expressed his mind that victory would only come with the "last million" of men that Great Britain should throw into the scale.

lege or advantage should accrue to any unit other than those to be extended to every section of the New Armies. Every formation must be standardised so as to fit exactly into its place in the military machine. That condition once observed, Kitchener valued the spirit of clannishness or comradeship which prompted men with social, local, or professional ties to serve together. It was the simple and plain desire to secure an unbroken military level which prevented him, to his great regret, from closing with the fine offer made by Mr. Redmond to raise a special force in Ireland.

But if the War Office rather than the Territorial Associations was thus to be constituted the central controlling authority, the Territorials were not to be deprived of golden opportunities, and Kitchener, to his last day, never tired of alluding to the splendid response of the Forty-third, Forty-fourth, and Forty-fifth Divisions when they were immediately asked to go to India. By this means, while Home Defence was duly provided for, substitutes could be found for the over-sea garrisons of Regular troops, who were at once recalled to form the Seventh, Eighth, Twenty-ninth, and mixed Anglo-Indian Divisions, and replaced by Territorial units. Thus, without impairing safety, Sir John French could be reinforced, when in the thick of his early fighting, with seasoned soldiers trained to the hour.

On August 8, 1914, Kitchener asked for 100,000 men, and within a fortnight he had them in camp. It was easy to get the men, but not easy to deal with them as they came. Four days earlier the Declaration of War had been followed by a rush to enlist. Such was the enthusiasm to join up on the day after the ultimatum that at the principal London recruiting office twenty policemen took twenty minutes to make a way through the crowd for the Chief Recruiting Officer. For many days the fine fever of military patriotism raged. Men of all classes would sometimes pass a whole day in the broiling August sun awaiting their turn to interview the recruiting officer. Not a few, after a weary trudge to a recruiting station, would for want of better accommodation lie down in a ditch for the night.

On a single day the number of recruits was over 30,000, or more than the quota obtained in a whole year in time of peace. The machinery creaked rather badly, but nothing would deter the men from presenting themselves. The popular ardour was allowed to suffer no chill, and during the fifth week of the war 250,000 men presented themselves for enlistment.[1]

The labour of enlisting a host of early applicants was overcome, but there succeeded the far greater difficulty of moulding them into a highly-trained army. For lack of equipment the stream of recruits had to be dammed for a time by raising the standard of physical fitness—a necessary expedient which proved rather embarrassingly effective. Those who had offered themselves out of a sheer martial longing to fight the Germans showed less eagerness in leaping again to arms. The call of the drum was succeeded by the call of duty. In time the first white-

---

[1] One of the German Emperor's spies, specially deputed to ascertain what efforts were being made to raise soldiers, is said to have reported in three different stages: (1) "I have been to London, east and west, north and south; there is nothing to be seen but soldiers." (2) "I have been in the provinces; there are soldiers everywhere." (3) "I have been to Wales, the home of pacifism, and there the very devils from hell [*i.e.* the miners] are coming up from below to join the Army."

hot enthusiasm lost something of its intensity. The fine recklessness of self-sacrifice gave place to a belief that perhaps the country did not immediately need every willing recruit. Where there had been a passionate determination to get accepted for the Army at any cost, there supervened a calmer mood —"when Kitchener wants us he will let us know." With the raising of the recruiting standard the tale of direct enlistments into the Regular Army dropped sharply, but a return to the lower scale induced an influx of recruits, stimulated by propaganda and by a felicitous proposal of "Pals" battalions.

It will stand to the undying credit of the Voluntary system [1] that in twelve months it secured for the land forces of the Crown 2,000,000 men, drawn from a non-military people. During one week in August 1915, when the war had run a year, 24,000 men came to the Colours. Kitchener admitted himself agreeably astonished: "We have been more and more surprised that recruiting should have kept up as it has; the success of the recruiting has been one of the most extraordinary features in the progress of the War."

[1] In December 1915 Sir Nevil Macready, hitherto Adjutant-General in France, brought his abilities to bear on the corresponding position at the War Office, in succession to Sir Henry Sclater. In bidding farewell to the latter officer, Kitchener spoke of the deep debt of gratitude due to him for his work in respect to the raising of the New Armies, the success of which was largely due to his infinite capacity for taking pains.

CHAPTER CXXXI

IN July 1915 there was passed the National Registration Act to draw up the nation on war lines. The Act was at once a precise inventory of the national resources, and a necessary preliminary to any legislation for universal service. It was no sooner passed than a vehement agitation was started for applying it to this very purpose, and for introducing forthwith a measure for Compulsory Service. This demand Kitchener deprecated as premature,[1] and therefore "harmful." The Voluntary system had within a year yielded 2,000,000 men; it was still producing approximately 20,000 men a week—and at that pace 1,000,000 men could be kept in the field for twelve months.

Before Conscription should supplant Voluntary Recruiting it was essential to know how many men it would find available—information only procurable from the still unclassified returns of the New Act. Apart from the difficulties inherent in the change of system under war conditions, it seemed unwise—until the returns could be examined and the new

[1] Mr. Walter Long, whom Kitchener had before taking office consulted as to man-power, joined the Coalition Government on the understanding that Conscription would be part of its programme. He only refrained from immediately pressing this condition on Kitchener's representation that the moment would almost surely, but had not yet, come. He was reminded that the War Secretary was the only Minister who could claim personal experience of Conscription.

plan prepared—to abandon existing methods which could still boast a yield of 1,000,000 men a year, and Kitchener would not "dislocate the whole machinery of the country for merely negligible results."

At the outset he had to choose between Voluntary Recruiting and Universal Service. He then had at one ear the apostles of Conscription, clamouring for a clean sweep of the Voluntary system and the immediate adoption of General Service; while into the other ear was being poured the gentler, but equally persistent, plaint of those who, not thinking in millions, believed that the Territorial framework could be stretched to accommodate any force which the country was liable or likely to raise.

He never expressed—it is by no means certain that he ever entertained—any fixed opinion on Conscription in the abstract. He looked on it now as an expedient rigorously exacted by pressing circumstances. Before the war, when questioned as to General Military Service, he always declined to commit himself—partly perhaps because he thought that his judgement, unless based on particular knowledge and pronounced *ex cathedra,* would possess but little practical utility. A prolonged absence from England had precluded the study of the subject in all its bearings, particularly with reference to the feelings of the working classes. He certainly had a latent fear lest economic conditions, no less than deep-rooted English tradition, might conflict sharply with any attempt to maintain a large Standing Army raised by Compulsion. When, on the declaration of war, the Recruiting question in all its complexities had to be squarely faced, the War Minister still disposed himself to treat General Service—whenever and however it might be required—not as a fixed policy, nor as a fundamental principle, but as meeting a simple military requirement of the hour. In his view, the keenest opponent of Conscription for a Standing Army could, quite consistently, allow Conscription as an emergency measure for maintaining an army in the field.[1]

Kitchener's deliberate purpose was to raise by the summer of 1917 a force which, by virtue of quality no less than quantity, should enable the Allies to outman, outgun, and overmaster the enemy. His tale of 70 Divisions was complete, and as the year 1915 matured he realised that a mighty effort must be made to ensure the necessary drafts. He already had a total of 2,500,000; within the twelve months from April 1916 to April 1917 he must obtain 1,500,000 more. If the year's Voluntary recruiting would issue in 1,500,000 men, instead of the calculated 1,000,000, Conscription might be set aside. At this juncture the War Minister entered into close consultation with Mr. Arthur Henderson, who represented Labour in the Cabinet. He impressed on his colleague the paramount importance of placing and preserving in the field a great force for the third year of the war. He told him frankly that he had made up his mind to ask early in 1916 for such legislation as would relieve our Commanders in the field from all further anxiety as to reinforcements. Mr. Henderson rose to the occasion. He could not, of course, pledge individual Members of Parliament, but he

[1] On January 31, 1915, Kitchener heard that—with wastage calculated at 150,000 a month—the reservoir of men would enable the French Army to be kept up to full strength for nine months more. On September 15 he knew that there were 4,350,000 Frenchmen in the field: 2,100,000 were at the front; and of the 2,250,000 in rear of the line, about 800,000 were efficient combatants.

could and did promise [1] that the Labour Party should not corporately oppose any legislative measure which the War Minister should pronounce indispensable to secure victory. He made the proviso that General Service, when asked for, should be labelled—to quote Kitchener himself—as a special requirement and not as a policy.

The matter thus comfortably settled, Kitchener was dismayed a few weeks later to hear a clamour, inspired by a patriotic "zeal not according to knowledge," for the immediate enforcement of General Service. He had himself always intended to ask, if and when necessity arose, for Compulsory powers; but he hoped to do this at the psychological moment when he could enlist at the same time the sense and sympathy of the people. The Compulsory Service proposal was now unfortunately regarded as a political move, with the result, as Kitchener said, "of bringing the big guns of the anti-Conscriptionists to bear" on the proposed Compulsion.[2]

A difficulty was thus rendered still more difficult by the action of well-meaning zealots, and Kitchener's only course was to inform the Prime Minister of his precise military requirements, and leave it to him to frame the necessary political measures.

The Labour men were much disturbed. To be asked for their consent to Compulsion by Kitchener, whom they trusted, was one thing; it was quite another to have it forced on them by politicians

---

[1] Mr. Henderson told the Cabinet that he was prepared in the last extremity to accept Compulsion for a definite and publicly stated object.

[2] "I have been watching since January very carefully," he said, "for the moment when it would be necessary to come forward, and it has been to me a most deplorable fact that this agitation has broken out, because, whatever I say now, I do not speak with as much force as I should have done had this agitation not arisen."

whom they distrusted, and whom they suspected of the desire to introduce industrial compulsion under martial law. He knew that anything like a *corvée* would be intolerable, and in case Labour opposition to Compulsion should assume threatening proportions, he kept ready a scheme which gave local responsibility for obtaining the necessary men—a compromise between the two systems.

To give Voluntary Recruiting its last chance,[1] Kitchener instituted the so-called Derby Scheme, marked by two distinctive features. The men "attested" their willingness to fight when wanted; they then entered the Reserve to be undisturbed in their employment until called up; the recruits were classified under the Group system according to their ages and whether married or single. The scheme flourished early, but faded somewhat during Kitchener's absence in the Dardanelles; and on December 11 recruiting of "groups" was formally closed. But Lord Derby had made no mean effort, for in two months 2,250,000 men had "attested" and 275,000 had actually enlisted.

The days of indiscriminate recruiting were evidently at a close. More men were wanted than the Voluntary system could yield; but no man must be taken if more urgently needed in other spheres of national work. There were eligible persons deaf to all appeals, and there were many who could not release themselves from family or business ties. A just and generous measure of Universal Service could no longer be retarded. In January 1916 a new Act was passed, imposing universal military service

---

[1] The National Register being now completed, every person in Great Britain—Ireland being excluded—between the ages of sixteen and sixty-five was registered on a separate card.

on all men of military age, groups being replaced by classes, and local tribunals deciding—as in the Derby Scheme—applications for exemption. But before Conscription was legalised, nearly 3,000,000 men had been enrolled by the time-honoured system of Voluntary Recruiting—and in great degree by virtue of Kitchener's name.

In the early days of 1916, Kitchener, who had always looked to the war being in full flood during this year, had suddenly to meet a representation, put forward by a section of the Cabinet, that we must choose between a diminution of the force of 70 Divisions and a reduction of our monetary advances to our Allies. He declined the dilemma. He did not think that England could present either of these conclusions to her Allies without proof positive that expenditure could not be reduced nor national income increased, that our administration was free from extravagance, that our taxable capacity was fully exploited, and that all parts of the Empire were pulling their weight. In this respect India, he was bound to say, was making no direct pecuniary contribution to the war. All extra military expenditure beyond the normal Indian Budget fell on England, who was, moreover, compelled to pay in advance. Kitchener calculated that the monetary position could be improved to the extent of £90,000,000—the sum required; and this without reduction, either of our own forces or of the advances necessary to keep our Allies fighting. The conflict of opinion was sharp and short, and with the upshot that the 70 Infantry Divisions were assured of their existence and their drafts, and the way was prepared for the "Kitchener Armies" to take their part in the battle

THE KITCHENER ARMIES 319

of the Somme, which he knew was planned for the coming summer.

He did not live to see the end, but he willed and fashioned the means. His untimely death was reproached with having snatched away the man before he had played all his part in winning the War and, even more, in establishing the Peace. But at least, as regards the creation and placing in the field of the great Force which was to hold high England's honour and spell victory for the cause of the Allies, he could review a finished work, for the last division of the Kitchener Armies to go oversea took ship the very day on which he himself set out on the journey from which there was to be no coming back.

"The great Armies that he called into being"— so ran the fine epitaph of the *Times* newspaper— "are his living monument, and no nobler monument has been raised to man."

APPENDIX TO CHAPTER CXXXI

INFANTRY DIVISIONS: ORDER OF FORMATION; DATES OF EMBARKATION

Guards'	{ Embarked as a Brigade 14.8.14. Formed in France as a Division 13.8.15	
1st	Embarked	9/22.8.14
2nd	"	9/22.8.14
3rd	"	9/22.8.14
4th	"	23.8.14
5th	"	9/22.8.14
6th	"	8.9.14
7th	"	4.10.14
8th	"	4.11.14

"K" Divisions

9th (Scottish)	Embarked	9.5.15
10th (Irish)	"	7.7.15
11th (Northern) . . .	"	1.7.15
12th (Eastern)	"	29.5.15
13th (Western)	"	13.6.15
14th (Light)	"	18.6.15 and 3.7.18
15th (Scottish)	"	7.7.15
16th (Irish)	"	{ 17.12.15 17.2.16, and 28.7.18
17th (Northern) . . .	"	12.7.15
18th (Eastern)	"	24.7.15
19th (Western) . . .	"	16.7.15
20th (Light)	"	20.7.15
21st	"	9.9.15
22nd	"	4.9.15
23rd	"	25.8.15
24th	"	30.8.15
25th	"	25.9.15
26th	"	19.9.15
27th	"	19.9.15
28th	"	15.1.15
29th	"	16.3.15
30th	"	9.11.15
31st	"	6.12.15
32nd	"	20.11.15
33rd	"	13.11.15
34th	"	7.1.16
35th	"	28.1.16
36th (Ulster)	"	3.10.15
37th	"	28.7.15
38th (Welsh)	"	1.12.15
39th	"	3.3.16
40th	"	1.6.16
41st	"	1.5.16

Territorial Divisions

42nd T. (E. Lancs) . .	Embarked	10.9.14
43rd T. (Wessex) . . .	"	9.10.14
44th T. (Home Counties) .	"	29.10.14
45th T. (Wessex) . . .	"	12.12.14
46th T. (N. Midland) . .	"	24.2.15
47th T. (London) . . .	"	9.3.15
48th T. (S. Midland) . .	"	22.3.15

INFANTRY DIVISIONS

49th T. (W. Riding) . .	"	12.4.15
50th T. (Northumbrian) .	Embarked	16.4.15
51st T. (Highland) . .	"	30.4.15
52nd T. (Lowland) . .	"	18.5.15
53rd T. (Welsh) . . .	"	14.7.15
54th T. (E. Anglian) . .	"	21.7.15
55th T. (W. Lancs) . .	⎰Embarked as Battalions on	
56th T. (London) . . .	⎱various dates; formed in France 3.1.16	
57th T. (W. Lancs) . .	Embarked	7.2.17
58th T. (London) . . .	"	20.1.17
59th T. (N. Midland) . .	"	17.2.17
60th T. (London) . . .	"	21.6.16
61st T. (S. Midland) . .	"	21.5.16
62nd T. (W. Riding) . .	"	5.1.17
63rd (Royal Naval) . .	"	Oct. 1914
64th T. (Highland) . .	Formed	Feb. 1915
66th T. (E. Lancs) . .	Embarked	26.2.17
67th T. (Home Counties) .	⎱	
68th T. (Welsh) . . .	⎬ Formed Feb. 1915	
69th T. (E. Anglian) . .	⎰	
74th T. (Yeomanry) . .	⎰ Formed in and embarked from Egypt Feb. 1917	
75th T.	⎰ Formed in and embarked from Egypt May 1917	

The newly constituted Territorial Divisions were largely composed of men surplus to the requirements of the Kitchener Divisions.

VOL. III

CHAPTER CXXXII

So much of Kitchener's life had been spent in the East that he had enjoyed little knowledge of domestic politics and little acquaintance with English politicians. It is possible to think that he never quite understood either of these. His entry into the Cabinet was, anyhow, a wholly novel experience. For the first time he had to adapt direct habits of thought to the exigencies of an atmosphere where compromise is daily exercised, and where side issues so often deflect policy from a clear course. In the political arena, from which partisanship is so hardly expelled, Kitchener always felt himself an amateur, and perhaps an amateur who, with the serious business of organising victory on hand, grudged the time to play that particular game. He never could understand, for instance, why the difficulties relating to war correspondents and conscientious objectors should be allowed to take on a political complexion. The French Government had determined that no correspondents should accompany the troops in the field, and Kitchener was obliged to lay down that, so long as the French Army largely exceeded ours in numbers, we must conform to their ruling on this subject; and this ruling had to be enforced at the cost of inflicting some disappointment and incurring some resentment. As soon as the British force was sufficiently large to justify independent action in this matter, he consulted the Commander-in-Chief as to his wishes, and, receiving the answer that he had an open mind on the subject, Kitchener made arrangements for special correspondents—at first in very limited numbers—to proceed to the front. As to conscientious objectors, it seemed to him that a very sharp line could, and should, be drawn between the men whose conscience really forbade them to take up arms, and those whose so-called conscience was a mere mask for apathy, selfishness, or disloyalty. For the latter he could only recommend the arm of the law. To the former—who were really a select band—he wished every consideration to be shown, and almost his last interview at the War Office was with three eminent Free Church Ministers, who were able to lay before him the case as they viewed it.

Neither his words nor his pen were a rapid or wholly effective vehicle for his thoughts, and this alone sufficed to place him at a disadvantage with his colleagues in the Cabinet. There were many who told him that he was too strong, too straight, too far-reaching, and, above all, too silent for any political enclosure; that the silence[1] itself was a constant source of irritation to his colleagues; that for his sake and theirs he would do well to withdraw himself.

Stories were frequent, but for the most part very ill-founded, of friction and difficulty; and it was asserted that the politicians had expressed themselves freely and strongly as to the inadaptability of

[1] Silence, if resented in the Council Chamber, seems to have appealed to the soldiers in the trenches. "Kitchener and Joffre are silent, but the politicians go on talking, talking," wrote a young officer just before he made the Great Sacrifice. (*The New Elizabethan*.)

any soldier to the Cabinet, and of the desirability of removing a soldier from it. These suggestions reached Kitchener himself from many sources, in many forms, and with many intents, but fell always on unheeding ears; unruffled by rumour and untraversed by intrigue, he pursued his path of public duty. "So long," he said, "as I honestly believe that I have the confidence of the public, so long, and not for a moment longer, will I retain my post."

And, if Kitchener differed deeply from his colleagues in opinions, in mode of life, and in outlook on it, he found and made some very sincere friends among them. "We are out to fight the Germans, not one another," was a phrase constantly on his lips. His loyalty to the Prime Minister was of a piece with the loyalty which he had always shown to his official chief, and to which such men as Cromer, Grenfell, and Roberts amply testified. Mr. Churchill and his military colleague—both large in their views—seldom saw eye-to-eye as to precise procedure; but neither ever sought for an instant to belittle the merits or the fame of the other.[1] " 'F. E.' has been a comfort in Cabinet to-day," was a not infrequent allusion to the Attorney-General, who was to ripen into the Lord Chancellor. Perhaps no two men contrasted more sharply in mentality, in method, than Kitchener and Mr. Lloyd George; but, holding

---

[1] Kitchener's personal relations with Mr. Churchill may be illustrated by an incident. When the Coalition Government was being formed, the ex-Lord of the Admiralty found himself without knowledge as to his own future, and without information, other than to be derived from the newspapers, as to what was taking place in the theatres of war. Kitchener on hearing this immediately ordered his motor-car and, in the middle of his day's work, drove to Mr. Churchill's residence to tell him the last news from Sir John French and Sir Ian Hamilton.

as they did the common creed that they should take no rest until the tyranny of Prussianism was overpast, their differences—when all things are made clear—may find their place in the province of detail.¹ Both opined that the war would convulse the world; both unswervingly believed that the Germans must, and would, be beaten; both were determined to devote to the uttermost time and thought and energy to serve the cause which should save humanity. And perhaps those among his co-workers who understood him the least were those who at heart trusted him the most.

Probably no War Secretary has ever spoken so little in the course of twenty-two months of office as Kitchener; three or four statements in the House of Lords, and two speeches in the City, about comprise his oratory. Curiously enough, his voice was to be heard in public for the last time—and when death had already thrown its shadow across his path—in the Parliament where his appearances had been so rare and where his lips had been so seldom opened. Just when his mission to Russia was decided, Kitchener heard that the House of Commons, collectively and individually, had grave and genuine doubts as to whether all was well in the military conduct of the war. Members had no wish to penetrate military secrets, but they felt themselves unduly in the dark, and sought information which they believed to be theirs of right. They had suggestions of solid value to offer, if only they could be sure that these would not be mislaid on their way to Kitchener's room. The War Secretary was determined that he

---

[1] "The little Welshman is peppery, but he means to win—which is what matters!" was the remark of Kitchener after a difference had occurred.

would not leave England without satisfying, so far as he could, a demand he deemed so reasonable. On the afternoon when the battle of Jutland was being fought, the Under-Secretary of State, Mr. Tennant, announced in the House of Commons that Lord Kitchener believed it would be of great advantage if he had an opportunity of conferring with any members who might wish to see him and put questions to him which he, under the seal of confidence, would as far as he was able gladly answer. The invitation was conveyed to all Members of the House irrespective of political colour, and on the morning of June 2 the War Secretary, who was accompanied by the Chief of the Staff, addressed an attentive expectant meeting:

"Mr. Whitley—In view of the many questions regarding Army administration which have lately been brought forward in the House of Commons, I decided that the best course would be to give Members of the House of Commons specially interested in questions of Army administration an opportunity of putting their views before me, and at the same time avail myself of the occasion to make a statement directly to them.

"I have always felt that it is unfortunate that circumstances prevent my being able to make my statements in the House of Commons, for, although no Secretary of State for War has ever had an abler or more loyal representative and colleague than I have had in Mr. Tennant, it is and must always be a handicap on a Minister to be obliged to meet criticism and to answer questions otherwise than personally.

"I have before now considered the possibility of such a meeting as this, but I have hitherto thought that such action on my part might be construed as showing a desire to avoid criticism in the House of Commons itself. However, the precedent of the Secret Session in the House, and the fact that the debate on my salary has taken place, has led me to adopt the course which brings us here to-day.

"I feel sure Members must realise that my previous work in life has naturally not been of a kind to make me into a ready debater, nor to prepare me for the various turns and twists of argument. However, since these questions are questions of plain matters of fact, and the criticisms which are made are obviously made solely for the purpose of advancing the cause we all have at heart, I know, Sir, that Members will overlook any of my shortcomings in this respect.

"When, therefore, Mr. Whitley, I have made my statement, I and my colleagues will be very glad to answer such questions as Gentlemen of the House of Commons desire to put to us, provided always that they deal with administration and not with operations.

"My reason for making this stipulation is that we must maintain secrecy in regard to operations—both past, present, and future—since the operations of our forces are, and must continue to be, a part of the combined operations of the Alliance, and it would be impossible to give our full reasons for undertaking operations without also communicating information regarding the contributing factors both political and material which do not concern us alone.

"Therefore, Mr. Whitley, although I am prepared

to give any facts which may be required regarding the administration and disposition of our own forces, I consider that I am not at liberty (even in a secret meeting such as is here assembled) to divulge any facts which refer to the decisions, policies, or intentions of the military and diplomatic advisers of the various Governments of our Allies.

"As briefly as possible, I will proceed to give those here present a general recapitulation of the situation.

"When I took over the office of the Secretary of State for War, I found myself confronted with a complicated emergency. The pre-war theory worked out by the General Staff on instructions from the Government of the day had been that, in certain eventualities, we should despatch overseas an Expeditionary Force of six divisions in all, or, in round numbers, 150,000 men; that the Territorial Force should take over the defence of these Islands; and that the Special Reserve should feed the Expeditionary Force. On this basis, the business of the War Office, in event of war, was to keep the Army in the field up to strength, and to perfect the arrangements for Home Defence.

"My immediate decision was that, in face of the magnitude of the war, this policy would not suffice. Whether our armies advanced, retired, or held their ground, I was convinced that, not only had we got to feed the existing Expeditionary Force, and maintain an adequate garrison here and in India, but, further, we had to produce a new army sufficiently large to count in a European war. In fact, although I did not see it in detail, I must ask Gentlemen of the House of Commons to recognise that I had, rough-hewn in my mind, the idea of creating such a force as would enable us continuously to reinforce our troops in the field by fresh divisions, and thus assist our Allies at the time when they were beginning to feel the strain of the war with its attendant casualties. By this means we planned to work on the up-grade while our Allies' forces decreased, so that at the conclusive period of the war we should have the maximum trained fighting army this country could produce.

"Such an idea was contrary to the theories of all European soldiers. Armies, it had always been argued, could be expanded within limits, but could not be created in time of war. I felt, myself, that, though there might be some justice in this view, I had to take the risk and embark on what may be regarded as a gigantic experiment. I relied on the energy of this country to supply deficiencies of previous experience and preparation, and set to work to build a series of new armies, complete in all their branches. However, I must point out here that the building of these armies was only a part of the task. The Expeditionary Force had to be kept going, and the Territorial garrison of these Islands had to be kept up to strength and given the training necessary to enable them to take the field against equal numbers of trained troops, and most splendidly have they realised our expectations.

"These two items, be it remembered, practically absorbed the whole of the Staffs and sources of military supplies which had been calculated upon in the days before the war.

"In passing, I must also mention that, in the early days of the war, the efficiency of the Home garrison was a matter of vital importance, for a raid of a desperate nature, though obviously doomed to failure as an attempt at conquest, might certainly have paralysed our industrial powers which are now playing so decisive a part in the struggle. The necessity for keeping these Territorial Divisions intact and at their war stations in day and night readiness for an emergency is a point which I think it well to mention now, as it is one apt to be overlooked by those whose attention is riveted on the actual points of enemy contact.

"My problem was therefore to produce a force independent of those forces which had formed a part of pre-war calculations. I think the way that force has been built up is pretty well known to those here present. It now transcends, both in size and efficiency, my own expectations, and it justifies in my own mind my original decision that, although the rapid formation of a European Army was in the nature of an experiment and a risk, it was an experiment which had to be made, and a risk which had to be taken.

"I also take the opportunity of mentioning that, while a New Army independent of the Regular Army and the Territorial Force was being built up, I further decided that, in order to secure the release of the Territorial Force, which was garrisoning this country and reaching a high state of efficiency, it would be necessary to reduplicate it by means of Second Line Divisions and Third Line units which should act as recruiting depots to both lines. It will be seen, therefore, that, side by side with creation or extemporisation of new armies, the full expansion of the only force capable of this process was also in progress.

"With a fighting army to keep up, garrisons at home and abroad to maintain, and no less than forty-nine Divisions in the course of construction, it may be imagined that there were many demands on our sources of supply in officers, in men, clothing, equipment, and munitions. That is to say, we had to find, in addition to what we had—

> Nearly two million suits of clothes,
> About 600,000 sets of equipment,
> Half a million horses,
> Over one million rifles,
> 4800 field-guns,
> 450 heavy guns,
> 500 millions S.A. ammunition for equipment, and 110 millions a month for upkeep,
> 110,000 rounds of ammunition for big guns a month,
> 2,600,000 rounds of ammunition for field-guns a month,
> 1500 machine-guns on the old calculation, and
> 100,000 transport wagons and general stores for the equivalent of over 100 years' peace administration,

besides housing accommodation for 760,000 men over and above the ordinary barrack accommodation. And all this in a country actually at war, with its existing military preparations strained to the utmost, and every one of these items of essential importance.

"Owing to the extraordinary zeal and loyalty of my subordinates, and the immense adaptability and enthusiasm of the people, this colossal task was accomplished.

"It was about this time, I think, that the first of the most serious criticisms of War Office administration was made. It was that we failed to anticipate the necessary supply of machine-guns, and neglected to supply an adequate proportion of heavy artillery, and to anticipate the proper supply of gun ammunition for such guns as we had.

"I will take the question of machine-guns first. The question of the value and use of machine-guns was one which had been hotly debated by various military schools before the war. Both ourselves and the Germans had decided upon the same proportion, that is, 2 per 1000 men. The moment actual fighting took place the true value of machine-guns became apparent, and the Germans were able to take advantage of their immense organised factories of war material, organised, be it remembered, *before* and not after the declaration of war, and immediately increased their proportion. We did our best. In September 1914 we made arrangements for the manufacture of 5000 machine-guns, or, on a basis of 8 guns per 1000 infantry, sufficient guns for over half a million men. The need, however, grew, and in January 1915 we told Vickers, the only manufacturers with the requisite plant, that we should want every gun they could supply, and made arrangements for the manufacture of 15,000 more, and in May for another 7000, that is to say, by May 1915 we had made arrangements for the manufacture of 27,000 machine-guns. Of these, 16,000 having been delivered to the Army up to date, the supply has been as rapid as circumstances permit.

"After due consideration has been taken of the facts,

(1) that the proportion required has risen from 2 to 18 machine-guns per 1000 men; and

(2) that the Army has expanded from 6 to 70 Divisions,

I cannot think that our results can be regarded as unsatisfactory.

"I have dealt with machine-guns in some detail. With regard to Field Artillery and Heavy Artillery, I would point out that, with the help of a Cabinet Committee which assembled in October 1914, arrangements were made in that month for the manufacture of 4000 field-guns, and howitzers of a heavier calibre than had yet been used in the field were also ordered.

"The supply of ammunition for this immense train of artillery and machine-guns exercised my mind, as I explained in the House of Lords on the 15th March 1915, though at that time I admit the use and development of artillery had not reached the pitch which it has since attained in the field.

"By December 1914 we had placed orders for the production by April 1915 of 1,300,000 rounds of gun ammunition a month, and this amount was about double that required for the guns which were in the field on 1st April 1915. We have now with the forces in the field in France, Egypt, and Salonika between seven and eight million rounds of gun ammunition.

"Any one who considers what I have already said, the figures I have quoted, and the magnitude of the task on which the War Office found itself embarked, will readily understand that, as time went on, the growth of administration and business on this head transcended the powers of one Department.

With the double growth of our forces in the field, and the proportionate expenditure of munitions by those forces, it was made very clear to me that the War Office must be relieved of some of its responsibilities.

"Munitions as such—that is, the provision of guns, rifles, and ammunition, and the financial responsibility pertaining thereto—had become something more than a Department's work, it required a Ministry to itself. You will realize what a relief it was to me when the Ministry of Munitions was formed and put under the able hand of the then Chancellor of the Exchequer. He and I have ever been in loyal co-operation, and from the day he took charge there has not been a single cause of friction between us.

"Before leaving this question I will give one figure which I think is of interest. Amidst all the points of criticism which have been raised there is one which might well have been raised—I always wondered why it was not,—and that is the supply of rifles. In September 1914 our output was 6000 a week, a figure barely sufficient to make good the wastage in France. Of 2,000,000 rifles ordered in America commencing with orders given in October 1914 for delivery in July 1915, not one had been delivered in April 1916.

"Mr. Whitley, two such figures as those are enough to give Gentlemen of the House of Commons some insight into the anxieties and disappointments which we have had to put up with. Notwithstanding these delays, there are two million rifles in the hands of our troops at this moment, and the American consignments are beginning to come in at last.

"I now pass to the second cause of criticism of the policy of the War Office, and that is to the question of Compulsory Service. Why did not the War Office demand Compulsory Service? I think that is easily answered. The question of a social change involving the whole country, and running counter to most ancient traditions of the British people, is not a matter for a Department to decide. My task and that of the War Office was to find men, clothe them, arm them, and organise them. So long as sufficient men came in, it was not my duty to ask for special means of obtaining men.

"I need not go into the details of that scheme or the legislation that followed it, which is fresh in your minds. I had foreseen this possible necessity and foreshadowed it when I said on the 25th August 1914:

> 'I cannot at this stage say what will be the limits of the forces required, or what measures may eventually become necessary to supply and maintain them.'

"In my opinion, compulsion came at the right time and in the right way as a military necessity and for no other reason.

"From these main criticisms of early administration, I now turn to more recent criticisms. I take those of Colonel Winston Churchill; and I may say that I reply to them in the spirit in which they are made. His criticism is of a constructive and not of a destructive order. His main charge is that one half of the Army in Flanders fights and one half does not fight. I have a Return here which shows the total number employed permanently and temporarily on the Lines of Communication, which I will ask one of my colleagues to read.

REPORT AS TO NUMBERS EMPLOYED ON LINES OF COMMUNICATION

S. of S.

With reference to the debate in the House of Commons last night, and Colonel Winston Churchill's speech in particular, I find the majority of it is such as would be answered by the C.I.G.S. and A.G.

So far as the comments go in my Department they refer chiefly to the Lines of Communication. For some time past there has been an under-current of criticism in regard to the numbers employed on the Lines of Communication. These have been most carefully scrutinised by myself, in conjunction with the Quartermaster-General of the Forces in France and the Inspector-General of Communications, and I do not consider that they are more than is necessary for the proper maintenance of the Armies in France. I attach in detail the numbers at present employed on the Lines of Communication, which works out at something between 5 and 6 per cent of the Force.

Any comparison in regard to rifles and ration strength, such as made by Colonel Winston Churchill, is totally misleading, as shown in the attached notes. In one place he says: "Of the half of the British Army abroad, half of it fights and half does not fight." This is a totally inaccurate statement, as is shown by the fact that 72,000 approximately are employed on the Lines of Communication, out of a force abroad of 1,400,000. Again, he states that "a great tail has grown up in France behind the Army outside the fighting formations," and ends by saying that "it contains large numbers of men in the prime condition of youth and military fitness." As you are aware, we have most carefully gone into this, and 16,000 men were able to be ear-marked for gradual replacement by older men. It must be remembered that older men cannot perform many of the very arduous duties in connection with the removal of very heavy weights, such as daily have to be undertaken; and in many instances again, such as the Ordnance Workshops, Mechanical Transport Depots, etc., the younger men are usually very highly skilled mechanics, whom we absolutely know we are at bedrock in obtaining—in fact we are thousands down in numbers.

The actual weight of stores, supplies, etc., entering the ports in France daily is 33,500 tons, and the Inland Water Transport on the canals from Dunkirk to Calais in addition is carrying about 2000 tons a day.

It must be remembered that it is by no means the "tail of the Army in France," it is really the vital neck of the bottle, so far as the ports in France are concerned; and it must also be remembered that we are almost entirely dependent on our own labour, and get very little assistance from our Allies. We have to send over all the Labour Companies, the men to cut down wood, etc. (and even all the stones for the heavy roads at the front, which amount to something like 500 tons a day). All these numbers are included in the 72,000 on the Lines of Communication, and taking into consideration the peculiar position we have in regard to our Allies, the French, no one can possibly criticise the percentage of between 5 and 6 per cent to maintain the Army.

Every ration, every round of ammunition, and every spare part, whether of gun or mechanical transport, has to be handled by the men engaged in disembarkation at each of the six or seven French ports. They have to be moved from the ship's side to storehouse, manned by our own storehousemen, and thence by rail to the front, and again from railhead to the trenches. In many cases the storehouse, where it is not available at the port of disembarkation, is at an intermediate point, such as Abaucourt, Abbeville, Audruicq, etc. This means everything being handled at the port, into the train, from the train to the storehouse, back again to the train, to railhead, and from thence to the trenches. At each of these different points strong and capable men are necessary, and I think we have reduced the numbers required to a minimum.

(Init.) J.S.C.
Q.M.G.

1.6.16

NOTE.—In addition to the 72,000 employed on the Lines of Communication in keeping up the whole Army as shown in the attached detail, there are of course all the Maintenance Services in each fighting formation—such as Division, Brigade, etc.—all of which have to be self-supporting and complete in themselves, as they may be detached at any moment. Reference to the composition of each fighting unit can be made in the recognised establishments for these formations, which have been carefully drawn up for many years and are under constant revision with a view to minimising the Maintenance Services as far as possible who are not actually fighting in the trenches.

Feeding Strength

The numbers of the various services employed on the Lines of Communication for the Maintenance of the Armies are shown as 72,277.

The strength of the Army in France, inclusive of those in hospital, is about 1,400,000.

The percentage therefore of services for work on the Lines of Communication in connection with the Army is just over 5 per cent.

The statement of Feeding Strength on the Lines of Communication is most misleading, for the following reasons:

(1) It contains the rations issued to all troops disembarking at the various ports and travelling up to the Army areas, which amount at times to quite 10,000.

(2) It contains the rations issued to all Convalescent Camps, which average 5000 to 6000 and sometimes more; we have accommodation for 9800.

(3) It contains the rations issued to men proceeding on

leave and returning from leave, viz. from 5000 to 6000 daily.

"With regard to the figures you have just heard read, it may appear to you that the numbers are excessive. My reply to that is that in every previous war in which British Armies have been engaged, there has been a breakdown at one time or another of these ancillary services on which the well-being of armies depend for food, medical attention, and comfort.

"In this war, immense as have been our fighting numbers, great and terrible as have been our battle casualties, there has been no serious breakdown of ancillary services, and the health of the Army, the attention to the wounded, and the physical fitness of the men have been satisfactory. To achieve this we have had to make ample provision—but, had we erred on the side of parsimony in this respect, we should not have saved in men, since the losses from sickness, bad nourishment, and ill-tended wounds would have far outweighed the numbers we should have gained by depleting the ancillary services; and I cannot help feeling that many of those who now criticise what they consider to be our excess in the manning of these services, would have been the first, and with justice, to blame us had our Army suffered for the want of proper attention.

"It may interest Gentlemen of the House of Commons to learn what our Intelligence Department compute the proportion of ancillary to fighting forces in the German Army: 1 to 3.

"The disposition and allocation of the Army in Flanders is a matter for the ultimate decision of the Commander-in-Chief of the Expeditionary Force.

His judgement we must rely upon with full confidence, and nothing would induce me to interfere with his arrangements in administrative affairs. To do so would most certainly weaken his authority, and that, I am certain, is not the desire of any one in this room.

"As regards the uses to which Indians and Africans may be put for fighting purposes in the field, we have given, and shall continue to give, this matter full consideration; but many factors have to be remembered—the state of feeling in India, the approval of the white populations of South, East, and West Africa, and the subsequent social and political dangers to which such a course might give rise. These expedients are in the nature of a last resource, their operation doubtful, and their practical difficulties in the question of officering, feeding, and organisation immense. However, they shall have my closest attention, and shall not be 'turned down' as their author seemed to fear merely because they occurred to him and not to me.

"Now with regard to Home Service, the same criticism is advanced that we are keeping too many men at home, just as we are keeping too many men on auxiliary services in France. The Army in England must be divided into four:

1. Home Defence.
2. Drafts for the Front.
3. Training staff.
4. Sick, wounded, invalids on light duty.

"With regard to Home Defence, I must ask Members not to press me, and to accept with confidence the decision of my colleague, the Chief of the

Imperial General Staff, Sir W. Robertson, in consultation with Lord French as to the number required.

"The responsibility for the safety of what is the financial and industrial capital of the Allies lies with us. We cannot afford its being worth our enemies' while to make even a desperate attempt. In this matter we take the precautions considered necessary.

"As regards drafts, our ideal is that we should have in hand, under training, men sufficient to supply drafts for three months to come.

"I so fully realise the necessity for keeping men in civil employment as long as possible, that we do all in our power to fill up the bucket as the water runs out.

"Before leaving this topic, I would remind Members that they must remember that there are normally in England about 20,000 men on leave. These men are naturally conspicuous at places of entertainment and in the streets, since they gravitate to our great cities, especially to London. The men on light duty and invalids swell the number of men that one sees in the streets, but I can give you no figure with regard to these owing to the fact that it is one which fluctuates from day to day according to casualties in the field.

"I have now given a summary of the situation as I see it. That there have been shortcomings I do not deny. I have endeavoured to explain what our general policy has been. Certain criticisms I have not dealt with, as, for example, the question of the hospitals in the Gallipoli expedition. That, I think, for certain reasons of Imperial importance, we should not go into now—the whole of that question we are subjecting to a close and searching scrutiny.

However, taking matters as a whole, I sincerely believe that the War Office has, in this immense and unprecedented emergency, risen to the occasion. We have been subjected to much criticism, and constructive criticism we welcome. There is another kind of pressure which, however, seems to me to serve very little purpose. On occasions, a need becomes apparent. We investigate the cause and decide upon action. By some means or other certain agencies become aware of our intentions and press us to do what we have already begun to do, and, when our action takes shape, claim to have pressed us into doing it. That, Mr. Whitley, neither advances our cause nor that of our Allies, and seems to me to have very little merit. However, that is a matter I only mention, as I do not wish Members of the House of Commons to imagine that I or my colleagues are inclined to adopt measures for any other reason than that they are necessary for military reasons.

"I have now concluded my statement. Before Gentlemen begin to ask me questions, there is one point which I would like most earnestly to lay before them. It is with regard to Questions in the House of Commons. It is no part of mine to shun Questions, but I do beg, on behalf of my staff and my colleagues, that Members will only ask such Questions as they deem to be of real importance. At the present moment the War Office staff is worked and overworked by the actual business in hand, and I am sure that Members do not desire to add to the labours of the Ministry except for such matters as really require elucidation. Many questions which only take a moment to write down, and are not matters of first-rate importance, mean the diversion of brains and energy from work which must be well done to be done at all."

The surrender of the Members was at discretion. They expressed themselves more than satisfied with the simple, straightforward, and explicit statement, which had removed the difficulties they had honestly felt; and they frankly expressed their recognition of what the War Secretary had done—and their admiration of the way he had done it. A vote of thanks was cordially proposed by Mr. William Crooks, and, somewhat curiously, seconded by an ex-Guards officer who a few days earlier had moved to reduce the salary of the man who was at once Secretary of State for War and Colonel of the Irish Guards.

CHAPTER CXXXIII

IF Kitchener did not travel quite easily along political lines, his close personal touch with the Allies formed not the least of his contributions to the war. From Rome the British Ambassador wrote that Kitchener's presence at the War Office inspired, even in the early days of the war, a strong feeling of confidence; that his largeness of view in at once insisting on the enrolment of new armies produced a deep impression and persuaded Italy that Great Britain would surely make good and carry her cause to final success.

His friendship with France gave him, so to speak, a flying start in gaining the best relations with her public servants. Before he even entered the War Office, he went to the French Embassy to see M. Cambon, to discuss with him matters of equal interest to France and England, and to beg that he might be placed and kept in closest touch with the French Commander. From then forward the War Minister and the French Ambassador held continuous and familiar intercourse. Many difficulties were overcome; many pitfalls avoided; many little sore places healed; many arrangements hastened; many important conditions adjusted. Kitchener was also able to be on the most comfortable terms with two such contrasting personalities as the dry, clever, somewhat unimaginative French War Minister, and the genial, courageous, warm-hearted soldier known to his troops as "le Père Joffre." With Joffre, indeed, Kitchener formed a sincere friendship, born of mutual respect and a mutual passionate determination to overcome a brutal enemy. Letters between them were frequent and intimate, without infringing the ritual of official routine, and Kitchener's last order before leaving London on his fatal journey was that his own motor-car should be placed at the disposal of Marshal Joffre, who was expected in London two days later. The love of France, bred in his bone and nourished by incessant interest in her defence, rendered relations with her from the outset easier than those with our other potential ally, Russia. He knew that the French and British General Staffs had always hoped that on the declaration of war Russia would concentrate against Germany whilst only adopting "containing" strategy as against Austria; but he himself doubted whether Russia's hatred of Austria would allow her to adopt this selfless line of action.

Russia's part in the War was to him a matter of vital importance, though he would not allow it to figure in his final calculations. He fully appreciated the weight of her human avalanche, but he regarded the advance into East Prussia rather as a powerful raid than as a great strategic move, and he never flattered himself with the idea that, if we could only hold Germany in grip in the West, the Russian "steamroller" would be entirely effective in the East.

He was quickly aware how deficient in munitions were the armies of the Emperor Nicholas, and how greatly depreciated they thus were as assessors to the Allies. The full gravity of the situation was not fully disclosed until early in 1915, but before then many communications had passed between him and the Grand Duke Nicholas, and the Englishman was no less dismayed than angry to note the gross bribery and corruption which marked Russia's attempts to furnish herself, and would not accept the explanation that the Russians were orientals, and what we called bribery and corruption was to them "dustouri."

By the time that the Central Powers delivered their great offensive on the Eastern front which carried their legions into the heart of the Tsar's dominions, Kitchener was thoroughly acquainted with the lamentable position in which the Eastern Empire stood in respect to war material, and was doing his utmost to bolster up an already rather tottering Ally.

L'état de Russie [he sent word to the French War Minister in the summer of 1915], est des plus alarmants, à quelque point de vue que l'on se place; social, politique, économique, et militaire; les parties anarchistes et révolutionnaires ne sont pas désarmés; la trahison est partout; l'influence allemande, malgré le Tsar et le Grand Duc Nicolas, continue s'exercer depuis le haut jusqu'au bas de l'échelle sociale; la mainmise par l'ennemi sur les Détroits scandinaves et ottomans isole la Russie et l'empêche de recevoir en échange de ses exportations de blé, les importations dont elle a un besoin urgent pour vivre et se défendre; le sentiment et la sensation de cet étouffement agissent presque autant sur le moral de la population que sur la vie économique; les Turcs combattent vigoureusement en Arménie; l'armement russe est insuffisant; la situation au point de vue des munitions est navrante et presque sans remède, étant donné l'isolement et les faibles resources industrielles de la Russie.

Kitchener, negociating with the Russian Government, had committed himself to serious responsibilities as to procuring rifles, machine-guns, and artillery—with their complement of ammunition—from the United States and from Japan, to arm the almost weaponless Russian hosts which were retiring before the armies of Germany and the Dual Monarchy. Huge contracts were placed in America and the Far East—particularly in the former—and placed in the first instance almost entirely on the security of the British War Minister's name. Nor was his influence in connection with the supply of munitions for the Russian fighting forces confined to the control and organisation of output from across the Atlantic and from the further side of Siberia. That influence stamped itself in Russia itself. His urgent representations and inspiring messages induced Russian high officials to consider the whole matter of munitions supply from a new angle, and efforts were put out within the Tsar's realm of a vigorous and prudent character previously unknown.

The results of these healthy reforms were not fully apparent for many months, but before the close of the campaign of 1916 a very marked change had taken place. The output from America and Japan started slowly, and it was not until the winter of 1916-1917 that shipments of war material—for which Kitchener had contracted eighteen months earlier —poured across the Atlantic and the Pacific to fit out the Russian armies for their great effort timed for the summer of 1917, which, but for the disastrous revolution in the spring, might well have brought final victory to the Entente. The principle established and the system created, Kitchener entrusted the control of Russia's supplies from America to General Ellershaw, an officer of extreme ability who knew Russia's needs to the core, and who was himself to share in Kitchener's fate. Establishments already existing for the manufacture of war material in America were enormously expanded and many new factories were set up; and, just as in the United Kingdom itself, where the elaborate organisation for munitions output began really to materialise eighteen months later—the credit for the work of others being taken by the Ministry of Munitions—so also did the results of Kitchener's labours in respect to the overseas contracts on behalf of the Russian Government only make themselves apparent when the great War Minister and his trusty lieutenant, Ellershaw, were no longer there to witness the fruits of their labours. But so great was the influence of Kitchener's personality, so unhesitating was the trust placed alike in his genius and his driving power, by Russians in high places, that the delays gave rise to little anxiety amongst those behind the scenes. Confidence that the Imperial levies would take the field fully equipped for the great contest of 1917 was maintained until the dire upheaval of March first broke the discipline of the Muscovite armies, and later brought about the shameful surrender of Brest Litovsk.

If it is difficult to account for, it is impossible to deny, the almost uncanny influence which Kitchener exerted throughout the great Eastern Empire. Except in the case of a few highly placed personages, who may have actually been brought into contact with him in the United Kingdom, or in the Near

East, or in Egypt, he was not personally known to the Russian people. Prominent soldiers no doubt had some acquaintance with his military record; leading officials would have read of him as an administrator who had accomplished great things in the basin of the Nile. But, when the crisis came and Russia was stretched upon the rack, the name of the British Soldier-Statesman was familiar to rank-and-file hanging on grimly to trenches on the Dvina and in the Ukraine who had never heard of Joffre; and it was sounded in the workshops of Putiloff and Tula by artificers ignorant of the existence of Elswick and Essen. This was a priceless asset, one of which the Emperor and the Russian Government took full cognisance, and of which they were determined to make the most. Thanks to this mysterious influence, Kitchener found himself in a position to criticise Russian methods with a freedom, to press his advice [1] with an insistency, and to adopt a tone of peremptoriness, that would have been tolerated at the hands of few foreigners in any case, and that would have been tolerated at the hands of no other foreigner not actually present in the country.

Early in May the Emperor caused it to be known that he had long cherished the wish that Lord Kitchener should pay a visit to Russia, in order that he might see for himself all the difficulties and possibilities attached to the prosecution of the war; that

[1] At the beginning of April 1915 Italy and Russia had not yet come to terms. Kitchener availed himself of his influence with the Grand Duke—who was just then elated by the capture of Przemysl—to telegraph that unless Italy quickly declared herself, some of the fruits of his success would be lost to him:

"Le Grand Duc Nicolas," so ran the significant answer on April 21, "partage entièrement l'opinion de Lord Kitchener sur urgence de la conclusion d'un arrangement avec l'Italie. Le Grand Duc fait son rapport officiel dans ce sens."

he might offer advice, which would be taken to the full—even if it included certain transfers of control into British hands. Kitchener himself was by no means averse to the proposal, and frankly said that he might well be able at least to discover how further help could best be rendered to an ally whom it behoved us to pillar up as much and for as long as possible. The British Sovereign gladly sanctioned the suggestion as submitted to him, and, on May 27, an intimation was sent to Sir John Hanbury-Williams, Chief of the British Military Mission in Russia:

Lord Kitchener intends to accept the gracious invitation of the Emperor. Please arrange for Nielson to meet Lord Kitchener at Archangel and to be attached to his Staff during his visit.

The party will consist of Earl Kitchener, Sir Frederick Donaldson, Brig.-General Ellershaw, Lieut.-Col. FitzGerald, Mr. O'Beirne, F.O., Mr. Robertson, Assistant to Sir F. Donaldson, 2/Lieut. McPherson, one clerk, one detective-inspector, and three servants. Should arrive Archangel 9th of June.

And three days later:

Lord Kitchener would like to pay a visit to G.H.Q. and some portion of the Front. The Russian Authorities will probably make all arrangements with the approval of the Emperor. Lord Kitchener thinks that it would be perhaps best if he saw the Finance Minister and Embassy at Petrograd, then visited G.H.Q. and some portion of the Front, and then returned to Petrograd *via* Moscow to deal with outstanding questions. His available time in Russia will be a week.

Then for a few days it seemed as if the fateful journey would not take place. On June 2 Kitchener telegraphed to Hanbury-Williams:

A VISIT TO RUSSIA

Mr. Bark has stated to our Ambassador that he thinks that my visit had better be postponed as he has to start for France on the 14th. I ought to arrive at Petrograd on or about the 11th, which would give me time to tell Mr. Bark all the financial points I have to communicate to him before he has to leave. Owing to the situation I cannot hope to have another opportunity of visiting Russia, so if my visit is postponed it will have to be put off altogether. Would you ascertain, underlying the action of Mr. Bark, if there is any desire that I should not come, in which case I should not think of doing so.

The answer was received the next afternoon:

Your telegram only received this morning. I thought it best to speak to the Emperor direct while avoiding any danger of placing him in the position of being obliged to answer me at once. I had a private and personal interview. I explained the position in regard to the dates named by you, and although I made it clear that if you did not come now you would not come at all, I said quite frankly at the same time that I knew you would not come if it were felt that your visit would be in any way embarrassing or entail extra work or make difficulties for any one. I twice begged His Majesty not to give his answer at once but to turn the matter over in his mind, to consult any one he wished, and to advise me later of the result. He repeated twice over that he wished you to come, and that he thought your visit was one of importance and should be of benefit to both countries. I trust that my action will be approved and that you will hold to the arrangements.

CHAPTER CXXXIV

THE final die was cast, and it was decided that Kitchener should embark at Scapa Flow on June 5 for Archangel. He was asked to examine thoroughly the whole Russian situation. He was given a free hand to make arrangements and conditions which he thought advisable; he was to use all the influence which he had already acquired with the Tsar and the Russian Military Authorities to set the Russian Military House in order; and he was asked to come back to England with all speed, as soon as ever his business was concluded.

He spent the evening of Saturday the 3rd, and part of Sunday, at Broome, still admittedly under the glow of the happy meeting with the House of Commons. He also that day made certain arrangements with regard to the development of his East African property, and told his devoted factor, Mr. Weston, to expect him within a month, when he looked forward to seeing the rose garden, in which he took infinite pleasure, in full summer bloom.

On his return to London in the late afternoon he found, as usual, a large number of papers awaiting his attention and signature, but, having completed them, he asked a friend to have tea alone with him,

DEPARTURE FOR RUSSIA

and accompany him to the station, to arrange several matters of personal concern to him.

At King's Cross Station some confusion occurred, as Mr. O'Beirne's servant had misdirected himself to the wrong station and left his master cipherless. The train was not, however, delayed, as it was thought better that Mr. O'Beirne should recover servant and cipher and follow by special train. Poor servant! if only he had been in question and not the cipher, he would have been spared his master's fate. Kitchener, as usual, entered the carriage immediately in order to escape more observation than was necessary. Then something unusual happened. He came back on to the platform and said very quietly—and a little sadly—to his friend, "Look after things while I am away"; thereupon, as if unable to explain to himself the impulse which had prompted him to have a last word, he quickly regained his seat and looked away out of the window until the train started.

On the morning of the 5th Kitchener crossed over with his Staff from Thurso on the destroyer *Oak,* and arrived alongside the *Iron Duke* at about noon. It was a very unpleasant day, with a heavy north-easterly gale blowing, but the passage from Thurso, being under the lee of the Orkneys, was fairly comfortable. The Admiral, Sir John Jellicoe,[1] received him on board, and entertained him to luncheon, having invited the Flag Officers of the Fleet to meet him. Kitchener told him the object of his visit to Russia, and laid some stress on the fact that he intended to be back at the end of three weeks' time, and seemed rather disappointed to learn the

[1] Later Viscount Jellicoe.

number of days that the passage between Scapa and Archangel would occupy. While discussing his mission to Russia he expressed delight at being relieved for a time from the labours of his office, and gave the Admiral the impression that he was looking forward to his visit with keen pleasure, no less than with real hope of its usefulness.

Kitchener's visit had not been made known, but as soon as the sailors recognised him they treated him to a great impromptu ovation, which he quite evidently keenly appreciated. He made a tour of the ship, watched the various drills going on, inspected the different gunnery devices for keeping officers and men efficient, and was told in detail all the tactics of the Fleet, before, during, and after the battle of Jutland.

At about 4.15 he left the Flagship and proceeded on board the *Hampshire*; the wind at Scapa having been north-easterly during the day the Admiral, with intent to make the passage to the northward as easy as possible, directed that the *Hampshire* should proceed on what, with that wind, would be the lee-side of the Orkneys and Shetlands. By an unhappy error of judgement an unswept channel was chosen for the passage of the cruiser; and Kitchener—the secret of whose journey had been betrayed—was to fall into the machinations of England's enemies, and to die swiftly at their hands. The faithful steward must suddenly give an account of his stewardship.

At five o'clock the *Hampshire* steamed from the Grand Fleet to her doom; she sped forward so fast and under such stress of weather that the destroyers who formed her titular escort turned about, leaving the vessel to her fate. When the crash came—the

LT. COL. O. A. FITZGERALD　　MR. H. J. O'BEIRNE　　JOHN JELLICOE　　LORD KITCHENER

LORD KITCHENER AND THE MEMBERS OF HIS STAFF BIDDING FAREWELL TO ADMIRAL JELLICOE FROM A PHOTOGRAPH TAKEN ON JUNE 5, 1916

death-knell of all but some thirteen souls on board —Kitchener was resting and reading in his cabin; he was summoned thence by the Captain and was seen standing on deck looking outwards, FitzGerald faithful at his side.

Nothing is known of what then happened to him —little indeed comes within just surmise. One thing is certain—that the brave eyes, which had faced so many difficult and dangerous passages in life, looked steadily into the face of Death; one thing in God's good mercy is possible—that to those eyes, always strained to pierce the future, there was vouchsafed in the storm and in the darkness, and in the death agony, the Vision of the Eternal.

The same electrical impulse which proclaimed Kitchener's death to the world induced an emotional current so intense and universal as to lack precedent or parallel. Men as great, and as greatly mourned, died in days when news travelled leaden-footed, and the West had forgotten before the East had learned; never, since man has made the lightning his messenger, did the passing of an individual so profoundly move humanity as a whole. For an instant a hush seemed to fall alike on soldier and citizen, on camp and council-chamber, as if in reverence for a great captain; men of the mart forgot their money and men of the parliament-houses forsook their politics; for once was true literally what has often been said in rhetorical insincerity—that a single thought dominated the Empire, from the central ring of its capital to its farthest township and remotest outpost.

And when that hush was broken and the gold of

the heart's tribute sought to express itself in the currency of tongue and pen, there was exposed then, if then only, the full extent of the sway which Kitchener had established over the hearts and imaginations of all sorts and conditions of men. For the next few weeks messages from everywhere, from every one, sent by every possible means—cable, telegraph, telephone, aeroplane, submarine, camel-back, and wireless—poured into the War Office. It was soon made clear that the one man in England who had taken least pains to win popularity was the hero of many peoples.

Little less than a year before, on the occasion of the last birthday he was fated to reach, Kitchener's post-bag bulged with many curious evidences of what he meant to many people. The bestowal of the Garter again had attracted many messages of another sort that might convince him of the confidence of what may be called the obscure Great. But the messages that arrived now spoke of a warmer sentiment—of affection refined, though not chilled, by a great reverence. In much of the official condolence this note was distinct. The Prime Minister, addressing the House of Commons—which a few days earlier had listened to Kitchener's own voice—spoke of no man having less reason to shrink from submitting his life to

> the sure eyes
> And perfect witness of all-judging Jove.

The same note was sounded no less clearly by a Labour Member, Mr. Wardle, who dwelt on the trust reposed by the working classes in Lord Kitchener; they regarded him as "absolutely straight"; they knew that his word was his bond, and that in his

TRIBUTES OF SYMPATHY

soul was no self-seeking found. Kitchener had not consciously done anything to win over the workingman; he had probably neglected much that a statesman in his position might well have attempted with that end in view, if only for policy's sake. Yet, both from the organised working-class and from that vast, inchoate, often inarticulate mass which is too often forgotten, though it forms four-fifths of the nation, there came irrefutable evidence that he had conquered where he had never fought.

Equally striking was the popular, as distinguished from official, mourning of the outer Empire. In Canada, where he had never set foot, the just word was said publicly by leading men, but the letters of private citizens brought to light the living reality of the universal feeling. It was long before Canada would believe him dead, and doubt when dispelled gave place to anger that such a life had been lightly risked. From Australia came the message that his work would live after him; and Louis Botha, mourning the man whom he had learnt to love before he had ceased to be his opponent, found himself for once the mouthpiece of a united South Africa.

Egypt had been Kitchener's home, and Egypt felt—and was to feel more deeply with succeeding years—a blank which nothing could replace. In India, whence came nearly a thousand letters of condolence, every prince and every public body added solemn and sometimes hyperbolic eulogy to the stream of condolence converging on Whitehall from every corner of Great Britain and in every language of civilised men.

The non-British world was perhaps even more emphatic than his own country in insisting on the loss to humanity and to the Allies of a man of Kitchener's stature. America, still neutral and still critical, had never been neutral or critical as to this man. There was in him a quality that deeply impressed the imagination of a virile people, at once strongly practical and highly sentimental. They believed in him as a master of organisation, an apostle of their own revered gospel of efficiency; but they also admired him because he looked the part, and still more because he acted it only in dumb show. The reticence and mystery of the man, his stoicism and self-dependence, coupled with his "thoroughly modern gift" of getting things done, made his personality for Transatlantic observers one "around which a legend twines like ivy round an oak."[1] They had always expressed faith in him alive; they now spoke of him dead with an appreciation always reverent in essence, if sometimes characteristically picturesque in expression.

In France, where 1870 was no more forgotten than 1914, this "brave and prolific organiser" was "mourned as if he had been a son of the Republic."[2] "The Field-Marshal with eyes of steel," wrote one, "disappears like the figure in a legend." "The fogs of the North," according to another, "threw over his death a cloud of apotheosis."

In Russia there were many parties, but only one sentiment; Kitchener was trusted by all beyond any Russian soldier, and beyond all statesmen of any nationality. In the general sorrow might be detected a sadness prophetic and almost selfish; the failure of the great Englishman to reach his destina-

[1] New York *Evening Sun*, June 8, 1916.
[2] Speech of M. Briand, the Prime Minister.

tion might well seem to Russians the destruction of the bridge which alone could save their country from the logical end, already visibly menacing, of her lonely travail.

In Italy, where a recent visit had reinforced the friendly respect in which he was always held by Italians, Kitchener's loss was mourned by all, from the King and the Commander-in-Chief down to the conscript who had read in a popular paper that Kitchener had said only a few months before, "Every Englishman has two fatherlands—Old England and Young Italy."

Far away on one side of the world, in Japan, the death of Kitchener was felt by men to whom every other Englishman's name was merely a fantastic arrangement of characters in an unfamiliar script; far away on the other side of the world, at Buenos Aires, was printed a tribute which, for its beauty and conviction, might well have been composed by a grief-stricken and gifted compatriot.

After attending the long and stately ceremony of Lord Roberts's obsequies, with all its soldiers' ritual, Kitchener said to a friend, "I lay a solemn charge on you: if anything should happen to me in this war, take care they do not give me a military funeral." A Higher Power secured what, in different circumstances, would probably have been denied. With the memorial service at St. Paul's Cathedral, the sensitive simplicity of the soldier and the reverent humility of the Christian could have found no quarrel. It was as little of a spectacle as such a thing could be, and not unfitting either the man of unobtrusive faith, or the multitude who, with that instinct for reality which saves them from the worst kind of errors, had faith in him. Simultaneously, at two-mile intervals from the sea to the Somme, British soldiers, with the sound of the guns punctuating the words of the chaplain, bade a *Vale* to their chief, while in all parts of the world where two or three Englishmen were gathered together the name and fame of a great Englishman were commemorated.

A permanent and practical memorial to the Great Soldier—the only Field-Marshal in history to die at the hands of the enemy—was at once inaugurated, with the object of assisting the sons of officers and men disabled in the War. The Queen Mother, whose kindly friendship Kitchener had deeply appreciated, placed herself at the head of the movement, and in answer to an appeal—based alike on sentiment and common sense—there poured in from every point of the Empire—from men and women and children of all colours, classes, and creeds—a stream of money which quickly secured a sum never before approached by a Memorial Fund. But, while the world was thus paying homage to its hero as he lay beneath the sea coffined in a man-of-war, there was offered a silent tribute, unnoticed by the temporary chronicler, but to which the historian may well turn to justify the Kitchener legend. On a blood-soaked field in Flanders there was found, among a group of British dead, the body of a young soldier on whom the German bullets had done their work. One hand still gripped his rifle; in the cold grasp of the other was a photograph of Lord Kitchener.

CHAPTER CXXXV

THE storm of welcome which greeted Kitchener on his return home after the capture of Khartum was for him the first revelation of the place he had won in the hearts of his countrymen. The Gordon tragedy had left the country in an agony of disappointment, disquieted by self-reproach and something of shame. The righting of the Sudan wrong relieved England's feelings, and the man whom she held to have vindicated her honour was then acclaimed and thereafter accepted as the man in whom England could repose her sure trust. Year by year the popular regard waxed stronger for the soldier of whom the last thing to be said would be that he courted attention; rather he shrank with unaffected dislike from it, and more especially from all its noisier manifestations; of the modern arts of self-advertisement he was ignorant; of rhetoric he had none.

The broad fact stands that Kitchener inspired multitudes whom he had never tried to draw to him, who had never set their eyes on him, who knew of him only by hearsay, with a sentiment much stronger than mere admiration—something quite appropriately describable as personal devotion. For a parallel one must perhaps go behind all history to the mythical heroic age—to the realm of saga and of legend; the mystery that in death wrapt round the blameless soldier and the persistent disbelief in that death belong to the same order as the Passing of Arthur.

What was the nature and the genesis of the attraction whose strength and depth surprised Kitchener's contemporaries and might well tempt the incredulity of posterity? To explain them is not easy; no explanation can be more than half true, no suggestion could be other than halting. To account for a moral phenomenon so extensive in its range and so intensive in its nature one must analyse and measure the great forces which lie behind it. The quest can only be pursued up to a certain point and no farther, but certain suggestible solutions can be ruled out at once. Neither in the multifold extent of its activities, nor in the variety and duration of official work, was Kitchener's life remarkable beyond that of many another man. Nor—though his abilities were great—can his sway over men's minds be thought due to any general intellectual superiority, or to a mastery of technique clearly denoting him a man apart, like Napoleon or Julius Caesar. And though pre-eminent as an organiser and administrator, and not far removed from a very great statesman, he can scarcely be described as towering conspicuously from any one point of view above some of his contemporaries—to say nothing of the great dead who challenge him across the centuries.

Is it to penetrate more nearly to the heart of the matter if one attributes his influence to the fineness of his soul? Yet even here it must be owned that there have been other men as clearly touched with spiritual nobility whose memories began to fade almost before their bodies grew cold.

Excelling as he did as soldier and statesman, as administrator and diplomat, as linguist and archaeologist, and proving his worth in other vocations, it is yet arguable whether any single element in his character or any event in his career stands out so boldly as to explain a domination which, without effort or intention, he exercised not only over those in close contact with him but over millions whom he never saw. It is perhaps true that a singularly happy combination of noble qualities, a singularly fine record of notable achievements, made him the least ordinary of men; but behind all these there was the man himself. No one could leave his company without the impression of a personality majestically solitary in an inexplicable distinction. It was by a subtle but sound intuition that the multitude in their regard for a man were rendering homage to a great ideal.

Kitchener's mind was as infinitely broad as it was accurately precise. He was above all the mathematician, and universality and exactitude together make up the soul of mathematics; algebraic truth does not vary, though it may be expressed in millimetres or millions of miles, and be employed equally "to measure Orion" or to "take the size of pots of ale." For this man nothing was too small, nothing too large, nothing too distant. He was never so engrossed in the task of the moment—when his faculties might seem to be stretched to its accomplishment—that he could not descry things on the far horizon. Some men take no thought of the morrow; others think of it to the detriment of the work of today; others again, while seeing the foreground and middle distance in fair detail, have but a blurred vision of things near the sky-line. He saw all, not as in a picture with the illusions of perspective, but as in a plan where dimensions and distances figure as they are and not as they seem. The solution of a problem over which others fluttered with many circuits, he was able to seize in a single swoop of the intellect; and, while working on that one problem, he discerned, not mistily and inconclusively, but with clear-cut certitude, the further stages in the argument.

This large prevision marked even his earlier life, when personal and professional ambitions naturally predominated; patient in subordination, he was nevertheless constantly preparing himself for promotion; when promotion came he had already fitted himself for the next step; arrived at great responsibilities he looked no longer months but years ahead; before he had reached the top of the military ladder his mind had already expanded to matters of administration and high statesmanship. So in his last and largest duty, while the minds of others were immersed—and forgivably so—in the waves of the moment, his prophetic intelligence, without thrusting aside immediate needs, foresaw and provided against requirements which no other had taken into the most distant consideration.

Nor was this forethought confined to the larger matters; it governed his own personal conduct. From the moment he went to the War Office he refused every sort of social engagement on the plea that they would interfere with his work. The plea was sincere enough, but behind it lay another consideration. He knew that any word falling from him would be widely repeated, and probably on occasion grossly distorted—that there must be gossip and there might be mischief; and he would not be made the subject of the one or the instrument of the other. The tendency to look ahead may not have been unaccompanied by the defects proper to it. He who marches head erect and thoughts concentred on a lofty object may meet minor troubles avoidable by the man who looks for the inequalities in the pavement and the contents of the gutter, and who learns the slippery qualities of orange-peel and the adhesive properties of mud.

"In all ages," says a student of the human mind, "the men whose determinations are swayed by the most distant ends have been held to possess the greatest intelligence."[1] Such a man surely was Kitchener, whose intellect was of that rare order which counts the day's work important chiefly as a preparation for the greater day's work to come. But this intellectual bias towards concentration on the greater vistas was reinforced, to a quite incalculable degree, by an imperious moral passion. His sense of duty was equally remarkable for the earliness and the completeness of its conquest of his personality; in no man was the pure gold more free from baser admixture. He was by no means insensible to the good things of life, or even oblivious of the power of money as a means to their attainment, and professional distinction must of itself have appealed to him; yet from his earliest manhood he seems to have regarded himself as merely the trustee of energies and capacities which were to be improved and spent in the service of his country. Devoting himself to that single end, he turned away from

[1] James's *Psychology*.

everything that might subtract from the complete surrender of all his energies to the work which he found to his hand. For him everything was dross compared with public duty. When he was entrusted with the expedition to Khartum, he asked his intimate friend, Mr. Arthur Renshaw, to look after his private affairs at home. The request was at once granted, and from that day Kitchener left the management of his own personal business entirely in the hands of the man whom he constituted trustee. "It is most awfully good of you," he wrote from Egypt, "to give me such help. As you know, I am quite helpless out here to look after things, and have my hands full and a lot of most anxious work in this most difficult country, where every obstruction has been put in one's way and has to be got over. Do whatever you please, and do not think I shall look blue if things do not turn out trumps."

Rigorous with himself, he was not inclined to be less exacting with others. Those who worked with him must accept his standards, and must reach—at least measurably near to—his ideals. He could not brook men who would not or could not attain to the degree of efficiency he demanded; they must be eliminated as nature herself gets rid of the unuseful —without harshness but without hesitation. From those he retained he exacted full service, and that with a certain outward hardness. Never expecting the impossible, he was not disposed to rhapsodise over the performance of the merely difficult. Good work never lacked approval, but it was for the most part silent approval; only on rare occasions was a meed of glowing praise offered. Yet there was a subtle kind of flattery in this restraint, which Kitchener's men learned to prefer to the outspoken congratulations of another chief; it assumed that they would always do their best, that their best must be always good, and that there was nothing remarkable in any given example of this best. And, if there was little praise, there was infinite trust, and to those who served him the Chief gave loyalty as illimitable as he expected from them.

Professional zeal and almost cloistral notions of discipline may well have served to provoke a soldier's admiration for the splendid military machine revealed in the German Army. He could but marvel at a gigantic effort—maintained for nearly half a century—which issued in a military organisation as complex in character as it was perfect in integration. But his military, no less than his human, sense was unutterably shocked by the baser uses to which a great engine of war was put. His own experience in contact with Germans had not been specially happy, but he had no reason to suppose that their fighting, however bitter, would be stained by positive dishonour. It was, therefore, with amazement, and some scepticism, that he received the first accounts of outrages in Belgium and France; and before accepting absolutely the reports of cruelties practised on British prisoners of war he caused the most careful inquiries to be made. But, when the truth was established to his full satisfaction, a marked change, to which he never hesitated to give expression, came over his feeling towards the enemy. The gross insults, the wanton torture, the more refined cruelties to which gallant folk were subjected, callously, constantly, and by authority, roused in him hot indignation. He knew how tragically the sufferings of the soldiers must react on their friends at home, and he knew to his grief that no exchange of prisoners could be effected before at least the equivalent of Germans was in our hands. "Until this maimed and scarred generation has passed away," he exclaimed to a friend, "no German should be allowed anything like permanent residence or social status in this country. Business must of course be done, but how can there be friendly relations?" A well-founded report of some more than usually diabolical outrages on wounded prisoners happened to reach him simultaneously with a note from a plutocrat of enemy birth, who asked him to be a guest on any evening he would name. "I am too busy fighting the Germans to dine with them," was the scornful comment.

Kitchener's private as his public life offered some curious contrasts. Although he disliked most social engagements, he still more disliked being entirely alone, and was only really happy within a strictly limited circle of intimates. A crowd of whatever calibre was distasteful to him; solitude even more so. The desire for some one near at hand had a very practical motive. Wholly self-reliant in great things, he was in the small circumstances of his own domestic life curiously dependent on others. He would with meticulous care compute the figures for a vast organisation, but he would be loath to file a paper himself. He would sustain through a long day at highest pressure a discussion on some weighty matter, but would be unwilling to open a Cabinet box or reply to a call on the telephone, and the key of an official box, if left in his custody, was liable to be found under the dressing-table.

"I have no home," he would often wistfully say. But the general loneliness of his life did not seem to oppress him, except in so far as the absence of child-life from it. He compensated for this as far as possible by an intense and somewhat pathetic interest in the children of his friends, in whose society he took great delight. *Maxima debet pueris reverentia.* He never talked down to his child friends, and they were never afraid of him and sought him instinctively as an ally. On him the nursery conferred its freedom. And as the boys grew older he would bestir himself on their behalf, and was especially pleased if he could guide them to the Army, when in many cases he would provide their outfits. Almost the only occasion during the Great War on which he completely broke down, and had to suspend work for an hour or two, was when he suddenly heard of the death in battle of the second of two brothers, both of whom he had known and watched from very babyhood. From the South African veldt he had ended one of his letters to them: "Now I must get back to work, so good-bye." "My work"—this it was that seemed to occupy every corner of his mind as well as every moment of his life. And as his work absorbed his life, so it ennobled it; if here and there rough corners could be discerned in the sculpture, no stain could be found in the marble.

The deep seriousness of his disposition was lightened by a genuine sense of fun and a keen eye for the ridiculous. A power of witty repartee was always latent, and he could riposte with ease and effect. He would fence lightly with questions indiscreet, inconvenient, or merely foolish. If he wished to avoid inquiry or importunity he did so with a disconcerting nimbleness, and an impertinent intrusion into his thoughts he could treat with unforgettable severity. Wit in others he appreciated keenly, and his stern features would relax and his steely eyes twinkle with almost schoolboy glee when his sense of the ridiculous was successfully assailed. But he had no joy in the thrust of a poisoned weapon or the double meaning of an unseemly jest. At a joke unlovely, unkind, or in any way irreverent he could not have laughed, simply because it would have been no joke to him. A friend who was with him on an occasion in Cairo, where a somewhat improper French light opera was given before a great party, wrote of Kitchener's unmistakable discomfort. He was half puzzled, half dismayed, that any intelligent person should care to see such a piece; interest in the veiled indecencies was as unintelligible to him as the indecencies were themselves intolerable.

Incapable himself of any meanness, viewing all personal questions from the standpoint of public interest, he was ever reluctant to believe that an attack on himself, however unfair or unreasonable, could proceed from malice. Sensitive by nature, he had schooled himself through long years to be stoical under criticism, and used even to exasperate detractors by neglecting to read their diatribes. He welcomed, indeed, all and any criticism from which something could be learned; but mere denunciation broke unavailing on his stately reserve. When he was told that a newspaper which had assailed him had been burned on the Stock Exchange, no expression of satisfaction could be extracted from him; he preferred to think that his critic had erred in ignorance of the facts and in honest conviction that he was performing a public service. In all such cases where his own personality was involved he was—perhaps unduly—indifferent. But let a word be said or written which could in the least degree tend to endanger a soldier's life, or give a scrap of information to the enemy, and swift and scathing would be the rebuke. "If you wish to sell your country, you should raise the price of your newspaper—a penny is too cheap," was the indignant message to an indiscreet correspondent.

Devotion to the Sovereign was a fixed point in his scheme of thought. The Throne was trebly sacred to him as a subject, as a soldier, and as a builder of the Empire, of which he regarded it as the symbol and the keystone. If the close and cordial correspondence which passed between Queen Victoria and himself was not continued in succeeding reigns, her successors appraised at their highest value the merits of a great Servant of the Crown, and Kitchener's admiration was unbounded for the masterstroke of Edward the Seventh in forging strong links of friendship between France and England, while he delighted to note how strikingly King Edward's most attractive traits were reproduced in the youthful Prince of Wales. Reverence for the monarchical principle at home seemed to open his eyes the wider to the errors and dangers of monarchy elsewhere. "The War will last many years, and many thrones will be vacant at the end of it," was one of his earliest remarks after he took office.

On one solemn subject—the arcana of a man's religion—to keep total silence would be to lose sight of the influence that unified and sanctified Kitchener's life. To those who lived near him, who never heard fall from his lips one word impure or ignoble, who could never detect in his mind the faintest ripple of an unworthy current, who witnessed day by day and hour by hour the selfless devotion to duty, the uncomplaining sacrifice of so much that so many men look upon as pleasant, it seemed as if a conflict between good and evil had been fought and decided in his soul at some early stage of existence, as if in respect of so many things that matter so much to the man of the world the prince of this world might come to him and would find nothing. His life was based on religion in the primary sense of the word—the binding himself up with God; and the sacramental truths in which he had steeped himself in early youth must have instilled in him—not less than the purity of mind—the reverence in which he held all sacred things. Christianity was to him not an attitude but an atmosphere—and an atmosphere wherein he could breathe freely, without stinting his admiration for the intensity of devotion which marks religion in that East where so much of his manhood was spent.

It was said—and with perfect truth—of Kitchener that "in life he knew no rest and in death he found no grave." And if, in any sense or degree, *laborare est orare,* may it not be thought of him that no life could present itself as a more proper prelude to the further life of full freedom and fair beauty, that no labour could claim more clearly

the rest
Inviolate, unvaried,
Divinest, calmest, best.

INDEX

Ababdeh, i. 61; Frontier Force, i. 64, 66–7, 68, 70, 72, 79, 80–81, 97, 216; Kitchener's escort, i. 71, 73, 77
Abbas Hilmi Pasha, Khedive, i. 184–86. *See* Khedive
Abdul Azim Bey, i. 216
Abdul Kader Pasha, i. 127, 138–39
Abdullah Bey, Kitchener as, i. 56
Abdullah Bey Ismail, i. 121, 125
Abdullah-el-Taaishi, the Khalifa, i. 132. *See* Khalifa
Abraham's Kraal, i. 302
Absarat, i. 202
Abu Anga, i. 122, 126
Abu Hamed, i. 64, 214–16
Abu Hamed—Halfa railway, i. 210–13
Abu Klea, i. 109, 112–14, 119, 214, 264
Abyssinia, expeditions against, i. 175
Abyssinians, i. 190–91, 232–33, 250, 253
Acca, Pasha of, i. 25
Achi Baba, iii. 138
Adarama, i. 217, 218
Adelaide, ii. 292, 293
Aden: sanatorium at, ii. 260–62; Turks threaten, iii. 158
Adererad tribe, i. 69
Admiralty: and Mombasa, i. 151–152; and forcing of Dardanelles, iii. 118, 122, 128, 129, 188
Adua, battle of, i. 191
Adye, Colonel (Major-General Sir John), i. 298, 304
Afghan War, ii. 133; in 1919, ii. 148 (*note*)
Afghanistan: German agents in, ii. 251, iii. 302; Russian advance and, ii. 145–50, 151–4, 241, 243; strength of, ii. 242
Afghanistan, Amir of, ii. 140, 147, 149, 150, 152–5, 164; visits India, ii. 242, 249–51;

Kitchener and, ii. 249–52; in Great War, ii. 251; assassinated, ii. 251
Africa: international rivalry in, i. 143; German ambitions in, i. 143, 144–45, 150, 151, 154, ii. 310–11; Portuguese interests in, i. 143–44, 146; Kitchener on strengthening British position in, i. 150–151
Afridis, ii. 161
Agadir incident, ii. 310–11
Aghavallin church, i. 2
Agordat, i. 189
Agra, Amir's visit to, ii. 249–50, 251
Agriculture, tropical, Kitchener and, ii. 322, 324–6
Ahmed Ali, i. 189
Ahmed-es-Senussi, ii. 344. *See* Senussi
Ahmed Fedil, i. 264, 265, 266, 267
Ahmed Khalifa, ii. 61, 81–82
Ahmedab tribe, i. 69
Aird, Sir John, ii. 110
Aisne, the, iii. 62, 64, 73
Ajit Singh, ii. 255
Akaba, i. 55, ii. 316
Akasha, i. 192, 193, 196, 199, 202
Alberts, ii. 60–61
Aldershot: Kitchener at, i. 7, 13–14; New Armies at, iii. 280
Aleigat tribe, i. 80
Alexandra, Queen, iii. 360
Alexandretta scheme, iii. 99, 104–5, 110, 190, 191
Alexandria: Kitchener in, during Arabi's rebellion, i. 47, 49; riots in, ii. 314; defence of, ii. 337; Gallipoli Expedition organised at, iii. 127, 128
Ali Agha Khan, i. 18, 23
Ali Wad Helu, i. 182, 240, 244, 267
Allenby, Gen. Sir E. (Field-Marshal Viscount), iii. 33, 38, 71
Alsace-Lorraine offensive, iii. 19

373

Altman Collection, ii. 299
Amalekites, i. 27
Amalgamated Society of Engineers, iii. 283
Amarar tribe, i. 69, 158–59
"Amatol," iii. 275
Ambukol, i. 85, 86, 87, 88, 96, 107
America: Kitchener visits, ii. 298–9; and Great War, iii. 9; munition supplies from, iii. 270, 271, 272, 276, 334, 347–8; and Kitchener's death, iii. 358
Amiens, concentration at, iii. 22, 25
Amir of Afghanistan. See Afghanistan
Ammunition shortage: in France, iii. 72, 74, 78–9, 91–2, 238–9, 240, 264, 291; in Gallipoli, iii. 140, 142, 176, 177, 238–9; efforts to remedy, iii. 268–9, 333. See High explosives
Ampthill, Lord, ii. 126, 198
Anafarta Sagir, iii. 163
Anatolia, i. 39, 51, 54, 90 (note), 93
Anglo-French Entente, ii. 238
Anglo-Japanese Treaty, ii. 238, 281
Anglo-Russian Convention, ii. 240, 241, 244–5, 247, 281, 282
Anglo-Sudanese agreement, i. 260, 261
Antwerp, iii. 67–8, 69–70, 107
Anzac Corps, iii. 98, 124, 131; landing of, iii. 133–6, 137; in Gallipoli, iii. 142, 143, 158, 161, 162, 165, 166, 168, 169, 177, 178, 180, 188–9, 206, 211–12, 213
Anzac Cove: landing at, iii. 133–6, 137; shelling of, iii. 142, 146; concentration in, iii. 161–2; sickness in, iii. 180–81; Kitchener at, iii. 189; evacuation of, iii. 190, 205, 211, 212–214, 216
Araba Valley surveyed, i. 53–6
Arabi, rebellion of, i. 47–8, 175, 178
Arabia: Turkey and British influence in, ii. 261–2; an independent State of, iii. 153–5, 261

Arabic, Kitchener's knowledge of, i. 16, 48, 55, ii. 333
Arabs: Kitchener and, i. 27–8, 55, 56–7, 66–8, 97–8, 155–158; his Reports on, i. 69, 70 (note), 74 (note), 75, 80 (note), 85 (note), 98 (note); his skill with, i. 55, 67, 73 (note), 79, 97–8, 100, 155, 156–157, 162, 163, ii. 333, iii. 154
independent Arab State, iii. 153–5, 261
Turks and, i. 27 (note), iii. 97, 98, 153–4, 155
Arbain, El, i. 33
Archaeology, Kitchener and, i. 23–4, 26, 28–9, 32, 33–5, 188
Archaeology, Society of Biblical, i. 15
Archangel, iii. 350, 352
Ardennes offensive, iii. 21, 28, 32, 35, 38
Arendt, Dr., i. 146
Argin, battle of, i. 165, 178 (note)
Arimondi, Colonel, i. 189
Armenians, iii. 99
Armentières, iii. 71, 72, 245
Armstrong, Sergeant, i. 57
Army Council: Kitchener and, ii. 263 (note), iii. 300; and high explosives, iii. 275, 276–8
Army expenditure, Kitchener and, i. 70–71, 173–74, 224, 254, 329; in India, ii. 198–9, 228, 277–9
Army Institute Fund, ii. 190–91
Arnold-Forster, Rt. Hon. H. O., ii. 201
Arras fighting, iii. 82, 83, 224, 229, 237, 241 (note), 246
Arthur, Sir George, iii. 260, 296
Artillery, supply of, iii. 264, 266–7, 290, 333; Sir John French and, iii. 266–7
Artois offensive, iii. 251, 253–7
Arundel, i. 272, 297, 309
Arya Samaj, ii. 254
Ascalon, i. 17
Asia Minor: British reforms in, i. 37, 44–6; Kitchener in, i. 37, 51, 54, 90 (note), 93

INDEX

Askwith, Sir George (Lord), iii. 283
Aspall, i. 3, 5 (*note*), ii. 111
Aspinall, Lt.-Col. (Brig.-Gen.), iii. 217
Asquith, Rt. Hon. H. H., Prime Minister:
and Viceroyalty suggested for Kitchener, ii. 302, 303-4; asks Kitchener to be War Secretary, iii. 3; and Maubeuge concentration, iii. 23; and French's proposed retreat, iii. 52; changes his Ministers, iii. 238, 239; arranges Paris Conference, iii. 201; refuses Kitchener's resignation, iii. 208; his tribute to Kitchener, iii. 356
Assuan, i. 64, 68; garrison needed at, i. 127, 128, 137; block of stores at, i. 212-213; Kitchener's farm near, ii. 322
Assuan Dam, i. 11, 190, ii. 110, 113, 316 (*note*), 345
Atbara, the, i. 182, 227-28; battle of, i. 229-32
Athens, iii. 197, 199; Kitchener visits, iii. 201-4
Auckland, N.Z., ii. 296
Australia: Kitchener's tour of, ii. 285, 289-96; defence of, ii. 290-91, 293-6, 297; railways in, ii. 292-3, 294; clears Pacific, iii. 83; and Kitchener's death, iii. 357
Australian Defence Act, ii. 295
Australian troops:
in South African War, i. 322-23, ii. 1, 290, 294
during Kitchener's visit, ii. 289, 290-91, 292, 293, 294, 299
in Great War: forces contributed, ii. 299-300
in Egypt, iii. 96, 98, 110
in Gallipoli, i. 322, iii. 113, 131, 137, 142, 143, 158, 161, 162, 165, 177, 178; at Sari Bair, iii. 166, 168, 169; sickness among, iii. 180; Kitchener and, iii. 188-9; and evacuation, iii. 206, 211-12, 213

Austria, Emperor of, and Kitchener, i. 12
Austrian manœuvres, i. 12-13
Austrians: against Russians, iii. 111, 120, 141; Italy declares war on, iii. 139
Aviation, Kitchener and development of, iii. 73
Ayas Bay scheme, iii. 191-5, 197, 201, 209
Azzazimeh Arabs, i. 27

Babington, Maj.-Gen. Sir James, ii. 35
Baden-Powell, Colonel (Lt.-Gen. Sir R.), i. 271, 312, 320, 321
Bagara tribe, i. 123, 125, 133-34, 183, 206, 229
Baghdad Expedition, ii. 283-4, iii. 259, 301-2
Baghdad Railway, ii. 281 (*note*), 282
Bailloud, General, iii. 175
Baird, Maj. A. W. F. (Brig.-Gen.), ii. 93 (*note*)
Baker, Mr., ii. 226, 227
Baker, Professor, iii. 235
Baker, Sir Samuel White, i. 41 (*note*), 63 (*note*), 73 (*note*), 79, 88 (*note*), 195
Baker Pasha, Valentine, i. 30, 168, 174
Baleli garrison, ii. 245, 246
Balfour, Rt. Hon. A. J., i. 269; Prime Minister, ii. 111, 145-6, 151, 201; Ministry falls, ii. 224; at Admiralty, iii. 188
Balkan War, ii. 337, iii. 273
Balkans, suggested Expedition to the, iii. 102, 104, 106-7, 108-9
Ballygoghlan, i. 2, 3, 4
Balmoral, Kitchener at, i. 257
Baluchistan, ii. 133, 147
Baptism of fire, Kitchener's, i. 8
Baratieri, Colonel, i. 190
Barghash, Seyyid, Sultan of Zanzibar, i. 144. *See* Zanzibar
Baring, Sir Evelyn, British Agent in Egypt (Earl of Cromer), i. 55, 62; and Dongola withdrawal, i. 128; on Kitchener, i. 163, 168, 171; asks Kitchener to reorganise Police, i.

376 INDEX

168, 171. *See* Cromer, Earl of
Bark, M., iii. 350–51
Barton, Maj.-Gen. Sir G., i. 320
Barttelot, Lieutenant, i. 115
Basra, iii. 98, 155
Basuto scouts, i. 304
Bathurst, ii. 290
Battenberg, Prince Louis of, ii. 336
Bayley, Mrs., ii. 130 (*note*)
Bayuda Desert, i. 106; campaign in, i. 109–116, 209, 213; Kitchener's route across, i. 209–10
Bazar Valley operations, ii. 143 (*note*), 161
Beatrice, Princess, letter to Kitchener from, i. 133 (*note*)
Beatty, Lieut. D., R.N. (Admiral-of-the-Fleet Earl), in Sudan, i. 206, 215 (*note*)
Bedawin: Kitchener's skill with, i. 40, 55; trained against Mahdi, i. 61, 64, 66–7; Government department for, i. 170; and Tripoli War, ii. 315; Turks intrigue with, iii. 97; Senussi and, iii. 155
Begum of Bhopal, the, ii. 130 (*note*)
Beirut, i. 23
Belgab tribe, i. 69
Belgian Army, iii. 21, 28; in Antwerp, iii. 34, 67; retires on the Yser, iii. 71, 72, 80; co-operating with British, iii. 82, 83, 86, 221, 245
Belgians, the King of the (Leopold): Gordon and, i. 104; and Nile Valley, i. 150
Belgium: Germans advance through, iii. 18, 19–20, 21, 28, 29, 34; British landing in, iii. 39, 68, 69, 70; scheme for clearing coast of, iii. 87–93, 94, 103
Bellairs, Commander, iii. 288 (*note*)
Bengal Army, ii. 124–5, 133, 203
Beni Amer tribe, i. 61 (*note*), 135, 136
Bennett, Mr., i. 5
Benson, Colonel, ii. 51–2, 57

Berber: key of Sudan, i. 63–64, 209, 217; attempt to reach, i. 63–4; Mahdists capture, i. 62, 68, 74, 84, 98, 137; routes to, i. 209–10; Hunter occupies, i. 216, 217–18, 223; concentration at, i. 226–27
Beris, attempted raid on, i. 181
Bertie, Sir Francis (Lord), iii. 88–9
Besant, Walter (Sir Walter), i. 16, 19; Kitchener's letters to, i. 20–21, 22–3, 38–40, 53–4, 56–7, 57–8, 62, 64, 68
Bethlehem Steel Corporation, iii. 271
Bethsaida, i. 34, 35
Bethulie bridge, i. 296–97
Bex, i. 5
Beyers, ii. 14
Bhopal, Kitchener in, ii. 130 (*note*)
Biddulph, Colonel, High Commissioner of Cyprus, i. 38, 41, 47, 49
Bikanir Camel Corps, iii. 96, 97
Bimbashi, i. 50 (*note*)
Binstead, i. 2
Birdwood, Gen. Sir William: commanding Anzacs in Egypt, iii. 98, 110; for Dardanelles, iii. 113, 114, 115, 121; doubtful of success of bombardment, iii. 121, 128; account of landing by, iii. 133–6; success by, iii. 142; and Admiral Thursby, iii. 143; account of Sari Bair by, iii. 166 (*note*), 166–9; unable to attack, iii. 177, 178; at Mudros conference, iii. 186, 206; and evacuation, iii. 206, 216; account of evacuation by, iii. 210–19
Bir-es-Saba, i. 27, 56
Bishara, Wad, i. 205, 206, 213
Bisharin, i. 61 (*note*); Kitchener's influence over, i. 97–8; his negotiations with, i. 66 (*note*), 67, 68, 79, 81; his Report on, i. 69; Mahdi and, i. 134, 135
Bismarck, Prince, i. 149
Bixschoote, iii. 83
Black troops: at Handub, i. 159,

INDEX 377

160; at Argin, i. 178 (*note*); frontier garrisons, i. 177–79; at Omdurman, i. 179; Hunter's brigade, i. 215
"Black Week," i. 268–69
Blockhouse system in South Africa, ii. 5–8, 29–30, 41, 43–4, 47, 53, 59, 97
Bloemfontein: Kitchener favours move on, i. 274–75, 278, 290; Roberts advances to, i. 301–303; Kitchener in, i. 305, 306–307, 327; supplies reach, i. 308–10; police posts round, ii. 7
Blood, Lt.-Gen. (Gen.) Sir Bindon, ii. 2, 27, 35
Blood River Poort surprise, ii. 48–9
Blow, Mr., i. 11
Blyth, Dr., Bishop of Jerusalem, i. 32, ii. 345 (*note*)
Boers: artillery of, i. 271, 299, ii. 5; Germany and, ii. 105; hope for foreign intervention, i. 308, 310 (*note*), 311, ii. 59, 97; independence of, impossible, ii. 18 (*note*), 19, 22, 87–8, 90, 93 (*note*), 96, 103; irregular warfare by, i. 313–14, 327–328, 330; their numbers, i. 330, ii. 1; peace proposals and, ii. 18, 55, 57–8, 61, 70, 86 (*note*), 90–92, 93 (*note*); their women and war, ii. 12
Bombay Army, ii. 124–5, 133, 203
Bordeaux, iii. 56, 58
Bordein, the, i. 104
Botha, Chris, ii. 32, 49
Botha, Louis (Gen. the Rt. Hon.): Boer improvement under, i. 307–308, before Pretoria, i. 313; at Diamond Hill, i. 314; on treatment of Boer women, ii. 13, 14; rumoured peace overtures by, ii. 16; interview with Kitchener, ii. 19–22, 25; Government answer, ii. 22–4; negotiations broken off, ii. 25, 34; at Boer council, ii. 32, 36; and London proclamation, ii. 46; Blood River Poort success, ii. 48; retreat from Natal, ii. 49–50; peace overtures by, ii. 54, 61, 91; Bruce Hamilton attacks, ii. 56–58; disappearance of, ii. 58–9; at peace conference, ii. 86, 93, 96, 97, 103; Peace Commissioner, ii. 98, 101
advises consultation of Kitchener on South African defence, ii. 305; on Kitchener's death, iii. 357
Botha, Mrs., ii. 19, 26
Boulogne emergency force, iii. 102
Bouwer, ii. 40
Boy Scout Movement, Kitchener and, ii. 313
Brabant, Maj.-Gen. Sir E., i. 296, 297
Braithwaite, Lt.-Gen. Sir Walter, iii. 131, 137, 161, 180
Brakfontein, i. 322–23
Brancker, Maj.-Gen. Sir W. S., iii. 74 (*note*)
Brand, ii. 33, 44
Brandwater Basin, i. 318
Bremner, ii. 86
Briand, M., iii. 260–61, 262, 294, 358
Brindle, Father, i. 248
Brisbane, ii. 289
British Agency in Egypt: Kitchener desires, i. 189, ii. 117, 263 (*note*); he obtains, ii. 312; status of, ii. 332
British Association, Kitchener addresses, i. 31–2
British Expeditionary Force: its original composition, iii. 4, 7–8, 16, 31, 39–40, 328; its rôle, iii. 16, 18, 25–6, 45, 50–52, 57; to concentrate at Maubeuge, iii. 21, 28, 30; Kitchener's message to, iii. 27; at Mons, iii. 30, 34; retreat from Mons, iii. 39, 42–4, 45, 46–7, 48, 50–56, 62; Le Cateau, iii. 39, 42, 62; superior to Germans, iii. 48–9; at the Marne, iii. 57–9, 60, 61–2, 63, 64; reaches the Aisne, iii. 64; its transfer to French left, iii. 65–66, 68; on Ypres front, iii. 68, 71, 74, 75, 76, 80; to occupy ex-

treme left, iii. 82-3, 86, 88-9; transfer to Balkans suggested, iii. 102, 104, 106, 107, 108 (note); the New Armies in, iii. 220-21; Neuve Chapelle, iii. 121, 225-6, 227, 228, 285 (note); Hill 60, iii. 229-30; Ypres gas attacks, iii. 231-4; Festubert, iii. 237-8, 239; Loos, iii. 148, 249, 252, 253; gas used by, iii. 235, 254, 255; holds line from Ypres to the Somme, iii. 305-6; its administration, iii. 335, 336-8

British Museum: Cyprus excavations for, i. 39; offers Kitchener work in Assyria, i. 43-4

British troops: in Sudan, i. 209, 226-27, 233; in South Africa, ii. 1-2; Native troops and, in India, ii. 166-7, 169-70, 177

Britstown, i. 304

Broadwood, Lt.-Gen. R. G.: at Omdurman, i. 242-43; ambushed at Korn Spruit, i. 309; pursues De Wet, i. 319, 320, 321, 322; Beyers evades, ii. 14; captures Free State notables, ii. 39

Brodrick, Right Hon. St. John (Viscount Midleton):
Secretary of State for War: Kitchener's reports to, i. 324, 328-30, ii. 4, 6, 7, 8, 19-22, 25-6, 29-30, 31, 33-4, 44, 46 (note), 48, 50, 51-2, 54-5, 61, 62, 68-9, 71, 76 (note), 84, 87 (note), 90, 91, 100-101, 104; his confidence in Kitchener, ii. 39, 84-5; on Concentration Camps, ii. 13; warns the country, ii. 67; on Tweebosch, ii. 68; on peace, ii. 26, 70, 95, 104; tries to get Kitchener to War Office, ii. 118-19, 120

Secretary of State for India: Kitchener's letters to, ii. 199-200, 201, 202, 206-7, 208, 209, 210-11, 222 (note): supports Kitchener, ii. 213, 219-23

Brooke, Col. Victor, V.C., iii. 71 (note)

Broome, Viscount, i. 3 (note), i. 64 (note)

Broome Park, i. 3 (note), ii. 313, iii. 2, 210, 352

Brussels, iii. 21, 29

Bulair, iii. 123, 131, 149-50

Bulgaria: Central Powers and, 100, 102, 104 (note), 108, 120, 139, 140, 172; Greek intervention and, iii. 106, 196, 197, 202-3; mobilises, iii. 176, 178

Bulgarians, Kitchener on, i. 30

Buller, General Sir Redvers; Kitchener appeals to, for protection to Stewart, i. 88, 89; in command of Desert Column, i. 110-16, 132; against abandoning Dongola, i. 128; asks Kitchener for Report on Sudan future, i. 130; public confidence in, i. 268, ii. 107; and siege of Ladysmith, i. 269, 272, 279; and Irregular Horse, i. 270-271; fails at Vaal Krantz, i. 279; relieves Ladysmith, i. 299; in Natal, i. 310; and public optimism, ii. 107

Bülow, General von, iii. 34, 44-5, 63-4

Burdett-Coutts, Baroness, i. 258

Burger, Schalk, ii. 60, 91; peace negotiations by, ii. 70-77, 86; at Vereeniging Conference, ii. 95-96, 97, 103

Burma, ii. 133, 241

Burn-Murdoch, Col. (Maj.-Gen.), i. 199-200

Byng, Lt.-Col. the Hon. Sir Julian (General Lord Byng): in South Africa, ii. 2, 41, 63-64, 65

and Boy Scouts, ii. 313 (note) in Gallipoli, iii. 170, 176, 177-8, 214, 217

Cabinet: and French's proposed retreat, iii. 51-2, 53; and Home Defence, iii. 69, 70; changes in, iii. 143, 144, 238, 239; and reinforcements to Hamilton, iii. 171-2, 250;

INDEX

and Gallipoli evacuation, iii. 184, 185, 207; secrecy in, iii. 209 (*note*)
Cabinet Committee on Munitions, iii. 267, 287
Cadorna, General, iii. 208, 302
Cairo, Kitchener in: in 1883, i. 50–52, 60; in hospital, i. 160, 161; hospitality as Sirdar, i. 188; desires British Agency at, i. 189, ii. 117, 263; during his term of office, ii. 317, 321
Calais, German menace to, iii. 70, 71–2, 235, 296
Calcutta: Amir visits, ii. 250, 252; Kitchener's hospitality in, ii. 248–9; speeches in, ii. 197, 240 (*note*)
Calcutta Volunteers, ii. 197
Camberley Staff College, ii. 173, 174, 175, 176
Cambon, M., iii. 45, 117, 344
Cambridge confers degree on Kitchener, i. 256
Cambridge, Duke of, i. 10–11
Cameron Highlanders, i. 179, 227 (*note*), 230, 231
Cameroons campaign, iii. 83
Campbell-Bannerman, Sir H., ii. 224
Canada and Kitchener's death, iii. 357
Canadian troops: in South Africa, i. 300; in France, iii. 40, 83, 87, 223, 227, 231–4
Cape to Cairo Railway, i. 211, ii. 310
Cape Colony rebellion, i. 298–299, 310 (*note*); Kitchener checks, i. 304; continued, ii. 15, 27; De Wet's invasion, ii. 16–17; Cape Government and, ii. 30–31; Smuts's campaign to further, ii. 38, 43–5; question of amnesty after, ii. 20, 23, 25–6, 99–100
Cape Town: Kitchener's arrival at, i. 271; speech in, after war, ii. 109; Botha's speech in, ii. 109
Capernaum, i. 34–5
Capernaum Synagogue, i. 32
Capitation Rate discussion, ii. 236–7

Capitulations, the, ii. 317, 318, 335
Carden, Admiral Sir S., iii. 113, 114, 115
Carrington, Sir F., i. 320, 322
Castelnau, General de, iii. 66, 243–244, 245
Cavan, Lt.-Gen. the Earl of, iii. 252
Cavell, Sister, i. 161
Ceres district invaded, ii. 45
Chaman-Kandahar line, ii. 147
Chamberlain, Rt. Hon. Joseph, i. 269, ii. 29, 88
Champagne, offensive in, iii. 175, 224, 227, 249, 251, 252, 256, 257, 258 (*note*)
Channel ports, iii. 36, 86, 245, 258
Chantilly, iii. 81, 186, 260, 294
Chanzy, General, i. 8, 9
Chapman, Major, ii. 49
Chatham: Kitchener at School of Military Engineering, i. 6, 9, 11–12, 12–13; his speech to Gordon boys at, i. 256; his visit to, ii. 112
Chermside, Lieut.-Col. (Maj.-Gen. Sir. H.), i. 52, 60, 61, 104, 129 (*note*), 131
Chesney, Sir George, ii. 177–8
Chetwode, Lt.-Gen. Sir P., iii. 33
Chevallier, Anne Frances (Mrs. Kitchener), i. 3, 4, 5
Chevallier, Dr. John, i. 3
Chicago, ii. 298
China: Kitchener ready for war in, i. 307; his visit to, ii. 265, 285, 286–7
Chitral, ii. 128
Cholera, outbreaks of, i. 18, 52, 201
Chorazin, i. 34
Chowder, ii. 15, 17
Christchurch, N.Z., ii. 296
Chunuk Bair, iii. 162, 171
Churchill, Rt. Hon. W. S.:
at Malta Conference, ii. 336; and campaign to clear Belgian coast, iii. 87–8, 90, 91; and Gallipoli campaign, iii. 98, 105, 109, 110, 115–16, 122, 127, 139, 208–9, 249–50; his faith in naval guns, iii. 87–8, 105, 116, 129, 189,

INDEX

208–209; asks for Twenty-ninth Division, iii. 115–16, 118; on Cabinet Committee of Munitions, iii. 267; criticises Army administration, iii. 335, 337; his personal relations with Kitchener, iii. 324

Churchmanship, Kitchener's, i. 12, 13, 22 (*note*), 32, ii. 276, 345 (*note*), iii. 371–2

Circassian atrocities, i. 37

Citadel Hospital, Cairo, i. 161

Clemenceau, M., iii. 224 (*note*)

Clements, Maj.-Gen., i. 296, 297, 305, 308, 318, ii. 14, 50

Colenbrander, Colonel, ii. 35

Colenso, battle of, i. 268, 269

Colesberg, i. 272, 273, 278, 297

Colinson's Egyptian brigade, i. 241, 244

Colonial Defence Force, ii. 34

Colonial troops: in South Africa, i. 274, 278, 300, ii. 1, 3, 4, 36

    in Great War. *See* Anzac Corps, Australians, Canadians, New Zealanders

Colt guns, iii. 270

Colvile, Lt.-Col. (Maj.-Gen. Sir Henry), i. 83, 106; in South Africa, i. 282, 286–87, 293

Colville, Commander (Admiral the Hon. Sir Stanley), i. 204, 205

Commando Nek, i. 321

Commando system, i. 330

Commissioners for Egyptian Debt, i. 222

Compulsory Service, iii. 313, 314–17, 334–5

Concentration Camps, ii. 12–14, 38, 46

Conder, Lieut. Claud: his friendship with Kitchener at Woolwich, i. 7; invites him to join Palestine Survey, i. 15, 16, 17; twice rescued by Kitchener, i. 17–18; disabled, i. 17, 18, 23 (*note*); Map of Palestine, i. 22, 23 (*note*); "Memoirs," 23 (*note*), 31

Connaught, Duke of, ii. 255 (*note*), 301, 302

Connaught Rangers, ii. 44

Conscientious objectors, iii. 323

Conscription, iii. 313, 314–17, 318, 334–5

Constantine, King, iii. 109, 120; Kaiser and, iii. 109, 196, 200, 202; Kitchener visits, iii. 197, 200, 201–3, 204

Constantinople, i. 30, 39, 284 (*note*); Kitchener and Embassy at, i. 189, 286 (*note*); his visit to, ii. 306; objective of Dardanelles Expedition, iii. 99, 103, 105, 106, 110, 115, 120, 123, 133, 182, 193, 249

Cook, Mr., ii. 285 (*note*), 289–90

Cookson, General, ii. 72–3

Coronation of Edward VII., ii. 89, 109–10; of George V., ii. 308–9

Coronation Durbar, ii. 122

Cotton cultivation: Egyptian, ii. 317, 323–4, 325; Sudanese, ii. 325–6, 333

Cowans, Gen. Sir John, iii. 17, 263, 336–8

Cranborne, Viscountess, Kitchener's letters to, i. 306–307, 314 (*note*), ii. 14, 89. *See* Salisbury, Marchioness of

Creedy, H. (Sir Herbert), iii. 7 (*note*)

Cromer, Earl of (*see* Baring): on Kitchener as economist, i. 71; nominates Kitchener for Sirdarieh, i. 172; and Khedive, i. 186, 191, ii. 342; and Dongola Expedition, i. 190, 191, 192, 193–95; and Abu Hamed—Halfa gauge, i. 211; Kitchener's resignation tendered to, i. 218, 223–25; and Atbara situation, i. 229; address to Sheikhs at Omdurman, i. 260; advice to Kitchener, i. 260–61, ii. 115; support given to Kitchener, i. 186, 194–95, 222, 234, 261; recommends Kitchener for British Agency, ii. 311–12; on National representation in Egypt, ii. 331; on Kitchener's administration, ii. 346;

INDEX

and Dardanelles Commission, iii. 117 (*note*)
Cronje, Gen., i. 273, 274, 276; pursued to Paardeberg, i. 280–81, 282–83, 285; frontal attack on his laager, i. 287–90, 291–95, 309; invested, i. 290–91, 294–95, 296; surrenders, i. 294, 297
Crooks, Rt. Hon. William, iii. 343
Crotta House, i. 3, 4
Ctesiphon battle, iii. 301
Cunningham, Brig.-Gen., ii. 38 (*note*)
Curium excavations, i. 43
Curzon, Lord (Earl) : letters to Kitchener in anticipation of his appointment, ii. 117–18; his Durbar, ii. 122; on Army renumbering and redistribution, ii. 127, 136; talks with Kitchener, ii. 129, 145 (*note*); on Frontier railways, ii. 148–9; on Frontier tribes, i. 159–60; and Samana valley question, ii. 162–4; on Dual Control, ii. 199, 201, 206 (*note*), 212–13, 214; his Minute, ii. 216–19; tribute to Kitchener's work, ii. 216–18; resignation, ii. 223; on expenses of Imperial defence, ii. 233; on Gallipoli evacuation, iii. 207; Mesopotamian Expedition and, iii. 301
Cyprus: British protectorate assumed, i. 36; Kitchener on British administration of, i. 44–46; shot at in, i. 41 (*note*); collecting and excavating in, i. 42–43; Land Registration, i. 41, 45; Map of, i. 36, 40, 41, 49, 68; Museum, i. 43; Survey, i. 36, 38–43, 49–50, 51, 68 (*note*); Kitchener leaves, i. 50
Turks and, i. 44
Czernowitz, iii. 111

Daiches, Dr., i. 24 (*note*)
Dakhila, i. 265
D'Amade, Gen., iii. 133, 143 (*note*)

Damant, Major (Lt.-Col.), ii. 43, 55
Damascus, i. 40
Dardanelles Commission, iii. 117–18, 127, 299–300
Dardanelles Expedition: urged by Churchill, iii. 98, 105, 109, 110, 115–16, 118, 122, 127, 139, 208–209, 249–50; Kitchener and, iii. 101, 104, 105, 110, 112–15, 116, 119, 120–21, 122–4, 127–9, 208, 217; Navy expected to force passage, iii. 106, 109, 112, 114, 115, 116, 121, 122, 125, 126, 128, 188; military support available, iii. 104, 105, 110, 112–15, 119, 120–21, 122–124, 128; instructions to Sir Ian Hamilton, iii. 122–4; bombardment, iii. 95, 112–13, 119–120; Navy fails, iii. 124, 128. *See* Gallipoli Expedition
Dar-es-Salaam, i. 150, 151
Darfur, i. 127, 128, 130, 134
Darfur, Sultan of, iii. 302
Darfur-Wadai frontier settlement, ii. 334, 335
Davies, Lt.-Gen. Sir F. J., iii. 177, 215, 217
Dawkins, Sir Clinton, i. 221
Dawson, Sir Henry, i. 8–9
De Aar, i. 297, 298, 304
Dead Sea, Survey's journey to, i. 55, 56 (*note*)
Deakin, Mr., ii. 292 (*note*), 293
Deane, Sir Harold, ii. 164, 165
Debbeh, i. 76–7, 81, 83, 84, 85, 116; Sheikhs refuse to go to, i. 80–81; Kitchener prepares defence of, i. 81–2, 83–4, 85, 107; Wilson visits, i. 85 (*note*), 96; stores at, i. 106–7
De Brath, Lt.-Gen. Sir E., ii. 260, 261
De Chasseloup Laubat, Marquis, iii. 280
Decorations, sale of, ii. 342–3
Delagoa Bay, i. 313
De la Rey, Gen.: leaves Driefontein, i. 303; attacks Clements, ii. 14; Methuen pursues, ii. 35, 47; for continu-

ing war, ii. 36, 71; in the Zwartruggens, ii. 53; De Wet and Steyn join, ii. 65; victory at Tweebosch, ii. 66-9; escapes great drive, ii. 72; in peace negotiations, ii. 73, 86, 90, 93; at Vereeniging Conference, ii. 97, 103; Peace Commissioner, ii. 98, 101
Delcassé, M., i. 249, iii. 108
Delhi Durbar and Manœuvres, ii. 122
De Lisle, Lt.-Gen. Sir. B., iii. 178
Denhardt, Herr, i. 149-50
Derby, Earl of, iii. 317
Derby Scheme, iii. 317
Derbyshire Militia, i. 314
De Robeck, Admiral Sir John, iii. 126, 127, 159, 188, 209
Dervishes: Kitchener on character of, i. 172; power in Sudan, i. 157-158, 163; invade Egypt, i. 164-66; defeated at Toski, i. 166-68; despise Egyptian cavalry, i. 179-80; raids by, i. 181-82; Italians and, i. 189-91, 220-21, 222; defeated at Firket, i. 199-200; rumours of British difficulties among, i. 205; defeated at Hafir, i. 205-206; lose Dongola, i. 206; lose Abu Hamed, i. 214-15; evacuate Berber, i. 216; defeated at the Atbara, i. 229-31; crushed at Omdurman, i. 237, 238-39, 240-41
Desert Column in Nile Expedition, i. 109-16, 132, 209, 213
Deville, General, iii. 278
De Wet, Christian: captures ox convoy, i. 277, 283; at Paardeberg, i. 289, 296; at Poplar Grove, i. 301-302; Korn Spruit and Reddersburg, i. 308-309; Smithfield and Wepener, i. 308-309; irregular warfare and, i. 313; exploits in Orange Free State, i. 314-15; nearly captures Kitchener, i. 315-17; in Brandwater Basin, i. 318; escapes encirclement, i. 319-22; takes Dewetsdorp, i. 326; invades Cape Colony, i. 304, 326, 327, ii. 15, 16-17; for continuing war, ii. 19, 21, 33, 36, 46, 54, 61, 95, 96-7, 97-8; escapes drive, ii. 54; Groen Kop victory, ii. 54-5; four columns attack, ii. 63-5; at peace conference, ii. 86, 93, 95, 96-7, 97-8, 103; Peace Commissioner, ii. 98-9, 101 in Great War, ii. 65 (*note*)
De Wet, Piet, i. 315
Dewetsdorp, i. 308, 326
Diamond Hill, i. 314
Diego Suarez, i. 149
Dinan, i. 8, 20
Discipline, Kitchener on, ii. 291
Dixon, Col. Sir Henry (Brig.-Gen.), ii. 35
Dixon, W. Hepworth, i. 22, 26
Dolling, Father, i. 14
Donaldson, Sir Frederick, ii. 350
Dongola: Mahdi threatens, i. 65; Kitchener in, i. 70-74, 78; Mudir of, i. 69, 72, 73-4, 76, 77-8, 80, 81, 83, 84, 85-7, 94-7, 98-101
evacuation question, i. 127, 128; Buller on, i. 128, 130; Kitchener on, i. 128, 130, 137, 138-41; the Mudirate of, 101 (*note*), 130-31, 140-42; suggested Vakilates of, i. 131, 140-42; Wilson on, i. 128-31; evacuated, i. 132
reconquest decided on, i. 191-92
Dongola Expedition: command of, i. 192-93, 194-95; strategy of, i. 195-96; transport difficulties, i. 196-98, 201, 202-4, 207; Egyptian forces, i. 198; Akasha taken, i. 196; Firket, i. 199-200; cholera and climatic troubles, i. 201-3; Hafir, i. 205-6; capture of Dongola, i. 206, 213; cost of, i. 254
Dongolawi and Shaikiyeh, i. 131, 136, 139-140, 141
Doornkop taken, i. 312
Douai, iii. 253
Douaumont, Fort, iii. 305
Douglas, Gen. Sir Charles, iii. 6, 103
Dover, i. 255-256

INDEX

Dreyer, ii. 40
Drives, system of, in South Africa, ii. 7, 8–10, 62–3
Druses, the, i. 23
Dthala sanatorium, ii. 260–62
Dual Control of Indian Army: fatal to economy and efficiency, ii. 199–202, 203, 205–8, 209–10; Kitchener's Minute on, ii. 203, 205–8, 210–11, 213–14; Military Member's position, ii. 177–8, 203–5, 207, 209–10, 215–16, 220; Roberts on, ii. 204, 208–9; Curzon and, ii. 199, 201, 206 (note), 212–13, 214, 216–19; Brodrick and, ii. 213, 219–22; Military Supply Department, ii. 220–21, 222–3, 226–30; Army Secretary, ii. 226–7; Military Finance Branch, ii. 227–8
Dublin, Kitchener lectures in, i. 31–2
Du Cane, Lt.-Gen. Sir John, iii. 279
Duff, Gen. Sir Beauchamp, ii. 266
Dulgo, i. 203
Dundee, Botha's dash for, ii. 48–9
Dunedin, N.Z., ii. 296
Dunkirk, iii. 70, 74–5
Dunottar Castle, Kitchener and Roberts on the, i. 270–71
Duntroon Staff College, ii. 295 (note)
Durbar, Coronation, i. 291
Dutch and South African War, ii. 27 (note); and Kitchener in Java, ii. 288–9

Earle, Maj-Gen. W., i. 109, 114
East, the: Kitchener's love of, i. 16, 22, iii. 153–4; his prestige in, i. 312–13, iii. 154; Gallipoli campaign and, iii. 104, 112, 129, 149, 187, 191, 192, 201, 205, 206 (note), 302
East Africa: Kitchener travels through, ii. 306, 307–8; his land in, ii. 307–8, 322, iii. 352
East African campaign, iii. 302, 304–305; Indian troops in, ii. 283
East Anglians and Kitchener, i. 256
Eastern school of war policy, iii. 102–3, 109, 111–12, 129, 139, 249
East Lancashire Territorial Division, iii. 96, 97, 137
Economy, Kitchener's: with Palestine Exploration Fund, i. 28, 31; in Egypt, i. 70–71, 170–4, 198, 223; in South Africa, i. 325, 326, 329, ii. 82–3, 277 (note); in India, ii. 198–9, 228, 277–9
Eden, Sir Ashley, ii. 205
Edgehill, Dr., i. 13
Edinburgh confers Freedom on Kitchener, i. 257
Education: Kitchener's own, i. 4–5; his work for Sudanese, i. 256, 257–59, ii. 113–14; higher Mohammedan, ii. 274 (note)
Education, Board of, and labour supply, iii. 283
Edward VII., King: confers O.M. on Kitchener, ii. 109; illness of, ii. 109–10; confers G.C.I.E., ii. 268; creates Kitchener Field-Marshal, ii. 301; and Mediterranean Command, ii. 301; and Indian Viceroyalty, ii. 302–3; dies, ii. 303; Kitchener's admiration for, iii. 371
Egeiga, i. 238, 239, 240
Egypt: Arabi's rebellion in, i. 47–8; cholera in, i. 52; Kitchener arrives in, i. 50–52; invasion of, foreseen by Kitchener, i. 65, 68; and her own preservation, i. 127, 138–39; Dervish invasion of, i. 164–66, 166–68; raids into, i. 181–82; Khedive and British authority in, i. 185–87, 191–92; French position in, i. 250, 252–254; Kitchener's love of, ii. 110, 346
Kitchener winters in, ii. 306
Kitchener British Agent in, ii. 312; changes in, ii. 316–17; German intrigues in, ii. 311,

338–40; Turco-Italian war and, ii. 314–16; administrative reforms in, ii. 317–21, 330–32, 345; cotton cultivation in, ii. 317, 323–4, 325; oil in, ii. 327; public health in, ii. 328–30; Mediterranean naval control and, ii. 336–7; Balkan war and, ii. 337
Kitchener leaves, ii. 346; return prevented, iii. 2–3
during Great War: Indian troops in, ii. 283, iii. 83, 96, 97; Anzacs in, iii. 96, 98, 304; Territorials in, iii. 96, 97; Germany and, iii. 95, 96–7, 302; Turkey and, iii. 40, 97, 103, 107; Senussi and, iii. 155–6
    defence of, iii. 96–8, 148–9, 187, 191, 192, 193, 194, 302, 303–4
    Gallipoli Expedition and, iii. 109, 110, 148–9, 187, 191, 192, 193, 194, 205–6, 207, 302
Kitchener's death and, iii. 357
disturbances after war in, ii. 331–2
Egypt, Sultan of, ii. 324
Egyptian agriculture, ii. 322–6
Egyptian Army: Kitchener joins, i. 50
cholera in, i. 52
composition of: fellahin, i. 175–77; blacks, i. 175, 178–79; artillery, i. 179; cavalry, i. 59, 62, 179–80; British staff, i. 180, 300 (*note*); native officers, i. 177
in Nile Expedition, i. 177; at Toski, i. 165, 166–68; in Dongola Expedition, i. 191–92, 198, 200, 203, 214, 225, 231, 235, 241
Kitchener's business management of, i. 173, 198; his training of, i. 174–75, 176–77, 208, ii. 115; European vigilance and, i. 173, 222; Khedive and, i. 184–86, 191; Kitchener resigns from, i. 132
Egyptian campaigns. *See* Dongola Expedition, Nile Expedition, Omdurman Campaign
Egyptian cotton, ii. 317, 323–4, 325
Egyptian fellahin: as agriculturists, ii. 324–5; as soldiers, i. 175–76, 176–77, 214, ii. 189 (*note*); sanitary improvements and, ii. 328–30; usurers and, i. 143, ii. 317–20
Egyptian Intelligence system, i. 183
Egyptian irrigation, i. 261, ii. 316 (*note*)
Egyptian Nationalism, i. 185, ii. 314, 317
Egyptian oil, ii. 327
Egyptian plots against Kitchener, ii. 334–5
Egyptian Police, i. 168–71
Eighth Division, iii. 74, 77, 310
Elandsfontein, i. 312
Elandskop, ii. 63
Eleventh Corps, iii. 252, 253
Eleventh Division, iii. 163, 164
Ellershaw, Brig.-Gen., iii. 347–8, 350
Elles, Lt.-Gen. Sir E., ii. 215
Elliot, Lt.-Gen. Sir E. L., ii. 34, 39, 40, 41, 42, 47, 54, 63, 64–5
Elliot, Sir Francis, iii. 197
Emmett, ii. 49
Engineering, Kitchener and, i. 11, 12, 197–98, 212–13
English Church Union, i. 14
Enteric: in South Africa; i. 291, 306; measures against, in India, ii. 270
Enver Pasha, iii. 158
Eritrea, i. 189–91
Ermelo, ii. 17, 48, 51
Esher, Viscount, iii. 295 (*note*)
Essex Regiment, iii. 164–5
Etman, i. 91–2, 93
Excavations, Kitchener's: in Jerusalem, i. 39; in Crete, i. 43; invited to conduct Assyrian, i. 43–4
Eye Hospitals in Egypt, ii. 328

Fachi Shoya, i. 266
Fanshawe, Maj.-Gen. Sir R., iii. 170, 176, 178
Farag Allah Bey, i. 116, 118

INDEX

Farag Pasha, i. 119–21, 124
Fashoda: occupied by French, i. 234; Kitchener and Marchand at, i. 250, 251–54, ii. 115
Fellahin, Egyptian: as agriculturists, ii. 324–5; as soldiers, i. 175–76, 176–77, 214, ii. 189 (*note*); sanitary improvements and, ii. 328–30; usurers and, i. 143, 321–24
Female labour, iii. 284
Ferdinand, Czar, iii. 176, 178
Ferreira, i. 283
Fertit, Sultan of, i. 139–40
Festubert, iii. 237–8, 239
Fifteenth Division, iii. 256
Fifth Division, iii. 31, 39
Fifty-fourth Division, iii. 141
Fifty-second Division, iii. 141, 144, 147
Fifty-third Division, iii. 180
Firket engagement, i. 199–200
First Division, iii. 31
Fisher, Admiral Lord, iii. 103
FitzClarence, Bimbashi, i. 215
FitzGerald, Captain (Lt.-Col.) O. A. G., ii. 249 (*note*); travels with Kitchener, ii. 285, 288 (*note*), 307; partner in East African scheme, ii. 308; saves Kitchener's life, ii. 334; letter to Ian Hamilton, iii. 138; on board the *Hampshire*, iii. 138, 350, 355
Five Feddan Law, ii. 318–20
Flanders, defence of, iii. 21, 65–6, 68, 70–71, 80, 224
Foch, General (Marshal): and size of Expeditionary Force, iii. 8 (*note*); at the Marne, iii. 57, 61, 63, 64; on Belgian front, iii. 72; meets Kitchener at Dunkirk, iii. 75; French's talks with, iii. 78; against offensive, iii. 78, 79; to attack Vimy Ridge, iii. 224, 229, 235, 236; in Ypres fighting, iii. 233; assaults Vimy Ridge, iii. 237, 246–7, 248, 249, 253, 255
Foreign Office: Kitchener working for, i. 36, 49, 143; and

Keneh-Kosseir Report, i. 61–2
Formidable sunk. iii. 91 (*note*)
Fort Jervois, ii. 296
Fort Lockhart, ii. 161
Fourteenth Division, iii. 239–40
Fourth Division, iii. 30, 31, 39, 62
France: Kitchener's education in, i. 5; Kitchener with Army of, i. 8–11; gratitude of, i. 9–10, iii. 344–5; and Kitchener's death, iii. 358
Francis Joseph, Emperor of Austria, i. 13
Franco-Prussian War, Kitchener's part in, i. 8–11, iii. 57 (*note*)
" Free institutions " in Egypt, ii. 330–32
French, Maj.-Gen. Sir John (Field-Marshal Viscount): in South African War, iii. 24–5; before Colesberg, i. 272, 273; on the Modder River, i. 278; relieves Kimberley, i. 279, 280; pursuing Cronje, i. 280, 281–82, 283; Queen's congratulations to, i. 282, 287; at Paardeberg, i. 292, 293, 295; at Poplar Grove, i. 301–2; cuts railway below Bloemfontein, i. 304; round Johannesburg, i. 312; first drive by, ii. 9, 16–17, 27; pursuing Kritzinger and Smuts, ii. 43, 44; in Cape Colony, ii. 76
Aldershot Command, iii. 24
in Great War: favours Maubeuge concentration, iii. 22; Kitchener approves choice of, iii. 24–5; his instructions, iii. 25–6, 28, 50–51, 92; on situation before Mons, iii. 28–9, 31–3, 34; in retreat, iii. 35–6; Le Cateau fighting and retirement, iii. 42–44, 45; suggests withdrawal from Allied line, iii. 46–7, 48, 50–51, 52–3, 54 (*note*); opposition of Kitchener and Cabinet, iii. 50–52, 53; Kitchener visits, iii. 53–6 on

the Marne, iii. 57-59, 60, 61-2; transference of forces to French left, iii. 65-6, 68, 70-71; and fall of Antwerp, iii. 67-8, 69-70; Antwerp relief force joins, iii. 69-70; on Flanders fighting, iii. 72, 75, 76; reports situation in December, iii. 77-9; conference with Joffre, iii. 80-83, 88; and operations on other fronts, iii. 86, 108 (*note*), 250, 258; plans campaign to clear Belgian coast, iii. 86-93, 94, 103; on amalgamation of New Armies, iii. 221; private visits to Kitchener, iii. 228, 234, 236, 237, 247, 249, 292, 295; offensive in preparation, iii. 223-4, 235, 239; Neuve Chapelle, iii. 121, 225-6, 227, 228; Hill 60, iii. 229-30; on use of poison gas, iii. 231-5; Festubert, iii. 237-8

ammunition shortage and, iii. 92, 228 (*note*), 238, 243, 291; high explosives and, iii. 86, 87, 239, 275, 276; communicates with *The Times* and political friends, iii. 238, 289-90

asks for Fourteenth Division, iii. 239-40; on importance of offensive, iii. 242-6; Loos, iii. 148, 249, 255-6; Salonika scheme and, iii. 86, 250, 258, 260

relieved of command, iii. 293, 295, 297; receives a peerage, iii. 295; commanding Home Forces, iii. 295, 310; writes *1914*, iii. 48 (*note*), 238

his personal relations with Kitchener, iii. 24-5, 70, 228 (*note*), 295-7; Kitchener's regard for, iii. 24-5, 63, 75, 263-4, 295

French, the:

Zanzibar Commission and, i. 146, 150; Khedive and, i. 184; in Congo, i. 209, 233; and Omdurman, i. 249; at Fashoda, i. 234, 250-54; rights in Sudan, ii. 334, 335; in Morocco, ii. 335; in Syria, iii. 154, 155, 193, 261

in Great War: and Belgian neutrality, iii. 20; strength of, iii. 18; General Staff, iii. 18, 19, 29, 81; supporting British, iii. 28, 29, 30, 31-4, 42; in retreat, iii. 35; success at Guise, iii. 44-5, 46, 49; early failures, iii. 48, 52-3; at the Marne, iii. 57-9, 60-64; reinforce Belgians, iii. 71, 72; in Flanders, iii. 74, 75, 80, 221; occupy British right, iii. 82, 83, 86, 223, 224-5, 231, 233; and Belgian coast campaign, iii. 88-9

co-operation in the East, iii. 108, 109, 258 (*note*); in Gallipoli campaign, iii. 124, 133, 136, 143-4, 148, 158-9, 174-6, 181; in Salonika, iii. 108, 176, 196, 198-9, 258, 260-61

gas attack on, iii. 231, 232, 233, 236; at their maximum strength, iii. 241 (*note*), 243, 319 (*note*); Champagne offensive, iii. 248-9, 251, 252, 256, 257; on Vimy Ridge, iii. 256, 257; at Verdun, iii. 305-6

munitions supply and, iii. 72, 276 (*note*), 277, 278, 279, 280 (*note*)

British relations with, iii. 239, 241 (*note*), 244, 258, 293, 344-5

Frere, Sir Bartle, i. 328, ii. 105, 324

Friendlies in Sudan campaign, i. 159, 160; occupy Berber, i. 216, 217; at Omdurman, i. 238

Frontier Militia in India, ii. 126, 135, 156, 157, 160-61, 163, 164-5

Frost, Mr. George, i. 6

Fukara, the, i. 81

Gaba Tepe, iii. 131

Gakdul, i. 109, 110, 115

Galilee: Survey of, i. 33-5; Synagogues of, i. 33-5

Gallieni, General, iii. 60, 63, 260-61, 294

INDEX

Gallipoli campaign: for preliminary operations *see* Dardanelles
Turkish defences, iii. 118–19, 122–3, 125, 133, 138; occupation not at first intended, iii. 120, 122–3; reconnaissance, iii. 125; military operations necessary, iii. 125, 126–7, 128; forces for, iii. 124; plans for landing, iii. 113, 114–15, 130–31, 150; landings, iii. 133–6, 137; battles of Krithia, iii. 136–7, 144–5; water difficulties, iii. 138, 140, 167, 168; strength of Turks, iii. 138, 140, 141, 142, 146; reinforcements for Hamilton, iii. 139, 140, 144, 145–6, 148, 149, 151, 250, 251; successes and checks, iii. 142, 143, 158; trench warfare established, iii. 146–7, 151–2, 177–8; Kilid Bahr, iii. 136, 144, 145, 146, 151, 189; Asiatic diversion, iii. 150–51, 158–60, 174–5, 181; Suvla Bay, iii. 160, 161–5, 171, 173, 176; Sari Bair, iii. 159–60, 165 (*note*), 166–9; Generals replaced, iii. 170; ammunition supply, iii. 140, 142, 176, 177, 238–9; shortage of men, iii. 171–4; Germans in, iii. 174, 177, 181, 290; sickness, iii. 180–81; troops required for Salonika, iii. 179–80, 181, 182–3
evacuation discussed in Cabinet, iii. 183; its effect on the East, iii. 149, 187, 191, 192, 201, 206 (*note*), 302; Robertson and Hamilton on, iii. 183; the French and, iii. 186, 261; Kitchener sent to decide, iii. 184, 185–8, 201; Mudros conference considers, iii. 190–91, 205; Kitchener's opinion, iii. 189, 205–6, 209; evacuation decided on, iii. 207, 209
evacuation of Peninsula, iii. 210; Birdwood's account of, iii. 210–19

value of campaign, iii. 190, 210
Ganneau, Clermont, i. 23 (*note*)
Gararish tribe, i. 70, 79–80
Garratt, Brig.-Gen. Sir Francis, ii. 41
Garstin, Sir William, i. 261 (*note*)
Gas used in warfare, iii. 231–5, 254, 255; Kitchener on, iii. 234–5
Gastrica excavations, i. 43
Gatacre, Maj.-Gen.: in Omdurman campaign, i. 227, 229, 234; at the Atbara, i. 228–30, 231; in South Africa, i. 297, 305, 308
Gedaref, i. 264
General Staff, British: in India, ii. 176; in Great War, iii. 4–6, 261–2, 297, 298, 300 (*note*)
George V., King: Coronation of, ii. 308–9; and Kitchener's appointment to British Agency, ii. 312; lands at Port Sudan, ii. 333; confers Earldom on Kitchener, ii. 346; French's visits and, iii. 228; visits the Front, iii. 77, 186, 260; Kitchener's visit to, iii. 186; Sudanese Sheikhs visit, i. 257 (*note*)
Germain, Captain, i. 251, 253
German, Kitchener studies, i. 14
German East Africa Company, i. 144
German Embassy, Kitchener at, iii. 2
Germans: in Africa, i. 143–154, 314–315; colonisation methods of, i. 144–45, 148–49, 152; Boers and, ii. 105; Egyptian intrigues by, ii. 311, 338–40; in Morocco, ii. 310–11
Kitchener foresees conflict with, i. 65, 150, ii. 244 (*note*), 282, 295–6, iii. 1–2; his attitude towards, iii. 234, 367–8
in Great War: plans of, iii. 18–19, 20–21, 22–3; forces of, iii. 18, 20; attack Belgium, iii. 19–20, 21, 28, 29, 34; hold off Russia, iii. 18, 51,

53; turning movement by, iii. 29, 30, 31, 33, 34–5, 40; launch main attack on British, iii. 38, 43; checked near Guise, iii. 44–5, 46, 49; inferior to British, iii. 48–9; prefer Paris to Channel ports, iii. 36, 56, 58; defeated at the Marne, iii. 57–9, 60–64, 112; on the Aisne, iii. 64, 65; take Antwerp, iii. 67–70; drive for Calais, iii. 71, 74, 76; withdraw forces to meet Russians, iii. 76, 78, 79, 88, 100–101, 223–224, 243; danger of their return, iii. 81–2, 86, 89, 92, 111, 243, 250, 256, 257; Belgian coast campaign by, iii. 87, 88–9, 91; use poison gas at Ypres, iii. 231–4, 235, 236; at Loos, iii. 257
 in colonies, iii. 83
 in Dardanelles, iii. 174, 177, 181, 290; compared with Turks, iii. 146, 147, 187
 Eastern ambitions of, ii. 281–2, iii. 97, 112, 156, 190, 192, 193, 194, 203–4, 302; agents in Afghanistan, ii. 251, iii. 302
Gezira cotton area, ii. 326
Ghaffirs, i. 170
Ghazis, the, ii. 161
Gibb, Sir George, iii. 284 (*note*)
Gibran, Sheikh Beshir, i. 67, 79–80
Gilgit, ii. 128, 129
Gillette, Mr., ii. 298
Ginnis, i. 164, 179
Girodin, Colonel, iii. 201 (*note*)
Girouard, Lieut. E. P. (Maj.-Gen. Sir Percy): in Sudan, i. 211–12, 213; in South Africa, i. 296, 297; Governor of East African Protectorate, ii. 308
Gladstone's Government: Gordon denounces, i. 104; withdrawal policy of, i. 128
Godley, Lt.-Gen. Sir A., iii. 166, 168, 217
Goldwoorintzicht, ii. 32
Goold-Adams, Sir H., ii. 58
Gordon, Colonel, i. 9

Gordon, General: tribes bribed to aid, i. 62, 70, 72, 74; Kitchener communicates with, i. 70, 74, 77, 80, 87, 102–5, 106; misunderstandings, i. 102–3; his admiration for Kitchener, i. 78; suggests Kitchener's Governor-Generalship, i. 78, 104–5; sends out Stewart expedition, i. 87, 90, 91; his papers, i. 87; King of the Belgians and, i. 104; Wolseley's letter to, i. 106; defence of Khartum by, i. 116–20; the Mahdi and, i. 117, 123–24; Farag Pasha and, i. 119, 121; death of, i. 110, 122–23; Sir Samuel Baker on fate of, i. 68–9; Wilson and blame for fate of, i. 112 (*note*), 132; avenged at Omdurman, i. 240–248; memorial service to, i. 248–49
Gordon, Lt.-Col. W. S., i. 162, 174 (*note*)
Gordon College: Kitchener's appeal for, i. 257–59, ii. 110; opening of, ii. 113; his visits to, i. 97, ii. 306
Gordon Home, Chatham, i. 256
Gorizia, iii. 208
Gorringe, Maj.-Gen. Sir G., iii. 153
Gorst, Sir Eldon, ii. 311, 312, 324, 332–3, 342
Gough, Colonel Hubert (Lt.-Gen. Sir Hubert), ii. 48, iii. 33
Gounaris, M., iii. 196
Gouraud, General, iii. 143–4, 158, 183
Graham, Sir Gerald, i. 128
Grand Clos, i. 5
Grant, Lieut. (Col.) S. C., i. 41, 49
Granville, Earl, i. 61, 62, 77
Great War:
 foreseen by Kitchener, i. 65, 150, ii. 244 (*note*), 282, 295–6, iii. 1–2; his estimate of its length, i. 65, iii. 9, 80, 90, 271, 274, 308, 309 (*note*), 371; lack of organisation for, iii. 4–6, 8–9, 10–11, 41
 landing of Expeditionary Force, iii. 17; Alsace-Lorraine of-

INDEX 389

fensive, iii. 19; invasion of Belgium, iii. 19–20, 28, 29; concentration at Maubeuge, iii. 21–3, 28, 30, 32; German enveloping movement, iii. 29, 30, 31, 33, 34–5, 40; battle of Mons, iii. 30, 34; Le Cateau, iii. 39, 42; retreat of Allies, iii. 42–4, 45, 57–9, 60–64; the Marne, iii. 36, 41, 57–9, 60–64; the Aisne, iii. 64; Ypres fighting, iii. 68, 71, 74, 75, 76; Dardanelles (see Dardanelles and Gallipoli); Egypt (see Egypt); Mesopotamia (see Mesopotamian Expedition); Neuve Chapelle, iii. 121, 225–6, 227, 228; Hill 60, iii. 229–30; second Ypres battle, iii. 231–4; Festubert, iii. 237–8, 239; Champagne offensive, iii. 175, 224, 227, 249, 251, 252, 256, 257, 258 (note); Loos, iii. 148, 249, 252, 253; situation at end of 1915, iii. 301–3; Verdun, iii. 305–6

Greece: and intervention, iii. 100, 102, 104 (note), 109, 120, 139, 140, 176, 186, 187, 200, 201–4, 261; afraid of Bulgaria, iii. 106, 196, 197, 202–3; and troops at Salonika, iii. 202–3

Greece, King of. See Constantine

Greeks in Egypt, ii. 314, 320, iii. 204

Green, Mary Emma, second Mrs. Kitchener, i. 3 (note)

Grenadier Guards at Omdurman, i. 241

Grenfell, Major Charles, i. 59

Grenfell, General Sir Francis (Field-Marshal Lord): on cholera outbreak, when Colonel, i. 52; Rundle and, i. 66 (note) Sirdar, i. 128, 188; and Handub, i. 159; at Suakin, i. 162; on Kitchener and tribes, i. 163; at Toski, i. 166–67; lends Kitchener for Police reorganisation, i. 169; resigns Sirdarieh, i. 172

G.O.C. Army of Occupation, i. 218, 224; Kitchener's letter to, i. 219–221; consulted on Atbara situation, i. 229; praises conduct of Omdurman campaign, i. 249

Grenfell, Lt.-Col. (Col.) H. M., ii. 66, 67

Grey, Earl, iii. 80 (note)

Grey, Sir Edward (Viscount), ii. 312, iii. 8, 54, 117

Grierson, Lt.-Gen. Sir James, iii. 31

Grobler, ii. 49, 51

Grocers Company and Gordon College, ii. 110

Groen Kop disaster, ii. 54–5

Guards Division, iii. 251, 252

Gubat, El, i. 110, 111–12, 114

Guildhall, Kitchener at the, i. 195 (note), iii. 289

Guise, French success at, iii. 44–5, 49

Gumal valley, ii. 128, 157

Gun Hill reverse, ii. 51–2

Gunsborough Lodge, i. 2

Gurkhas, ii. 126, 178; in Gallipoli, iii. 144–5, 165

Gwynne, Dr. Bishop of Khartum, ii. 345 (note)

Habibullah, Amir of Afghanistan, ii. 140, 147, 149, 150, 152–5, 164, 242, 249–52

Haddai, Sheikh El, i. 83, 84, 85, 98 (note)

Hadendoa tribe, i. 61 (note), 69 158

Hafir engagement, i. 205

Haifa-Jaffa ride by Kitchener, i. 19

Haig, Sir Douglas (Field-Marshal Earl):
in South Africa, ii. 15, 35
in Great War: commanding First Corps, iii. 31, 38, 43; advances on Ypres, iii. 71, 73; commanding First Army, iii. 222–3; prepares for Neuve Chapelle, iii. 225; Loos, iii. 253, 254–5; Commander-in-Chief, iii. 293; relieves pressure on French,

iii. 305–6; Kitchener and, iii. 293, 294, 339
Haking, Lt.-Gen. Sir R., iii. 252, 253
Haldane, Mr. John, iii. 234
Haldane, Rt. Hon. R. B. (Viscount): Secretary of State for War, ii. 224, 231–2, 235; on North-West Frontier results, ii. 143 (*note*); and extension of Kitchener's term, ii. 263; and Mediterranean Command, ii. 301; Kaiser visits, ii. 308; presses Kitchener's appointment as War Secretary, iii. 3; and the Expeditionary Force, iii. 16; on Committee of Munitions, iii. 267
Halfa: Khedive's review at, i. 185–186; railway work at, i. 197–198; garrison, i. 127, 128, 137, 192, 196, 214
Halfa—Abu Hamed line, i. 210–213, 218, 222, 223
Hamilton, Gen. Sir Bruce, i. 310, ii. 34; pursuing Smuts, ii. 40, 41, 42; pursuing Botha, ii. 49–50, 56–7, 58, 60
Hamilton, Col. Hubert (Gen.), i. 294, 297 (*note*), iii. 71
Hamilton, Gen. Sir Ian: leads column into Transvaal, i. 310; takes Doornkop, i. 312; round Pretoria, i. 313; collar-bone broken, i. 318; pursuing De Wet, i. 320, 321, 322; goes home with Roberts, ii. 2; on blockhouses, ii. 8; Chief of the Staff, ii. 52, 77 (*note*), 82; controls drive against Kemp, ii. 73–4, 88–9; final drive by, ii. 9, 74, 76–7
in Russo-Japanese War, ii. 174 (*note*), 286
in Gallipoli campaign: Kitchener's instructions to, iii. 122–4; reconnaissance of Peninsula, iii. 125; strong military operations needed, iii. 125, 126–7; his plans, iii. 130–31, 150; on the torpedoing of the *Manitou*, iii. 131–2; on the landing, iii. 133, 137; his difficulties, iii. 137–9, 140; reinforcements for, iii. 139, 140, 144, 145–6, 149, 151, 171, 250, 251; on trench warfare, iii. 145–7, 151–2, 177–8; on Bulair landing, iii. 150; on campaign on Asiatic side, iii. 151, 158–9; on Suvla Bay, iii. 150, 160, 161–5, 171, 173, 176; replaces Generals, iii. 170; and shortage of men, iii. 171–4; and unity of command, iii. 175; on difficulty of offensive, iii. 176–8; and withdrawal of troops to Salonika, iii. 179–182; on evacuation, iii. 183; asked to tour Near East, iii. 183
Kitchener's letter to, on Paardeberg, i. 291–95; on Kitchener's character, ii. 73 (*note*); their relations, ii. 52, iii. 138–9, 143, 159, 161, 170
Hammersley, Maj.-Gen. F., iii. 163, 170
Hampshire, the, iii. 354–5
Hanbury-Williams, Sir John, iii. 350, 351
Handub, i. 158, 159–60
Hannay, Colonel: pursues Cronje, i. 280, 282, 283; at Paardeberg, i. 287, 288, 293, 294; killed, i. 288, 294
Hannington, Bishop, murdered, i. 149
Hanover, Kitchener in, i. 14
Hansell, Consul, i. 122
Harazi, Jebel, i. 108
Harper, Mr., i. 16
Hart, Maj.-Gen. Sir Fitzroy, ii. 43, 44
Hart's River drive, ii. 73–4
Hartebeestfontein, i. 327
Hasheesh smugglers, iii. 156–7
Hassan, i. 92, 93
Hassan Bey Bahnasawy, i. 122
Hassaniyeh tribe, i. 74 (*note*), 85 (*note*), 88, 98, 108
Hatfield, ii. 111, 264 (*note*)
Hatzfeldt, Prince, ii. 338
Hauhauin tribe, i. 74 (*note*), 98–9, 107

INDEX 391

Hauran Survey, i. 38–9
Havre, iii. 36, 44
Hawatat, i. 56
Hebbeh, Stewart disaster at, i. 88–9, 91–3, 94–5
Hebrew, Kitchener studies, i. 7
Heilbron Road Station, i. 314, 315
Hejaz, the: bombarded, ii. 316; made a kingdom, ii. 332
Heligoland exchange, i. 154 (*note*)
Helles, Cape, iii. 130, 138, 146, 164, 189; sickness at, iii. 181; evacuation of, iii. 183, 190, 205, 215, 216, 217–18
Helvetia captured, ii. 15
Henderson, Mr. Arthur, iii. 315–16
Henderson, Col. (Lt.-Gen. Sir David), ii. 78, iii. 300 (*note*)
Herat, ii. 147, 152
Hertzog, ii. 16, 33; at peace conference, ii. 86, 93, 95; Peace Commissioner, ii. 98–9
Hickman, Captain (Brig.-Gen. T. E.), i. 159 (*note*), 160, 173 (*note*)
Hicks-Beach, Sir Michael (Earl St. Aldwyn), ii. 277 (*note*)
Hicks Pasha, disaster to, i. 55, 172, 175, 218, 265
High explosive, supply of, iii. 274–5
High explosives: Sir John French and, iii. 86, 87, 239, 275, 276; needed in Gallipoli, iii. 140, 176; Kitchener and supply of, iii. 272–4, 275–9; Army Council and, iii. 276–8; Ministry of Munitions and, iii. 287–8
Highland Light Infantry, ii. 44
Hill 60, iii. 229–30
Hill 70, iii. 255, 256
Hipperley, Mr., i. 41 (*note*)
Hobart, ii. 293
Hobhouse, Miss, ii. 13 (*note*)
Hohenzollern Redoubt, iii. 257
Holland offers mediation in South Africa, ii. 70
Home Defence, iii. 10, 31, 40, 69, 70, 328, 330, 340

Home Office and labour supply, iii. 283
Homogeneous Brigades in India, ii. 135–6, 166–7
Hong-Kong, ii. 265, 286, 288
Hor, Mount, i. 54–5
Hore, Colonel, i. 322–23
Horne, Maj.-Gen. Sir H. (General Lord), iii. 170, 206
House, Colonel, iii. 9 (*note*)
House of Commons, Kitchener's speech to Members of, iii. 325–343, 352
House of Lords, Kitchener in, ii. 310, iii. 285–6
Hudi, i. 227–28
Hull, Prof. Edward, i. 53, 54, 55–6
Hum, Tell, i. 34–5
Hunter, Maj.-Gen. (Gen.) Sir Archibald:
in Sudan, i. 205, 207–8; takes Abu Hamed, i. 214–215; occupies Berber, i. 216, 217–218; on the Atbara, i. 229; proceeds to Roseires, i. 264–65; goes to India, i. 229
in South Africa, i. 310, 318, 319
commanding Bombay troops, ii. 138
Hunter, Surgeon, i. 161
Hunter-Weston, Lt.-Gen. Sir A., iii, 177
Hussars, 20th, at Toski, i. 167
Hussein Pasha Khalifa, i. 61 (*note*), 63, 67 (*note*), 74, 78
Hussein, Prince Kamil, ii. 324

Ibrahim Bey Fauzi, i. 123
Ibrahim Bey Rushdi, i. 122
Idris, El Said, ii. 344
Imbros, iii. 140, 205
Imperial Cadet School, ii. 179
Imperial Defence Committee, ii. 145, 174, 238; Kitchener a member of, ii. 305
Imperial Institute, Kitchener lectures at, ii. 322 (*note*)
India: Kitchener on leave in, i. 168; desires Indian Command, ii. 117–21; becomes Commander-in-Chief in, ii. 112, 115–16; plans defence of, ii. 134–5, 145–50, 151–4,

206, 238–9, 241, 243, 281; Frontier Railways, ii. 146–7, 148–50; the incidence of Army expenses in, ii. 232–7, iii. 318; German menace foreseen, ii. 281–2; Kitchener suggested as Viceroy of, ii. 302–4; his prestige in, i. 316 (*note*); unrest in, ii. 253–9, iii. 302; and Japanese success, ii. 238–9, 242, 281

Roberts in, i. 270, ii. 204

in Great War: Egypt kept secure by, iii. 83; Territorials in, iii. 77, 310; war material supplied by, ii. 200, 277, iii. 267; and military expenditure, iii. 318; unrest in, iii. 302; and Kitchener's death, iii. 357

Indian Army:
Curzon on need for reform in, ii. 117–18, 122, 123
Dual Control of. *See* Dual Control
Kitchener's reforms, ii. 123–4, 27 *i* ; re-numbering, ii. 124–7; Reorganisation and Redistribution, ii. 132–7, 139–44, 184–5, 196, 198–9, 214, 244–7, 278–9, 280–82; Frontier Militia, ii. 126, 135, 156, 157, 160–61; Mixed Brigades and Homogeneous Brigades, ii. 106–7, 135–6, 169–70; Divisional System, ii. 167–9, 283; " Kitchener test," ii. 171–2; Staff College, ii. 173–6; General Staff, ii. 176; standing of Native officers, ii. 177–83; improved conditions for British officers, ii. 184–7, 280; for British troops, ii. 190–193, 235–6, 270–76, 280; for native troops, ii. 189 (*note*), 193–7, 231, 245; health and morals of the troops, ii. 270–76, 280, iii. 27 (*note*) : finances of Kitchener's reforms, ii. 277–9; his farewell order, ii. 279–80

Morley's economies: administrative, ii. 224, 226, 227–30;

proposed reduction of British troops, ii. 231–5, 238–43; apportionment of Army expenses, ii. 232–7; Redistribution scheme suffers by, ii. 244–7
seditious propaganda in, ii. 253–259
in Great War, iii. 40, 339–40; in East Africa, ii. 283; in Egypt, ii. 283, iii. 83, 97; in France, ii. 185, 283, iii. 65, 73, 79, 259, 260; in Gallipoli, iii. 148, 162; in Mesopotamia, ii. 283–4, iii. 98, 132, 259, 302–3

Indian Criminal Law Amendment Act, ii. 258

Ingouville-Williams, Maj.-Gen. Edward, ii. 35

Intelligence Department in Egypt, i. 183

Invasion possibility, iii. 10, 308, 329–30

Invincibility, the tradition of Kitchener's, i. 316–17

Irish rebellion, iii. 96 (*note*)

Iron Duke, the, iii. 353–4

Irrigation: Egyptian, i. 261, ii. 316 (*note*); Sudanese, ii. 326 (*note*)

Ismailia, Kitchener's journey to, i. 56–7

Itala fighting, ii. 49

Italians: Abyssinians and, i. 190–191; Dervishes and, i. 189–91; evacuate Kassala, i. 220–21, 222, 225; at war with Turks in Tripoli, ii. 314–16, 344; and purchase of Mariut Railway, ii. 340; Senussi and, ii. 316, 341, iii. 155–6

Italy: and Great War, iii. 85, 100, 102, 108, 120; joins Allies, iii. 139, 241 (*note*), 302; Russia and, iii. 349 (*note*); and Kitchener's death, iii. 359

Italy, King of, Kitchener visits, iii. 207–8

Jaalin tribe, i. 135, 213, 214, 238
Jacobsdal, i. 283
Jacob's Well, i. 29–30

INDEX

Japan: Afghanistan and, ii. 154; Kitchener visits, ii. 285, 287–8; clears Pacific, iii. 83; and Kitchener's death, iii. 359
Japanese munitions, iii. 280 (*note*), 347
Japanese Staff, ii. 174
Japanese success and Indian opinion, ii. 238–9, 242, 281
Java, Kitchener visits, ii. 288–9
Jehadia riflemen, i. 159
Jellicoe, Admiral Sir John (Viscount), iii. 353–4
Jerabin tribe, i. 56
Jerusalem, i. 15, 17, 27, 29–30; Bishop of, i. 32, ii. 345
Jevzad Effendi, i. 99, 100
Jews and Synagogues of Galilee, i. 33–4
Joffre, General (Marshal), iii. 16; his strategy, iii. 18–21; and Maubeuge concentration, iii. 22; French meets, iii. 28; Ardennes offensive by, iii. 32, 35, 38; new dispositions by, iii. 42, 44, 46, 47, 48; opens Marne offensive, iii. 56–7, 58, 61; and Antwerp, iii. 67–8; in Belgium, iii. 72; support at Ypres from, iii. 74; meets George V., iii. 78; on fresh offensive, iii. 78, 79; on Russian situation and contingencies in France, iii. 81–2; plans attacks at Arras and Rheims, iii. 82, 83; and Belgian coast campaign, iii. 89, 103; agrees to new arrangement of forces, iii. 221, 223–4; and Twenty-ninth Division, iii. 117; and Eastern schemes, iii. 103, 186, 250, 258, 260; protests against further drafts for Dardanelles, iii. 174–5; eager for offensive, iii. 224, 241 (*note*), 243; his letter on situation and need for British assistance, iii. 241 (*note*), 251; his Champagne offensive, iii. 248–9, 251, 252; and Loos, iii. 255; Haig and, iii. 294, 305–6; at Verdun, iii. 305–6; Kitchener's friendship for, iii. 345

Johannesburg: occupied, i. 312; stables raided, ii. 3 (*note*); mines reopened, ii. 27–8, 33, 92; Kitchener's dislike for, i. 323; his speech at, ii. 106
Johnsonville, ii. 296
Joubert, i. 307
Judaea, Survey of, i. 16
Jutland battle, iii. 326, 354

Kababish tribe, i. 70, 72, 74, 75, 98, 164
Kabul, ii. 140, 141, 147–8, 149
Kaffir franchise, ii. 20, 24
Kaiser Wilhelm II.: Mohammedan world and, ii. 282; meetings with Kitchener, ii. 308; rancour against British, iii. 43; and King of Greece, iii. 109, 196, 200, 202
Kalamon, i. 25
Kandahar, ii. 140, 141, 147
Karee hills, i. 307
Kassala, i. 189, 190; Italians evacuate, i. 219–21, 222–25
Kastamuni, i. 37–8, 51
Kavanagh, Lt.-Gen. Sir C., iii. 170
Kebir, Tel-el-, i. 175
Kekewich, Col. (Maj.-Gen.), i. 272; against De la Rey, ii. 53, 66, 67; at Roodeval, ii. 73–4
Kelly-Kenny, Gen. (Sir Thomas): at Klip Drift, i. 278–79; pursuing Cronje, i. 282, 284; at Paardeberg, i. 286, 287, 288–89, defeats De la Rey, i. 302–3
Kelvin, Lord, ii. 268
Kemp: Vlakfontein success by, ii. 35; attacks Methuen, ii. 47; in the Zwartruggens, ii. 47, 53; defeated at Roodeval, ii. 73–4, 88; at Vereeniging Conference, ii. 97, 103
Keneh, i. 60–61
Keneh-Kosseir roads, Kitchener's Report on, i. 61–2
Kenhardt, i. 298, 304
Kennedy, Lord John, i. 42 (*note*)
Keriyat tribe, i. 74 (*note*)
Kerma, i. 204, 205, 209
Kerreri hills, i. 240, 242, 243; plains, i. 227, 236

Keyes, Commander (Rear-Admiral Sir Roger), iii. 188, 209
Khaibar line, ii. 148–50, 162
Khaibar Rifles, ii. 160
Khalifa, the (Abdullah-el-Taaishi), i. 132, 156, 158, 165; revolt against, i. 164; settles in Omdurman, i. 182–83; prepares against attack, i. 186, 213, 214, 218, 234, 236; confident, i. 213, 214, 236; at battle of Omdurman, i. 237, 240; escapes to Kordofan, i. 247; pursued, i. 265–66; killed, i. 266–67
Khalifa, Sheikh, i. 108
Khartum: invested, i. 62, 65, 68–9; Kitchener's reconnaissances near, i. 77, 82; messages into, i. 70, 74, 77, 80, 102–3, 106; starving, i. 109, 117, 119; Gordon's defence of, i. 116–20; news of fall of, i. 110, 120–125; Kitchener's account of fall of, i. 112 (note), 116–125, 133–134
Expedition reaches, i. 248, 250; Gordon memorial service held in, i. 248–49
Gordon College, i. 97, 257–59, ii. 110, 113, 306
new city planned, i. 262, ii. 304
Khartum Cathedral, ii. 306
Khash'm-el-Mus, i. 100, 131
Khedive, i. 68, 184–86, 191–92; intrigues of, during Kitchener's Agency, ii. 314, 339–41, 344; sale of decorations and religious property, ii. 341–3; threatened with deposition, ii. 343
Khen, Sheikh Wad-el-, i. 108
Khurbet Kefr-es-Samir, i. 25
Khurbet Minieh, i. 34–5
Kilid Bahr, iii. 136, 144, 145, 146, 151, 189
Kilimanjaro range, i. 154
Kimberley: besieged, i. 271–72, 273–74; relief force, i. 278, 279; relieved, i. 280, 290; Kitchener in, i. 299–300
King's Own Scottish Borderers, i. 162
Kirbekan, i. 113
Kirk, Sir John, i. 148

Kirster, ii. 40
Kitchener, Arthur (brother), i. 3
Kitchener, Frances Emily Jane (sister), i. 3
Kitchener, Frederick Walter (Maj.-Gen. Sir Walter) (brother): in Egypt, i. 265–66; in South Africa, ii. 50, 73; Governor of Bermuda, i. 3 (note)
Kitchener, Henry Elliott Chevallier (brother), 2nd Earl, i. 3, 64 (note)
Kitchener, Henry Horatio, Colonel (father), i. 2–3, 8–9
Kitchener, Herbert Horatio, Field-Marshal Earl Kitchener of Khartoum:
ancestry and parentage, i. 1–3
appearance, i. 4, 6, 23 (note), 41, 60
career:
1850: birth and christening, i. 2, 3
1850–1863: childhood in Ireland, i. 3–4
1863: family goes to Switzerland, i. 4
1864–1866: his mother's death, i. 4–5; studies in France and Switzerland, i. 5
1866–1868: cramming for Woolwich, i. 5
1868–1870: Cadet at Woolwich, i. 5, 6–8; friendship with Claud Conder, i. 7–8
1871–1874: in Franco-Prussian War, i. 8–11, iii. 57 (note); commission in Royal Engineers, i. 11; at Chatham, i. 6, 9, 11–13; friendship with H. R. Williams, i. 11–12, 13; religious interests, i. 12, 13–14; attends Austrian manœuvres, i. 12–13; at Aldershot, i. 11, 13–14; in Hanover, i. 14
1874–1875: joins Palestine Survey, i. 15–16; fever, i. 17, 19, 20; twice saves Conder, i. 17–18; Safed outrage, i. 17–19, 23; returns to England, i. 19;

INDEX 395

Kitchener, Earl (*contd.*)—
Book of *Photographs* of Biblical Sites, i. 19-21
1876: in London, preparing Map of Palestine, i. 22
1877–1878: Survey resumed, i. 23-8, 31-2; Reports to Fund, i. 23-5, 26, 27-8; Northern Survey completed, i. 26-7; in Jerusalem, i. 27, 29-31; Jacob's Well, i. 29-30, 32; Capernaum Synagogue, i. 32; Russo-Turkish War, i. 25-6, 30, 40; in England, i. 30; hands his contributions over to Fund, i. 31-32; lectures to British Association, i. 31-2; monographs, i. 33-5
1878–1881: Cyprus Survey begun, but discontinued, i. 36; Military Vice-Consul at Kastamuni, i. 37-8, 51, 54, 90 (*note*); Survey Director in Cyprus, i. 38-43; shot at, i. 41 (*note*); Land Registration remodelled, i. 41, 45; wins steeplechase, i. 42; offered excavation work by British Museum, i. 43-4
1882–1883: takes part in campaign against Arabi during leave, i. 47-9; desire for service in Egypt, i. 47, 49, 50; leaves Cyprus, i. 50; joins Egyptian cavalry, i. 50-53; Captain, R. E., Bimbashi, Egyptian Army, i. 50 (*note*); reputation in Cairo, i. 50-52, 60
1883–1885: Sinai Peninsula Survey, i. 53-8, 59; journey to Ismailia, i. 56-7; eyesight injured, i. 57, ii. 329; with his regiment, i. 59-60, 62; sent to Keneh, i. 61; Report on Keneh-Kosseir route, i. 61-2; Bedawin force suggested, i. 61, 62; sent to open up Berber-Suakin route, i. 63-5; at Korosko, i. 64; fore-

Kitchener, Earl (*contd.*)—
sees peril to Egypt, i. 65, 68; the Ababdeh Frontier Force, i. 66-7, 68; negotiations with Arab tribes, i. 66 (*note*), 67-8, 70, 79-81; sent to Dongola, i. 70, 72-4, 76; relations with Mudir, i. 73-4, 76, 78, 80-82; examines routes for Relief Expedition, i. 75, 76-7, 81, 103; promoted Major, i. 76 (*note*), 80; suggested return to Korosko, i. 79, 80-82; defences of Debbeh, i. 81-2, 83-4, 85; with Mudir to Merawi, i. 85, 86-7; attempts to avert disaster to Stewart, i. 87-92; his account of Stewart's fate, i. 90-93; Intelligence Officer with Relief Expedition, i. 94; difficulties with Mudir, i. 95, 98-101; success in intertribal politics, i. 97-100; communications with Gordon, i. 77, 102-5, 106; at Debbeh, i. 106-7; at Ambukol, i. 107-8; with Sir Herbert Stewart, i. 109
1885–1886: with Desert Column under Buller, i. 110-116; cuts enemy water-supply, i. 114-15; back at Debbeh, i. 116; Report on Fall of Khartum, i. 112 (*note*), 116-25; on Mahdi's position and Sudan policy, i. 126-127, 128, 130-32; his Sudan Report, i. 133-142; resigns from Egyptian Army, i. 132; returns to England, i. 133; presented to Queen Victoria, i. 133; on Zanzibar Commission, i. 143, 146, 147, 148, 149, 150-52, 153-54; German intrigues and, i. 148-50, 152-153; suggests acquisition of Mombasa, i. 150-52
1886–1888: becomes Governor-General of Eastern

Kitchener, Earl (*contd.*)—
    Sudan, i. 155–158, 162–63; wounded at Handub, i. 159–161; Brevet-Colonel, i. 160; Adjutant-General, i. 162; siege of Suakin, i. 162
    1889: at battle of Toski, i. 166–168
    1890–1891: reorganises Egyptian Police Force, i. 168–171
    1892–1896: becomes Sirdar, i. 172; the preparation of the Egyptian Army, i. 172–180, 198, ii. 115; his Intelligence system, i. 183; incident with the Khedive, i. 184–86; knighthood, i. 186; social life, i. 188–89; mobilises Army, i. 191–92; in command, i. 193
    1896: Dongola Expedition: Cromer's support, i. 194–95; plans of campaign, i. 195–96; transport difficulties, i. 196, 198, 201, 203–4, 207; Firket victory, i. 199–200; delays and disappointments, i. 201–204, 207; Hafir battle, i. 205–206; Dongola taken, i. 206; instructed to proceed, i. 209
    1897–1898: Omdurman Campaign: alternative routes, i. 209–10; the Halfa—Abu Hamed railway, i. 210–13, 218, 222, 223, 226; at Merawi, i. 214, 215, 217; Berber occupied, i. 216, 217–218; the taking-over of Kassala and financial difficulties of campaign, i. 219–225; resignation tendered, i. 218, 223–24, ii. 209; discussion in Cairo, i. 224; concentration at Berber, i. 226–27; the Atbara victory, i. 228–32; command confirmed and reinforcements promised, i. 232, 233–234; his forces, i. 235; the eve of battle, i. 237–39; the

Kitchener, Earl (*contd.*)—
    battle of Omdurman, i. 240, 246, 263–64; entry into town, i. 246–47, 248; at Gordon memorial service in Khartum, i. 248–49; receives peerage, i. 5 (*note*), 249, 257; Fashoda incident, i. 251–54, ii. 115; reception in England, i. 255–57, iii. 361; success of appeal for Gordon College, i. 256, 257–59
    1899: becomes Governor-General of Sudan, i. 260, 261–62; Cromer's advice, i. 260–61; charges of cruelty refuted, i. 263–64; Wingate to succeed him, i. 266, 267
    1899–1900: South African War: Chief of the Staff, i. 269–70; voyage with Roberts, i. 270–271; difficulties and deficiencies, i. 271, 274–76, 307, 329–330; transport arrangements, i. 271, 275–78, 299, 311, 329; pursuit of Cronje, i. 279–85; in supreme control at Paardeberg, i. 284–85; his frontal attack, i. 286–90, 291, 295, 309; relations with Roberts, i. 269, 284, 285, 294, 304, 305, 309, 324, ii. 17; at Arundel, i. 297, 309; Cape Colony rebellion, i. 298–99, 304; letter on situation to Lord Salisbury, i. 299–300; messages from Queen, i. 301, 305; reorganisation at Bloemfontein, i. 306–7; checks De Wet, i. 309; in Kroonstad, i. 311; Pretoria entered, i. 314 (*note*); pursuing De Wet, i. 314–15, 319–23; two narrow escapes, i. 315–17; relieves Hone, i. 322–23; in Pretoria, i. 323; desires Indian Command, ii. 117–21
    1900–1902: Commander-in-Chief, i. 324–25; speed and economy urged by Govern-

INDEX 397

Kitchener, Earl (*contd.*)—
ment, i. 325-26, ii. 29-30, 107; reply describing position, i. 328-30; calls for mounted troops, ii. 4-5; blockhouses and drives, ii. 5-10, 20-30, 40, 43-4, 59, 62-3; Concentration Camps, ii. 11-14, 38, 46; Cape Colony rebellion, ii. 15-16, 20, 23, 25-6, 30-31, 38; De Wet turned back, ii. 16-17; peace negotiations with Botha, ii. 16, 18-26, 34, 54; acting as High Commissioner, ii. 28-9; pursuit of Smuts, ii. 40-45; blockhouse system extended, ii. 46-7, 51, 53; on Benson's death, ii. 51-2; a run of ill-luck, ii. 54-5; on Boer attitude, ii. 55, 57-8, 61; drive for De Wet, ii. 63-5; Tweebosch disaster, ii. 66-9; Roodeval success, ii. 73-4, 88, 89; his character, ii. 75-7, 78-80, 84-5; his methods, ii. 75-80, 81-4, 169; hostile criticism, ii. 12-14, 108; peace negotiations, ii. 70, 86-89, 91, 93-4, 95; at Vereeniging Conference, ii. 95, 98, 99, 100-101, 103, 104; urges clemency to Boers, i. 299, 328, ii. 19, 21-2, 25-6, 71, 87 (*note*), 94, 104-6, 116; peace signed, ii. 104; returns to England, ii. 109; receives Order of Merit, ii. 109; public honours, ii. 110-11
becomes Commander-in-Chief in India, ii. 112, 115-21; opens Gordon College, ii. 113-114; lands in India, ii. 122; Curzon's welcome, ii. 117-18, 122-123
1903-1904: re-numbering of Native regiments, ii. 124-7; tour of North-West Frontier, ii. 128-9, 160; social life at Simla, ii. 130-31; Army Redistribu-

Kitchener, Earl (*contd.*)—
tion and Reorganisation, ii. 132-7, 139-144, 160-65, 166-72, 214, 244-247, 277-9; financial grants for, ii. 278-9; his leg broken, ii. 129 (*note*), 138-9; North-West Frontier defence against invasion, ii. 135, 140-43, 145-150, 151-5, 240-43, 281; against Frontier tribes, ii. 155, 157-65, 241-2; the Divisional system, ii. 167-9; Army training, ii. 169-72; Indian Staff College scheme, ii. 173-6; the standing of Native officers, ii. 180-83; British officers, their number, promotion, and payment, ii. 184-8; his care for the British soldier, ii. 189-93, 235-6, 260-62, 270-76; for the Native, ii. 187-8, 189 (*note*), 193-7; on health and morals of the Army, ii. 271-276, iii. 27 (*note*); on Army expenditure and Dual Control, ii. 198-201
1905-1907: Minute on the Dual Control, ii. 203-11, 213-14; Curzon's attitude, ii. 199, 201, 206 (*note*), 212-13, 214, 216-19; Secretary of State supports Kitchener, ii. 209-210, 213, 220-22; Cabinet's decision, ii. 219-23; Morley's departmental reforms, ii. 224-230; the incidence of military taxation, ii. 233-4, 236; opposes reduction of forces, ii. 238-43, 245-6; the Redistribution scheme and the Morley economies, ii. 236-7, 240, 244-7; travels and social life, ii. 247-9; visit of the Amir of Afghanistan, ii. 249-52; seditious propaganda and Indian Army, ii. 253-9; the Dthala sanatorium, ii. 260-62; extension of his' term of office,

Kitchener, Earl (*contd.*)—
ii. 262–5, 267, 268; attacks of fever, ii. 264, 265, 267; his absence considered inadvisable, ii. 265–7; receives G.C.I.E., ii. 268–9

1908: on Eastern question and German designs, ii. 281–2

1909: Budget speech on finances and results of his schemes, ii. 277–9; farewell to India, ii. 279–80; the fruits of his work, ii. 283–4

offered Mediterranean Command, ii. 285, 301, 302; invited to advise on Australian defence, ii. 285, 289; visits China, ii. 286–7; on Manchurian battlefields, ii. 286–7; in Japan, ii. 287–8; in Java, ii. 288–9

1910: in Australia, ii. 289–93; on Australian defence, ii. 290–291, 292, 293–6, 297; in New Zealand, ii. 296–8; in United States, ii. 298–9; reaches England, ii. 301

receives Field-Marshal's baton, ii. 301; suggested Viceroyalty, ii. 302–4; death of King Edward VII., ii. 303; a brief holiday, ii. 304; joins Committee of Imperial Defence, ii. 305; visits Turkey, ii. 306

1911: visits Sudan, ii. 306–7; tour through British East Africa, ii. 307–8; acquires land there, ii. 307, 308, iii. 352; recalled, ii. 308; visited by German Emperor in Venice, ii. 308; in command of troops at Coronation of George V., ii. 308–9; the question of his employment, ii. 310; the Agadir incident, ii. 310–11

appointed British Agent

Kitchener, Earl (*contd.*)—
in Cairo, ii. 311–12; leaves England, ii. 313

1912–1914: Italo-Turkish war and Egyptian feeling, ii. 314–316; changes in Egypt, ii. 316–17; fellahin freed from usurers, i. 143, ii. 317–18, 320; the Five Feddan Law, ii. 318–320; arranges transport for produce, ii. 320–21; furthers cotton cultivation in Egypt and Sudan, ii. 317, 322–4, 325–6, 334; supports oil industry, ii. 327; his sanitary reforms, ii. 328–30; administrative reforms, ii. 330–31, 345; revives prestige of his position, ii. 332–3; King and Queen land at Port Sudan, ii. 333; at the Malta Conference, ii. 336–7; the Balkan war, ii. 337; attempted assassination, ii. 334; German intrigues in Egypt, ii. 311, 338–40; Khedive's intrigues, ii. 339–44, 345; Kitchener visits Sudan, ii. 333–4; settlement of French rights, ii. 334, 335; plots against his life, ii. 334–5; the scope of his work, ii. 344–346; receives Earldom, ii. 346; leaves for England, ii. 346

August 1914–1915: return to Egypt prevented, iii. 2–3

becomes Secretary of State for War, iii. 3–4, 7, 322–5, 364–365; the war long foreseen, i. 65, 150, ii. 244 (*note*), 282, 295–296, iii. 1–2; his estimate of its duration, i. 65, iii. 9, 80, 90, 271, 274, 308, 309 (*note*), 371; Chief of the Staff, iii. 6, 103; "no Army," iii. 7–8, 15; plans for seventy divisions, iii. 9, 10, 307, 315, 318; invasion possibility, iii. 10, 308, 329–30; trusted by

Kitchener, Earl (*contd.*) —
the people, iii. 12–15, 356–7; creation of his New Armies, ii. 116, iii. 8, 13–14, 39–40, 59, 93, 220, 240, 265, 280, 308–10, 328–31; importance of secrecy, iii. 17, 209, 327; personal regard for Sir John French, iii. 24–25, 63, 75; instructions to Sir John French, iii. 25–6, 28; message to troops, iii. 27; foresees German movements, iii. 21–3, 28, 29–30, 33, 34, 35; on importance of keeping touch with the French, iii. 36, 50–52, 55, 57; supply of reinforcements, iii. 39–41, 45, 62, 65, 77, 83; and French's proposed independent retreat, iii. 45–6, 50–52, 53; Kitchener visits French, iii. 54–6; on supply of officers, iii. 64–5; plan for relief of Antwerp, iii. 67–70; the defence of Egypt, iii. 95–6, 98; ammunition shortage, iii. 72, 74, 78–9, 265–7; Cabinet Committee on Munitions, iii. 267; contract with Bethlehem Steel Corporation, iii. 271; high explosive production, iii. 274–5; supply of high explosives, iii. 272–4, 275–9; letter defending von Donop, iii. 279–80; work for aviation, iii. 73; meeting with French President at Dunkirk, iii. 74–5; the fruits of his work in India, ii. 283–4; and Arab movement in Syria, iii. 153–5, 250–51

1915: considering operations elsewhere, iii. 85–6; Alexandretta scheme, iii. 99, 104–105, 110, 190, 191; on Belgian coast campaign, iii. 88–90, 91–93, 104; not prepared for large military operations in Gallipoli, iii. 99, 101, 104, 105,

Kitchener, Earl (*contd.*) —
110, 116, 120–21; visit from Millerand, iii. 280; his relations with the French, iii. 344–5; refuses to weaken Western front, iii. 104, 111, 223; New Armies in France, iii. 220, 223, 227–8; French's secret visits, iii. 228, 234, 236, 237, 247, 249, 292, 295; troops available for Gallipoli, iii. 109, 110, 113–15, 116, 120–121, 124, 141; Russia in difficulties, iii. 101, 110–11, 345–8; the Twenty-ninth Division detained, iii. 106, 109, 110, 111–12, 117–18, 119, 121, 125; Neuve Chapelle, iii. 121, 227; instructions for Gallipoli attack, iii. 122–124; large operations found necessary, iii. 126, 127–9, 131, 133; the East and operations against Turkey, iii. 111, 112, 129, 142, 149, 185, 190–91, 192, 193, 194, 209; on battle of Shiva, iii. 132–3; reinforcements for Hamilton, iii. 136–7, 139, 141–2, 171, 172; on use of poison gas, iii. 234–235; provision of munitions, iii. 268–9, 271, 272; Labour and munitions output, iii. 282–6; Ministry of Munitions, iii. 287–9; Sir John French asked to lend ammunition for Dardanelles, iii. 238–9, 289; French's political manœuvre, iii. 238–9, 289–290; receives the Garter, iii. 290, 356; Fourteenth Division sent, iii. 240; Joffre's appeal for British support, iii. 241, 246, 251, 258 (*note*); suggested Bulair landing, iii. 149; operations against Senussi, iii. 155–7; Perim and Aden attacked, iii. 157–8; formation of Guards Division and Territorial reor-

Kitchener, Earl (*contd.*)—
ganisation, iii. 251-252;
National Registration Act,
iii. 313-14, 317 (*note*);
and Compulsory Service,
iii. 313; landing on Asiatic side of Peninsula, iii.
158-9, 160, 174-175; Suvla Bay, iii. 159-60; unsuccessful Generals replaced,
iii. 170; and unity of command, iii. 175, 261-2; Salonika operations, iii. 179,
182-3, 186, 187, 198-9,
260-261; Derby Scheme,
iii. 317; his work for the
supply of munitions, iii.
264-9, 270-72, 274-6, 278-81, 282-6, 287-91
sent to decide evacuation question, iii. 184,
185; rumours of his supersession, iii. 185-6; interview with Joffre in Paris,
iii. 186, 260-261; his views
on evacuation, iii. 183,
187-8, 189, 190-91, 205-6,
209-10, 261; Mudros conference, iii. 186, 188-9,
205; Gallipoli visited, iii.
188-9; Ayas Bay Scheme,
iii. 191-5, 197, 201,
209; Greek recalcitrance,
iii. 186, 197, 202-3;
Salonika visited, iii. 195,
198-9; interview with
King of Greece at Athens,
iii. 197, 200, 201-4; report on evacuation and
Egyptian situation, iii.
205-6, 207, 208-209; opposes suggestion that he
should go to Egypt, iii.
205, 206, 207; King of
Italy visited, iii. 207-8;
returns to London, iii.
208; his resignation refused, iii. 208; situation
at end of 1915, iii. 301-3
1916: relations with Haig, in
command in France, iii.
293-5; relations with Robertson, Chief of Imperial
General Staff, iii. 297-300,
303; assistance to French

Kitchener, Earl (*contd.*)—
during Verdun battle, iii.
305; operations in Egypt,
iii. 303-304; question of
Compulsory Service, iii.
314-18, 334-5; and suggested reduction of forces
or money supplied, iii.
318-19; and conscientious
objectors, iii. 323; debate
on his salary, iii. 327,
343; his speech to the
House of Commons, iii.
326-43; his influence in
Russia, iii. 348-9; his mission to Russia, iii. 325,
349-51, 352; talk on East
African property, ii. 308,
iii. 352; leaves London,
iii. 353
June 5, 1916: at Scapa Flow,
iii. 353-4; lost with the
Hampshire, iii. 354-5
world-wide tributes, iii.
355-360; service at St.
Paul's, iii. 359-60
Characteristics:
archaeological interests, i.
23 (*note*), 24, 32, 33-5,
188, iii. 363
artistic tastes, i. 42-3, 50, ii.
248 (*note*), 249, 279, 287,
288
china, fondness for, i. 42-3,
ii. 287, 288
clemency, i. 299, 328, ii. 19,
21-22, 25-6, 71, 87 (*note*),
94, 104-6
confidence in subordinates, i.
208, ii. 76-7, iii. 299-300
consideration for troops, i.
13, 24 (*note*), 287, ii. 13,
14, 182-3, 189 (*note*),
190-93, 193-7, 235 (*note*),
270-76, iii. 72, 75, 185
detail, care for, i. 24, 25, 31
diplomatic gifts, i. 252-54,
ii. 115, 312, 315, 332, 340-43, 344-6, iii. 201-4, 363
duty, devotion to, i. 24
(*note*), iii. 364-6
East, love of the, i. 16, 22,
iii. 153-4
economy, i. 28, 31, 70-71,
173, 174, 223, 254, 256,

INDEX 401

Kitchener, Earl (*contd.*)—
325–6, 329, ii. 82–3, 198–201, 233–4, 277–279
education, zeal for, i. 256, 257–259, ii. 113–14, 274 (*note*)
energy, i. 6, 13, 23 (*note*), 50, 55–6, 58–9, 69, 156, 158, 208, 224, ii. 2 (*note*), 81–2, 117, 217
engineering, love of, i. 11, 12, 197–8, 212–13
financial ability, i. 70–71, 254, 256, 329, ii. 82–3, 198–9, 233–234, 277–9
flowers, love of, i. 3, 24, 188, ii. 249, 264 (*note*), 279
foresight, i. 65, 68, 111, 163, 172, 173 (*note*), 175, 268, 291, ii. 93–4, 105, 263 (*note*), 279, 281–2, 296, iii. 8, 9, 15, 22–3, 80 (*note*), 95, 111, 264, 265, 270–72, 274–5, 307–8, 346–8, 363–4
gratitude, i. 161, ii. 79–80
horsemanship, i. 6, 7, 42, 188
hospitality, i. 188, ii. 130–31, 248–9, 279, 333
humour, ii. 250, iii. 369–70
impatience of formality, i. 274–275, ii. 76, 123–4, 131
justice, ii. 68–9
knowledge, range of, ii. 292 (*note*), 336, iii. 6, 153–4, 299, 363–4
loyalty: to colleagues, iii. 201, 324–5, 367; to the Throne, ii. 301, iii. 371
moral fibre, ii. 276, iii. 362, 365, 370
organising ability, i. 197, ii. 75–76, 83–4, iii. 2, 358, 362
religious impulse, i. 12, 13–14, 22 (*note*), 32, ii. 276, 345, iii. 359, 371–2
reticence, i. 4, 7, 42, 50, 208, 261, ii. 75–6, 84–5, iii. 323–4, 358
self-reliance, i. 23, 219, 224, ii. 75–6, 77–8, 115, iii. 299–300, 368
sensitiveness, i. 232, 248, 263–264, ii. 13, 14, 73, iii.

Kitchener, Earl (*contd.*)—
185, 290, 359, 369, 370–71
shyness, i. 42, 51, ii. 263 (*note*), iii. 361
sociability, i. 6–7, 52, 55, ii. 111–12, 130–31, 247–9, iii. 368
statesmanship, i. 252–54, ii. 115, 312, 344–6, iii. 201–4, 363
three Kitcheners, i. 51–2
unselfishness, iii. 2, 365–6
warmth, love of, i. 27, 39, 60, ii. 306
Letters, to:
Amir of Afghanistan, ii. 252
Asquith, Rt. Hon. H. H., iii. 189–90, 192, 193, 194–95, 197–8, 198–9, 202–4, 205–6, 207, 260–261, 279–80
Baring, Sir Evelyn (Earl of Cromer), i. 156–7
Bertie, Sir Francis (Lord), iii. 88–9
Besant, Walter, i. 20–21, 22–3, 38–9, 39–40, 53–4, 56–7, 57–8, 62, 64, 68
Birdwood, Gen. Sir W., iii. 114, 115, 120
Blyth, Dr., Bishop of Jerusalem, i. 32, ii. 345
Botha, Gen. (Rt. Hon. Louis), ii. 22–4
British Museum, i. 43–4
Brodrick, Rt. Hon. St. John (Viscount Midleton): from South Africa, i. 324, 328–30, ii. 4, 6, 7, 8, 19–22, 25–6, 29–30, 31, 33–4, 44, 46 (*note*), 48, 50, 51–2, 54–5, 61, 62, 68–9, 71, 76 (*note*), 84, 86 (*note*), 87 (*note*), 90, 91, 100–101, 104, 120; from India, ii. 162–3, 199–200, 201, 202, 206–7, 208, 209, 210–11, 222 (*note*)
Buller, Gen. Sir R., i. 130–31
Bullough, Colonel, i. 49–50
Churchill, Rt. Hon. W. S., iii. 101
Conder, Miss, i. 22 (*note*)
Cranborne, Viscountess (Marchioness of Salis-

Kitchener, Earl (*contd.*)—
bury), i. 306–307, 314 (*note*), ii. 14, 89
Cromer, Lord (Earl of), i. 223–225
Curzon, Lord (Earl), ii. 160–61, 164
Dawkins, Sir Clinton, i. 221
Dixon, W. Hepworth, i. 26, 27–8
French, Sir John (Field-Marshal Viscount), ii. 235 (*note*), iii. 25–6, 29–30, 39–41, 52, 54, 55–6, 57, 63, 65, 67–8, 69–70, 73–4, 85–6, 90–94, 223, 227, 234, 238, 240, 246, 252, 290–291
"a friend," i. 271, 311, ii. 27 (*note*), 31, 119, 124, 231 (*note*), 244 (*note*), 249 (*note*), 254, 281 (*note*), 293 (*note*), 301
Gordon, General, i. 77, 104–5
Gordon, Lt.-Col. W. S., i. 174 (*note*)
Grenfell, Gen. Sir Francis (Field-Marshal Lord), i. 162, 219–20
Haig, Sir Douglas (Field-Marshal Earl), iii. 305
Hamilton, Gen. Sir Ian, i. 291–295, iii. 122–4, 126, 127, 132, 133, 137, 139–40, 141–2, 144, 145, 149, 150, 158–9, 160, 170, 172, 173, 174–5
Hanbury-Williams, Sir John, iii. 350–51
Imperial Defence Committee, ii. 146, 174–5, 176
Joffre, Gen. (Marshal), iii. 57 (*note*)
Kitchener, Colonel, i. 105
Maxwell, Gen. Sir John, ii. 255 (*note*), iii. 113, 114–15, 120, 157
Millerand, M., iii. 258 (*note*), 346
Minto, Earl of, ii. 149–50, 253–4, 256–7
Morley, Rt. Hon. J. (Viscount), ii. 180–81, 187–8, 225–6, 227, 228, 233–5,

Kitchener, Earl (*contd.*)—
235–6, 259 (*note*), 261–2, 264–5, 265–6, 267, 268–269
Ralli, Mr., i. 90–93, 274–75, 300 (*note*), ii. 13 (*note*), 93 (*note*), 119–20
Renshaw, Mr. Arthur, i. 225 (*note*), ii. 336
Roberts, Field-Marshal Earl: as Chief of Staff, i. 280–81, 289, 297; as Commander-in-Chief, i. 315 (*note*), 327, ii. 3 (*note*), 11–12, 13, 14–16, 16–17, 22, 27–8, 34, 36, 52–3, 55, 57–8, 60, 63, 67, 78, 79 (*note*), 82, 85 (*note*), 89 (*note*); from India, ii. 127 (*note*), 129, 135 (*note*), 167, 168; in 1914, iii. 266 (*note*)
Rundle, Bimbashi Leslie (Gen. Sir L.), i. 79 (*note*), 80–81
Salisbury, Marchioness of, ii. 129 (*note*), 132 (*note*), 145 (*note*), 169 (*note*), 189 (*note*), 247 (*note*), 248 (*note*), 249–50, 264 (*note*), 288 (*note*), 298 (*note*), 306
Salisbury, Marquis of, Prime Minister, i. 263–64, 299–300
Salisbury, 4th Marquis of, ii. 238 (*note*)
Stewart, Colonel, i. 74, 102
Times, The, ii. 306 (*note*)
Ward, Sir Joseph, ii. 297
Willcocks, Gen. Sir James, iii. 73
Wilson, Maj.-Gen. Sir Charles, i. 89–90, 98–101
Wolseley, Sir Garnet (Field-Marshal Viscount), i. 108, 126–127, 161
Wood, Sir Evelyn, Sirdar (Field-Marshal), i. 71, 72, 74, 78, 79–80, 81–2, 83–4, 85, 86, 87
Kitchener, Kawara (step-sister), i. 3 (*note*)
Kitchener, Mrs. (mother), i. 3, 4–5
Kitchener, Thomas (great-great-great-grandfather), i. 2

INDEX 403

Kitchener, William (grandfather), i. 2
Kitchener legend, the, i. 316–17, iii. 358, 360, 361–3
Kitchener's Armies: seventy divisions required, iii. 9, 10, 307, 315, 318; their creation, iii. 8, 13–14, 39–40, 59, 93, 220, 240, 265, 308–10, 328–31; methods of recruiting, iii. 13–14, 310–12, 313–19; in training, iii. 280; in France, iii. 220–21, 239–40, 250, 256–7, 259, 305, 306, 319; in Gallipoli, iii. 145, 161, 162, 164–5, 166, 167; list of, iii. 320
Kitchener's Horse, i. 274, 282, 289, 293
Klerksdorp, ii. 72, 73
Klip Drift, i. 279, 281
Kluck, General von, iii. 34, 39, 41, 44, 45, 55, 57, 60–64
Knowles, Maj-Gen. Sir C., i. 192, 193
Knowsley, ii. 111
Knox, Maj.-Gen. Sir Charles, i. 280, 281, 282, ii. 34, 41
Kohat, ii. 163
Kordofan: Emir with army from, i. 84, 85; prison at, i. 88; revolts against Mahdi, i. 125, 126–7, 128, 130, 133–36, 137; revolts against Khalifa, i. 164
Korn Spruit, i. 308
Korosko: Kitchener at, i. 64, 68; reconnaissance from, i. 66–7; Rundle left in, i. 72; Kitchener's return to, suggested, i. 80–81; outposts at, i. 128
Korosko—Berber route, i. 63
Korti: Mudir's victory at, i. 83, 86, 123; Wolseley takes Mudir to, i. 98 (*note*); forces concentrated at, i. 106, 109, 110; Desert Column returns to, i. 116
Kosheh, i. 201, 202, 203
Kosseir route reconnoitred, i. 61
Krithia battles, iii. 136, 137, 144–5
Kritzinger, ii. 8, 16, 43, 44, 47, 61

Kroonstad: entered, i. 310; conference at, ii. 60, 71
Kruger, President: keeps up Free State resistance, i. 290; with De Wet, i. 301, 302; in favour of blowing up mines, i. 312; leaves Pretoria, i. 313; suggested conference with, ii. 32; for holding out, ii. 37; manifesto inspired by, ii. 38–9
Krugersdorp, ii. 38 (*note*)
Kulmon, i. 25
Kunur, i. 227
Kuram valley, ii. 128, 148, 160, 162–163
Kut-el-Amara, iii. 259, 302, 303
Kynoch, Messrs., iii. 288 (*note*)

La Bassée, iii. 71, 80, 224, 237, 241 (*note*), 253
Labour: and war requirements, iii. 281; organised by Kitchener, iii. 282–6; and Conscription, iii. 315–16, 317; its trust in Kitchener, iii. 12–13, 356–7
Labour Battalions, iii. 290
Ladybrand, i. 306
Ladysmith, i. 268, 269, 272
Lahej, iii. 158
Laj-pat Rai, ii. 255
Lakenheath, i. 2
Lambart's Bay, ii. 16
Lancers, 21st, at Omdurman, i. 241, 243
Land Registration in Cyprus, i. 41, 45
Lanrezac, General de, iii. 28, 29, 34, 35, 44–5, 46, 49
Lansdowne, Marquis of, i. 233, 269, ii. 70
La Panouse, Vicomte de, French Military Attaché, iii. 276 (*note*)
La Terrière, Captain, i. 59, 60
Launceston, ii. 293
Lausanne Treaty, ii. 316
Laval, Chanzy's H.Q. at, i. 8–9
Lawley, Col. the Hon. R., ii. 60
Layard, Lady, ii. 308, 334
Layard, Sir Austen, i. 37, 38
Learmonth, Col., iii. 71 (*note*)
Le Cateau: H.Q. at, iii. 28, 29; battle of, iii. 39, 42, 62

Leggett, Major, ii. 93 (*note*), ii. 308
Leicester, address at, ii. 313 (*note*)
Lemaire, M., i. 152
Le Mans, i. 9, iii. 47
Lemnos, iii. 113, 140
Lens, iii. 253
Lewis, Colonel, i. 202, 230, 241, 244, 266
Lewis guns, iii. 253
Lichtenburg, ii. 67
Liebenberg, i. 298, 299, 304, ii. 72
Liége, siege of, iii. 20, 21, 105
Lille, iii. 71
Lillers, iii. 256
Lincolns in Sudan, i. 227 (*note*), 230, 231, 244, 245–6
Lindley, i. 314
Lines of Communication, iii. 335, 336–8
Lister, Lord, ii. 268
Listowel, i. 2
Liverpool, ii. 112
Liverpool Camp, ii. 290
Lizerne, iii. 232, 233
Lloyd, Col. Clifford, i. 168
Lloyd George, Rt. Hon. D., iii. 14 (*note*); of the Eastern school of war policy, iii. 102–3, 104, 106–7, 108, 109, 111; and labour organisation, iii. 284 (*note*); and munitions supply, iii. 267, 287, 289; his relations with Kitchener, iii. 324–5, 334
Local Government Board, iii. 283
Lockhart, Sir William, ii. 162
Loi Dakka, ii. 148
Loi Shilman line, ii. 148–9
London: confers Freedom on Kitchener, i. 256; and Gordon College Fund, i. 259
London, Bishop of, i. 32
London Scottish, iii. 76
"Lone Pine," iii. 165 (*note*)
Long, Rt. Hon. Walter, iii. 313 (*note*)
Loos, battle of, iii. 148, 249, 252, 253, 255–8
Lorenzo Marques, i. 300, 310 (*note*)
Loyal North Lancashires, ii. 67
Lucas, Lord, iii. 267

Ludendorff, General, iii. 257
Lushington, Eleanor Fanny, i. 3 (*note*)
Luxemburg, iii. 18, 19, 28
Lyttelton, Lt.-Gen. (Gen. the Rt. Hon.), Sir N., i. 241, 244, 315 (*note*), ii. 2, 17, 48, 49, 50

Ma'azi Arabs, i. 56
Maccabees, tombs of the, i. 33
MacDonald, Gen. Sir Hector: at Akasha, i. 196; at Suarda, i. 201; marches to Absarat, i. 202; at the Atbara, i. 230; at Omdurman, i. 179, 241, 244; in South Africa, i. 282, 293, 305
Macdonald, Gen. Sir J., ii. 148 (*note*)
Machadsdorp, i. 313
Machera, Mt., i. 40
Machine-guns, iii. 264, 270, 332–3
McKenna, Rt. Hon. R., iii. 267
McMahon, Col. Sir Henry, iii. 186, 191, 192, 197, 206, 207
MacMunn, Col. (Maj.-Gen.) Sir G., iii. 217
McMurdo, Major, ii. 308
McPherson, 2nd Lieut., iii. 350
Maconchey, General, ii. 268
Macready, Gen. Sir Nevil, iii. 312 (*note*)
Madras Army, ii. 124–5, 126, 133, 203
Mafeking: besieged, i. 271–72, 273; relieved, i. 312
Magato Pass, i. 321
Magersfontein, i. 268, 276, 280
Mahdi, the: advance of, i. 62, 63, 64–5, 68, 129–30; Bisharin and, i. 67; Sheikh Saleh and, i. 70 (*note*); Mudir of Dongola and, i. 73, 76, 77; defeated at Korti, i. 83; tribes with, i. 74 (*note*), 133–138; Khartum garrison and, i. 117–18, 119, 123–125; and death of Gordon, i. 117, 123; predicts massacre of infidels at Omdurman, i. 213, 236; Kordofan revolts against, i. 125, 126–127, 128, 130, 133–36, 137; Kitchener on position of, i. 130, 133–38, death

of, i. 132; his son and George V., i. 257 (*note*)
Mahdi's tomb destroyed, i. 237, 238, 246; Kitchener's reasons, i. 263-64
Mahdist movement, menace of, i. 62, 63, 64-5, 68, 157-158
Maher Pasha, i. 184, 187
Mahmud Ibn Mohammed, Emir, i. 84, 85; at Metemma, i. 214, 215; Kitchener on movements of, i. 85, 219, 224; defeated at the Atbara, i. 227-28, 229-32
Mahon, Maj.-Gen. (Lt.-Gen. Rt. Hon.) Sir Bryan, i. 312, iii. 163, 170, 199, 284 (*note*)
Mahsuds, the, ii. 156-9
Malan, ii. 8, 44
Maliks, the, ii. 156, 158
Malleson, Maj.-Gen., ii. 268
Malta Conference, ii. 336
Manchuria, Kitchener visits, ii. 286-7
Manitou, the, iii. 131-2
Maoris and Kitchener, ii. 296
Marchand, Major, i. 251-54
Marine Contingent, iii. 83
Mariut Railway, ii. 339-40, 343
Marker, Major (Col.), ii. 93 (*note*), iii. 71 (*note*)
Markey, Brigade-Surgeon, i. 161
Marne, battle of the, iii. 36, 41, 57-9, 60-64
Marseilles, iii. 186
Marshall, Lt.-Gen. Sir W., iii. 302
Martin, Colonel, i. 243
Mary, Queen, lands at Port Sudan, ii. 333
Mason, Maj.-Gen. H. M., ii. 260
Massawa, i. 225
Master-General of the Ordnance, iii. 263, 273, 274, 278-80, 287
Mathews, General, i. 146 (*note*)
Maubeuge, iii. 21-3, 28, 30, 32, 38, 43, 64, 78
Maude, Gen. Sir F. Stanley, iii. 170, 178, 302, 303
Maunoury, General, iii. 44, 55, 57, 58, 63
Maxwell, Major (Col.) F., V.C., ii. 285 (*note*), iii. 71 (*note*), 228

Maxwell, Maj.-Gen. (Lt.-Gen. Sir John): in Sudan, i. 230, 241, 244, 246; in South Africa, i. 313; in India, ii. 255 (*note*)
in Great War, iii. 2; organising defence of Egypt, iii. 96-7, 155-6, 206; on Alexandretta scheme, iii. 99, 105; on Suez Canal victory, iii. 107; supplies forces for Dardanelles, iii. 113, 131, 148; on Turkish defences on Peninsula, iii. 118-19; on Turks and Senussi, iii. 155-6; at Mudros conference, iii. 186; and Ayas Bay scheme, iii. 191, 192; and Irish rebellion, iii. 96 (*note*)
Mecca, Sherif of, i. 27 (*note*), iii. 154-5
Mediterranean: German policy and, ii. 310-11; naval control of, ii. 336-7
Mediterranean Command, Kitchener and, iii. 288, 301, 302
Melbourne, Kitchener at, ii. 249 (*note*), 290-93
Melek of Argo, i. 129, 131, 139, 140
Melek of Berber, i. 140
"Memoirs" by Conder and Kitchener, i. 31
Memorandum to the Mudirs, i. 262
Memorial Fund to Kitchener, iii. 360
Menelik of Abyssinia, i. 232-33
Merawi, i. 81; defence of, i. 84, 85, 86; Kitchener and Mudir at, i. 86-8; Mudir ordered to, i. 95; Egyptian Army at, i. 214
Mersa Matruh, iii. 304
Mesopotamia, autonomy promised to, ii. 332
Mesopotamian Expedition, iii. 83, 98, 132, 153, 259, 301-2, 303-4; Indian troops in, iii. 83, 98, 259, 302-3
Messines, iii. 75
Metaxas, Colonel, iii. 203, 204
Metemma: Desert Column attacks, i. 109-10, 111, 114, 119, 132; Jaalin hold, i. 213;

Mahmud at, i. 214, 217–18; bombarded, i. 218
Methuen, Maj.-Gen. Lord (Field-Marshal), i. 272, 278, 310; pursuing De Wet, i. 314–15, 318, 319, 320, 321, 322; against De la Rey, ii. 35; repulses Kemp and De la Rey, ii. 47, 53; Tweebosch disaster to, ii. 66–9, 74
Meuse fortresses, iii. 21
Middelburg Conference, ii. 19–22, 88, 99, 100
Middlesex Hospital, ii. 304
Mikado and Kitchener, ii. 288
Military Department and Redistribution, ii. 136, 219, 220, 221, 226
Military Finance Branch, ii. 227–8
Military Member of Viceroy's Council; Redistribution and, ii. 136; under Dual Control system, ii. 177–8, 203–5, 207, 209–10, 220; Minute by, ii. 215–16
Military Supply Department, ii. 220–21, 222–3, 226–30, 266
Military training, Kitchener on, ii. 111
Millerand, M., iii. 175, 258, 260, 280, 345, 346
Milner, Sir Alfred (Viscount): on Cape rebellion, i. 298; on Transvaal advance, i. 310 (*note*); on Boer women, ii. 12 (*note*); Boer feeling against, ii. 20; Kitchener acts for, ii. 28–9; meets Boer delegates, ii. 88; views on peace terms, ii. 25, 26, 92–3, 102; drafting peace formula, ii. 98–9; introduces Kitchener in House of Lords, ii. 310
Kitchener on, ii. 25, 26, 100, 109
Minto, Earl of: Khaibar line and, ii. 149; accepts Militia Reserve recommendations, ii. 165; on Dual Control controversy, ii. 218 (*note*), 219 (*note*); and Army Secretary, ii. 226–7; and Supply Department, ii. 229 (*note*);

and unrest in Army, ii. 253, 259; and Kitchener's extension, ii. 263 (*note*), 264; farewell speech by, ii. 279; in favour of Viceroyalty for Kitchener, ii. 303; on Kitchener at War Office, iii. 13 (*note*)
on Kitchener's character, ii. 189 (*note*), 218 (*note*), 219 (*note*), 224 (*note*), 263 (*note*), 279; on his avoidance of frontier campaigns, i. 164 (*note*); on his work for Army, ii. 169 (*note*)
Kitchener on, ii. 302
Miranzai valley, ii. 162
Mixed Brigades in India, ii. 135–6, 166–7
Mixed Tribunals in Egypt, ii. 335, 339
"Moabite" idols, i. 30
Modderfontein Nek, ii. 38 (*note*)
Modder River, i. 272, 278, 287, 289, 292–93
Moedwil, ii. 53
Mohammed, Stewart's pilot, i. 91, 92–93
Mohammed Ahmed. *See* Mahdi
Mohammed Bey Abud, i. 129, 131, 139, 140
Mohammed Bey Mustafa, i. 122
Mohammed el Misir, i. 92–3
Mohmands, the, ii. 149
Moltke, von, i. 110
Mombasa, i. 150–52, ii. 307
Monasir tribe, i. 88, 91, 93
Monro, Gen. Sir Charles, ii. 214; in Gallipoli, iii. 183–4, 186, 192, 206, 217; in France, iii. 241, 251
Mons: battle of, iii. 30, 34; retreat from, iii. 30, 35–6, 37–8, 39, 42–4, 45–7, 48–9, 50–56
Montagu, Rt. Hon. E. S., iii. 108 (*note*)
Morley, Rt. Hon. John (Viscount): strategic railway scheme and, ii. 150; on Native officer question, ii. 179–80; on responsibility and overwork, ii. 213; relations between Kitchener and, ii. 224–6, 234 (*note*), 237, 302;

administrative economies of, ii. 227–30; on the apportionment of military charges, ii. 232–4, 236–7; "Kitchener Reforms" and economies of, ii. 150, 231–3, 236–7, 240, 244–7; and Dthala sanatorium, ii. 260–62; proposes extension of Kitchener's term, ii. 262–4, 265, 267, 268; his objections to Kitchener's absence, ii. 266, 267; to Kitchener on his G.C.I.E., ii. 268–9; presses Mediterranean Command on Kitchener, ii. 301; opposes offer of Viceroyalty to Kitchener, ii. 302–3; introduces Kitchener in House of Lords, ii. 310
Morocco: Anglo-French agreement over, ii. 335; German policy in, ii. 282, 310–11
Morto Bay, iii. 130, 158 (*note*)
Moslems attack Palestine Survey, i. 17–19
Mosters Hoek, i. 309
Mosul Consulate, i. 43
Moulton, Lord, iii. 274, 275
Mounted Infantry: raised, i. 274–75, 281 (*note*), 297 (*note*), ii. 1, 3–4; pursue Cronje, i. 280–81, 282; at Paardeberg, i. 286, 287, 288, 293, 294; take Doornkop, i. 312; Brand defeats, ii. 44
Mounted troops in South Africa: need for, i. 270–71, 297 (*note*), 300; Army of, ii. 1–5
Mudir of Dongola, Mustafa Yawer, i. 72; Kitchener and, i. 73–4, 76, 78, 80, 82, 85, 86, 87, 95, 98–101; Mahdi and, i. 73, 76, 77, 84; Mahdi defeated by, at Korti, i. 83, 85–6, 123; goes to Merawi, i. 86–8; ordered back, i. 86–7; Stewart's murder and, i. 94–5; ordered to Merawi, i. 95–6; Sir H. Stewart and, i. 95–6; insulting behaviour of, i. 96–7; Wolseley and, i. 96–7, 98 (*note*), 100, 101; made K.C.M.G., i. 96–7; intrigues with tribes, i. 98–9; attitude to English, i. 96–7, 99–100; expulsion of, i. 98 (*note*)
Mudirate of Dongola, Kitchener's proposed new, i. 101 (*note*), 130–131, 140–42
Mudirs: Memorandum to the, i. 262; police reform and, i. 168, 169
Mudros, iii. 110, 130, 189; conference at, iii. 186, 188, 190, 205
Mukden, ii. 286, 287
Mule transport in South Africa, i. 276–77
Mulhouse occupied, iii. 19
Mullah, the, ii. 156, 158
Muller, ii. 36, 38, 59, 103
Munitions: shortage in France, iii. 72, 74, 78–9, 91–2, 238–9, 240, 264, 291; shortage in Gallipoli, iii. 140, 142, 176, 177, 238–9; Kitchener and the supply of, iii. 264–9, 270–72, 274–6, 278–81, 282–6, 287–91; high explosives controversy, iii. 272–80; Labour and the supply of, 282–6
Munitions Act, iii. 284
Munitions Advisory Council, iii. 267 (*note*)
Munitions, Cabinet Committee on, iii. 267, 287
Munitions Committee, iii. 287
Munitions, Ministry of, iii. 287; its achievements and Kitchener's, iii. 287–9, 348; Kitchener and, iii. 287, 334
Murat Wells, i. 211
Murray, Gen. Sir Archibald, iii. 222
Murray, Lt.-Gen. Sir James Wolfe, iii. 103, 299–300
Murraysburg, ii. 30
Musa Jebel, i. 54
Mustafa Yawer. *See* Mudir of Dongola

Naauwport, i. 296, 297, ii. 15, 17
Nablus, i. 28–9
Nakheila, i. 228
Namur, iii. 30, 34, 35, 105
Napier, N.Z., ii. 296
Natal: Buller in, i. 310; Botha's dash on, ii. 48–9

Natal rebellion and amnesty, ii. 20, 23, 25-6, 99-100
National Registration, iii. 313-14, 317 (*note*)
Native officers: Egyptian, i. 177; Indian, ii. 177-83
Native troops: British troops and, ii. 166-7, 169-70, 177; Kitchener's work for, ii. 189 (*note*), 193-7, 231, 245
Naval concentration in North Sea, ii. 336, 337
Navy: and Belgian coast campaign, iii. 82, 87, 88
expected to force Dardanelles, iii. 106, 109, 112, 114, 115, 116, 121, 122, 125, 126, 128, 188; bombardment by, iii. 95, 112-13, 119-20; its failure, iii. 124, 128; its work in Gallipoli campaign, iii. 133, 134, 137, 150, 164; and evacuation, iii. 211, 212, 215, 217
Nazareth, i. 24, 27
Nazarieh, iii. 153
Nejumi, Wad-el-, i. 135, 164-167
Nepal Army and Kitchener, ii. 126
Neufeld, i. 183
Neuve Chapelle, iii. 121, 225-6, 227, 228
New Armies, iii. 9, 10, 307, 315, 319; creation of, iii. 8, 13-14, 39-40, 59, 93, 220, 240, 265, 308-10, 328-31; recruiting of, iii. 13-14, 310-12, 313-19; in training, iii. 280; in France, iii. 220-21, 239-40, 250, 256-7, 259, 305, 306, 319; in Gallipoli, iii. 145, 161, 162, 164-5, 166, 167; list of, iii. 320-21
New York, ii. 298-9
New Zealand: Kitchener visits, ii. 293, 296-8; defence of, ii. 297-298; clears Pacific, iii. 83; forces contributed to Great War, ii. 300
New Zealanders: in Egypt, iii. 96, 98; in Gallipoli, iii. 162, 166-7, 168, 213; Kitchener and, iii. 189. *See* Anzac Corps

Nicholas, Grand Duke, iii. 346, 349 (*note*)
Nicholas, Tsar of Russia, iii. 349-50, 351, 352
Nicholson Commission, 1912, ii. 200 (*note*)
Nicola, Consul, i. 123
Nicosia, Kitchener at, i. 38, 42, 43, 47
Nieuhardt, ii. 103
Nieuport, iii. 80, 221, 245
Nile Expedition: preparations for, i. 59-69, 70-76, 83-6, 94, 106-8; route of, i. 74-5, 77, 82; concentration at Korti, i. 106, 109; Desert Column sets out, i. 109; Abu Klea, i. 109; Herbert Stewart killed, i. 110; Buller joins Column at El Gubat, i. 110-11; news of fall of Khartum, i. 110, 111; Buller withdraws, i. 111-12; running fight at Abu Klea, i. 112-13; contradictory orders, i. 113-14, 132; Kitchener fills in the wells, i. 115; retirement to Korti, i. 114-16; River Column, i. 66, 113, 123
Nile Valley, authority over, i. 250
Nineveh excavations, i. 44
Ninth Corps at Suvla, iii. 163, 164, 168, 171
Nixon, Gen. Sir John, iii. 301
Nokoto, ii. 288
Northbrook, Earl of, i. 261
Northcliffe, Viscount, iii. 3
North Midland Division, iii. 227
North Staffordshire Regiment, i. 196, 203, 205
Northumberland Fusiliers, ii. 67
North West Frontier: fourteen battalions for, ii. 126; Kitchener's tour of, ii. 128-9, 160-161; defence against Russia, ii. 140-44, 145-50, 151-4, 241, 243; against Frontier tribes, ii. 154-9, 241-3
Norval's Pont bridge, i. 296
Nubar Pasha, i. 79, 86, 96
Nur Angara, i. 134, 264

O'Beirne, Mr., iii. 350, 353
O'Creagh, Gen. Sir Moore, ii. 280

INDEX

Odessa, iii. 95
Officers, British, Kitchener and: to understand financial side of their work, i. 71 (*note*), 329, ii. 198–9; to be willing to take responsibility, ii. 139–40, 169, 170–71, 280; their general training, ii. 68–9, 169–71; his treatment of, ii. 79–80
 in Egyptian Army: selection of, i. 180; Khedive threatened with resignation of, i. 185–86
 in Indian Army: on their behaviour to Native officers, ii. 182–184; better conditions obtained for, ii. 184–7; Staff College for, ii. 173–6; on their moral influence, ii. 271–2
 in Great War: losses of, iii. 64–5
Officers, Native: Egyptian, i. 177; Indian, ii. 177–83
Ohrwalder, Father, i. 183
Oil, Egyptian, ii. 327
Oil-fields, Anglo-Persian, iii. 98
Olifants Nek, i. 321, 322
Olifants River, i. 315 (*note*)
Oliphant, Laurence, i. 40
Olivier, ii. 86
Omdurman: cut off from Khartum, i. 116, 118, 124; Mahdi's prisoners at, i. 124, 125; Khalifa's preparations at, i. 182, 190, 213, 214, 218, 219, 234, 236; Abyssinians at, i. 233; Cromer addresses sheikhs at, i. 260
Omdurman, battle of: bombardment, i. 237–238, iii. 273; Osman Azrak's force destroyed, i. 240–42; gun-boats cover Broadwood, i. 242–43; the 21st Lancers, i. 243–44; MacDonald's brigade, i. 179, 244–46; town entered, i. 246–47, 248; losses at, i. 247
Omdurman Campaign: alternative routes, i. 209–10; the Halfa—Abu Hamed line, i. 210–13, 218, 222, 223, 227; Abu Hamed taken, i. 214–15; Berber occupied, i. 216, 217–218; Khalifa's preparations, i. 213, 214, 218, 219; financial difficulties, i. 219–25; Kassala, i. 219–21, 222–23, 225; concentration at Berber, i. 226–27; the Atbara, i. 227–232; reinforcements, i. 232, 233; battle of Omdurman, i. 240–46; Khartum entered, i. 248, 250; cost of campaign, i. 254; Kitchener accused of cruelty in, i. 263–64
Orakzais, the, ii. 161
Orange Free State: Paardeberg and, i. 284, 287, 290; rebellion in, i. 298; attitude to war of, i. 299, 308; Roberts and, i. 306; annexed as Orange River Colony, i. 312; irreconcilables in, ii. 33; Elliot sweeps, ii. 35; questions of amnesty and payment of debts for, ii. 23, 24, 100–101, 102
Orange Free Staters: council of, ii. 36; and peace, ii. 33, 38, 61, 86 (*note*), 90, 91–2, 97–8, 103
Osborne, Kitchener at, i. 133
Oshoek, ii. 56–7
Osman Azrak, i. 213, 240, 241–42
Osman Digna, i. 128, 155; at Handub, i. 158–160; attacks Suakin, i. 162, 182, 198; ordered to retake Kassala, i. 190; posts left under, i. 214; at Adarama, i. 217, 218; captured, i. 301
Osman Sheikh-ed-Din, i. 240, 242, 245
Ostend, iii. 69, 87–93, 94
Ox convoys, i. 277, 283
Oxford confers degree on Kitchener, i. 256 (*note*)

Paardeberg: Cronje pursued to, i. 280–84, 286–87; Kitchener's frontal attack at, i. 287–90, 291–95, 309; Cronje surrenders at, i. 294, 297
Paget, Maj.-Gen. (Gen. the Rt. Hon. Sir Arthur), i. 318, 327, iii. 242, 246

410   INDEX

Palestine: Kitchener's lifelong interest in, i. 32, 39, 40; Roman roads in, i. 28
Palestine Exploration Fund, i. 15; Kitchener's Reports to, i. 23–5, 26, 27–8; his contributions handed to, i. 31; and his Sinai Survey, i. 53–8
Palestine Survey, i. 15, 16, 17; cholera and Safed outrage interrupt, i. 17–19; resumed, i. 23–8, 31–2; Russo-Turkish War and, i. 25–6, 40; Reports on, i. 23–5, 26, 27–8; Northern, completed, i. 26–7; Memoirs on, 23 (note), 31; Conder's work for, i. 15, 16, 17–18, 19, 22, 23 (note), 31; Hauran Survey, i. 39–40
Palmer, Sir Edwin, i. 220, 222, 223, 224
Panther, the, ii. 310
Paris: besieged, 1871, i. 8, 9 (note); Kitchener in, ii. 113, iii. 186, 260; Germans near, iii. 36, 56, 58, 224 (note)
Paris Conference, iii. 195, 201
Paris, Major (Maj.-Gen. Sir A.), ii. 66, 67
Parker, Mr. H. R., i. 3 (note)
Parr, Lt.-Col. (Maj.-Gen. Sir Hallam), i. 52
Parsons, Colonel (Maj.-Gen. Sir Charles): takes over Kassala, i. 225; takes Gedaref, i. 264; in South Africa, i. 298, 304; in India, i. 292
Pathans, ii. 126, 161, 178
Patriarch, the Greek, i. 29
Patrimonio, M., i. 146
Peking, ii. 286
Perim, i. 150, iii. 157
Péronne, iii. 38, 39
Perth, Australia, ii. 292
Peters, Karl, i. 144
Petra, Kitchener at, i. 54, 55
Peyton, Captain (Maj.-Gen. Sir William), i. 214, iii. 148, 170, 178
Philistia, Survey in, i. 16
Phoenicia, Survey in, i. 26–7
Photographs of Biblical Sites, Kitchener's *Book of*, i. 19–21
Piet Retief, ii. 48, 50

Pietermaritzburg, ii. 16
Pieters Hill, i. 299
Pilcher, Maj.-Gen. T., ii. 43
Pilgrims Club banquet, ii. 299
Pilgrim's Rest, ii. 59, 60
Pissouri, Kitchener shot at in, i. 41 (note)
Pivaen Bridge, ii. 50
Plumer, Maj.-Gen. (Field-Marshal Lord):
  in South Africa, ii. 2; heads De Wet off Cape Colony, ii. 17; pursuing Botha and Viljoen, ii. 35; in drive for Smuts, ii. 42, 43; Botha evades, ii. 57, 58
  in Great War, iii. 235
Poincaré, President, iii. 74–5
Police: Egyptian, reorganised by Kitchener, i. 168–171; English, and labour supply, iii. 283; Indian, ii. 135
Poona School of Cookery, ii. 192
Poplar Grove, i. 297, 301–2, 304
Porro, General, iii. 208
Port Arthur, ii. 286–7
Port Darwin, ii. 289
Port Lyttelton, ii. 296
Port Sudan, ii. 333
Portuguese in Africa, i. 143–144, 146
Potgieter, ii. 74
Potter, Archdeacon, ii. 345 (note)
Powis, ii. 111
Presidential Armies, ii. 125, 127, 133, 203
Press Law in India, ii. 254, 255 (note), 256, 257
Pretoria entered, i. 313–14; Kitchener in, i. 314 (note), 323, ii. 81–4
Prieska revolt, i. 298, 304–5, 309 (note)
Prinsloo, Martin, i. 319
Prinsloo, Michael, ii. 59
Prospect, ii. 49
Prüfer, Dr., ii. 338–9
Prussian Guards, iii. 76
Przemysl, iii. 120, 141
Public Worship Regulation Act, i. 13–14
Punjabis, ii. 124, 126, 255

INDEX 411

Quartermaster-General, iii. 17, 263
Queen Elizabeth, the, iii. 105, 208–9
Quetta, ii. 140, 141, 147; garrison, ii. 245
Quetta Staff College, ii. 173–6

Rafa'ah, ii. 316
Raffray, M., i. 146, 147, 148, 149, 152
Railways, strategic, in India, ii. 146–7, 148–50
Ralli, Mr., Kitchener's letters to, i. 90–93, 274–75, 300 (note), ii. 13 (note), 93 (note), 119–20
Rawal-Pindi manœuvres, ii. 168–9
Rawlinson, Gen. Sir Henry (Lord):
  in South Africa, ii. 2, 35; pursues Smuts, ii. 43; pursues De Wet, ii. 63, 64, 65; in drive against Kemp, ii. 73–4
  in Peking, ii. 285 (note)
  in Great War, iii. 2, 68, 69, 70, 71
Recruiting, iii. 310–12, 314, 315, 317
Reddersburg, i. 308–9, ii. 43
Redmond, John, M.P., iii. 310
Regimental Institutes, ii. 190–91
Regular Army in Great War, iii. 7, 31, 39–40, 77, 106, 308
Reitz, ii. 39, 54
Religion, Kitchener and, i. 12, 13, 22 (note), 32, ii. 276, 345 (note), iii. 371–2
Renkh, i. 251, 266
Rensburg, i. 272, 297
Renshaw, Mr. Arthur, i. 225 (note), iii. 366
Reservists in Great War, iii. 8, 40
Rheims, iii. 82, 83
Rhenoster River Bridge, i. 314, 315
Rhodes, Rt. Hon. Cecil, i. 211, 273–274, 279, ii. 107, 310
Riding, Kitchener's love of, i. 6, 7, 42
Ridley, Brig.-Gen. Charles, i. 320

Rifles, supply of, iii. 272, 334
Rimington, Brig.-Gen. (Maj.-Gen.) Michael Frederic, ii. 63
Robatah tribe, i. 91
Robb, Maj.-Gen. Sir F. S., iii. 45
Roberts, Countess, i. 305
Roberts, Field-Marshal Earl:
  in India: on strategic railways, ii. 150 (note); on Native officers, ii. 177; creates Army Institutes, ii. 190; and Dual Control, ii. 204, 208–9
  in South Africa: given command, i. 269; voyage with Kitchener, i. 270–71; plan of advance, i. 273–74, 276, 310 (note); reaches Paardeberg, i. 290; on frontal attack, i. 295, 309; Cronje surrenders to, i. 295, 297; advances on Bloemfontein, i. 301–303; Queen Victoria and, i. 305, 324 (note); occupies Karee hills, i. 307; gives Kitchener plenary powers, i. 309; advances into Transvaal, i. 310–11; annexes Free State, i. 312; occupies Johannesburg, i. 312; Diamond Hill, i. 314; and De Wet, i. 318, 319; goes to Johannesburg, i. 323; Commander-in-Chief in England, i. 324; optimistic speech by, i. 324–25, 327, ii. 106, 107; gets reinforcements sent, ii. 4, 5 (note)
  Kitchener's relations with, i. 275, 305, 309, 324 (note), iii. 324; their achievements compared, ii. 106–7; his application for Indian Command supported by, ii. 117, 118 (note), 120; letters from, ii. 4 (note), 5 (note), 13, 22 (note), 118 (note); letters to: from South Africa, ii. 3 (note), 11–12, 14–16, 16–17, 22, 27–8, 34, 36, 52–3, 55, 57–8, 60, 67, 68–9, 78, 79 (note), 82, 85 (note), 89 (note); from India, ii. 127 (note), 129, 135 (note), 167, 168; during Great War, iii. 266 (note)

military service campaign, iii. 1; funeral, iii. 359
Robertson, General Sir William: Chief of the Staff in France, iii. 183, 222, 256; on Gallipoli evacuation, iii. 183; Chief of Imperial General Staff, iii. 6, 297-9, 300, 303, 340
Robertson, Mr., iii. 350
Rochfort, Maj.-General Sir A., ii. 41
Rogers, Lt.-Col. Sir J. G., i. 220
Roman roads in Palestine, i. 28
Romans and Jewish synagogues, i. 34
Rome, iii. 208
Roodeval, i. 314, ii. 73-4, 88-9
Rosebery, Earl of, i. 149, 151, 258
Rossignoli, Father, i. 183
Rothschild, Lord, and Gordon College, i. 259 (note)
Roux, i. 318
Royal Air Force, iii. 74
Royal Artillery entertain Kitchener, i. 256
Royal Engineers:
Kitchener training for, i. 5, 6; commissioned in, i. 11; at Aldershot with, i. 13, 14; entertained by, i. 256
Palestine Survey and, i. 15-16
Royal Flying Corps, ii. 73 (note), 78
Royal Irish Regiment, i. 110, 112, ii. 60
Royal Naval Division, iii. 69, 109, 124, 131, 145, 152
Royal Scots, iii. 151-2
Royan, i. 235
Royle, Captain, iii. 304 (note)
Rumania and Allies, iii. 85, 100, 102, 108, 139, 187, 261
Runciman, Rt. Hon. W., iii. 267
Rundle, Leslie, Bimbashi (General Sir Leslie), i. 52; with Ababdeh Frontier Force, i. 63, 64, 66, 67 (note), 79; suggests Kitchener's return to Korosko, i. 80-81; his friendship with Kitchener, i. 82, 208; Adj.-General of Egyptian Army, i. 174; Chief of the Staff, i. 208; refutes accusations of cruelty, i. 263 (note); in South Africa, ii. 34; Governor of Malta, ii. 336
Russell's Top mine, iii. 178 (note), 212, 213-14, 216
Russia:
Afghanistan and, ii. 145-50, 151-4, 241, 243; India and, ii. 134-5, 145-50, 151-4, 206, 231, 233, 238-9, 241, 243, 281
in Great War, iii. 18, 20; attracts Germans from West, iii. 76, 78, 79, 88, 100-101, 223-4, 243, 345; conference on situation in, iii. 80-82, 83, and Dardanelles Expedition, iii. 120, 121, 123, 124, 140, 141, 249; Turks and, iii. 100, 101, 105, 346; in need of help, iii. 101, 105, 172, 224, 241 (note), 302; munition shortage in, iii. 345, 346, 347-8; corruption in, iii. 346
Kitchener's influence in, iii. 347, 348-9, 352, 358-9; his mission to, iii. 325, 349-51, 352
Russia, Tsar of, iii. 349-50, 351, 352
Russo-Japanese War, ii. 231, 233; Indian opinion and, ii. 238-9, 242, 281; Kitchener visits scenes of, ii. 286-7
Russo-Turkish War, i. 25-6, 30

Saarburg, iii. 19
Safed outrage, i. 17-19, 23
Said Agha, i. 129, 130, 131, 140
Saigon, ii. 285
St. Gond marshes, iii. 64
St. Nazaire, iii. 44
St. Omer, Kitchener at, iii. 74 (note)
St. Paul's, memorial service at, iii. 359
St. Quentin, iii. 39
Sala, Sheikh, i. 81
Salamat, i, 20, 91
Saleh, Sheikh of the Kababish, i. 70, 72, 75, 81, 98
Saleh Bey Wad-el-Mek, i. 139, 140, 164
Salisbury, Marchioness of, Kitch-

ener's letters to, ii. 129 (*note*), 132 (*note*), 145 (*note*), 169 (*note*), 189 (*note*), 247 (*note*), 248 (*note*), 249-50, 264 (*note*), 288 (*note*), 298 (*note*), 306
Salisbury, Marquis of: Foreign Secretary, i. 31, 37, 38, 44 Prime Minister: on Kitchener's economy, i. 71; and Zanzibar Commission, i. 148; insists on having Kitchener in charge of Omdurman Campaign, i. 226 (*note*); supports Kitchener's action at Fashoda, i. 253 (*note*); Kitchener explains destruction of Mahdi's tomb to, i. 263-264; stipulates that Kitchener shall be Chief of the Staff, i. 269; Kitchener's letter to, on South African situation, i. 299-300; suggests blockade of Boers, i. 300-301; gravely ill, ii. 128
Salisbury, 4th Marquis of, ii. 238 (*note*)
Salisbury Ministry: withdrawal policy of, i. 128-129, 190; decides for reconquest of Dongola, i. 191-192
Salonika, iii. 86, 176, 194; French co-operation at, iii. 108, 176, 196, 198-9, 258, 260-61; troops required for, iii. 179-80, 181, 182-3, 186, 187, 194, 258, 260-261; Kitchener visits, iii. 195, 198-9; position at, iii. 198-9, 302
Samana Rifles, ii. 160, 161, 162
Samana valley defence, ii. 160, 161, 162-3
Samrat Fiddan, i. 55
San Francisco, ii. 298
Sandys, Dr., i. 256 (*note*)
Sanitary measures in Egypt, ii. 328-30
Sari Bair, iii. 159-60, 162, 165 (*note*), 166-9
Sarrail, General, iii. 174, 175, 198-9
Saunalisport, ii. 44
Sawarab tribe, i. 74 (*note*), 85 (*note*), 98-9, 101, 107

Sayed Abderrahman Mohammed Ahmed, i. 257 (*note*)
Scapa Flow, iii. 352, 353
Schleswig-Holstein scheme, iii. 103
Schmidt, Dr., i. 146, 147-148, 149, 152, 153
Schupers, ii. 45
Schwab, Mr., iii. 271
Sclater, Sir Henry, iii. 300, 312 (*note*)
Scott, Maj.-Gen. Sir C., ii. 226, 228, 229
Scout Movement, Kitchener and, ii. 313
Seaforth Highlanders, i, 227 (*note*)
Sebastopol, iii. 95
"Second Army" of the Loire, i. 8
Sedd-el-Bahr, iii. 113, 130, 138
Selim Isawi, Sheikh, i. 75
Sennar, i. 134
Senussi, the: Italo-Turkish war and, ii. 316, 341, iii. 155; Germans and, ii. 339, iii. 156; Khedive intrigues with, ii. 339, 341, 344; during Great War, iii. 97, 155-6, 157, 302, 304
Sepoy, Kitchener's work for the, ii. 193-7
Serbia: expedition to suggested, iii. 86, 182, 194, 261; Lloyd George in its favour, iii. 102, 106-7, 108; Greece and, iii. 196, 204; overrun, iii. 100, 176, 187
Settle, Lt.-Gen. Sir Henry, i. 298, 299, 304
Seventh Division, iii. 40, 62, 65, 67, 68, 69, 70, 77, 310
Seymour, Admiral Sir Beauchamp (Lord Alcester), i. 47
Shabluka gorge, i. 236
Shaikiyeh tribe: Dongolawi blood-feud with, i. 85 (*note*), 131, 136, 139-140, 141; Kitchener and, i. 83, 85, 98, 101; Mahdi and, i. 83, 85, 123, 135, 137, 140
Shambat, Khor, i. 238, 246
Shamyun, i. 67, 68
Shanghai, ii. 286

Shaw, Lt.-Gen. Rt. Hon. Sir F., iii. 166, 168
Sheikh-Sayed, iii. 157
Shekan, i. 265
Shellal, i. 197
Shendi, i. 228
Sherif of Mecca, i. 27 (*note*), iii. 154, 155
"Shirkela reconnaissance," i. 265–266
Shiva, iii. 132
Shukuriyeh tribe, i. 135, 136
Sidi Osman, i. 135–136
Sidney, Kaimakam, i. 215
Sikhs, ii. 39, 178
Silladar cavalry, ii. 197
Simla: Kitchener's arrival at, ii. 130; his hospitality at, ii. 130, 131, 248–9, 279; his accident at, ii. 129 (*note*), 138–9; his departure from, ii. 279–80
Simla Conference of Lieut.-Generals, ii. 136, 166, 179, 187
Sinai, Archbishop of, ii. 345
Sinai Desert campaign, iii. 103, 107, 148, 304
Sinai Peninsula Survey, i. 53–8
Singapore, ii. 265, 285
Sirdars of Egyptian Army: Wood, i. 52; Grenfell, i. 129 (*note*); Kitchener, i. 172
Sixth Division, iii. 39–40, 41, 62
Skouloudis, M., iii. 196, 202, 203
Slatin Bey (Sir Rudolf, Pasha), i. 183, 190
Smith, Sir F. E. (Lord Birkenhead), iii. 117 (*note*), 324
Smith, Colonel Holled (Maj.-Gen. Sir Charles), i. 52, 162
Smith-Dorrien, Maj.-Gen. (Gen. Sir H.):
    in South Africa, i. 282, 293, 310, 320, 321
    visits Morley, ii. 268
    in Great War: commanding Second Corps, iii. 31, 38, 39, 43, 73; commanding Second Army, iii. 222-3, 229; at second battle of Ypres, iii. 232, 233; replaced, iii. 235; in East Africa, iii. 305
Smithfield, i. 309
Smuts, J. C. (Gen. the Rt. Hon.):
    in South African War: Cape Colony rebellion and, ii. 8, 38; at Transvaal council, ii. 32; successful 1100-mile trek by, ii. 40–45; and peace, ii. 91; at Vereeniging Conference, ii. 96, 98; negotiates with Milner, ii. 98–9
    in Great War, iii. 305
Snowdon, ii. 130, 279
Sogaro, Mgr., i. 163
Sokotra, i. 150
Sollum, ii. 315, 340, iii. 155
Solomon, Hon. Sir Richard, ii. 29, 99
Somali tribes in East Africa, i. 143–144
Somme battles, iii. 251, 319
South Africa: Crown Colony government of, ii. 23; suppresses rebellion, iii. 83
South African Constabulary, ii. 1, 7, 41, 42, 43, 47, 56
South African Defence, ii. 305
South African War: Kitchener's warning, i. 65, 264, 267; public over-confident, i. 268, ii. 106–7; "Black Week," i. 268–69; Ladysmith besieged, i. 268, 269, 272, 279; Mafeking besieged, i. 271–272, 273; Kimberley besieged, i. 271–272, 273–274; plans of campaign, i. 273–274; difficulties and deficiencies, i. 271, 274–276, 307, 329–330; Kimberley relieved, i. 279–280, 299–300; Paardeberg, i. 280–284, 286–295, 297, 309; Ladysmith relieved, i. 299; Cape Colony rebellion, i. 272, 298–9, 304, ii. 15–16, 27, 30–31; Bloemfontein entered, i. 301–303; Boer hope of foreign intervention, i. 308, 310 (*note*), 311, ii. 59, 97; Mafeking relieved, i. 312; Orange Free State annexed, i. 312; Johannesburg occupied, i. 312; Pretoria entered, i. 313–314; drive for De Wet, i. 318–322
    Kitchener Commander-in-Chief, i. 324; economics of campaign, i. 325–26, 329;

INDEX 415

blockhouses and drives, ii. 5–10, 29–30, 40, 43–4, 46–7, 51, 53; Concentration Camps, ii. 11–14, 38, 46; peace overtures begin, ii. 18–26, 32–3, 36, 37; Vlakfontein, ii. 35–6; Smuts's campaign, ii. 38–45; London proclamation, ii. 46; Botha's campaign, ii. 48–50, 56–9; Gun Hill, ii. 51–2; Groen Kop, ii. 54–5; drive for De Wet, ii. 63–5; Tweebosch, ii. 66–70; Roodeval, ii. 73–4; peace negotiations, ii. 70, 86–94; Vereeniging Conference, ii. 95–8, 102–3; Pretoria Commission, ii. 98–101; peace signed, ii. 104

ammunition expended in, iii. 268

South Wales Borderers, iii. 151
South-West African campaign, iii. 83
Special Reserve, iii. 8, 328
Spion Kop, i. 278 (*note*)
Spragg's Convoy, i. 314
Staff: in England, 1899, i. 269–70; in South Africa, i. 287–88, ii. 174; in Great War, ii. 176
Staff College, Australian, ii. 295; Indian, ii. 173–6
Standerton, ii. 37
Stanton, Father, i. 13
Steenekamp, i. 298, 304
Steenstraate, iii. 232, 233, 234
Stephenson, Lt.-Gen. Sir Frederick, i. 157–158
Stephenson, Maj.-Gen. T. E., i. 293
Stewart, Sir Herbert: Kitchener Intelligence Officer to, i. 94, 96, 106, 107, 108, 109; Mudir and, i. 95–6; commands Desert Column, i. 109–10, 132; killed, i. 110
Stewart, Colonel J. D. H.: with Kitchener in Anatolia, i. 90 (*note*), 93; Kitchener communicates with, i. 74, 77; leaves Khartum for Dongola, i. 87; Kitchener's attempts to save, i. 88–91; wrecked and murdered, i. 88–9, 91–3

Steyn, President: at Koedoesrand, i. 283, 289; keeps up Free State resistance, i. 290, ii. 32–3, 38, 46, 54; with De Wet, i. 301, 319; hopes for foreign intervention, i. 311; prevents blowing up of mines, i. 312; enters Cape Colony, ii. 16; narrow escape, ii. 39; at Kroonstad conference, ii. 60; breaks through with De Wet, ii. 65; and peace negotiations, ii. 86, 87, 89, 90, 93, 95, 102
Stock Exchange, Kitchener's speech in, i. 259
Stopford, Maj.-Gen. Sir L., iii. 163, 164, 168, 170
Storks, Sir Henry, i. 261
Stormberg, i. 268, 297
Stuart-Wortley, Major (Maj.-Gen. the Hon. E.), i. 236
Suakin, i. 63, 65, 67, 128; Kitchener Governor-General in, i. 155, 157, 158, 162–163; Osman Digna besieges, i. 162; Indian garrison at, i. 198–199
Suakin—Berber route, i. 63, 65, 218
Suarda, i. 201
Submarine campaign, iii. 87, 91
Sudan, the:
 campaigns in. *See* Dongola Expedition, Nile Expedition, Omdurman Campaign
 English policy in, i. 127–132, 250–52
 reconquest decided on, i. 191–192; natural obstacles to, i. 201–203, 207; cost of, i. 254
 Khalifa's rule in, i. 182–183
 Kitchener and, i. 97–8; Report on future of, i. 130–131, 133–42; Governor-General of, i. 260, 261–262, ii. 115; work for education of, i. 256, 257–259, ii. 113–14
 reforms in, ii. 304; cotton cultivation in, ii. 325–6, 334; French rights in, ii. 334, 335
Sudan, the Eastern: fighting in, i. 128, 158–162; Kitchener Governor-General of, i. 155, 156–157, 163; province re-

stored to Egyptian rule, i. 168, 171
Sudanese Loan, ii. 326
Sudanese Sheikhs visit King George V., i. 257 (*note*)
Sudanese troops, i. 84, 159, 175, 178–179, 198; take Abu Hamed, i. 214–215; at the Atbara, i. 231; at Omdurman, i. 241, 242, 244–245, 246
Suez Canal, ii. 314; German designs on, iii. 95, 97; Turks attack, iii. 97, 103; Turks defeated on, iii. 107; defence of, iii. 191, 192, 193, 206 (*note*), 303
Sufsaf Synagogue, i. 34
Suleiman Wad Gamr, i. 88, 90–93
Sultan of Egypt, ii. 324
Sultan of Turkey, i. 39, 40
Sultan of Zanzibar, i. 144, 146, 147, 151, 152–153, 154
Surgham, Jebel, i. 237, 240, 243–244, 245
Surveys: of Cyprus, i. 36, 38–43, 49–50, 51, 68 (*note*); of Palestine, i. 15, 16, 17–19, 23–8, 31–2, 39–40; of Sinai Peninsula, i. 53–8, 59
Sussex Regiment, i. 107
Suvla Bay: landing in, iii. 150, 159–160, 161–5; sickness in, iii. 181; evacuation of, iii. 190, 205, 211, 212, 214
Suweiteh, Wadi, i. 55
Switzerland, Kitchener educated in, i. 4–5
Sword of Honour presented to Kitchener, i. 256
Sydney, ii. 289–90
Sykes, Lt.-Col. Sir Mark, iii. 154
Synagogues of Galilee, i. 33–5
Syria: Arab movement in, iii. 151, 153–5, 261; autonomy promised to, ii. 332; French rights in, iii. 154, 155, 193, 261

Taher Arabi, ii. 334
Tashi Lama's letter to Kitchener, ii. 269
Tasmania, Kitchener visits, ii. 293

Taylor, Colonel, i. 59
Teb, El, i. 175
Teck, Prince Francis of, ii. 304
Tenedos, iii. 140, 205
Tennant, Rt. Hon. H. J., iii. 326
Tenth Division, iii. 163, 164, 180
Terauchi, Viscount, ii. 286
Territorials: at outbreak of war, iii. 7, 308; Home Defence by, iii. 8, 10, 31, 40, 308, 328, 330, 340; relieve Regular garrisons, iii. 77, 83, 96, 97, 310; in France, iii. 65, 73, 75, 76, 87, 89, 91, 227, 229, 244, 250, 251, 296, 310; in Gallipoli, iii. 141, 145; divisional formation of, iii. 250, 251–2; list of divisions of, iii. 320–21; and creation of New Armies, iii. 308, 309, 310, 314, 329
Theodosia, iii. 95
Third Army formed, iii. 241–2
Third Division, iii. 31, 39, 71
Thorneycroft, Maj.-Gen. A., ii. 43
Thubron gunboats, i. 201
Thursby, Admiral Sir C., iii. 142, 143
Thursday Island, ii. 289
Tiberias, i. 23, 34
Tibet: Expedition to, ii. 209 (*note*); Tashi Lama of, ii. 269
Tigersfontein, i. 320
Times, The, French's communication to, iii. 238, 289
Tireh, i. 25
Tochi valley, ii. 128, 157
Togoland, iii. 83
Tokar: battle of, i. 168, 171, 182; cotton-growing at, ii. 326
Toski, battle of, i. 166–168
Town Planning Conference, ii. 304
Townshend, Maj.-Gen. Sir Charles, iii. 259, 301–2, 303
Trade, Board of, and labour supply, iii. 282–3
Trades Unions and supply of munitions, iii. 284 (*note*), 286
Transport: in Dongola Expedition, i. 196–198; in South Africa, i. 271, 274–76, 299, 329, ii. 83–4
Transvaal: question of amnesty

INDEX

and payment of debts for, ii. 21-2, 23, 24, 100-101, 102; Government in flight, ii. 56, 60; peace negotiations, ii. 70
Transvaalers: and Free Staters, i. 299, ii. 86 (*note*), 90, 91-2, 97-8; council of war of, ii. 32; and peace, ii. 86 (*note*), 90-91, 91-2, 97-8; in Great War, ii. 39-40
Trichardt, Louis, ii. 36
Trinitrotoluol, iii. 275
Tripoli, Italo-Turkish war in, ii. 314-16, iii. 155
Troödos, Mt., i. 40
Tsar and Kitchener, iii. 349-50, 351, 352
Tulloch, Colonel (Maj.-Gen. Sir A. B.), i. 47-8
Turco-Italian war, ii. 314-16, iii. 155
Turkey:
 and Dthala scheme, ii. 261
 Egypt and wars involving, ii. 314-315, 337, 345, iii. 107
 Germany and, ii. 306, iii. 86, 95, 97
 Kitchener and our relations with, ii. 281 (*note*), 306, iii. 95
 in Great War, iii. 40, 86, 95, 96-9. See Turkish Army
Turkish, Kitchener's knowledge of, i. 40, ii. 281 (*note*)
Turkish Army, i. 24, 30; soldiers at Debbeh, i. 81, 83-4, 85 (*note*), 99
 in Great War:
  Aden menaced by, iii. 157-8
  in Caucasus against Russians, iii. 100, 101, 105, 346
  in Egypt: preparations against, iii. 40, 95-9, 103; defeated on Canal, iii. 107, 109; and Senussi, iii. 97, 155-6, 157; Sinai Desert campaign against, iii. 103, 107, 148, 304
  in Gallipoli campaign: defences of, iii. 114, 118-19, 122-3, 124, 125, 133, 138; Germans and, iii. 146, 147, 177, 181, 190; ammunition supply of, iii. 142-143, 151, 152; reinforcements of, iii. 140, 141, 146, 151, 173; successes and repulses, iii. 143-4, 151-2, 166-9; during evacuation, iii. 213-14, 215-16
  in Mesopotamia, iii. 132-3, 153, 259; capture Kut, iii. 301-2, 303
  in Syria, iii. 97-8, 153-5
Turkish courtesy, ii. 333 (*note*)
Turkish misrule: in Asia Minor, i. 37-8; in Cyprus, i. 44; in the Sudan, i. 78, 130, 134, 139
Turks and Arabs, i. 27 (*note*), iii. 97, 98, 153-5
Turner, Major (Maj.-Gen. Sir Alfred), i. 98 (*note*)
Tweebosch disaster, ii. 66-9, 74
Twenty-eighth Division, iii. 77, 87, 93, 186, 199, 227, 260, 261
Twenty-ninth Division, iii. 77, 310: for France, iii. 87; for Eastern campaign, iii. 106, 109, 228; delay in despatching to Dardanelles, iii. 110, 112, 115-16, 117-18; Joffre requires, iii. 117-18; voyage of, iii. 121, 124, 131-2; in Gallipoli, iii. 130, 133, 145, 180
Twenty-seventh Division, iii. 77, 186, 199, 260
Tyre cathedral, i. 33

Udine, iii. 208
Umdabia, i. 229, 230
Um Debreikat, i. 267
United Services Club banquet at Simla, ii. 279
United States. See America
Unity of command, iii. 175, 261-2

Vaal Krantz, i. 279
Vaal River crossing, i. 310, 312
Vakil, the Mudir's, i. 86, 87, 95, 96, 99 (*note*), 100
Vakilates of Dongola, suggested, i. 131, 141-142
Valenciennes, iii. 32
Van der Venter, ii. 40, 43
Vendutie Drift, i. 283

Venereal disease in Army in India, ii. 271–6
Venice, ii. 308, 334
Venizelos, M., iii. 120, 176, 203
Verdun, iii. 305–6
Vereeniging Conference, ii. 90, 95–8, 102–3
Verner, Lieut.-Col. Willoughby, i. 110–11, 115
Versailles War Council, iii. 262
Viceroy of India: and Dual Control, ii. 204, 205, 207–8; Kitchener proposed as, ii. 302–4. *See* Curzon, Minto
Vickers, Messrs., iii. 270, 332
Victoria, Queen: Kitchener presented to, i. 133; her regard for Kitchener, i. 133, 160, ii. 329 (*note*), iii. 371; Khalifa's threat to, i. 158; confers peerage on Kitchener, i. 249; entertains Kitchener at Balmoral, i. 257; supports Sirdar's Fund, i. 258; congratulates French, i. 282; letters to Kitchener by, i. 301, 305; Roberts on his audience with, i. 324 (*note*); and Kitchener's employment, ii. 118; and courtesy to Indians, ii. 182
Victorian Mounted Rifles, ii. 36
Viljoen, Ben: captures Helvetia, ii. 15; at Transvaal council, ii. 32; in Middelburg district, ii. 38; pursued by Benson, ii. 50–51; at Pilgrim's Rest, ii. 59; captured, ii. 60; and peace, ii. 61
Viljoen, Piet, ii. 56, 57, 59, 60
Vimy Ridge, iii. 224, 237, 246–7, 248, 249, 253, 255, 256
Vitry-le-François, iii. 28, 61, 63, 64
Vlakfontein, ii. 35, 36
Voluntary enlistment, iii. 13–14, 312, 314, 315, 317, 318
Volunteer movement in India, ii. 197
Von Donop, Lt.-Col. Sir Stanley (Maj.-Gen.), ii. 67, iii. 263, 273, 274, 278–80, 287
Vorbeck, General von Lettow, iii. 302
Vrieheid, ii. 15

Wakfs, ii. 341–2, 343
Wales, Prince and Princess of (King George and Queen Mary), in India, ii. 169, 333
Wales, Prince of: service in France, i. 316, iii. 228; Kitchener and, i. 316, iii. 371
Wallace, Maj.-Gen. A., iii. 304
Wantage, Lady, iii. 13
War correspondents, iii. 322–3
War Council: formed, iii. 98; on Belgian coast campaign, iii. 90–94; discussions of Easterners and Westerners in, iii. 98, 109, 139; decides on Dardanelles attack, iii. 106; Robertson on its functions, iii. 298
Ward, Sir Joseph, ii. 297
Wardle, Mr., iii. 356
Wardrop, Major, i. 112–13, 115
War Office: and South African war, Kitchener on, i. 275; offered to Kitchener, ii. 118–19, 120
Warren, Colonel (Maj.-Gen. Sir Charles), i. 15
Warwicks in Omdurman campaign, i. 227 (*note*), 230, 231
Waterval conference, ii. 37
Waterval Drift, i. 284
Wauchope, Maj.-Gen., i. 241, 244
Waziris, the, ii. 156–9, 161
Waziristan, ii. 157, 160
Welbeck, ii. 111, 112
Wellington, N.Z., ii. 296, 297
Welsh Division, iii. 141
Welsh Guards, iii. 251
Welshpool, ii. 111
Wemyss, Admiral Sir R., iii. 209, 211, 217
Wepener, i. 309
Western policy, Kitchener and, iii. 111, 129, 223
Westminster, Duke of, iii. 304
Weston, Mr., iii. 352
West Point, ii. 295, 298
White, Field-Marshal Sir George, i. 268, 269
Whittingehame, ii. 111
Wildflower Hall, ii. 138, 279
Wildfontein, ii. 32
Wilge River campaign, ii. 64–5
Wilhelm II., German Emperor,

INDEX

ii. 282, 308, iii. 43, 109, 196, 200, 202
Willcocks, Gen. Sir James, ii. 143 (*note*), iii. 73
Williams, Lt.-Col. (Col.) W. H., ii. 41
Williams, Captain H. R. (Colonel), i. 11–13
Willowmore, ii. 16
Wilmansrust, ii. 36–7
Wilson, Maj.-Gen. Sir Charles: Palestine explorations by, i. 15; Consul-General in Asia Minor, i. 37, 38, 39, 90 (*note*); on Kitchener's Survey, i. 53, 58; Head of the Intelligence in Egypt, i. 61–2, 94, 95, 96, 97; on negotiations with Arabs, i. 67 (*note*); Mudir and, i. 96, 99, 101; communications between Kitchener and, i. 98–101, 103 (*note*); with Desert Column, i. 110; and blame for Gordon's end, i. 112 (*note*), 132; Kitchener defends, i. 112 (*note*)
Wilson, Lt.-Col., iii. 151
Wilson, Lt.-Gen. (Field-Marshal Sir H. H.), iii. 66
Windsor, Kitchener at, i. 257
Wingate, Maj.-Gen. Sir Reginald: Colonel in charge of Secret Service, i. 183, 190, 205; defeats and kills Khalifa, i. 266–267; Sirdar-elect, i. 267; urges development of Sudan cotton resources, ii. 326
Kitchener confers with, ii. 334
Wintri, Khor, i. 198
Wodehouse, Colonel (Gen. Sir Josceline Heneage), i. 52, 165, 166, 172
Wolmaranstad, ii. 65, 67, 89
Wolseley, Sir Garnet (Field-Marshal Viscount): High Commissioner of Cyprus, i. 36; and Kitchener's application for Egyptian service, i. 47, 49 (*note*); Adjutant-General, i. 61; and Kitchener's promotion, i. 76 (*note*); arrives in Egypt, i. 83, 94; at Halfa, i. 76 (*note*), 95; Mudir and, i. 96–7, 98

(*note*), 100, 101; foresees crisis, i. 106; writes to Gordon, i. 106; and Debbeh stores, i. 107; and Stewart's death, i. 110; orders to Desert Column from, i. 113–14; to Kitchener on his wound, i. 160–161; on Kitchener's strategy, i. 196, 229
Wood, Sir Evelyn (Field-Marshal): Sirdar, i. 50, 52, 67 (*note*); and Merawi situation, i. 85, 86, 87; General of Lines of Communication, i. 94; Chief of the Staff, i. 109
Wood, Surgeon-Major, i. 161
Wools-Sampson, Col. Sir Aubrey, ii. 51–2
Woolwich Arsenal, iii. 264
Woolwich, Kitchener at, i. 5, 6–8
Worcestershire Regiment, iii. 151
Wynyard, ii. 111
Wytschaete, iii. 80, 223, 245

Yakub, Khalifa's brother, i. 240
Yeomanry: in South Africa, ii. 1, 3, 4, 5, 45, 54, 66; in Gallipoli, iii. 148, 176–7
Yorkshire Brigade, iii. 163
Yosemite Valley, ii. 298
Younghusband, Maj.-Gen. Sir G., iii. 157, 158
Ypres, iii. 71–2; first battle of, iii. 62, 70, 76, 77; positions round, iii. 80; defence of salient, iii. 223, 225, 227, 235; second battle and gas attack, iii. 231–4, 235–6; withdrawal opposed, iii. 245
Yser, the, iii. 71
Yussuf Pasha's mission, i. 158

Zafir, the, i. 203–204
Zakka Khel expedition, ii. 161
Zanzibar Delimitation Commission, i. 143–154
Zanzibar, the port of, i. 150
Zanzibar, Sultan of, i. 144, 146, 147, 151, 152–3, 154
Zastron, ii. 43
Zeebrugge, iii. 69; plan to seize, iii. 87, 94
Zhob valley, ii. 128, 160
Zohrab Bey, Colonel, i. 101
Zwartruggens, the, ii. 47, 53

PRINTED IN THE UNITED STATES OF AMERICA